BEYOND THE PALE OF PITY

Key Episodes of Elite Violence in Brazil to 1930

R. S. Rose

BEYOND THE PALE OF PITY
Key Episodes of Elite Violence in Brazil to 1930

R. S. Rose

Austin & Winfield, Publishers
San Francisco - London - Bethesda
1998

Library of Congress Cataloging-in-Publication Data

Rose, R. S., 1943-
    Beyond the pale of pity : key episodes of elite violence in Brazil
    to 1930 / R.S. Rose.
      p. cm.
    Includes bibliographical references and index.
    ISBN 1-57292-123-4 (hardcover : alk. paper). -- ISBN 1-57292-122-6
    (pbk : alk. paper)
    1. Violence--Brazil--History. 2. Political violence--Brazil-
    -History. 3. Elite (Social sciences)--Brazil--History. I. Title.
    HN290.Z9V56   1998
    303.6'0981--dc21   98-15185
                                                  CIP

Editorial Inquiries:
Austin & Winfield, Publishers
7831 Woodmont Avenue, #345
Bethesda, MD 20814
(301) 654-7335

To Order: (800) 99-AUSTIN

TABLE OF CONTENTS

List of Illustrations ix

Preface. xiii

Acronyms xv

Introduction 1

Chapter I - Slavery. 7

Chapter II - Order not Progress. 45

Chapter III - The *cangaço*: Rural Bandits? 89

Chapter IV - Cleaning Up the Capital. 119

Chapter V - "O Cravo Vermelho" 139

Epilogue. 187

Appendix 189

Selected Glossary. 197

Bibliography. 203

Index. 225

LIST OF ILLUSTRATIONS

Figures (All figures are located on the unnumbered pages between Chapters III and IV):

1. Branding irons used on slaves before and/or after shipment from Africa.

2. Shackles that bent slaves over, imprisoning the hands and feet, making sleep nearly impossible.

3. Two of the metal masks used to keep slaves from drinking liquor or from committing suicide by eating dirt.

4. A *feitor* in action.

5. A public thrashing.

6. Galley or chain-gang prisoners, including one white inmate, bringing food to their fellow convicts.

7. The log chained to one ankle, iron leg rings, and the *libambo*.

8. Francisco Alberto Teixeira de Aragão.

9. The Aljube.

10. The lime bath of 1823 in the hold of the brig *Palhaço*.

11. A policeman in the 1840s.

12. A black *capitão do mato* escorting his black victim.

13. A slave being taken to the Casa de Correção to be whipped for a "small sum."

14. *Revista Illustrada*, February 18, 1886, pp. 4-5.

15. "Viva the Republic or the Marshal?"

16. *Coronel*-Senator Pinheiro Machado in 1911.

17. "The Black Admiral."

18. Lt. Colonel Candido Rondon in 1911.

19. Antônio Conselheiro dead in October of 1897.

20. The second João Maria.

21. José Maria.

22. Survivors of Canudos, erroneously said to be *"jagunços"* and *"jagunças"* as well as 400 in number.

23. Survivors of the Contestado War.

24. Antônio Silvino on August 30, 1938 after arriving in Rio de Janeiro.

25. Getúlio Vargas arranging a job for Antônio Silvino.

26. Lampião and a part of his gang in their prime in 1936.

27. The heads of Lampião and some of his group after Angicos.

28. A police execution squad in Juazeiro do Norte in early 1928.

29. A *Batalhão Patriótico* in Juazeiro do Norte in 1926.

30. *Coronel*-Dr. Floro Bartolomeu and *Padre* Cícero.

31. Benjamin Abraão and *Padre* Cícero.

32. "The Separation on the Island of the Snakes."

33. "Big Daddy" inaugurating Avenida Central.

34. "Actualities."

35. "Police Inquiries."

36. An unsigned characterization of Artur Bernardes in December of 1928.

37. One-armed General Tertuliano Potyguara.

38. Chief of Police, General Fontoura.

39. Carlos Reis.

40. Waldemar Loureiro, Director of the Casa de Correção.

41. "Prisoner 2308."

42. Meira Lima, Director of the Casa de Detenção.

43. View of the galleries at the Casa de Detenção in the mid-1920s.

43. View of the galleries at the Casa de Detenção in the mid-1920s.

44. "Mello das Creanças."

45. General Santa Cruz alias "Scalped Coconut."

46. The announcement of the "suicide" of José Nadyr Machado.

47. Attila Neves.

48. Conrado Niemeyer, dead on the Rua da Relação sidewalk.

49. A lad in knickers mopping up Niemeyer's blood.

50. Niemeyer's body covered with newspapers at the Polícia Central beneath the second-story window.

51. Chico Chagas, Moreira Machado, Pedro Mandovani, and "Twenty-Six" on the first day of their trial.

52. Washington Luís and Artur Bernardes "directing the band."

53. Coriolano de Góis.

54. Luís Carlos Prestes in the 1920s.

Maps (All maps are located on the pages following this page):

1. Brazil in the Early Twentieth Century.

2. A Partial View of Metropolitan Rio de Janeiro and Surrounding Suburbs in 1925.

3. Downtown Rio de Janeiro in 1925.

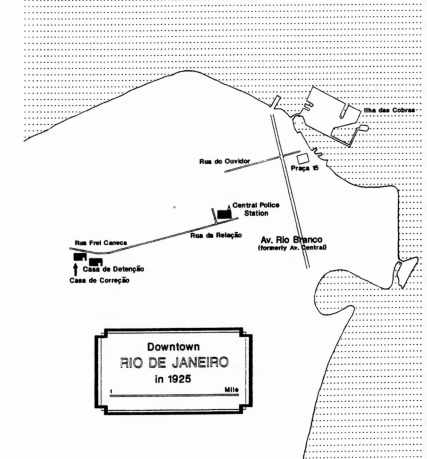

GUANABARA BAY

Ilha das Cobras

Rua do Ouvidor

Praça 15

Central Police
Station

Rua da Relação

Av. Rio Branco
(formerly Av. Central)

Rua Frei Caneca

Casa de Detenção

Casa de Correção

Downtown
RIO DE JANEIRO
in 1925

1 ──────────────── Mile

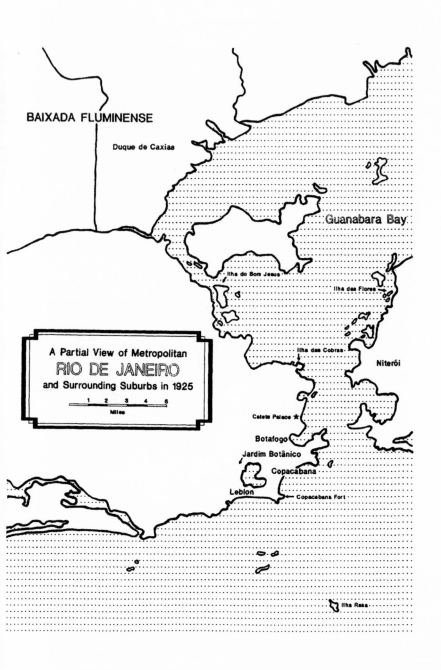

BAIXADA FLUMINENSE

Duque de Caxias

Guanabara Bay

Ilha do Bom Jesus

Ilha das Flores

Ilha das Cobras

Niterói

A Partial View of Metropolitan
RIO DE JANEIRO
and Surrounding Suburbs in 1925

1 2 3 4 5
Miles

Catete Palace ★

Botafogo

Jardim Botânico

Copacabana

Leblon

Copacabana Fort

Ilha Rasa

PREFACE

Numerous people deserve a bigger pat on the back for this book's coming to life than simply to have their names appear in the preface. Each encouraged me along the way. Some might feel puzzled that I am thanking them at all. Others nurtured my ideas and inspired me in such profound ways that I can never express my complete gratitude. Knut Sveri is the first in line. Du har gitt meg så mye Knut. En kjempestor takk skal du ha! Then comes Peter Wickman, Luís Carlos Prestes, Generosa Alencar, Fátima Menezes, and two of the sons of the great "Rifle of Gold": Manoel Batista de Morais Filho and Severino Batista de Moraes.

John W.F. Dulles unselfishly sent me many indispensable things from his own files and put up with my pestering phone calls and letters over the years. Michael Ormsby did a commendable job of proofreading. Also supportive were Nilo Batista, J. Barry Gurdin, Robert M. Levine, Paulo Sérgio Pinheiro, and my publisher, Robert West. One of the people who gave me unique help was Anonymous-1.[1] And only Anonymous-3 knows what he did. Only he knows how much I owe him (You see, I did keep my promise. No one will ever know your identity).

Not to be left out are Peter M. Beattie, Aldenor Alencar Benevides, Marcos Bretas, J.J. Chiavenato, Michael Conniff, Douglas Corbishley, Paulo Couto, Kevin Cronin, Eduardo and Grasiella Freire, José Joffily, Jeff Lesser, Isabel Lustosa, Luis Cláudio and Cecilia Marigo, Ginger McNally, Tania Mara Guimarães di Motta, Rosa del Olmo, Waldecy Catharina Magalhães Pederia, Eliane Perez, Anita Leocadia Prestes, Lygia Prestes, Ivan W. Rodrigues, José Augusto Jesuino dos Santos Jr., Nicolau Sevcenko, Nelson Werneck Sodré, Pedro Tórtima, and all the

---

[1] Note on anonymous sources followed by a number: since this narrative is not aimed at harming the innocent, several individuals who disliked having their names revealed are listed anonymously. All of these persons feared physical injury or some negative impact on their careers should they be connected to the information they provided. Keep in mind that mere gossip was not accepted. In all situations, the unidentified informant was in a position to give an eyewitness' or an expert's account.

people who answered the phones, let me use their facilities, or asked their superiors if I could look at restricted documents in Argentina, Brazil, England, Sweden, and the United States.

A special note of appreciation is also due to the individuals at the Arquivo Leuenroth, Arquivo Nacional, Arquivo Nirez, Arquivo Público do Estado do Rio de Janeiro, Arquivo Público Mineiro, Centro de Documentação do Exército, Fundação Casa Rui Barbosa, and everyone at the Biblioteca Nacional who cordially helped me time and time again. Not to be left out are the people across town at the Fundação Getúlio Vargas' CPDOC, and this includes their colleagues in the library down on the 7th floor who came to my rescue so often. Muito obrigado Guara, Ligia e vocês duas Denises.

For my mother, I can only express my love. For my father, Claude Murphy Rose, who was always in my corner, I dedicate this book. He passed away before it could be published.

R.S. Rose

ACRONYMS

AAB	Arquivo Artur Bernardes (Artur Bernardes Archive)
ADOPS	Arquivo do Departamento de Ordem Política e Social-Rio de Janeiro (Archive of the Department of Political and Social Order-Rio de Janeiro)
AEL	Arquivo Edgard Leuenroth (Edgard Leuenroth Archive)
AML	Arquivo Maurício de Lacerda (Maurício de Lacerda Archive)
AN	Arquivo Nacional (National Archive)
APM	Arquivo Público Mineiro (Public Archives of the State of Minas Gerais)
BN	Biblioteca Nacional (National Library)
CPDOC	Centro de Pesquisa e Documentação de História Contemporânea do Brasil (Center for Research and Documentation of Contemporary Brazilian History)
GAP	Generosa Alencar Papers
HAHR	*Hispanic American Historical Review*
JLAS	*Journal of Latin American Studies*
JSH	*Journal of Social History*
LAP	*Latin American Perspectives*
LARR	*Latin American Research Review*
LBR	*Luso-Brazilian Review*
MPC	Memorial Padre Cícero (*Padre* Cícero Memorial Institute)
RBH	*Revista Brasileira de História*
RLAS	*Review of Latin American Studies*
USNA	United States, National Archives

INTRODUCTION

For first-year students of Brazilian Studies it is a curious thing that no texts exist outlining the centuries of downwardly directed, inter-caste and inter-class violence that has plagued South America's largest country. This volume is an attempt to fill in some of that void. It is written not from the point of view of the elite, or power-brokers, within that social system but from the perspective of the non-elites, the victims, or the large bulk of the Brazilian people.

Studies of social elites invariably include definitions of the stratification relationships between the groups being examined. These kinds of explanations are important for the reader to understand who or what sector of a society is being placed above and below one another. Here, elite will be used to mean everyone from so-called functional elites on up. This is to say that the various degrees of the upper classes are naturally included; but so too are some members of the clergy, medium-size land owners, rank and file politicians, junior officers and their superiors in the armed forces, plus the budding industrialists and entrepreneurs who increased in size and importance as Brazil grew from colony to independent state. Many members of the functional elite are hence classified here in the same category as those on the very top of society.[1] Persons who had ascribed status as elites are thus lumped together with those few who achieved this status. In a word, just about anyone with money or power or both qualified to be lifted out of the sewer of grinding poverty that comprised the immense underside of the Brazilian community. Racially, the vast majority of the better-off group was usually some shade of white.[2] As for their respective size and strength, when the Old

---

[1]This is a modification of the schemata presented by Frank McCann and Michael Conniff, "Introduction," *Modern Brazil: Elites and Masses in Historical Perspective*, Michael Conniff and Frank McCann (eds.), Lincoln: University of Nebraska Press, 1989, p. xi. See also *infra*, chap. ii, 21n.

[2]Since the terms Afro-Brazilian and Euro-Brazilian, etc., are not used in Brazil they will not be used in this text. To do so in any case would be to impose American cultural definitions in a foreign setting. Instead, simple generalized translations from the Brazilian Portuguese will be utilized whenever possible. This will mean that persons of predominately African heritage will

Republic was founded in 1889, a visitor to Brazil, French author Max Leclerc, outlined how the country's business and agricultural elite were in *de facto* control of the new nation. Of European origin and small in numbers, their opposites, the despised *povão*,[3] were said to be totally uninterested in the country's affairs.[4]

Admittedly this discourse is taking on a familiar feel of the Marxian paradigm of oppressed and oppressor. The opponents of such thinking might look at this famous duality and call attention to the fact that in the Brazilian sense elites were rarely if ever united. Thus, would run their reasoning, how could they ever have engaged in repression as a coherent group? And if not, they could only be called oppressors individually or when they acted in some coalition against their inferiors.

This project would call attention to the first of these objections. The Brazilian ruling classes were often splintered as befitted the degrees of power retention and aspirations of each member. Yet it is erroneous to believe that this was perpetually the case on all topics of concern to them. One of the unifying factors that brought this group together perhaps better than anything short of war, was the civil war it waged unremittingly against the lower stratum of society. The watchwords of the rich during these contests were that "order had to be kept" (read: "keep the *povão* in its place"). This common denominator, at times open, at times hidden, but understood by all, united countless generations of higher-rank Brazilians whenever they unmasked proletarian threats to their own statuses or to one of their sought-after goals.

One might conclude that such an analysis could be applied to the upper and lower classes in a number of countries in the same time frame as this effort (1500-1930). That elites would react against their own countrymen first with coercion and then with violence through the auspices of "sub-elites," or surrogate enforcers, might be what one would expect in numerous social settings. The ideas first put forward by Marie Kolabinska, which were reaffirmed by Vilfredo Pareto on

---

be called African or "black." Individuals of obvious mixed ancestry will be referred to as *mulato* during the years of colonization and more often as "brown" thereafter. Those coming mostly from European backgrounds will be called "white." And, Native Brazilians will be designated by the commonly used *índio,* or Indian. See also *infra,* chap. i, nn. 33-35, 34n-35n, and chap. iv, 7n.

[3]*Povão* literally means the great mass of working-class Brazilians. It translates as "the people," and carries an aura of upper-class distaste when used by this latter segment of society.

[4]Leclerc, Max, *Cartas do Brasil,* Sérgio Milliet (trans., pref., & com.), São Paulo: Nacional, 1942, pp. 31, 124, 164-65.

governing elites and non-governing elites, have accordingly been expanded here to include this new category of individuals.[5] For this study, I characterize sub-elites as being situational and transitory muscle-providers. Examples would include the police, guards, bodyguards, and all types of bullies in the employ of some higher authority. Note that the Brazilian lower classes (including trustworthy non-whites) were and are easily fitted into the fleeting roles of sub-elites.

The validity of this larger construct is not the question here. What is of significance is that in Brazil, the violence component associated with it often tended to be excessive. Again, this state of affairs could also be found in many places. In some of these areas, such as the United States, time and civilization are supposed to have caught up with and mollified the reaction (although others might argue differently). In Brazil too, the workings of time had a softening effect, but to a lesser degree.

Why this was so is directly tied to the days of Brazilian slavery. A lineage of greed and violence not found in North America was the problem. In their lust after profits, the Portuguese and the Brazilians succeeding them imported so many Africans into the country to toil as slaves, that they themselves became a white minority in a sea of black faces.[6] It was a potentially threatening environment in which masters and immigrants tended to overreact out of fear of slave rebellions.[7] They interrupted their literal safety as being at stake. Reinforcing this definition was the comfortable justification that it was their God-given right to treat their possessions in any way they so chose. This blend of economic legacy, too many numbers, and divine exoneration resulted in an atmosphere where stern examples were believed to be necessary and normal. Africans were to be maintained in check and the frequency of their outbursts kept unflinchingly at zero.

One of the more subtle turning points in Brazilian history came when the spirit of these slave control methods was refined and applied not simply to members of a caste, but just as easily and just as readily to all individuals from the lower classes. For centuries masters had conducted the bulk of their dealings with

---

[5]*Cf.*: Kolabinska, Marie, *La circulation des élites en France*, Lausanne: F. Rouge, 1912, p. 6; and Vilfredo Pareto, *The Mind and Society*, A. Bongiorno and A. Livingston [trans.], A. Livingston [ed.], New York: Harcourt, Brace, 1935, vol. iii, pp. 1423-25.

[6]See *infra*, chap. i, nn. 38-39.

[7]See *infra*, chap. i, nn. 64-68.

bond servants as a form of life insurance. However, as legal servitude began to come to a close, following the 1860s, Brazil opened her doors to needy European immigrants to do the work of those slaves. By then, excessive social control reactions were entrenched as the norm regarding the country's varying degrees of non-whites. It was only natural that these measures be carried over and fully applied to the large numbers of impoverished newcomers and anyone else ready to stand with them.

Again and again in the first decades following the formal collapse of slavery, those in command found that the best techniques were the most tried and true techniques. As major events unfolded, each could be (and often times was) concluded with superfluous violence on the part of those in power. That the lower classes sometimes fought back in kind was but one manifestation of a deterministic collective consciousness, a cultural trait, in the way they had come to perpetrate, understand, and accept domination from above.

The examples selected here all unfolded from this common core. In Chapter I, slavery, avarice, and the role of the Church are discussed. The foundations of enforcement are likewise gone into, especially as elites discovered that the might they controlled could be turned even against the capital itself with relative safety. Chapter II deals with many of the ordeals in Brazilian society brought on once servitude wound down to its official demise. The resulting change in relationships between immune elites and immigrants, both urban and rural, virtually exploded against this tense backdrop. *Ordem e Progresso* indeed! Chapter III moves to the Northeast to look into the often misunderstood institution of rural banditry and its relation to these events. Chapter IV picks up the narrative in Rio de Janeiro when it was decided to beautify the nation's most important city and cleanse it of undesirable elements, come what may.

In the final chapter, we continue in the old federal district some two decades after the government focused its power and urban design schemes on the poor. The administration of Artur da Silva Bernardes in the mid-1920s is a landmark in Brazil's recent past. On the one hand his years in power produced a reaction in the army that resulted in rebellion and the birth of the *tenente* movement. Their quest would simmer beneath the surface of Brazilian politics until several of its officers claimed the ultimate prize in the *golpe* of 1964. Bernardes' years in office, however, propagated another large and hitherto ignored milestone. In his tenacity to stay at the helm, he utilized the same repressive tactics designed for the *povão* against targeted members of his own class. Such occurrences, when they infrequently came to pass before, were quickly hushed up and forgotten. But the murder of Conrado Niemeyer in 1925 and the subsequent trial of his police assassins (after Bernardes left office) was an aberration. For the first time in the twentieth century, elites fought back in the courts in an affair given wide coverage under the spotlight of an unchained mass media. For coming generations of police, what happened to the accused represented the first acid test of the die set generations earlier. This one trial confirmed what until then had only been taken for granted. The impunity of sub-elites had become so ingrained and impetuous that it could withstand any type of scrutiny. There was nothing to fear. Even the rulers were prisoners to the violence they created.[8]

---

[8]Support for this preposition was provided after these lines were written by Lygia Prestes, sister of Luís Carlos Prestes (see *infra*, chaps. iii and v). As a young woman in Rio de Janeiro, Lygia lived through the Bernardes presidency. Lygia Prestes, interview, Rio de Janeiro, August 6, 1994.

Chapter I

SLAVERY

By the third decade of the sixteenth century, the lower social orders in Portuguese America, particularly the non-white, had long been dominated and exploited by individuals in positions of power. In fact they had known no other way. The Portuguese brought this system of suffering with them. It was based in large measure on the ages-old duality of who would own versus who would work the land.[1]

As one person, group, or family came to rule over pieces of the new territory, so too grew their interests in controlling those who labored on or dug things out of their terrain. A whole host of enforcers and protectors came into existence in this way with at least the part-time jobs of carrying out the broader security requirements of the owners. Initially, devoted assistants had this combined assignment. But soon men like the *cabra*, *jagunço* and *capanga* thugs on the landed estates, and the *bundões* where mining operations were carried out, were given or took over these roles. Although the terms *cabra*, *jagunço* and *capanga* came to be used almost interchangeably, along with a number of others, a *cabra* was often a strong farm hand or other able-bodied worker who sometimes committed murder for his master. The *jagunço* likewise did the killing for his bosses when called upon to do so. In more normal times his usual responsibility was to oversee the slaves on the *fazendas*, or large estates. The *capanga*, however, was a privately contracted, armed bodyguard. Besides assassinations, he saw work whenever the landlords needed someone intimidated.[2]

---

[1]*Cf.*: Burns, E. Bradford, *A History of Brazil*, New York: Columbia University Press, 1970, pp. 23-24, 418; and Júlio José Chiavenato, *Cangaço: a força do coronel*, São Paulo: Brasiliense, 1990, p. 7.

[2]*Cf.*: Freyre, Gilberto, *The Masters and the Slaves: a Study in the Development of Brazilian Civilization*, Samuel Putnam (trans.), 2nd ed., New York: Alfred Knopf, 1966, pp. 48n, 66n-67n; *The Mansions and the Shanties: the Making of Modern Brazil*, Harriet de Onis (ed. and trans.), New York: Alfred Knopf, 1963, p. 41; Chiavenato, pp. 10-11; Affonso Henriques, *Ascensão e queda de Getúlio Vargas: o maquiavélico*, Rio de Janeiro: Record, 1966, vol. i, p. 53; Francisco Julião, "The Practice and Preaching of Revolution," *Revolution in Brazil: Politics and Society in*

8

When utilized together, these ruffians were the first extermination groups to appear in the young colony. They were regularly given such additional duties as tracking down escaped bondsmen or instigating practically anything else that was deemed appropriate or necessary. By way of their muscles and guns each came to have but one reason for existence: to implement the wishes of their employers. It was a part in which ruthless force was concentrated in their hands alone, while the capriciousness of commanding their talents awaited but the lone flick of a master's finger.

In reality the social function of this monopolistic control of violence was always for successive and concurrent concentrations of influence to use it, normally by way of sub-elites,[3] to reinforce their preoccupation with order and domination.[4] Many of the original Portuguese understood this. For them the resulting fury and suffering were either inflicted or received.[5] There was no middle ground and no room for discussion.

Viewing the antecedents of violence in the Brazilian sense in this way, however, is somewhat incomplete. It can be granted that there were responses in self-preservation conflicts wherein the gentry and even local governments acted with vigorous means against one another simply to stay in power. Yet we should remember that instances of this kind were the proverbial exception and not the rule. In any case, local elites habitually used these occasions to rid themselves of lower-class nuisances. What is more, the use of violence by this select group

---

a Developing Nation, Irving Horowitz (ed.), New York: E.P. Dutton, 1964, p. 35n; Peter Singelmann, "Political Structure and Social Banditry in Northeastern Brazil," Journal of Latin American Studies [hereafter JLAS], vol. vii, no. 1, May 1975, p. 61; and Jorge Amado, The Violent Land, Samuel Putnam (trans.), 4th ed., New York: Avon, 1979, pp. 189, 220, 275-76. See also infra, chap. iii, nn. 2-4, 3n.

[3]See supra, introduction, nn. 4-6.

[4]Keith, Henry, "The Nonviolent Tradition in Brazilian History: a Myth in Need of Explosion," Conflict and Continuity in Brazilian Society, Henry Keith and S.F. Edwards (eds.), Columbia: University of South Carolina Press, 1969, pp. 235-36. While the urban and rural poor may well have been able to rebel successfully against this system on occasion, such outbursts had dubious long-term results in the face of elites who could wait patiently to impose their will, and where possible take revenge. For an example of one of these events, the Quebra-Quilo Revolt, together with the opposite interpretation, see Roderick Barman, "The Brazilian Peasantry Reexamined: the Implications of the Quebra-Quilo Revolt, 1874-1875," Hispanic American Historical Review [hereafter HAHR], vol. lvii, no. 3, August 1977, pp. 401-24.

[5]Lobo, Antonio de Sousa Silva Costa, Historia da sociedade em Portugal no seculo xv, Lisbon: Nacional, 1903, p. 236.

towards their inferiors never really subsided with the end of any given inter-elite brawl. Such was not limited to isolated affairs but continuously a part of daily life. In fact, a deeper look reveals that it was always there. It loomed as an ominous threat designed and utilized, due to its absolute ferocity, as a barricade against the lesser levels of society. So it was that future inhabitants to the new country, who found themselves on the bottom social tiers, discovered that they were to be kept fearfully silent, ignorant, cooperative, and resigned to their prescribed destinies as cheap labor.

Much of this had occurred earlier in Portugal. But after discovery of the immense land across the sea, it all gained a new intensity. The excuse was that God wanted Christians to expand their proselytizing among his enemies in the old world to those noble savages in need of his blessings in the new. The latter were red, which was close enough to white to warrant paternalistic attention and second-class citizenship. Following the Papal Bull by Paul III in 1537,[6] native Brazilians were not to be enslaved, despite sporadic efforts being made to press them into servitude anyway. Why the Vatican limited its pronouncement (it was reaffirmed by Urban VIII in 1639) to Native Americans, while excluding Africans, presented questionable motives based in part on indirect economic ties the Church had to African slavery. Observe also that the enslavement of the *indio*, or Indian, in Brazil was prohibited by the Portuguese in the late 1750s, some two centuries after Paul III's Bull. This was over 130 years before such legislation was enacted, albeit by the independent Brazilians, in defense of the black man.[7]

This delay in following ecclesiastical authorities, or in enacting statutes earlier, can be placed directly at the feet of king profit. In Brazil the chase after money began with the first colonists. It rapidly displaced anything but superficial religious concerns as the predominant reason, for most people, for the entire

---

[6]Hemming, John, *Red Gold: the Conquest of the Brazilian Indians*, Cambridge: Harvard University Press, 1978, pp. 146, 278.
[7]Bethell, Leslie, *The Abolition of the Brazilian Slave Trade: Britain, Brazil and the Slave Trade Question, 1807-1869*, Cambridge: Cambridge University Press, 1970, p. 2. For a discussion of the Church's failure to take an early stand against the enslavement of blacks in Brazil, see Robert Toplin, *The Abolition of Slavery in Brazil*, New York: Atheneum, 1972, pp. xv, 5, 34, 117-19, 234, 240. Definitions of the racial terms used in this text can be found in *supra*, introduction, 2n.

undertaking in the new colony.[8]   Moreover, in order to reap the financial rewards envisioned by the Europeans, the backbreaking part of the equation was to be provided as it always had been.   Prisoners, non-believers, and the enemies of Christian civilization and social order would be forced to do whatever was demanded of them, providing their labor through enslavement.

In Portugal, as in the rest of Europe, the institution of slavery had been part of the social fabric for many centuries.   By the time the first pioneers set foot in Brazil, there were already several ways one could be forced into this most degrading of human predicaments.   Routinely included were the offspring of all females who were slaves; so too were persons who could not pay their bills or live up to their end of agreed upon contracts; those who married bondsmen; those who kidnapped the slaves of important people, or their children, in order to sell them to unbelievers; and female servants along with their newborn if the child was fathered by a priest.   Even being a good Christian resulted in a sentence of servitude if one sold wood, arms, munitions, or iron to infidels.[9]   There was an important flaw in these procedures, however, because they were never designed to produce large numbers of slaves for forced-labor purposes.   Complicating the picture was the fact that the laws governing enslavement were becoming more narrowly defined by the fourteenth century,[10] to say nothing of the effects of disease and migration in succeeding periods.

The Portuguese confronted this difficulty by turning elsewhere for their menial needs.   One of the first places they looked was Northwestern Africa.   This corner of the nearby continent had already been the source of a number of Moorish slaves.[11]   It was perhaps to be expected then that from the thirteenth century on their southern neighbor came to be viewed anew with greater attention.   The fact that the Moors were Muslims helped as well because this meant that they were additionally the mortal enemies of Christ.   A formidable people, the Moors had

---

[8]Costa, Emilia Viotti da, "The Portuguese-African Slave Trade: a Lesson in Colonialism," *Latin American Perspectives* [hereafter *LAP*], vol. xii, no. 1, Issue 44, Winter 1985, pp. 41, 43.
[9]*Ibid.*, p. 46.
[10]*Ibid.*, p. 50.
[11]Perhaps due to Shakespeare's *Othello: the Moor of Venice*, any people erroneously believe that all the Moors were black.   They were actually made up of blacks and whites, the exact proportion of which is still being disputed.   Wayne Chandler, "The Moor: Light of Europe's Dark Age," *African Presence in Early Europe*, Ivan van Sertima (ed.), New Brunswick: Transaction, 1985, p. 144.

invaded and occupied the Iberian Peninsula for a time in the eighth century. This distasteful interlude left the Church nervous. Rome was worried that the "Saracens," as all Muslims were derisively labeled, might once again gain a foothold in Western Europe. Such was no idle fear as the two sides fought on now and again for several hundred years. A solution was needed, and it was not long before one was suggested.

The impetus was provided by Portuguese King Afonso V who beseeched Rome for permission to enslave all those opposed to the divine word who were living in Africa. Afonso, of course, was not merely drawn to dealing with non-believers over questions of faith. If the truth be known he was just as fascinated by whatever he could make in the bargain. Pope Nicholas V was only too willing to oblige. On January 6, 1454, the Holy See issued *Romanus Pontifex*. In this teaching the Church gave its approval for Afonso to use force against the infidels to turn them into Christians. This was to be accomplished by capturing anyone with whom his explorers and traders came into contact.

> ...By means of our other letters we conceded among other things the clear and free power of invading, conquering, storming, subduing, and subjugating whatever Saracens and Pagans, and other enemies of Christ wherever found, and also their kingdoms, dukedoms, principalities, dominions, possessions, mobile and immobile goods, whatever is controlled and possessed by them; and of reducing their persons to perpetual slavery; and of adding and appropriating, to themselves and their descendants, the kingdoms, dukedoms, counties, principalities, dominions, possessions and goods; and of converting them to the advantage and use of themselves and their descendants....[12]

Acknowledging that the Portuguese monarch had already been active along the African coast, the Papal Bull added that

> ...many Guineans and other Negroes having been captured by force, a certain number by command were transferred, through the exchange of unprohibited goods or by another legitimate contracts of purchase, to the

[12]Marques, João Martins da Silva, *Descobrimentos portugueses: documentos para a sua história publicados e prefaciados por João Martins da Silva Marques professor da faculdade de letras de Lisboa (1147-1460)*, Lisbon: Instituto para a Alta Cultura, 1944, vol. i, p. 505. An earlier version of Nicholas the 5th's *Romanus Pontifex* can be consulted in Antonio Caetano de Sousa, *Provas da historia genealogica da casa real portugueza, triadas dos inſtrumentos dos archivos da Torre do Tombo, da sereniſſima caſa de Bragança, de diverſas cathedraes, moſteiros, e outros particulares deſte reyno*, Lisbon: Sylviana, 1739, book i, pp. 448-54.

kingly realms; in the great number of whom there were found converts to the Catholic faith, and it is hoped that with the help of divine clemency, if progress of this kind is continued among them, either the people themselves will be converted to the faith, or at least the souls of a great number of them will be won for Christ.[13]

Nicholas' dictum was reaffirmed by three subsequent leaders of Christendom: Calixtus III in 1455, Sixtus IV in 1481, and Leo X in 1514. The stance taken by these pontiffs allowed the Portuguese to convert all Muslims (and anyone else) from Morocco to India. When and where resistance was encountered, the guilty parties could be enslaved through the neat but dubious axiom of the "justified war."[14] It was all befittingly written out in the legal language of the time. Yet the way it worked was another matter since Portuguese missionaries were never too successful nor concerned about converting anyone.[15] What they were interested in, more and more, was using the justified war option for the creation of more African bondsmen.

Gradually the Portuguese sailed further south along the west coast of Africa. Wherever their ships dropped anchor, the men on board were supposed to be interested in trade and new adherents for Christ. At the slightest problem, however, they would claim that the natives were obstructing the Christianizing process or killing merchants or soldiers, or even representatives of the crown. Accusations might be made that the Africans joined forces with the enemies of Portugal or destroyed Portuguese property. Any of these charges warranted declaring a justified war and, after a lopsided victory, enslaving the prisoners. The Church also came to support justified wars against Africans who renounced their conversions to Christianity. Tribal rulers who tormented their subjects or committed offenses against nature could be enslaved as well, as could any African who failed to abide by the rules of hospitality.[16]

---

[13]Marques, *loc. cit.*

[14]*Cf.*: Coutinho, José Joaquim da Cunha de Azeredo, *Concordancia das leis de Portugal, e das bullas Pontificias, das quaes humas permittem a escravidão dos pretos d'Africa, e outras prohibem a escravidão dos indios do Brazil*, Lisbon: João Rodrigues Neves, 1808, pp. 8-9; and Costa, p. 45.

[15]Boxer, Charles, *Race Relations in the Portuguese Colonial Empire, 1415-1825*, Oxford: Clarendon, 1963, p. 6.

[16]*Cf.*: Brasio, Antonio (ed.), *Monumenta missionaria africana*, 2nd ser., Lisbon: Agencia Geral de Ultramar, 1958-1964, vol. ii, p. 552; and Costa, pp. 54, 56.

By the middle of the sixteenth century, once Portugal was firmly established in Africa and Brazil, the demand for slaves had multiplied a hundredfold. Bondsmen were needed in ever increasing numbers for sugar production, in the mines, and for all kinds of servile labor. It was at this moment that the Church's barrier to the enslavement of the easily identifiable African began to soften. Slaves obtained in justified wars were just too few. The whole procedure was a bother anyway in the face of massive profits that were beginning to be made in open slavery. This point was not lost on those African leaders who were themselves involved in the slave trade. They speeded up its development by embracing the lucrative institution as never before. At the start of the seventeenth century neither Church nor king stood in the way any longer. The floodgates of economic greed lay gapingly open.[17]

In regard to the victims abducted to Brazil, their life spans would average between two to seven years. This brief period was the best that a new slave could hope for in many places.[18] Some didn't even make it that far as whole batches died *en route* on the slave ships. Others were so weak from lack of food, disease, crowded, and unsanitary conditions during their journeys, that they were sent to recovery centers on arrival. Once rested, these prisoners could often be

> ...seen taking the Air, in the Suburbs, under the care of a *Capataz*, or Keeper, who generally bears the Badge of his Office--a Whip.... These miserable Creatures, actually reduced to Skin and Bone, have the appearances of Scarecrows, and it is sometimes extraordinary how such emaciated Beings can muster sufficient strength to walk about.[19]

---

[17]*Cf.: ibid.*, pp. 56-59; Boxer, *Race Relations in the Portuguese Colonial Empire*, pp. 7-9, 21, 34, 49-51; and Robert Conrad, *Children of God's Fire: a Documentary History of Black Slavery in Brazil*, Princeton: Princeton University Press, 1983, p. 12.

[18]For one of the better general descriptions of the fate that awaited African slaves, see Charles Boxer, *The Golden Age of Brazil, 1695-1750: Growing Pains of a Colonial Society*, Berkeley: University of California Press, 1962. For a more specific accounting, see Mary Karasch, "Slave Life in Rio de Janeiro, 1808-1850," PhD thesis, Department of History, University of Wisconsin, 1972. An example of what has come to be called a seignorial position, by the man who started the myth of Brazilian "racial democracy," can be found in Freyre's *The Masters and the Slaves*. Freyre would become friendly with at least the first of the post-1964 military dictators. Joseph Page, *The Revolution that Never Was*, New York: Grossman, 1972, p. 218.

[19]Chamberlain, Henry, *Views and Costumes of the City and Neighbourhood of Rio de Janeiro, Brazil: from Drawings Taken by Lieutenant Chamberlain, Royal Artillery, during the Years 1819 and 1820 with Descriptive Explanations*, London: Thomas McLean, 1822, plate 29. The *capataz* in the painting being described is black.

Portuguese warriors, colonists, and priests, accordingly, came from a milieu embracing profound God-fearing convictions and just as significant racist conventions.[20] They were a people convinced of their religious mission who placed making a profit above all else. The slave trade was one of the quickest roads to riches. The journey by one party of Portuguese settlers perhaps tells this tale best. Led by Paulo Dias de Novais, the group was given seed, supplies and a royal charter in the early 1570s. They were instructed to build a community in a specific section of Angola.

> But when Paulo Dias' expedition arrived off Luanda in February 1575, the slave-trade was already in full swing; malaria and other tropical diseases proved an insuperable obstacle to white colonization for the next three centuries; and the high ideals of the royal charter were soon abandoned for the unrestrained procurement of *peças*, 'pieces', as Negro slaves were termed.[21]

The travelers who embarked for Portuguese America became involved with these same *peças* in another way. They put them to work mainly in the plantation economies or in the pursuit of precious mineral deposits. It is important to remember, as well, that those who became the masters over men in Brazil were not just from the better-off classes or from those who were often their relatives: the clergy.[22] Unsuspectingly eager for a better life in the new world, and just as enthusiastic about the enterprise of slavery, were the landless peasants.

Finally, as was the custom with other European powers, prisoners together with rounded up petty criminals and other undesirables were all deported on the same ships bringing the immigrants to Portuguese America. This took place because the discovery of Brazil in 1500 failed to stimulate much in the way of emigration from the mother country. In consequence, Lisbon began granting

---

[20]Aside from Africans, individuals of mixed backgrounds, Moors and other Muslims, Indians from the subcontinent, Gypsies, and Native Americans, the Portuguese discriminated against Jews both before and after the Inquisition, whether they had converted to Christianity or not. For an accounting of these persons with *sangue infecto*, or "infected blood," see Maria Luiza Tucci Carneiro, *Preconceito racial: Portugal e Brasil-colônia*, 2nd ed., São Paulo: Brasiliense, 1988, pp. 12, 19, 58-68, *et passim*.

[21]Boxer, *Race Relations in the Portuguese Colonial Empire*, p. 23.

[22]*Cf.*: Sveri, Knut, interview, Stockholm, April 10, 1985; and Martha Knisely Huggins, *From Slavery to Vagrancy in Brazil: Crime and Social Control in the Third World*, New Brunswick: Rutgers University Press, 1985, p. 16.

15

hereditary tracts of land to court favorites. The new landlords were given near total power in their realms across the Atlantic on the sole promise that they settle the largely uncharted territories and defend the king's laws.[23]

This last aspect of the agreement the Portuguese of this period were certainly capable of doing. For in addition to whatever other unique traits they possessed, many of the individuals who would sire the dominant social layer in Brazil were long noted for mean streaks in their dispositions. They were typically described as independent, uncouth teetotalers who usually spoke their minds without stopping to consider the consequences. If being circumspect was not a usual quality, neither was constraint nor convention. It is said that they had mystical imaginations, harsh temperaments, and frequently possessed a cruel vindictiveness only matched by a thorough lack of mercy.[24]

The then system of justice repeatedly empowered the darker side of these idiosyncrasies. At one time the theft of as little as a silver coin was punishable by death. Forgers were burnt at the stake and had their property confiscated by the crown. The king could order the severing of the hands and legs plus the gouging out of the eyes of anyone convicted of perjury. When this penalty was later reduced in severity, those found guilty of lying had their tongues ripped out in public while being thrashed, bound to a whipping post.[25]

Ordinary men were perhaps as afraid of the sovereign's discipline as they were of each other. Those who could afford the expense went about armed to the teeth for their own protection. Although carrying weapons had long been customary in Europe, the remarks of an Englishman who visited Portugal much later, in the first part of the eighteenth century, pointed out that the Portuguese were second to none.

All Degrees of them from the Nobleman to the Beggar [except slaves and Moors] wear *Spado's* [or swords]. If a Porter is called to carry a Burden, or to go on an Errand, though he has neither Shirt, Shoe nor stocking, he will not fail of his *Spado*, which is generally five, and ſome ſix Foot long, which as they walk, eſpecially on the Declivity, trail on the Ground after

[23]*Cf.*: Conrad, p. 483; and Dauril Alden, *Royal Government in Colonial Brazil: with Special Reference to the Administration of the Marquis of Lavradio, 1769-1779.* Berkeley: University of California Press. 1968, pp. 30-31.
[24]Lobo, p. 235.
[25]*Ibid.*, pp. 235-36.

them; on their Right ſides they were [*sic*] Daggers, as long as our
Swords; and under their Cloaths, a Weapon called a *Faca da Punta*, or
pointed Knife, made like a Bayonet, with a ſarp Point and Edge, but the
Back of it notch'd like a Saw; and often beſides theſe Arms, in their
Pockets a Brace of Piſtols. Thus they go armed to meet thoſe Miſchiefs,
their implacable Jealouſies as often make fatal, as obvious to them.[26]

By 1860, individuals from the Religious Tract Society in London noted that
all of these ingredients had taken root in Brazil. In that year one of their members
wrote that "...the frequent occurrence of murders [are] committed... from motives
of revenge and hatred.... Every one you meet upon the road is armed with pistols
and long knives....[27]

The first years of Portuguese America hence produced a largely rural society
made up of vast estates, or *sesmarias*. Each was totally dominated by an often
times unforgiving patriarchal donee, his descendants, and those who would
become his peers. Many of these men deftly drew upon their positions for political
as well as other administrative ends.[28]   Much of their proficiency in these
endeavors arose from the fact that the threat of Napoleon's armies forced the
House of Bragança to move the capital of the empire from Lisbon to Rio de
Janeiro in the year 1808. The obvious advantages of proximity to the emperor and
familiarity with the host country paid off in numerous ways, one of which was the
number of titles that were handed out in Brazil. Presenting such rewards was
usually done to promote the continued loyalty of the in-some-way powerful. With
an absentee monarch, investitures of this type had proceeded at a subdued but
steady level. After the royal yacht dropped anchor in Rio de Janeiro, however, the
practice expanded *ad nauseam*.

Possibly even before the Braganças disembarked, and certainly by the start of
the 1830s, the proper term of respect in referring to provincial patriarchs thus

---

[26]*Cf*.: Brockwell, Charles, *The Natural and Political History of Portugal: from...1090 Down to
the Present Time...to Which is Added, the History of Brazil, and All Other Dominions Subject to
the Crown of Portugal in Asia, Africa, and America*, London: T. Warner, 1726, pp. 20-21; and
Conrad, p. 246.
[27](Anonymous), *Brazil: its History, People, Natural Productions, etc.*, London: Religious Tract
Society, 1860, p. 201.
[28]Pang, Eul-Soo, *Bahia in the First Brazilian Republic: Coronelismo and Oligarchies, 1899-
1934*, Gainesville: University Presses of Florida, 1979, p. 4.

17

became an address from the armed forces. This was whether or not they had ever seen any active service with the military. Until their power began to be questioned by an impatient army after 1889, and then weakened mainly in the larger urban areas with the first national government of Getúlio Vargas in 1930, if they used a title at all, these men typically allowed themselves to be called *coronel.*[29]

To guard the Braganças a police force was established in the new capital the year they arrived. Later, in 1825, another was put together for ceremonial occasions up in Salvador. But these two bodies were kept small in size, and allowed to become so unscrupulous in practice, that they were of little use beyond the coastal enclaves.[30] A formal army existed, but for budgetary and other reasons

---

[29]Literally "colonel," there are two main schools of thought concerning the origins of the word in Brazil. There are those who say that *coronel* came into use as a sign of respect during the Period of Empire, after the formation of the National Guard in 1831. Others claim that its use pre-dates this period. As this discussion is not a central issue here, it was decided to retain the position of the acknowledged standard work on *coronelismo* by Leal (Victor Nunes Leal, *Coronelismo, enxada e voto: o município e o regime representativo no Brasil,* 3rd ed., São Paulo: Alfa-Omega, 1976). Excellent source material for both sides is presented in Pang (pp. 1-2, 1n). Pang continues (p. 7) with the observation that

> The title of coronel [*sic*] was overshadowed by five categories of nobility grades, *duque, marquês, conde, visconde,* and *barão* [duke, marquis, count, viscount, and baron], in descending order; furthermore, the academic titles of *bacharel* for a lawyer and an engineer and *doutor* for a physician [or any college graduate] drew greater prestige than 'coronel.' The honorific commendations and academic degrees, however, remained beyond the reach of most Brazilians, making the paramilitary commissions more accessible and appealing. In the process, 'coronel' became an inferior title, having a parvenu, if not pedestrian, connotation. Such a class distinction was even more accentuated in the late nineteenth century.

See also *infra,* chap. ii, 21n.

[30]*Cf.*: Brazil, *Collecção das leis do Brazil de 1808,* Rio de Janeiro: Nacional, 1891, pp. 26-27, warrant of May 10, 1808: and ___, *Collecção de decretos, cartas imperiaes e alvarás do Imperio do Brazil de 1825,* Rio de Janeiro: Nacional, 1885, pp. 18-19, decree of February 17, 1825. Limiting her comments to the city of Salvador, another English visitor, Lady Callcott, who traveled to the area in 1821 (Maria [Dundas] Graham Callcott, *Journal of a Voyage to Brazil and Residence There during Part of the Years 1821, 1822, 1823,* London: Longman *et al.*, 1824, pp. 131-32), at a time when officials were still using the military to carry out policing tasks, wrote as follows:

> The police here is in a wretched state. The use of the dagger is so frequent, that the secret murders generally average two hundred yearly, between the upper and lower towns. To this evil the darkness and steepness of the streets mainly contribute, by furnishing almost a certainty of escape. The nominal *intendente da policia* is also the supreme judge in criminal cases. No law, however, has yet determined the limits or scope, either of his power, or that of the lieutenant-colonel of police, who calls upon a few soldiers from any of the garrisons whenever he has to act, and who appoints military patroles also from among the soldiers on duty. It often happens that persons accused before this formidable

it was usually not very large and not very professional. This meant that only the colonial militias could be called upon at a moment's notice. The militias were primarily composed of civilians acting as a second-line army of reservists. Freed persons of African and *indigenas* (plural adjectival of *indio*) descent, either wholly or in part, were accepted into the lower echelons of the militia.[31]

It was into the hands of the white, rural estate owners then that all true might outside the main cities descended from a grateful crown. This was so because many of these men were not only the noble heads of their properties, families and assorted clans, but frequently leading officers in the militias as well.[32] Moreover, it was only to be expected, once family and clan members acquired power, that nearly anything any of them coveted could be and often times was obtained. If their wishes were not satisfied through lawful means and alliances, they could be dealt with or fulfilled through legally sanctioned and condoned violence. Desired

---

officer are seized and imprisoned for years, without ever being brought to a trial; a malicious information, whether true or false, subjects a man's private house to be broken open by the colonel and his gang; and if the master escapes imprisonment it is well, though the house scarcely ever escapes pillage. In cases of riot and quarrels in the street, the colonel generally orders the soldiers to fall on with canes, and beat people into their senses. Such being the state of the police, it is, perhaps, more wonderful that murders are so few, than that they are so many. Where there is little or no public justice, private revenge will take its place. *Ibid.*, pp. 140-41. See also *infra*, nn. 72-81, 81n.

[31]Arraes, Miguel, *Brazil: the People and the Power*, Lancelot Sheppard (trans.), Middlesex: Penguin, 1972, pp. 107-8.

[32]Leal, pp. 20n-21n. Callcott (p. 141) went on to state that the militia in the city of Salvador consisted of

...one company of mounted gentlemen, forming the government guard of honour;... one squadron of flying artillery;... two regiments of whites, almost all tradespeople;... one regiment of mulatoes; and... one of free blacks amounting altogether to 4,000 men, well armed and equipped; but the black regiment is unquestionably the best trained, and most serviceable, as a light infantry corps. The regiments of country militia, as those of Cachoera, Piaja, &c. are much stronger, and with those of the city, amount to about 15,000 men. The officers are chosen from among the most respectable families, and with the exception of the majors and adjutants, who are of the line, receive no pay.

That the officers were indeed "...chosen from among the most respectable families...." seems to be born out by the comments of another traveler who first reached Pernambuco on December 7, 1809. He observed that even in these freed black and brown regiments, many of the officers were white or at a minimum had whiter skins. Henry Koster, *Travels in Brazil*, London: Longman *et al.*, 1816, pp. 1, 391-99. If this were not enough, there was a concerted effort, apparently for reasons of security, to compose non-white companies with a mixture of blacks, *mulatos*, and *indios*. A.J.R. Russell-Wood, "Colonial Brazil," *Neither Slave nor Free: the Freedman of African Descent in the Slave Societies of the New World*, David Cohen and Jack Greene (eds.), Baltimore: Johns Hopkins University Press, 1972, p. 118.

goals could also be pursued by one's own brow beaters, normally without much worry, in any event.

There was a sexual side to all of this too, since the forceful and the men under them were long known for their total disregard of the taboos against miscegenation. In part this was due to the small number of women leaving Portugal on each ship destined for the young colony. But to a larger degree, it was probably a manifestation of the same power relationships played out and imitated by all levels of Portuguese men when they and their male children interacted with non-white females. The result was a wide range of racial hybrids as the newcomers formed sexual unions, welcomed or otherwise, with the *indios* and their own African servants.

The fruit of these relationships fell into a definitional dilemma. This is to say that pigmentation, facial features, and hair qualities evolved into basic criteria, instantaneously checked before assigning social status to one and all.[33] In 1815, over three-hundred years after the first Portuguese waded ashore, the ship carrying German Prince Maximilian Wied-Neuwied tied up and docked in Rio de Janeiro. The prince later remarked on the general rank orderings based on the foregoing physical qualities then in existence in the city. First were the native Portuguese, or "*filhos do reino*" ("children of the kingdom"). Then came the *brasileiros* (Brazilians or Portuguese born in Brazil of European parents); *mulatos* (African and European blood); *mamelucos* (also called *mestiços*: persons of *indígenas* and European backgrounds); *negros* (native Africans); *crioulos* (Africans born in Brazil); *caribocos* (mixtures of *indios* and Africans); and pure-blooded *indios*.

---

[33] And, as Harry Hutchinson (*Village and Plantation Life in Northeastern Brazil*, Seattle: University of Washington Press, 1957, pp. 98-99) points out,

white masters who had children by dark slaves often raised them as legitimate if they were light-skinned, that is, if the difference between father and child was not too great. In such a case the child could become a member of the upper end of the social hierarchy, with education, family, and a position in which he could command others rather than do any manual labor. This was particularly the case when the white master did not have a legitimate, European wife to bear him children. If the difference between father and offspring was too great for the child to be easily acceptable as the son of a European, the child was nevertheless not infrequently partially recognized and helped by the father in some fashion. He then took his place among the *gente pequena* (["small people" or Europeans and persons of European and other racial backgrounds without any real power)], free but illegitimate and rather dark-skinned. With marked Negroid features his status was even lower than the European *gente pequena*. An illegitimate child who proved to be clearly Negroid was likely to be left in bondage with its mother.

Índios who most approximated the ways of the Portuguese were known as *caboclos*. They were considered to be almost civilized.[34]

While Wied-Neuwied didn't know about regional differences, nor a whole gamut of sub-combinations,[35] the arguments used to promote and support the resulting classifications were grounded on several conventional if bigoted beliefs. At this period of European history such views were of course commonly held. Each was a rationalization ascribing the attributes of Christian society, and consequently "civilization," to settlers of direct European extraction. Towards the other end of this scale, native peoples and Africans represented unknowns, therefore pagan, therefore barbarous, entities. At various times, for example, both Native Americans and Africans were commonly thought to be carrying the mark and hence the guilt of Cain.[36]

Thus it was during these former days that along with everything else a caste-like atmosphere, still present in many aspects today, established anticipations as expectations. *Mulatos* were described as presumptuous and proud, and some of the poorer ones were said to think they were the equal of whites. Africans were seen by the Portuguese, just as they would later be viewed by numerous whiter Brazilians, as lazy, devious, and stupid.

For their part bondsmen did not necessarily go meekly into this long night. Despite the imposed definitions, their overt behavior was often only situationally defined. Inside, many of them dreamed of, and even participated in, a whole host

---

[34]Wied-Neuwied, Maximilian, *Reise nach Brasilien in den Jahren 1815 bis 1817*, Frankfurt: Brönner, 1820, vol. i. p. 28. Wied-Neuwied may have been given incomplete information on one of his groupings. *Caribocos* were not the products of Africans and *indios*. Their parents were European, often Portuguese, and *indio*. They themselves were dark-skinned with coloring between that of an African and a *caboclo*. Also, while it was true that a *caboclo* was a civilized, pure-blooded *índios*, the term has grown to encompass individuals of white and *indigenas* backgrounds, or a copper-colored *mulato* with straight hair, or even a lower-class peasant from the North or South. See also *infra*, 35n.

[35]By the mid-1950s, in Vila Recôcavo, Bahia, Hutchinson (pp. 117-21) distinguished between seventeen different groupings of persons pigeonholed by race from white through *indio* to black. While skin color was an important, hair texture, nose shape and thickness of the lips were all part of the classification process. Combined with this was the social class of the individual, i.e., if he was dark and had some Negroid features; but had a good economic position, he may have been called one of the sixteen types closer to white. Conversely, if he *was not* wealthy he was probably called something closer to black. See also, *supra*, 33n-34n.

[36]Boxer, *Race Relations in the Portuguese Colonial Empire*, pp. 96, 104-5, 110-11.

of defiant acts. Protests ranged from unpleasant expressions all the way to situations that masters considered deliberately malicious. By the late eighteenth century, one form of resistance slave owners repeatedly found unbearable were the black clubs that practiced a high-kicking dance called *capoeira*. Performers sometimes had razors, knives, or other objects attached to their feet. Unless it was agreeable to their masters, slaves were not to have anything to do with such groups. Then again, when it suited men of influence, members of a *capoeira*, or those who wanted others to think they knew what they were doing, were employed as *capoeira*-adept bodyguards. Such circumstances didn't occur often, however, as the authorities regularly attempted to crush *capoeiras* and discipline all those associated with them. Whippings of up to 150 lashes for slaves involved in the activity were not uncommon.[37] Owners felt that an unyielding approach was called for in order to insure the function of their property.

The penalties for *capoeira* were only a small part of this chastisement picture. Control of slave labor was a paramount concern since slaves had become absolutely vital by the turn of the sixteenth century.[38] Much more so than in North America, bondsmen by this point were so common in Brazil that they were utilized by everyone except the poorest whites. Slaves could be found in all aspects of plantation slavery, in almost all professions where physical exertion was required--including prostitution--and in the entire area of domestic duties and chores. At the peak of the sugar boom some years later, Africans had been imported into Portuguese America in such numbers that they exceeded whites by a margin of up to three to one. In sum, while only 500,000 slaves eventually entered the United States, some 4,000,000 were taken to Brazil.[39]

---

[37]*Cf.*: Holloway, Thomas, *Policing Rio de Janeiro: Repression and Resistance in a 19th-Century City*, Stanford: Stanford University Press, 1993, pp. 40, 223-25; ___, "A Healthy Terror': Police Repression of *Capoeiras* in Nineteenth-Century Rio de Janeiro," *HAHR*, vol. lxix, no. 4, November 1989, pp. 648-49, 648n; and Gilberto Freyre in Felix Cavalcanti de Albuquerque Mello, *Memorias de um Cavalcanti: trechos do livro de assentos de Felix Cavalcanti de Mello (1821/1901) escolhidos e annotados pelo seu bisneto Diogo de Mello Menezes*, São Paulo: Nacional, 1940, p. 29. Holloway (*Policing Rio de Janeiro*, pp. 8-9) interestingly enough points out that *capoeira* was not made illegal until 1890. Nevertheless, the police arrested and whipped people for decades prior to it ever formally being declared a crime. See as well *infra*, nn. 62-63.
[38]Boxer, *The Golden Age of Brazil*, p. 2.
[39]*Cf.*: Huggins, p. 19; Conrad, pp. 129-32, 176-78; and *Newsweek* (New York), December 8, 1997, p. 62. Not merely was prostitution a way for owners to make money, Conrad (p. 110) writes that

To legally safeguard their investments in human flesh, Brazilian slaveocrats were duly elected by themselves to represent themselves against any inclination that anyone might have about making changes in the laws governing slavery. Of course, this included unruly non-whites. Fear of transgressing the law had to be instilled and in some instances beaten into bond servants. It is not surprising then that the Portuguese had a wide range of reprimands in their American colony for just such purposes.

One of the least severe measures was the slapping of palms with a holed wooden paddle known as a *palmatória*, or ferule. This device was used until the first part of the twentieth century in Brazilian schools and jails. Without the holes and clandestinely, it is still utilized by the police in Rio de Janeiro. Further down the list, especially in rural areas, were the stocks. Shackles could be found somewhere in between; even shackles that bent slaves over, imprisoning both hands and feet in a single iron unit. From the year 1603, slaves who killed their masters had their hands cut off before being strung up to suffer a "natural death through hanging," as it was termed. After 1801, this grim sentence was usually commuted to lifetime servitude. There were cases, however, where the king was petitioned to punish slaves with the old method when bond servants were found guilty of such crimes. Cities often had galleys or chain-gang prisoners, one method of imprisonment with forced labor. Occasionally white faces could be found among such inmates; but they had to have committed some particularly heinous crime since whites were not usually sent to the galleys.[40] Still, the fact that now

as in the United States, slaves were often hired out to others, including industrial establishments. In Minas Gerais, to cite one example, rich slaveholders rented hundreds of slaves to British gold-mining companies.... Even more often, city slaves were urged to work on their own, with the understanding that they pay for their personal needs and that each day they bring their masters a certain sum of money.... These *prêtos de ganho*, or earning blacks, were a common sight on Brazil's streets, selling merchandise or produce, working as craftsmen or laborers, or hiring themselves out as porters or sedan chair carriers. 'We are not the least inventive,' wrote a critic of slavery in 1823, 'because whoever possesses a slave sends him out to earn money; it does not matter if he robs, assaults, or kills, as long as he brings the stipulated daily amount.'
A *prêto de ganho* was likewise referred to as an *escravo de ganho* or "earning slave." Pierre Verger, *Flux et reflux de la traite des nègres entre le golfe de Bénin et Bahia de todos os santos du dix-septième au dix-neuvième siècle*, Paris: Mouton, 1968, p. 488.
[40]*Cf.*: Karasch, p. 154; Jean Debret, *Voyage pittoresque et historique au Brésil*, Paris: Frères, 1835, vol. ii, plate 29; Maurice Rugendas, *Voyage pittoresque dans le Brésil*, Paris: Engelmann, 1835, part iv, plate 10; and Candido Mendes de Almeida (ed.), *Codigo philippino ou ordenações*

and again they were, and that they were chastised there along with non-whites, presents a link to the realities imposed on poor Europeans who migrated to Brazil in large numbers at the end of the nineteenth century.[41]

Slaves in the provinces, especially in the North, may have been treated more severely than those in Rio de Janeiro. One observer noted that in Bahia it was not an "...uncommon thing to tie... [the] hands and feet [of slaves] together, hoist them off the ground, and then 'beat them as near to death as possible."[42] The man who made these remarks, Manuel Ribeiro Rocha, was a Portuguese priest stationed in Bahia in the 1750s. He continued, recording that

> ...although flogging with the *chicote* ([a] rawhide knout or whip) was limited to a maximum of forty lashes under Portuguese law, ...Brazilian slave-owners thought nothing of inflicting two-, three-, or even four-hundred lashes. He also states that there were some slave-owners who, whenever they bought a new slave, had him soundly flogged straightaway, simply out of a sadistic determination to show that they would stand no nonsense. He advocates the abolition of such barbarous punishments as flogging with the *chicote*, pricking the victim's buttocks with a pointed knife, cauterizing the wounds with drops of hot wax.... [and or]... with salt, lemon juice, and urine....[43]

---

e leis do Reino de Portugal recopiladas por mandado d'El-Rey D. Philippe I, 14th ed., Rio de Janeiro: Instituto Philomathico, 1870, book v, pp. 1190-91, titulo xli. In respect to palm slapping, see *O Globo* (Rio de Janeiro), April 9, 1997, 3rd ed., p. 8. Also of interest is *infra*, 43n, and chap. v, nn. 69-70, 82-83, 97-98, 102-4. A scene showing slaves in the stocks is located in Debret, vol. ii, plate 45. Comments to Debret's rendition can be found in Robert Conrad, *The Destruction of Brazilian Slavery, 1850-1888*, Berkeley: University of California Press, 1972, plate 11. The shackles that doubled-up its victim (here, Figure 2) are from Thomas Ewbank (*Life in Brazil: Or a Visit to the Land of the Cocoa and the Palm*, New York: Harper, 1856, pp. 437-38). For an example of one instance that took place in 1815, where perhaps only the sex of the criminals saved them from antiquated penalties, see Biblioteca Nacional [hereafter BN], Manuscritos, document, C 453, 10 n. 1-2. Galley prisoners are depicted in Debret, vol. ii, plate 41; Chamberlain, plates 20 and 35 (here, Figure 6); and Rugendas, part iv, plate 14. Following the Bahian slave revolt of 1835, slaves who murdered their owners or one of his family were subject to the death penalty via a new capital punishment statute. *Cf.*: Karasch, p. 393; and José Alípio Goulart, *Da palmatória ao patíbulo: castigos de escravos no Brasil*, Rio de Janeiro: Conquista, 1971, pp. 144-45. The 1835 revolt in Bahia is discussed at *infra*, nn. 65-68.

[41]For more on European immigration to Brazil, see *infra*, chaps. ii and v.

[42]Ewbank, p. 438.

[43]*Cf.*: Boxer, *Race Relations in the Portuguese Colonial Empire*, p. 112; and ___, *The Golden Age of Brazil*, p. 8. Rocha urged, however, that the scourge (whip), cane, *palmatória* and jails all be retained. They evidently were! A few years before abolition, the custom of whipping slaves with *chicotes* dipped in some substance, so as to cause extra pain and even infection, was still being practiced. The Rio de Janeiro newspaper *Revista Illustrada* (February 18, 1886, pp. 4-5) published a remarkable group of etchings in this regard. One of these drawings (here, among

In addition to the human waste, a slave might well count on religious decorum becoming a part of his punishment. For all too many *fazendeiros*, or larger landholders, were known to take retribution

> ...in a manner cynically based on religious practice, ordering that their slaves be whipped for either nine or thirteen successive days, just as the Catholic Church was accustomed to hold religious devotions called *novenas* or *trezenas* for nine or thirteen successive days. This was done, says one informant, 'to remain in harmony with religious practice.' If the slave sinned on the day of St. Anthony, said another of the many reports of the practice, he was given a *trezena* of whippings.... If he sinned on some other saint's day, he received a *novena*.[44]

Should the slave still prove obstinate he was flogged to death or hung. In unusually cruel situations he was thrown into a furnace[45] or even boiled alive. Some female slaves were beaten and kicked to death by masters or his subordinates, angry with the woman's reduced work load in the final months of a pregnancy.[46] Both sexes and all ages were forced to work sixteen hours a day[47] or more.

All of this mistreatment produced a slave population that repeatedly resorted to escapist reactions. Some turned to the solace of alcoholism, which in a many instances resulted in a metal mask being locked onto their heads to keep them from drinking. There were those who smoked *diamba* (marijuana) for the fleeting release it offered.[48] But the most desperate group, unable to cope with their lives in bondage, took the supreme step and committed suicide.

There is evidence to suggest that some of the several styles of masks mentioned above were used to keep the enslaved from eating dirt, one morbid

---

those in Figure 14) depicts a slave being whipped with a *chicote* that had been soaked in vinegar and then covered with sand before being used.

[44]Conrad, Robert, "Nineteenth-Century Brazilian Slavery," *Slavery and Race Relations in Latin America*, Robert Toplin (ed.), Westport, CT.: Greenwood, 1974, pp. 159-60.

[45]*Cf.*: Boxer, *The Golden Age of Brazil, loc. cit.*; and Jorge Benci, *Economia Cristã dos senhores no governo de escravos: livro brasileiro de 1700*, 2nd ed., Serafim Leite (ed.), Porto: Apostolado, 1954, p. 139. See also Figure 14.

[46]*Cf.*: Ewbank, p. 439; and *Revista Illustrada*, February 18, 1886, p. 5. See also Figure 14.

[47]Conrad, "Nineteenth-Century Brazilian Slavery," p. 161.

[48]Karasch, pp. 382-83. Pictures of the masks appear in several publications among which are Debret, vol. ii, plate 10; Ewbank, p. 437; Kidder and Fletcher, p. 131; and in Luiz Edmundo, *O Rio de Janeiro no tempo dos vice-reis*, 4th ed., Rio de Janeiro: Conquista, 1956, vol. i, p. 71. Two masks are presented here as Figure 3.

method of slave suicide. Perhaps an even more frantic way of achieving this same end was the swallowing of one's own tongue, which as bizarre as it sounds did occur. In the province of Rio de Janeiro, slaves took their lives usually through hanging or drowning, averaging eighty or more per year. Looking at these numbers another way, in 1865 in Rio de Janeiro, nearly 70% of all suicides involved someone who was black. Further to the north, in Sergipe, this figure was even higher at eighty percent.[49] During his trip around South America, Charles Darwin learned of the way one Brazilian slave who had run away, threw herself "...from the summit [of a] mountain" rather than be recaptured. He accordingly remarked in his diary on April 8, 1832 that "in a Roman matron this would have been called the noble love of freedom: in a poor negress it is mere brutal obstinacy."[50]

Numerous slaves, particularly newly arrived African males,[51] attempted to escape. Sometimes those who succeeded used forged letters of manumission to obtain what must have been humble employment elsewhere as freed men. At other times runaways, *indios*, and even the odd military deserter (many of the latter may well have been black), formed *quilombos*. These were free, semi-independent villages of fugitives. Up until the start of the seventeenth-century *quilombos* (or "war camps" in the Jagan language from Africa) were called *mocambos* ("hideouts" in the Ambundu language). By whatever name, it was common that they developed close to communities populated by whites. One notable exception was the most famous of these societies, Palmares. It existed as a near nation-state in what is now Alagoas from about 1605 to 1694 before being crushed. Slaves were also known to hide themselves by living among the poor on the outskirts of cities and, at least in Rio de Janeiro, with master shoemakers. In this last instance they no doubt traded their labor for the double protection afforded by the leather they could put on their feet. It must be added that the enslaved, the imprisoned, and the liberated were distinguished from one another by a single article of dress.

---

[49]*Cf*.: Schlichthorst, Carl, *O Rio de Janeiro como é, 1824-1826: huma vez e nunca mais*, Rio de Janeiro: Getulio Costa, 1943, p. 134; Edmundo, *loc. cit.*; Karasch, pp. 384-85; Ewbank, pp. 281, 440-41; Kidder and Fletcher, p. 132; Robert Walsh, *Notices of Brazil in 1828 and 1829*, London: Westly and Davis, 1830, vol. ii, p. 359; and *Jornal do Brasil* (Rio de Janeiro), May 30, 1988, sec. 1, p. 11.

[50]Darwin, Charles, *The Voyage of the Beagle*, New York: Collier, 1909, p. 30.

[51]*Cf*.: Karasch, pp. 368-69; and Schlichthorst, p. 136.

Neither bondsmen nor prisoners were allowed to wear shoes.[52]

As with *capoeiras*, the ruling classes routinely weeded out *quilombos* when and where it suited their needs. In these crackdowns, elites employed so-called *capitães do mato* ("forest captains") and *capitães de estrada* ("road captains"). The purpose of the former was to capture and return any runaway, besides destroying each encountered *quilombo* encampment. The goal of the *capitães de estrada* was to collar escaped slaves and all the other likely suspects they could detain. Of course these jobs differed in reality very little. Both were customarily carried out under the direction of a stern white or a fair colored *mulato* boss. The *capitães* themselves were usually freed slaves or mixed-race individuals including persons with some *indigena* blood. As for the bondsmen they apprehended, in Minas Gerais by the middle of the eighteenth century, runaways who resisted recapture were often decapitated. Their heads were then brought back to the slave's former master for a monetary compensation. Other retaken fugitives were put up for sale by their captors to new proprietors elsewhere. The idea was to cash in on the larger profits from selling slaves instead of accepting the smaller rewards paid out by legal owners.[53]

Innumerable Africans were branded like cattle to indicate to whom they belonged. This flesh-burning ordeal took place before setting sail from Africa or after arrival in Brazil. It was also common when slaves were sold between masters and could even be seen on the cheeks of slaves as a sign of owner displeasure. Some bond servants had the letter "F," which stood for *fujão*, or escapee, seared onto one shoulder. It was a living notice to everyone. When so marked slaves tried to flee again, their ears were cropped off. A third attempt usually resulted in the malcontent's execution. There was even the suggestion in 1755, later turned

---

[52]*Cf.*: Kent, R.K., "Palmares: an African State in Brazil," *Journal of African History*, vol. vi, no. 2, 1965, pp. 164-65, 174; Karasch, pp. 372-80; Renato Mocellin, *A história crítica da nação brasileira*, 5th ed., São Paulo: Editora do Brasil, 1987, p. 49; Karasch, pp. 365-66; Chamberlain, plates 20, 29, 35; and "Fantástico," Rede Globo, February 21, 1988. Other works claim slightly different dates concerning Palmares. See for example, Abdias do Nascimento, *O quilombismo*, Petrópolis: Vozes, 1980, p. 47.
[53]*Cf.*: Karasch, p. 368; Kent, p. 162; Chiavenato, pp. 11-12; Koster, p. 391; and Conrad, *Children of God's Fire*, p. 383. See Figure 12 (which is taken from Rugendas, part ii, plate 11) for a depiction of a black *capitão do mato*, singular of *capitães do mato*, and his prisoner. Called a *capitão do campo* in Pernambuco, these same people were often in charge of discipline in the slave quarters on individual estates in that province. Chiavenato, p. 12.

down in Lisbon, that recaptured slaves should have their Achilles tendon severed in one foot. This would prevent them from further attempts to escape since it would dramatically reduce their mobility. It would not, however, keep them from hobbling to work.[54]

With the start of the nineteenth century there were a number of penal institutions for the enslaved. When necessary, the choice of their use depended on the offense, available space, and impulse of the official. The main facilities included several military installations, the old Santa Barbara Prison on the island of the same name, and a stockade on Ilha das Cobras, or Island of the Snakes. The last two were just offshore from the capital itself. There also existed an authentic dungeon called the Aljube, which was located on one side of the Morro da Conceição (Hill of the Conception). The Aljube was originally a place of confinement for wayward members of the cloth. In 1808, the government took out a lease on all but one upper-story room in the building. The Church would not rent out the entire parcel because it still needed a niche for its own rule breakers. As soon as non-ecclesiastical arrivals began entering the Aljube, they were roughly dropped through a hatch in the floor into a set of nine-reeking vaults. One of these chambers was the dismal area known as the "Guiné." Any prisoner who could not come up with some kind of bribe was kept there. In the heat and humidity of nearly endless tropical summers, droves of captives died from suffocation in the Guiné. Besides the lack of food, the cockroaches, rats, and filth, 4'7" by 8' was the total expanse allocated to each man. Yet more than once, three living bodies were

---

[54]*Cf.*: Boxer, *Race Relations in the Portuguese Colonial Empire*, p. 111; and ___, *The Golden Age of Brazil*, pp. 170-73. In respect to the branding of Africans, such activities had gone on in several areas run by the Portuguese for many years. *Cf.*: Costa, p. 59; and Antonio Brasio (ed.), *Monumenta missionaria africana: Africa Ocidental (1469-1599), suplemento ao século xv e xvi*, Lisbon: Agencia Geral de Ultramar, 1954, vol. iv, pp. 123-33. For a description of the practice in Brazil, *cf.*: Conrad, "Nineteenth-Century Brazilian Slavery," p. 161; ___, *Children of God's Fire*, pp. 20, 22, 59, 115, 186, 289-92, 338, 340, 365; and Gilberto Freyre, *O escravo nos anúncios de jornais brasileiros do século xix*, Recife: Universitária, 1963, unnumbered plates between pp. 62-63, 64-65, 80-81 and pp. 98-103, 217-24. A picture of the owner's symbol on the business end of two slave-branding irons can be found in Marfa Barbosa Vianna, "O negro no Museu Histórico Nacional," *Anais do Museu Histórico Nacional*, vol. viii, 1947, Rio de Janeiro: Ministério da Educação e Cultura, 1957, p. 96, plate 8 (here, Figure 1). See also the unnumbered plate in *Isto É* (São Paulo), April 20, 1988, p. 40.

packed into this same limited space.[55] A witness described the Aljube as

> ...the sink of every kind of wretchedness and vice. Persons occasionally confined by order of the Magistrates, are put down into the lowest Cells, amongst the worst and most desperate Outcasts, unless they comply with all the exhorbitant demands of the Gaoler, and thus forced to concent to whatever sums he chooses to extort as the price of breathing a less fetid air, and of release from Wretches so abandoned that their bare touch is a contamination, the thought of which makes one shudder. Unfortunately no redress is to be obtained for such practices.[56]

There was a fundamental difference in these places of incarceration in the early nineteenth century. Each of them, including the Aljube, were confines for people thought to have transgressed some military or civil statute. One final option existed. It was the specific establishment to which slaves were taken to be physically castigated.[57]

For those *carioca* (residents of the city of Rio de Janeiro) slave owners too busy or too refined to do so themselves, thereby adhering to the letter of the law,[58] bond servants "...to be chastised for disobedience or for common misdemeanors," could be sent to the Calabouço.[59] Until 1837 this structure was situated slightly west of today's Santo Dumont Airport. The word Calabouço was derived from

---

[55]*Cf.*: Holloway, *Policing Rio de Janeiro*, pp. 22, 55-57; and Karasch, p. 157. A rendition of part of the Aljube is presented here in Figure 9.

[56]Chamberlain, comments following plate 35.

[57]Karasch, pp. 157-58.

[58]The Portuguese tried to dampen what criticism there was by promulgating laws in 1688, 1698, and 1714, making it a crime to abuse slaves. Boxer, *Race Relations in the Portuguese Colonial Empire*, p. 103n. Karasch (pp. 182n-183n) mentions that later

> the Constitution of 1824, Article 179, paragraph 19, forbade the torture and whipping of slaves by private citizens. According to the Criminal Code, Article 14, paragraph 6, of November 11, 1835, the masters had the right to punish their slaves moderately--as the father his sons, and the teacher his students. It was forbidden to burn slaves, wound them, drown them, or kill them in any way--which suggests that masters did all of this.

[59]Kidder, Daniel and James Fletcher, *Brazil and the Brazilians: Portrayed in Historical and Descriptive Sketches*, Philadelphia: Childs and Peterson, 1857, p. 131. One of the authors went on to point out that in sending slaves to such places, "they are received at any hour of the day or night, and retained free of expense as long as their masters choose to leave them. It would be remarkable if scenes of extreme cruelty did not sometimes occur...." Daniel Kidder, *Sketches of Residence and Travels in Brazil: Embracing Historical and Geographical Notices of the Empire and its Several Province*, Philadelphia: Sorin and Ball, London: Wiley and Putnam, 1845, vol. i, p. 100. That violence against the incarcerated slave did take place is evident from the work by Moreira de Azevedo, *O Rio de Janeiro: sua história, monumentos, homens notáveis, usos e curiosidades*, 3rd ed., Rio de Janeiro: Brasiliana, 1969, vol. ii, pp. 437-59.

the bilge compartment of a ship; amply descriptive of the dreadful things that went on in the Rio de Janeiro version. In 1837 the facility was moved west, across town, to the site of the Casa de Correção (House of Correction, or prison). At either place, for a minimal charge, difficult slaves were whipped. By mid-1835, the fee imposed by the authorities for this service appears to have been 160 *réis* (or 12.4 cents in that period's American currency) for each 100 lashes.[60]

When masters desired something a little less severe, jailers at the Calabouço could attach one or several devices to bondsmen given over to them for their attentions. There was a log that was chained to an ankle, iron leg rings, and even a metal collar called a *libambo*. *Libambos* had at least one "...extremity projecting upward by the side of the head,"[61] making running into the bush as well as rest and sleep difficult if not at times impossible. These were austere procedures indeed, but they were vastly overshadowed by the number and brutality of what at times were the spectacles of daily whippings.

For example, the proscribed penalty for being the leader of a *quilombo* was three-hundred lashes to death; for running away, two-hundred lashes; and for other

[60]*Cf.*: Gardner, George, *Travels in the Interior of Brazil: Principally through the Northern Provinces and the Gold and Diamond Districts, during the Years 1836-1841*, London: Reeve, 1846, p. 18; [José Gabriel de] Lemos Britto, *Os systemas penitenciarios do Brasil*, Rio de Janeiro: Nacional, 1925, vol. ii, p. 148; Conrad, "Nineteenth-Century Brazilian Slavery," p. 160; *Jornal do Commercio* (Rio de Janeiro), June 20, 1835, p. 1; *New Orleans Price Current, and Commercial Intelligencer*, June 20, 1835, p. 4; Karasch, pp. 156-58; and Holloway, *Policing Rio de Janeiro*, pp. 55, 204. Thomas Holloway ("The Brazilian 'Judicial Police' in Florianópolis, Santa Catarina, 1841-1871," *Journal of Social History* [hereafter *JSH*], vol. xx, no. 4, Summer 1987, p. 737. See additionally his pp. 745 and 751 for Santa Catarina), adds that most slave arrests took place at the request of the slave's owners. For a portrayal of a bond servant (he does not have shoes, see *supra*, nn. 51-52) being taken to the House of Correction in the latter part of the 1840s, see [Pedro Ludwig and Frederico Guilherme Briggs], *The Brasilian Souvenir: a Selection of the Most Peculiar Costumes of the Brazils*, Rio de Janeiro: Ludwig and Briggs, 1846-1849, plate 17 (here, Figure 13). If only in the places of incarceration in Rio de Janeiro, Karasch (p. 184n) adds that black slaves were whipped by other blacks; with the men whipping men, and possibly the females being whipped by other black women. The canvas she is alluding to as a basis for this comment is by Augustus Earl, and can be seen in James Henderson, *A History of Brazil*, London: Longman *et al.*, 1821, p. 73. Until 1941, the Correção was under the control of the chief of police. In that same year it was renamed the Central Penitentiary of the Federal District. A second name change took place in 1957 when the structure began to be called the Professor Lemos Brito Penitentiary. Elizabeth Cancelli, "O poder da polícia e o mundo da prisão na era Vargas (1930-1945)," pre-publication manuscript, p. 5n.

[61]Kidder, *loc. cit.* These items are also reported in Ludwig and Brigs, plate 9; Kidder and Fletcher, pp. 131-32; Ewbank, pp. 77-78, 437-38; Karasch, p. 380; Debret, vol. ii, plate 42 (here, Figure 7); and Chamberlain, plate 35. Chamberlain (*ibid.*) mentions the leg rings.

improper acts, up to two-hundred lashes. Just being more than two leagues (8.2 miles) from home without approval resulted in one-hundred lashes to the slave and prison costs to the owner. By law, whippings could be administered in public until the early 1830s.[62] Slaves found guilty of any of several crimes, one of which was being a member of a *capoeira*, were nonetheless whipped in public after this period in spite of the ordinance. If the number of lashings was high they were customarily administered on several different dates, and where possible, in various squares in any given community. Later, those arrested for practicing *capoeira* in the capital were taken straight to the Casa de Correção, and immediately subjected to between 100 and 150 lashes. No trial was necessary. This policy existed into the 1850s, after which time forced military service and imprisonment came to be used more often. When a master was still not satisfied, he could hire the special services of an overseer or *feitor*. Such individuals probably functioned as private "slave tamers" as well. *Feitor* advertisements notifying the literate public of their talents for pacifying rowdy slaves appeared often in two Rio de Janeiro newspapers of this period.[63]

It must have been an incredible sight that met the eyes of the unaccustomed visitor. English clergyman Robert Walsh no doubt was one of those who felt ill-at-ease with some aspects of his travels in Brazil. In 1828 and 1829 he was in Rio de Janeiro and commented on his stay as follows:

> I never walked through the streets of Rio, that some house did not present to me the semblance of a bridewell, where the moans and cries of

---

[62]*Cf.*: Karasch, pp. 159, 162, 546n; and Holloway, "A Healthy Terror," pp. 649-54, 673-74. In addition to the painting of a whipping at the House of Correction mentioned toward the end of *supra*, 60n, there are renditions of public thrashings in Rugendas, part iv, plate 15, and in Debret, vol. ii, plate 45 (here, Figure 5). Note the way the prisoners waiting to be whipped, standing to the left, in Figure 5 are tied with a rope around their necks. This is the same form of constraint sometimes used by the police even today. As an example, see the series of photographs in one of Rio de Janeiro's most respected independent dailies, *Jornal do Brasil*, September 30, 1982, sec. 1, pp. 1, 8.

[63]Walsh, vol. i, p. 491. In his reference to "slave tamers," Walsh must have been speaking about *feitors* who had many functions besides those of administrators or foremen on the *fazendas*. An illustration of a *feitor* in action can be viewed in Debret, vol. ii, plate 25 (here, Figure 4). Business oriented and South America's third oldest tabloid, the *Jornal do Commercio*, along with the *Diário do Rio de Janeiro*, ran these kind of advertisements for many years. That even foreigners who spoke limited Portuguese were allowed to do this type of work was perhaps indicative of the social status ascribed to it. See in this regard, *Jornal do Commercio*, January 8, 1830, p. 3n.

the sufferers, and the sound of the whips and scourges within, announced to me that corporal punishment was being inflicted. Whenever I remarked this to a friend, I was always answered that the refractory nature of the slave rendered it necessary, and no house could be properly conducted unless it was practised. But this is certainly not the case; and the chastisement is constantly applied in the very wantonness of barbarity, and would not, and dared not, be inflicted on the humblest wretch in society, it he was not a slave and so put out of the pale of pity.[64]

While it is plausible to believe that most bondsmen tried to accommodate themselves to their predicament, even in the most tranquil of times there might exist a tense relationship between owners and those under their supervision. Now and then it seemed that the slightest ember could ignite pent-up emotions and result in full-blown insurrections. Plans for slave mutinies were uncovered or actually put into effect in the provinces of Bahia, Maranhão, Minas Gerais, Pará, Pernambuco, Rio Grande do Sul, and São Paulo. Bahia led the list. Intrigues or genuine outbreaks came to light there perhaps as early as 1798 and flared up continuously until a major uprising in 1835.[65]

This last insurrection originally began in Africa in 1804 as a *jihad*, or Muslim holy war, pitting neighbor against neighbor. Some belligerents were captured by slavers and freighted across the South Atlantic in chains. They arrived in Bahia with their old hatreds in tow. Many of these new bondsmen spoke or understood one of a handful of African languages well enough to use them as a means of communication. This was not the case down the coast in Rio de Janeiro where plots were uncovered once in awhile, but where no large slave rebellion ever took place. Due to their religion, and owing to the ability to speak a *lingua franca* other than Portuguese, much of the anguish of the Bahian captives was easily redirected towards the alien social structure that kept them in bondage. In 1835, out of 286 individuals of African descent found guilty of revolting, 126 or 44.1% were former slaves. It also may well have been that the English--trying to put a

---

[64]Walsh, vol. ii, pp. 354-55.

[65]*Cf.*: Conrad, *Children of God's Fire*, pp. 192-94, 228, 360, 394-97, 412-13; ___, "Nineteenth-Century Brazilian Slavery," pp. 160-61; Donald Pierson, *Negroes in Brazil: a Study of Race Contact at Bahia*, Carbondale: Southern Illinois University Press, 1967, p. 7; Jose Carlos Ferreira, "As insurreições dos africanos na Bahia," *Revista do Instituto Geográfico e Histórico da Bahia*, vol. x, no. 29, 1903, pp. 95-119; Verger, pp. 325-50, 351n-354n; and R.K. Kent, "African Revolt in Bahia, 24-25 January 1835," *JSH*, vol. iii, no. 4, Summer 1970, pp. 343, 348. Several of the above authors disagree as to which years were involved.

damper on the slave trade[66]--had a hand in arming the rebels.

Despite the veracity of London's involvement, the really revealing aspects of the revolt lay in the penalties applied by the Bahian authorities and in the new statutes enacted in the post-1835 atmosphere to toughen things up. Although the provincial records are incomplete they do show that of eighteen slaves sentenced to a natural death by hanging, only five were finally executed. Since no hangman could be found, a firing squad carried out the sentence. Four others were given simple imprisonment of eight years. One person was given twenty years, three received twelve years, and nine others were sentenced to eight years, all at hard labor. Two were imprisoned for fifteen years in the galleys, while thirteen were ordered to spend the rest of their lives there. A total of twenty-three blacks were whipped in public. The largest number of lashes was 1,200 and the lowest fifty. The law stipulated that the whippings were to be administered in bunches of fifty a day over a period of time sufficient for the offender to recuperate enough to withstand the next session. Whether or not this was followed in all cases no one knows. One man did die as a result of the thrashings he received. His owner, as were all the owners, was made to pay for the application of justice.

When the appropriate number of strokes had been carried out, chains complete with a crucifix were locked around the necks of the bleeding blacks, or shackles were attached to their ankles. Masters were responsible for seeing that each item remained in place as long as his slave was in Bahia. Because these final impediments lessened one's ability to work, many of the rebellious slaves were soon sold to new owners in other parts of the country.

As a guarantee that there would be no further outbursts, the Bahian authorities passed a statute allowing the detention of any freed man suspected of promoting an uprising. He could be held in custody until such time as his "re-exportation" to another province might be arranged. This same law mandated that all former slaves were to pay a tax of 10,000 *réis* (written 10$000, which was equivalent to US$7.78 by mid-1835) to live in Bahia. The only exemptions were the incapacitated, the destitute, and those working in a factory, especially factories producing sugar or cotton.

There was a catch, however, for this last group. Black mill workers had to

---

[66]See *infra*, chap. ii, nn. 5-6.

33

comply with the following conditions: 1) they had to have a written contract from their employer valid for a period of not less than three years, 2) the proprietor of the establishment was to be responsible for their conduct, and 3) they were to live in the factory or in one of the owner's houses. In addition they were to be registered with the local *Juíz de Paz*.[67] All freed persons refusing to work, or those who could not present documents showing that they were registered, were to be sentenced by police judges (but probably by anyone in a police uniform) to prison for a period of six to sixty days at forced labor. Non-whites refusing to pay the 10$000 tax could be incarcerated at labor for whatever period it took to earn 20$000. Ex-slaves were forbidden from owning any kind of property. There was a 100$000 fine for renting or leasing houses to slaves or freed men without special permission. All masters were to Christianize their slaves or face a 50$000 penalty. Recidivists were subject to a 100% increase of their sentences with each new offense. As a final incentive, any bondsman uncovering a planned rebellion was to be given his immediate freedom, a 100$000 reward, and would be exempt from the 10$000 residence tax.[68]

One third of the way into the nineteenth century, the 1835 Rebellion demonstrated that only minuscule changes had taken place. Elites continued to cling to their old belief systems. In the years immediately prior to the Bahian insurgency, Darwin gave a stirring account of just what the old ways produced in Brazilian bondsmen:

> I may mention one very trifling anecdote, which at the time struck me more forcibly than any story of cruelty. I was crossing a ferry with a negro, who was uncommonly stupid. In endeavouring to make him understand, I talked loud, and made signs, in doing which I passed my hand near his face. He, I suppose, thought I was in a passion, and was going to strike him; for instantly, with a frightened look and half-shut eyes, he dropped his hands. I shall never forget my feelings of surprise,

[67]See *infra*, nn. 84-87.
[68]*Cf.*: Pierson, *loc.cit.*; Bethell, p. 291; Walsh, vol. ii, p. 330; Verger, pp. 326-27, 347-50, 355-64, 352n-353n; Manuel [Raymundo] Querino, *A raça africana e os seus costumes*, Rio de Janeiro: Progresso, 1955, p. 113; Brazil, *Collecção das leis e resoluções da assemblea legislativa da Bahia, sanccionadas e publicadas nos annos de 1835 a 1838*, Bahia: Antonio Olavo da França Guerra, 1862, vol. i, pp. 22-27; *Jornal do Commercio*, June 20, 1835, p. 1; and *New Orleans Price Current, and Commercial Intelligencer*, June 20, 1835, p. 4. See also *supra*, 40n, and *infra*, chap. iv, nn. 0-4, 2n.

disgust, and shame, at seeing a great powerful man afraid even to ward off a blow, directed, as he thought, at his face. This man had been trained to a degradation lower than the slavery of the most helpless animal.[69]

It mattered little if slaves flared up individually or rebelled in alliance with some group. Typically, the mind-set of masters displayed distinctive roots. Their Portuguese ancestry nurtured a violence hammered out on the anvil of survival in a land with too much selfishness and, in their view, too many non-whites. Exacerbating this situation was the fact that with each passing year an increasing number of former slaves--most of whom were women and *mulatos*--entered the free population.

Women and persons of mixed backgrounds had a vastly better chance for manumission than darker-skinned males. Perhaps the ratio was as high as two to three in their favor. This resulted from intimacies, forced or voluntary, with their owners. Freed slaves, on the other hand, were virtually helpless because they were forbidden by law from holding elected office (this even included the white husbands of ex-slaves); from being electors; from becoming attorneys; or from joining the diplomatic corps. Additionally, they could not become council to the government, magistrates, bishops, or priests. They were also prohibited from carrying any kind of weapon or from wearing certain kinds of clothing or jewelry. They could not in theory become itinerant peddlers or own slaves themselves. Still, bribery and having a lighter skin no doubt helped a select few skirt around some of these statutes.[70]

Right up until slavery was formally done away with, and most notably in 1887 and 1888, the enslaved were granted their liberty several different ways: 1) by serving in the military with distinction, 2) through an intercession of the crown or other authority (sometimes occurring, for example, when a slave turned in criminals), 3) through self-purchase, 4) via third-party purchase, and 5-7) by childhood release, conditional release, or unconditional release by one's owner. All of this

[69]Darwin, p. 35.

[70]*Cf.*: Conrad, *Children of God's Fire*, p. 317; Russell-Wood, pp. 99-102; Stuart Schwartz, "The Manumission of Slaves in Colonial Brazil: Bahia, 1684-1745," *HAHR*, vol. liv, no. 4, November 1974, p. 611, 611n; Agostinho Perdigão Malheiro, *A escravidão no Brasil*, Rio de Janeiro: Typographia Nacional, 1866, vol. i, p. 182; Katia M. de Queirós Mattoso, *To Be a Slave in Brazil, 1550-1888*, Arthur Goldhammer (trans.), New Brunswick: Rutgers University Press, 1986, p. 164; and *Isto É*, April 20, 1988, p. 40.

was not entirely what it seemed since there was one drawback. Former masters could revoke their voluntary emancipations at any time. This was done to keep ex-slaves under control even after they had been freed.[71]

It should be pointed out that as the number of manumissions slowly increased, the ruling classes did not really relinquish anything. They simply substituted for the role of the *jagunço* with that of another just as cooperative sub-elite: the policeman. Brazilian police forces came into being as entities focusing their punitive attention in the first instance on every black and person from a mixed-racial background. No distinction was made between the enslaved and the freed, as every non-white was suspect. For the years 1810 to 1821, as many as eighty percent of those coming before some kind of magistrate were slaves. Of these, only five percent had not been born in Africa.[72]

The expanded interest in all *gente de cor* (persons of color) produced a ripple of administrative change that spread slowly to the rest of the country until 1841. By 1808, among other things these modifications created were the *Guarda Real de Polícia* or Royal Police Guards. The *Guardas* were privately funded, and they waded into their task. They quickly became well known, led by police chiefs who molded forces of men infamous for their repressive tactics.[73]

Though not formally in charge, one of these early police pacesetters was Major Miguel Nunes Vidigal. The real boss, Paulo Fernandes Viana, was Rio de Janeiro's first *intendente* (a director modeled along the lines of an eighteenth-century French police administrator). Being number two did not bother Vidigal. He began his activities in the militia before transferring to the *Guarda* in 1809. Viana gave him wide powers and he became a kind of jack-of-all-trades in carrying out the law.[74] In the consummate work by Manuel Antônio de Almeida, Vidigal is described as an

---

[71]*Cf.*: Bethell, pp. 67-69; 380-81; Karasch, pp. 491-516, 536; and Russell-Wood, pp. 93-94.

[72]Holloway, *Policing Rio de Janeiro*, p. 39. Many slaves were arrested for insignificant crimes in Rio de Janeiro. Silva, p. 109n. Confirmation of Holloway's analysis, albeit with slightly more conservative figures can be found in Patricia Aufderheide, "Order and Violence: Social Deviance and Social Control in Brazil, 1780-1840," unpublished PhD thesis, Department of History, University of Minnesota, 1976, p. 137.

[73]*Cf.*: *Jornal do Brasil*, March 11, 1985, sec. 1, p. 2; and Holloway, *Policing Rio de Janeiro*, pp. 31-34. See also *supra*, nn. 29-30, 30n.

[74]Holloway, *Policing Rio de Janeiro*, pp. 32-35, 37.

...absolute king, the supreme arbitrator of anything that concerned... his branch of the government. He was the judge who passed sentences and administered punishments, and at the same time, the policeman who hunted down suspects. In cases taking place within his immense jurisdiction, there were no depositions, no explanations, and no trials. He adjudicated everything himself [and considered] his 'justice' infallible. There was no appeal from his pronouncements. He did what he wanted and answered to no one. In short, he practiced a type of police inquisition.[75]

Vidigal and his men, who were chosen for their imposing size, utilized a very uncomplicated procedure to effect social control. With long-handled whips, they simply flogged or beat anyone they ran into who looked questionable. These fiascoes came to be referred to by the locals as "Shrimp Dinners," because of the similar fracas put up by shrimp when being eaten alive. Vidigal's human shrimp often included persons caught in the act of some offense, as well as vagrants and escape slaves from nearby *quilombos*. More than a few of the runaways they came across were gruesomely tortured and executed.

Other victims came from *batuques*, or nighttime gatherings of slaves and free blacks who met to drink sugarcane brandy known as *cachaça*, dance, sing, and listen to the African music that pulsated through the suburbs.[76] One of the tunes was not of African origin but sung anyway since it was indicative of the fear that Vidigal inspired. Loosely translated its title, *Papai lêlê seculorum*, meant "It will be great when 'Papa' [i.e., Vidigal] is dead." For obvious reasons it was not performed openly by Rio's non-white inhabitants. Some of the lyrics went:

> Avistei o Vidigal,
> Fiquei sem sangue;
> Se não sou tão ligeiro
> O quatí me lambe[77]
>
> . . . .
>
> I caught sight of Vidigal
> My blood ran cold
> If I'm not quick

---

[75]Almeida, Manuel Antônio de, *Memórias de um sargento de milicias*, São Paulo: Martins, 1941, p. 46.

[76]*Cf.*: Holloway, *Policing Rio de Janeiro*, pp. 35, 38, 221; and Epitácio Torres, *A polícia: uma perspectiva histórica*, Porto Alegre: Bels, 1977, p. 69.

[77]Almeida, pp. 9-10.

The coatimundi will devour me

While Vidigal was one of the most vicious, he was far from being the only ruthless official during the formative years of the *carioca* police. Consider for example Rio's sixth *intendente*, Francisco Alberto Teixeira de Aragão. A less malignant but just as heartless personality, Aragão had resided for a time in France after taking a law degree from prestigious Coimbra University in Portugal. He was thought of in certain circles as being a rogue whose time in Paris had familiarized "...him with the worst abuses of the post-Revolution French secret police and with personal excess, but not with... Brazilian reality."[78]

In 1825 Aragão issued orders prohibiting blacks and *mulatos* from stopping on the streets at any time, from making any unnecessary noise, even whistling. This final proviso came about because whistling was a ritualistic part of the practice of *capoeira*. That same year, a curfew was enacted to contain the occasional sailor on leave from his ship, or any black who happened to be foolish enough to be on the streets. Known as the "Curfew of Aragão," it began precisely at 10 P.M., each evening when the bell at the São Bento Monastery and the one at the São Francisco Church started ringing for thirty minutes. This was the signal for everyone to get indoors. In the summer, the bewitching hour was changed to 9 P.M., and it was sometimes as soon as sunset.[79] The report of two observers to this nightly dash for safety underlines the seriousness with which it was taken.

> When the great bells ring at the hour of ten, every slave 'heels it;' and woe be it to him that is caught out after the tocsin tolls the time when the law prescribes that he should be in his master's house; for if dilatory, the police seize José and commit him to durance vile until his owner ransom him by a smart fine.[80]

All of this was *pro forma*, however, because slaves could be stopped and searched at any time of the day or night. The curfew was consequently a way of letting bondsmen and any free man know that they had better not be outside or in precarious places after the decisive hour. Every non-white who broke this rule

---

[78]Aufderheide, p. 134. Aragão in profile is depicted here as Figure 8.

[79]*Cf.*: Barreto Filho, [João Paulo de] Mello and Hermeto Lima, *História da Polícia do Rio de Janeiro, aspectos da cidade e da vida carioca, 1565-1831*, Rio de Janeiro: S.A.A. Noite, 1939, p. 274; and Holloway, *Policing Rio de Janeiro*, pp. 40, 46-47, 79. See also *ibid.*, pp. 125-26 and *infra*, chap. iv, nn. 2-4.

[80]Kidder and Fletcher, p. 124.

was to be thrashed. In this, Aragão's critics accused him of promoting two kinds of police: one for the citizen, who was always white, and the other for any person of color who caused trouble. The police serving the former were supposed to be men of great knowledge, judgement, prudence, and integrity. Those destined to have charge over the city's *gente de cor* only needed the ability to use a whip or cane.[81]

On different occasions lawmen didn't have to resort to corporal violence. They merely exercised the threat of three-years imprisonment for all blacks and miscegenated persons without obvious employment. Under the provisions of a *termo de bem viver* (terms of good behavior), which in theory even the jobless might be forced to sign, the accused had to find a suitable trade within fifteen days. Adults failing to do so were subject to up to three-years incarceration. Minors were not bothered with this formality. They were dispatched straight away to industrial projects[82] where the state or private businessmen cashed in on their labor at the least possible cost.

The value of these legal arrangements was two fold. First, they provided a labor pool of reserve workers, one which could also be used as cannon fodder in times of conflict. During the Paraguayan War (1864-1870), for example, some battalions were composed of 90% black "recruits." This came about because of the promised manumissions. Whites who had been drafted could send a slave in their place and receive the luxury of an indemnity in the process. It was also as a result of the problems the provincial authorities had in meeting their recruitment quotas. The police and military were then instructed to pick up males lacking

---

[81]Aufderheide (pp. 134-35) adds that down in the ranks

the police became, like the army, a refuge for the unemployed or unskilled. It provided work for the urban poor in its newly formed... [detachments]. The reliability of the police was always suspect. Travellers reported them sloppy or lazy in their pursuit of reported crime. One traveller in 1819 remarked that the police 'is suspected of committing half the robberies about the city, and it is thought without much injustice.' Urban residents only reluctantly accepted the police, a force largely composed of the same suspicious types as formed the criminal population.... Police forces were drawn from the poor, separated from their peers by a small government salary. They existed to suppress marginal activity within their own social group. *Ibid.*, pp. 141-42. See also *supra*, nn. 29-30, 30n.

For a rendition of one keeper of the peace, who perhaps had charge over a number of black men in the early 1830s, see Rugendas, part iv, plate 14.

[82]*Cf.*: Brazil, *Collecção das leis do Imperio do Brasil, desde a independencia: 1832 e 1833*, Ouro Preto: Silva, 1833, vol. iv, p. 436, art. 12, sec. 2; and Huggins, p. 71. See also *infra*, chap. v, nn. 8-9.

gainful employment. A majority of individuals shanghaied in these conscription dragnets came from rural areas of the North, Northeast, and Southeast.[83]

Being in the wrong place at the wrong time or lacking a *termo de bem viver* also allowed for the periodic ouster of the lower classes. This proved to be a not uncommon stratagem when such individuals became a criminological nuisance, or when their numbers grew to either morally or demographically dangerous levels in the minds of the elite. Examining only Recife during the last decade or so of the nineteenth century supports this assertion. There, the police were used to pick up and dispose of selected segments of the city's indigent population. Sometime the victims were only run out of town; sometimes they were killed and thrown into the Capiberibe and Beberibe Rivers.[84]

It should also be mentioned that assisting the long arm of the law in this general preoccupation with blacks and those of mixed-racial backgrounds were the *Juizes de Paz* (Justices of the Peace). They began sharing the policing role in 1827, and until being stripped of nearly all authority on December 3, 1841, the *Juizes* took full advantage of an impunity afforded by what in effect was summary power.[85] The president of the province of Alagoas, Manoel Felizardo de Souza e Mello, commented on the period immediately prior to the demotion of the *Juizes de Paz* by stating that the shameful quality of service performed by these men

...forms a black page in the reports of all the presidents of provinces,

---

[83]*Cf.*: *Folha de São Paulo*, July 30, 1987, p. A-15; *Jornal do Brasil*, May 12, 1988, sec. Cidade, p. 1; and Peter Beattie, "National Identity and the Brazilian Folk: the *Sertanejo* in Taunay's *A retirada da Luguna*," *Review of Latin American Studies* [hereafter *RLAS*], vol. iv, no. 1, 1991, p. 13; and ___, "Exacting the Tribute of Blood: Army Impressment and the Troop Trade in Brazil, 1850-1916," pre-publication manuscript, p. 21. Beattie goes on to mention (*ibid.*, p. 24) that coercive methods were used on more than two-thirds of all army recruits in the 1850s. By the period 1870-1882, such tactics were utilized less, but still on at least half of all new inductees. See also *infra*, chap. ii, nn. 0-1, 1n. For what awaited blacks once they returned home, they were considered free if they came back alive, note the scene in *A Vida Fluminense* (Rio de Janeiro), June 11, 1870, p. 184, depicting a former bondsman arriving home to see his still enslaved mother being whipped.

[84]Levine, Robert, *Pernambuco in the Brazilian Federation, 1889-1937*, Stanford: Stanford University Press, 1978, p. 52. Levine goes on to point out (p. 198) that although he failed to find any evidence, the opinion that itinerants are murdered in Recife was still heard at the time of his research there.

[85]*Cf.*: Aufderheide, p. 137; Holloway, "The Brazilian 'Judicial Police' in Florianópolis," p. 736; Hermes Vieira and Oswaldo Silva, *História de Policia Civil do São Paulo*, São Paulo: Nacional, 1955, p. 154; and Thomas Flory, "Judicial Politics in Nineteenth-Century Brazil," *HAHR*, vol. lv, no. 4, November 1975, p. 668.

indicating that others besides ourselves have to struggle with the overwhelming evils of an absolute lack of justice, and of the delinquencies of the very men who are charged with its administration. Our justices of the peace pursue their wonted course; either doing nothing through indolence and cowardly restraint, or practising notorious injustice when instigated by selfish passions, or by men of influence in their neighborhood.[86]

The police and the *Juizes* thus had a recurring managerial function in this procedure. They or their superiors decided which poor people to harass and when to harass them. One can detect the application of these policies in the writings of Walsh and another Englishman and pastor, Daniel Kidder. In 1828, only one year after the *Juizes de Paz* were formed, Walsh wrote that "...it is highly creditable to the citizens of Rio that no native beggars are ever seen in their streets."[87] While this may have been the situation in 1828, Kidder states that "this was far from being the case in 1838,"[88] just ten years later. As luck would have it he was in Rio de Janeiro when Eusébio de Queiroz, head of the *Polícia Civil* (or plain clothes Police[89]), decided to clean things up. A reward of 10 *milréis*, or about $5, was offered to all constables

...for every mendicant they could apprehend and deliver at the house of correction. In a few days not less than one hundred and seventy-one *vagabundos* [(vagabonds)] were delivered, over forty of whom were furnished with employment at the marine [navy] arsenal. The remainder were made to labor at the penitentiary till they had liquidated the expense of their apprehensions. This measure had a most happy effect, and the streets were thenceforward comparatively free from mendicity, although persons really deserving charity were permitted to ask for aid at their pleasure.[90]

[86]Kidder, vol. ii, pp. 99, 101-2.
[87]Walsh, vol. i, p. 473.
[88]Kidder, vol. i, p. 98.
[89]See *infra*, nn. 90-92.
[90]Kidder, vol. i, pp. 99, 351. Holloway (*Policing Rio de Janeiro*, pp. 110, 133) in his penetrating analysis of these events notes that

if the full 10$000 bounty was paid for each beggar brought in, the ...[office of Eusébio de Queiroz] disbursed enough in bonuses in one week to pay the wages of a police soldier (at [640 *réis*] per day) for almost four and a half years, and a pedestre [enforcers within the police secretariat] (at [400 *réis*]) for more than seven years. Other rewards paid in this period were 4$000 for apprehending a runaway slave and 5$000 for capturing a conscript fit for military service, so 10$000 for a beggar was indeed an extra incentive.

Even before the demise of the *Juizes* in 1841, the helpless were kept at bay with an apparently new arrangement. When the *Guarda Real* proved disloyal in the turmoil following the April 7, 1831 abdication of Emperor *Dom* Pedro I, Minister of Justice Diogo Antônio Feijó replaced them with a professional, militarized police force. Other units had been tried briefly only to prove unsatisfactory. Thus, on October 10, 1831, Feijó handed the policing role to a freshly minted entity that was the direct predecessor of today's *Policia Militar*, or Military Police.

Initially they were called the *Corpo de Guardas Municipais Permanentes* (Corps of Permanent Municipal Guards), and referred to as "*Permanentes.*" In 1858 their name was shortened to *Corpo de Guardas Municipais*. In 1866 it was expanded into the *Corpo Militar de Policia da Corte* (Military Police Corps of the Court). This lasted until 1920 when they began being called simply the *Policia Militar*. Along with the name variations, the years brought several structural modifications and changes. One of these occurred in 1833 when the forerunners of the *Policia Civil* came into being.[91]

The *Policia Civil*, together with various layers of secret police, would gradually become more and more important in the twentieth century. At this early juncture, however, it was onto the shoulders of the looming *Policia Militar*, led by such bulwarks of authority as army Major Luís Alves de Lima e Silva, that responsibility was placed for insulating the elite from the larger and poorer populace. During the Balaiada uprising of 1838-1840, Lima e Silva was the leader of Rio de Janeiro's *Policia Militar*. In that capacity, he was named to the combined post of governor of the province of Maranhão and commander-in-chief of the administration's troops. Once his forces were assembled and in place the new military leader spared nothing. In the name of duty, God, and country, Lima e Silva himself led in a needless massacre of vanquished peasants, or *sertanejos*. He also took personal charge of the pacification of Maranhão once hostilities ended. His efforts were a success and for them he was made the Baron of Caxias by a

---

[91]*Cf.*: Aufderheide, pp. 139-41; Azevedo, p. 428; Brazil, *Collecção das leis do Brazil de 1808*, pp. 26-27; Eduardo Tourinho, *Revelação do Rio de Janeiro*, Rio de Janeiro: Civilização Brasileira, 1964, p. 240; Barreto Filho and Lima, p. 201; and Holloway, *Policing Rio de Janeiro*, pp. 50, 65-70, 80, 88. Until well into the twentieth century, governors, and the string-pullers behind them, used the *Policia Militar* as virtual private armies (see *infra*, chap. v, nn. 11-13, 25-26).

thankful regency. Later military feats, including the slaughter of black rebels surviving the Battle of Porongos in the Farroupila Revolution, would bring a still more exalted title: the Duke of Caxias (*Duque de Caxias*). Lima e Silva's accomplishments turned him into the gilded knight of the army. Ever since he has been touted as the very essence of Brazilian patriotism.[92] Yet over the years his name lived on with another kind of fame as a northern suburb in the once great national capital. It came to be a repulsive honor but some might contend characteristic of the man. Duque de Caxias, in the Baixada Fluminense, is home to many of Rio's lower-class workers. It is also the place where since the mid-1950s, modern day death squads have killed more of their countrymen than those lost in any war or conflict in which Brazil has been involved bar none.

The future Duke of Caxias' version of the *Policia Militar* differed from their earlier colleagues in that they received a modest salary, stayed in military-style barracks, and were not subject to civilian courts. They wore uniforms. Meals and medical treatment were provided, such as they were. As for the similarities, the main occupational requirement was the same one delegated to all the sub-elites that had gone before: keep the have-nots (who were usually non-white) from the haves (who tended towards the opposite end of the racial scale). In a word, the role of the police was the repression of any crime against the owners of real property; not the equal protection of the country's inhabitants. This philosophy was ingrained for generations to come in the police at large. It actually mattered little in what political era or year one found oneself. The differences were insignificant. The baton had passed once again, this time into the hands of the *Policia Militar*.[93]

All, however, was not set in stone. There was a new subtlety at work and it exploded as 1879 became 1880. At issue was a series of events that shocked the

[92]*Cf.*: Souza, Paulo Cesar, *A Sabinada: a revolta separatista da Bahia, 1837*, São Paulo: Brasiliense, 1987, pp. 43-47, 113, 137-57; Mocellin, pp. 118-19; Leslie Bethell and José Murilo de Carvalho, "1822-1850," *Brazil: Empire and Republic, 1822-1930*, Leslie Bethell (ed.), New York: Cambridge University Press, 1989, p. 75; and Chiavenato, p. 9. Mocellin claims (p. 116) that the Balaiada lasted until 1841.
[93]Holloway, *Policing Rio de Janeiro*, pp. 171-73, 182-83, 240-41, 283-86. For a rendition of one policeman in the 1840s keeping a watchful eye on things, including the slave (he has no shoes [see *supra*, nn. 51-52]) with a basket to his left, see Ludwig and Briggs, plate 7 (here, Figure 11). This drawing appeared in an inverted view in Kidder and Fletcher (p. 125).

nation. In the new year, it became clear that the authorities were ready to employ the full weight of their repressive apparatus--up until then used only against *gente de cor*--against mobs in the capital that included sizable numbers of poor whites. At first the Vintem Riot was a protest march in Rio de Janeiro by members of the lower-middle class opposed to a tax increase of one *vintem* (about 1 cent) on trolley fares. Four days passed, and on January 1, 1880, needy workers together with "persons of little importance"[94] began breaking up selected streetcar lines and erecting barricades on Rua Uruguayana. The economic situation of these individuals was so precarious that they could ill afford the increase in transportation costs.

When the *Policia Militar* could not control the situation, the army appeared and a combined contingent of soldiers plus cavalry totaling 600 strong was charged with restoring order. After taking up their positions, the infantry wasted little time. With rifles at the ready they began moving on one barrier after another. It is possible that the secret police, acting on orders, provoked the unified military force to open fire. Not far away, at the Largo do São Francisco, mounted troops galloped into a group of protesters trying to block a tram. When the last horse was reined in, the losses from the day's actions were three civilians dead and fifteen to twenty wounded. For the first time in the history of the city, the police and army had teamed up to maintain the urban *povão*.

Months later, the government fell, the *vintem* tax was repealed, and the monarchy weakened due to the clumsy way *Dom* Pedro II dealt with the protest. Increasingly, the public began to discuss what the legislature was doing. One thing they failed to talk about or notice were the directives that passed down the chain of command. Soon police *tropas de choque*, or shock troops, were formed to deal with future urban disturbances.[95] The knowledge that the *carioca* public caved into their might, coupled to the prospect of using choice *tropa de choque* units, would serve the elites and their associates well at the start of the coming century.

---

[94]Graham, Sandra Lauderdale, "The Vintem Riot and Political Culture: Rio de Janeiro, 1880," *HAHR*, vol. lx, no. 3, August 1980, pp. 440-41.

[95]*Cf.: ibid.*, pp. 431, 437, 440, 440n, 446; and Holloway, *Policing Rio de Janeiro*, pp. 261-62.

Chapter II

ORDER NOT PROGRESS

The colonial militias were replaced in 1831 in the general fervor of nationalism that gripped Brazil following the abdication of *Dom* Pedro I. The new group of men in part responsible for internal security would be called National Guards. Africans, freed or otherwise, were excluded from their ranks. But they were allowed into the emerging *Policia Militar*, and especially into the regular army to help maintain Brazil's external security concerns.[1] Entrance into the National Guards was made more difficult, even for those possessing the requisite skin color. It was no longer enough to be white. One had to be an eligible voter in order to enlist in the Guards. All officers in the new body, as they had been in the militias, came from the landed gentry or the classes nearby in socio-economic standing.[2]

Before the militias were done away with, they were overseen by the minister of justice. Next, and more importantly in the chain of command, came the semi-autonomous provincial governors who were often addressed as *presidente*. Theirs was the power of appointment, and by far the most prophetic of these designations was the *coronel* selected to command the militia within the province. Those given this role were routinely catapulted as well into leadership positions in the political machine of the regional administration. The party in power was accordingly labeled in any one area as the *partido do coronel*, or "party of the colonel," which

---

[1]*Cf.*: Kraay, Hendrik, "As Terrifying as Unexpected': the Bahian Sabinada, 1837-1838," *HAHR*, vol. lxxii, no. 4, November 1992, p. 512; Aufderheide, p. 110; and Karasch, pp. 310-17. The Urban Guards, established later in 1866, and large numbers of the *Policia Militar* were sent to fight and die in the Paraguayan War. Holloway, *Policing Rio de Janeiro*, p. 158. See also *supra*, chap. i, nn. 62-63, 82-83, 83n.

[2]*Cf.*: Kraay, p. 514; and Pang, p. 8. As concerns the infantrymen in the National Guard. In the capital and the surrounding suburbs,

...the rank and file was made up of [*petit bourgeois*] 'citizens who live from their labor,' including artisans, petty merchants, clerks, and others of the lower orders of free [white] society. As of 1849, the guard in the municipality of Rio de Janeiro had a total of 6,544 members, nearly 13 percent of the 51,037 free male Brazilians in the city's population. Of the total, 624 were cavalry troops and 4,052 were soldiers of the lowest rank, distribute among the eight infantry battalions in the city. Holloway, "A Healthy Terror," p. 666.

For more on the racial composition of the militias, see *supra*, chap. i, 32n.

also just happened to be the local *partido do presidente*, or "party of the president."[3]

What made the situation advantageous for the *coronéis* was the fact that patronage positions, of which ordinary police commissions were a part, were usually drawn from the large reservoir of poor people. These appointees in turn could be counted on to help bring in the vote from their districts, or in other ways provide services to their protector.[4] The rural political system and to a sizable degree even the national one were thus headed by the emperor on paper. Day-to-day reality, however, took place on a different stage. It was directed by regional *coronéis* under whom powerful umbrellas of kinship relations and obligations called *parentelas* worked their way down into the peasant population.[5]

The ups and downs of political life were of course such that any provincial *presidente*, and the *coronéis* who stood behind him, could be replaced by a new *presidente* and his respective *coronéis*. When this happened, unless an individual was able to retain his position through some kind of alliance with the incoming clique, he was destined to wait out the intervening period, often languishing under the vengeance of the new rulers. All this made for individual policemen who were only concerned with keeping their jobs, and thus dedicated to enforcing every wish

---

[3]Singelmann, p. 69.
[4]The *coronéis* had (*ibid.*, pp. 71, 76) a couple of mottos relevant to this situation:

Para os amigos pão
Para os inimigos pau
. . . .
For friends, bread
For enemies, the stick
-and-
Para os amigos todas as facilidades
Para os inimigos a lei
. . . .
For friends, everything
For enemies, the law

Jorge Amado's analysis, however, does not waste time with adages:

Homem que não mata
não tem valia pro coronel
. . . .
The *coronel* has no use for
any man who is not a killer

Cf.: Jorge Amado, *Terras do sem fim*, 45th ed., Rio de Janeiro: Record, 1981, p. 25; and ___, *The Violent Land*, p. 9.
[5]Lewin, Linda, "The Oligarchical Limitations of Social Banditry in Brazil: the Case of the 'Good' Thief Antonio Silvino," *Past and Present*, no. 82, 1979, pp. 128-29.

and whim of their *coronel* patron, or *patrão*.

For rural autocrats, everything started to get complicated with the demise of the militias. Yet within three decades a much more serious event began to unfold. It would shake the established structures to their very foundations. Slowly and painfully, slavery was coming to an incomplete end.

The first stirrings of the Brazilian abolition movement occurred in 1807 when England outlawed slavery in the British Isles. In 1833, London applied this same policy to her overseas colonies and was determined to see that the rest of the Western Hemisphere followed suit. It is meaningful to remember, however, that Britain's desire to end slavery in the Americas was not an outgrowth of benevolent motives. She was actually more motivated by commercial interests in the sugar industry. England's own production of this commodity was confined to several Caribbean islands. As bondage was made progressively illegal, the only alternative was more expensive free labor.

Gradually the English came to feel that they could better compete on the world market if the Portuguese ended slavery in Brazil, and as a result, lost their monopoly on cheaply manufactured sugar. Portugal had already done away with bondage in its corner of the Iberian Peninsula in 1761. This was not applicable to Portuguese America, however, because of the huge need there for the manual labor provided by slaves. The outcome turned Portugal into the largest trader in slaves south of the Equator. Nonetheless, things changed dramatically when the House of Bragança moved to Brazil during the Napoleonic Wars. It was not long before King *Dom* João IV agreed with his Britannic majesty's representatives to a gradual end to the business of importing slaves from abroad. This grew out of his dependence on the English fleet for protection. It was also sweetened with a £600,000 "loan."

There followed British anti-slave trade agreements with Portugal in 1815 and 1817, Spain in 1817, Holland in 1818, Spain again in 1822, Portugal and Holland in 1823, independent Brazil in 1826 and 1827, France in 1831 and 1833, Spain in 1835, Portugal and the United States in 1842, and again with France in 1845. All of these negotiated treaties, either directly or indirectly, attempted to regulate and then to stop the shipment of African bondsmen to Brazil. Each was a failure in respect to this second objective. The English government subsequently tried an unilateral edict, the porous Palmerston Act of 1839, but it too brought little change.

The real stumbling block was the entrenched economic system itself. The Brazilians were the weak link. They avoided, procrastinated or refused to enforce their end of any of these agreements right from the very start, let alone those to which they were not a party. At the same time, Rio de Janeiro attempted to convince London that they were complying with existing legislation, and that whatever non-compliance the English detected was due to factors beyond their control. It was all a bluff. So much so that an expression entered the vocabulary and has remained a part of Brazilian Portuguese. "*Só para inglês ver,*" or "Only for the English to see," is still used when one wants to indicate that something is being done in less than a serious capacity.

Thoroughly frustrated, Britain reluctantly came to rely on the Aberdeen Act, a harsher measure, which it promulgated into force in 1845. This newer decree permitted the English to treat slavers as pirates when encountered on the high seas. Once the new law took effect, the Royal Navy stationed several men-of-war just off the Brazilian coast. Backed up by such muscle, an end to the Africa-to-Brazil slave trade was realized in the early 1850s.

Domestically things went slower. Initial reforms commenced in 1831 with a virtually ignored statute that released all slaves entering Brazil after this date. Although they may well have been freed technically, the so-called *Africanos Livres* were declared wards of the state, and then apprenticed out and reabsorbed back into the slave population. In 1864, some thirty-three years later, Rio de Janeiro finally granted liberty to these same slaves under more English pressure. The following year the end to the whipping of slaves serving sentences in labor gangs was ordered. In 1866, using bondsmen in governmental works was prohibited. Freedom was also granted to those slaves that the regime owned who joined the military in the war against Paraguay.

By 1871 the newborn children of the enslaved were deceptively declared free under the *Lei do Ventre Livre*, or "Law of the Free Womb." These infants were to be their master's property until they became eight years of age. At that time they could be released for a state compensation, or they could continue to be supported in exchange for their labor by their mother's owner until they reached twenty-one. The lawful possessors of most slaves chose the second alternative. In the 1880s the province of Ceará and the Amazonas territory endeavored to end legal bondage within their borders. Rio Grande do Sul then allowed its slaves to go free, provided that they serve an additional and specified number of years in servitude. The total number of years, though, were usually decided upon at the fancy of their masters.

In 1885 all slaves over the age of sixty were given their liberty through the *Lei dos Sexagenários* ("Law of the Sixty Year Olds"). Of course, one might ask how many slaves lived to such a ripe old age when they were consistently sent to do the most dangerous work possible. For those few who did, the Law of the Sixty Year Olds actually allowed masters to escape the burden of supporting old and decrepit slaves. The year 1886 brought a ban on all public whippings as a legal punishment for bond servants. São Paulo then joined the abolitionist movement using the service contract idea developed in Rio Grande do Sul. Finally, on May 13, 1888, Princess Isabel, representing her sick and absent father, *Dom* Pedro II, signed the *Lei Áurea* or "Golden Law," formally putting a *de jure* end to the institution.

Even though debt peonage smoldered on until our own times, Brazil won the distinction in 1888 of becoming the last nation in the New World to declare enslavement illegal.[6] As for the newly released slaves, their reward was in believing that they were suddenly and dramatically without bonds. They did not understand that setting a particular group of people free was an actuality only in that these people could then join the rest of Brazil's workers to look for employment. The emancipated were henceforth to exchange their labor for staples instead of being given staples for their labor as slaves.

It was obvious, what is more, that at the time of the Golden Law not many slaves had much to fall back on by way of contacts or education beyond those that they had before 1888. Virtually nothing was done to ease them into new economic roles. These shortcomings in turn were accompanied by the view held by most whites that was the *raison d'être* of the abolitionist's urging all along. For it was not due to noble reasons and concerns that whites wanted slavery abolished. Proof is plainly evident by the fact that after abolition, in 1890, the immigration of blacks was essentially prohibited and remained so until 1950. No, whites felt that there

---

[6]Rose, R.S., "Slavery in Brazil: Does it Still Exist?" *RLAS*, vol. iv, no. 1, 1991, pp. 97-98, 101-7.

were simply too many persons of African heritage in the Brazil. Quite often their view was that the country had been "...inundated without measure by a rude and stupid race... [and that] the population Brazil wanted was a white one...."[7]

Not only did the government make migration to Brazil virtually impossible for all persons of African heritage, they likewise prohibited Asians from taking up residence the country. The ban against the Japanese and Chinese was revoked a two years later, in 1892, when commercial treaties were signed between the three nations. But this did not lead to an immediate flood of immigrants from Japan or China. In part that would come later, beginning in 1908, when the Japanese were persuaded by the same former slaveocrats to move to São Paulo and work in the coffee fields. The Chinese, however, remained secretly in the inadmissible category for Brazilian immigration officials despite the written agreement.[8]

So if not sold off first when the abolition of sorts finally came along, freed slaves stayed right where they were if there was a weak local economy or a shortage of white laborers. For those favored enough to get regular employment in the cities, apprenticeships in numerous trades, as well as a monopoly on being barbers was what men could hope for. Black women might find a job as a maid or midwife.[9] On an everyday level, all the years of racial subjugation left their mark in countless areas of contemporary Brazilian society. Just one of these is the obsession of the middle and upper classes with having maids--the more maids, the

---

[7]Cf.: Bethell, p. 72, 72n; Jeff Lesser, "Are African-Americans African or American?: Brazilian Immigration Policy in the 1920s," *RLAS*, vol. iv, no. 1, 1991, pp. 115-30; and Arthur Corwin, "Afro-Brazilians: Myths and Realities," *Slavery and Race Relationships in Latin America*, p. 402. The 1872 and 1890 censuses (*indios* are sadly listed in the "Brown" category) shows the following Brazilian racial breakdowns:

	1872		1890	
	Total	% of Total	Total	% of Total
Black	1,954,452	19.7%	2,097,426	14.6
Brown	4,188,737	42.2	5,934,291	41.4
White	3,787,289	38.1	6,302,198	44.0

Source:
Brazil, Conselho Nacional de Estatística, *O Brasil em números*, Rio de Janeiro: IBGE, 1966, vol. ii, p. 25. That blacks continued to be viewed in stereotypes in the newspapers of the city of São Paulo after abolition, can be seen in Lilla Moritz Schwarz, *Retrato em branco e negro: jornais, escravos e cidadões em São Paulo no final do século xix*, São Paulo: Compania das Letras, 1987.
[8]Lesser, pp. 116-17, 131n.
[9]Fernandes, Florestan, *The Negro in Brazilian Society*, Phyllis Eveleth (ed.), Jacqueline Skiles, A. Brunel and Arthur Rothwell (trans.), New York: Columbia University Press, 1969, pp. 3, 23.

more status. These "house servants" are often of African or mixed-racial backgrounds. At the same time, many members of the better-off groups are typically lazy around the house, refusing to do the slightest household task. These individuals invariably state that such things as cooking a meal, or picking up after oneself, are maid's work, i.e., slave's work.[10]

After 1888, former slaves who left the farms and mines to seek a better life invariably found a harsh climate when they decided to try their luck in the cities. Some simply moved to nearby *fazendas* in cases where grudges were still being harbored against former masters. Few if any of these newly liberated persons possessed or understood the competitive character of the landless peasants and salaried rural workers who were also struggling to subsist. A good portion of these last two groups were made up of Italian immigrants who streamed unendingly into the country and to the coffee plantations.[11]

Other Europeans were encouraged to move to Brazil throughout the 19th and 20th centuries. Bringing in large numbers of provincial Italians from the 1880s on, however, was the first serious attempt by the agricultural *coronéis* in São Paulo to whiten their labor forces.[12] As the project unfolded, special light-skinned

---

[10]A similar view can be found in Conrad, *Children of God's Fire*, pp. 139-40, 221-25.

[11]Arruda, Marcos, *et al.*, *The Multinational Corporations and Brazil: the Impact of Multinational Corporations in the Contemporary Brazilian Economy*, Toronto: Latin American Research Unit, 1975, p. 1.

[12]*Cf.*: Hahner, June, *Poverty and Politics: the Urban Poor in Brazil, 1870-1920*, Albuquerque: University of New Mexico Press, 1986, pp. 45-46; and Thomas Skidmore, *Black into White: Race and Nationality in Brazilian Thought*, New York: Oxford University Press, 1974, p. 125. That this undertaking produced the desired results can be seen by looking at the immigration figures for Austrians (Germans were lumped into this category), Italians, Portuguese, and Spaniards for the fifteen year period between 1870 to 1884, and then again for the fifteen years after 1885 until the end of the century. These countries would continue to send large numbers of their citizens to become new white Brazilians until the end of the 1920s.

	1870-1884	1885-1899	Rate of Increase
Austrians	260	17,416	66.0%
Italians	10,698	567,610	52.6
Portuguese	5,787	77,497	12.4
Spaniards	995	91,837	91.3

Source: Brazil, Instituto Brasileiro de Geografia e Estatística, *Repertório estatístico do Brasil: quadros retrospectivos no. 1*, Rio de Janeiro: IBGE, 1941, p. 17. See also *infra*, 13n. At one time, the person in charge of this venture in Europe was José Maria da Silva Paranhos. Known by his royal title of *O Barão do Rio Branco* (The Baron of White River), he would go on to become Brazil's minister of foreign relations and receive countless homages, many after his death. The post-1964 military dictators had his likeness placed one more time on a Brazilian bank note:

teams were sent to Italy to point out that free transportation and jobs could be had by all those able-bodied peasants ready to immigrate to São Paulo.[13] It was hoped that dirt-poor Italians would be so grateful for this opportunity that they would tolerate the terrible conditions awaiting them. Not only would they be expected to do the work of slaves, but order would be kept as it had been before among the enslaved.

To the north, the state of Minas Gerais fared a little differently. French observer Pierre Denis traveled to the region at the start of the twentieth century and noted that

> in 1888, blacks were the largest majority among rural workers. Today, as well, when visiting the *fazendas* in Minas, one will notice hardly anything except black laborers. Why is it that they have returned to the jobs they once deserted?[14]

They returned because even though Minas Gerais tried to attract new Italians, they were never as successful at this as the *paulistas* (persons from the state of São

---

their 1,000 *cruzeiro* bill. Besides being a renowned whoremonger (Freyre, *Order and Progress*, pp. 57-58, 57n-58n), he used his *capangas* to rig elections (Hahner, pp. 57-58), was a monarchist at heart (Gilberto Freyre, *Order and Progress: Brazil from Monarchy to Republic*, Rod Horton [ed. and trans.], New York: Alfred Knopf, 1970, pp. 200, 202, 337-38), and was one of the most important personalities behind this whiten Brazil effort in general. *Cf.*: *ibid.*, pp. 202-3, 205; Skidmore, pp. 125, 252n; and José Maria Bello, *A History of Modern Brazil, 1889-1964*, Stanford: Stanford University Press, 1968, p. 239.

[13]See also *supra*, 12n. The state of São Paulo provided this free transportation to 283,982 Italians between 1894 and 1897. Eventually, there may well have been two Italians for every native-born Brazilian in the city of São Paulo by 1897. Out of a state population of 2,282,279 in 1900, one-half were probably first or second generation Italian immigrants. *Cf.*: Richard Morse, *Formação histórica de São Paulo: de comunidade à metrópole*, São Paulo: Difusão Européia do Livro, 1970, p. 240; Brazil, Ministerio da Agricultura, Industria e Commercio, *Annuario estatistico do Brazil, 1908-1912*, Rio de Janeiro: Directoria Geral de Estatistica, 1916, vol. i, p. 289; and Pierre Denis, *Le Brésil au xxᵉ siècle*, Paris: Armand Colin, 1909, pp. 131, 145. Another way of looking at this influx is provided by Paulo Sérgio Pinheiro ("O proletariado industrial na Primeira República," *História geral da civilização brasileira: o Brasil republicano: sociedade e instituições, 1889-1930*, Boris Fausto (dir.), Rio de Janeiro: Difel, 1977, book iii, vol. ii, p. 139). Of the industrial workers in the city of São Paulo in 1893, 82.5% were Italians. In 1900, and again in 1912, the number of Italians working in industry was 81% and 65% respectively. It is likewise important to remember that all through these years, organized labor felt that the policy of sponsored immigration produced a malleable work force unwilling to strike nor form forceful unions. Michael Hall and Marco Aurélio Garcia, "Urban Labor," *Modern Brazil: Elites and Masses in Historical Perspective*, p. 162. See in this regard *infra*, chap. v, nn. 3-6.

[14]Denis, pp. 255-56. From 1894 to 1897, Minas Gerais imported 51,259 Italians. A first and second generation figure was not given. See also *supra*, 13n.

Paulo). In part this was due to the intermittent problems Minas Gerais was having with its coffee crop that made imported white labor an expensive luxury.[15] It was also a result of another consideration. Scores of Italians, provided free passage to Minas Gerais and several other states, consistently wanted to go (and eventually did) to the place with the largest Italian settlement...São Paulo.

Consequently, in Brazil's then two most important states, São Paulo and Minas Gerais, and on a smaller scale in Rio de Janeiro, the opportunities for newly released slaves lessened in many places. Or, there was no real change from what went on before. The sad reality was that most ex-slaves stayed at or near, or even came back--hat in hand--to their old masters. Jorge Amado, South America's most widely read author, perhaps had this national disgrace in mind when he had one of his characters in *Terras do sem fim* mutter the following lines:

> Eu era menino no tempo da escravidão... Meu pai for escravo, minha mãe também... Mas não era mais ruim que hoje... As coisas não mudou, foi tudo palavra...
>
> . . . .
>
> ...I was a lad in the days of slavery.... My father was a slave, my mother also. But it wasn't any worse then than it is today. Things don't change; it's all talk.[16]

What in fact had happened was that the black man, and in some cases the brown, lost his special niche in the system of production. He had quite literally been shoved aside and replaced. What was largely a caste question before now shifted and became primarily a class question. It was a grim truth that produced a situation in which poor whites generally came to be preferred over non-whites for the few jobs that were available. With or without work, the *classe conservadora*, or dominant class, looked down on each and every one of these individuals for performing what in their opinion was the menial work formerly carried out by those in perpetual servitude.[17]

One of the consequences of this policy could be seen as the number of immigrants increased in São Paulo. Slowly, there was a concomitant expansion of the

---

[15]Denis, p. 256.

[16]*Cf.*: Amado, *Terras do sem fim*, p. 98; and ___, *The Violent Land*, p. 85. Note that Samuel Putnam's translation of these lines for *The Violent Land* fails to capture the bad Portuguese used by Amado to indicate that an uneducated (and probably poor) person is doing the talking.

[17]See also *infra*, chap. v, nn. 3-6.

provincial police forces whose role it was to keep these newcomers submissive, violently if need be. Following a visit to the area in 1899, an Italian official complained to no end about the brutality of the local police.[18] The scale of this ruthlessness evidently went so far as to be condemned in the Italian Parliament. An unsuccessful bill was even introduced in that body to prevent the subsequent emigration of Italians to Brazil.[19] Had these disgruntled representatives of the *Parlamento Italiano* had the opportunity to visit São Paulo they would have discovered that their fears were justified. From roughly the early 1890s through the first years of the new century, arrest rates in the city were about double those of London. Perhaps even more suggestive was the fact that of those picked up less than ten percent were ever charged with a formal offense.[20]

The only crime that had been perpetrated in the minds of Brazil's real rulers were the new, expensive labor arrangements ushered in by the Golden Law. In 1889, one of the first reactions by the *coronéis* and other men of power[21] was thus

[18]Hall, Michael and Paulo Sérgio Pinheiro, "The Control and Policing of the Working Class in Brazil," paper presented to the Conference on the History of Law, Labor and Crime, University of Warwick, September 15-18, 1983, p. 4.

[19]Dallari, Dalmo de Abreu, "The *Força Pública* of São Paulo in State and National Politics," *Perspectives on Armed Politics in Brazil*, Henry Keith and Robert Hayes (eds.), Tempe: Arizona State University Press, 1976, p. 86.

[20]Hall and Pinheiro, p. 5. The exact years the authors cite in reference to the London data were 1892-1904.

[21]With the changing times there were many new individuals who were accepted into the select company of the *coronéis*. See *supra*, chap. i, nn. 28-29, 29n. Pang (pp. 36-39) lists the seven main types by the overthrow of the monarchy as: 1) *coronel*-landowner, 2) *coronel*-merchant, 3) *coronel*-industrialist, 4) *coronel*-priest, 5) *coronel*-warlord, 6) *coronel*-party cadre, and 7) *coronel*-ward boss. While the power of these people may have been less, equal to, or even superior to the original planter-patriarchs, it was not necessarily so that they were called *coronel*.
In practice, a *coronel* was anyone important who did not have a bachelor's degree. Those who had this diploma were called *doutor*. Those who did not, but who were important because of political position, leadership, money, or because they were from old established families, were normally addressed with a National Guard rank from *capitão* [captain] to *coronel*. Centro de Pesquisa e Documentação de História Contemporânea do Brasil [hereafter CPDOC], oral history, "Osvaldo Trigueiro," 1977, p. 57.
In the cities, other terms often came to be preferred such as *patrão*, *chefe* (chief), *figurão* (person of eminence), and the ubiquitous *doutor*. It is interesting to observe, moreover, that as the years rolled by, the elite often kept discreetly in the background. Writing in 1973, one author (Marcio Moreira Alves, *A Grain of Mustard Seed: the Awakening of the Brazilian Revolution*, Garden City, NY: Doubleday Anchor, 1973, pp. 48-49) stated that they represent the more dynamic economic sectors and are part
of a modern and international world. Their wealth is a key to any door. They defend

a push, finally carried out by an ever more outspoken army, to get rid of the enfeebled monarchy. It was to be a largely non-violent affair. Most of the fatalities were ex-slaves who attempted to defend the old system that begrudgingly set them free--hardly anything of concern to the incoming administration.

There followed a period of veiled military rule. When the new republic's first head of state, army marshal and dictator Deodoro da Fonseca, was forced to resign in 1891, Brazil's second military autocrat, Floriano Peixoto, seized office. This provoked cries from thirteen fellow officers and *Jornal do Brasil* editor Rui Barbosa, that Peixoto had violated the just written constitution. The document stipulated that direct elections should be called. But Floriano had a mind of his own and ignored the provision. He declared marshal law and had the thirteen military opponents arrested. They were quickly placed aboard the steamer *Pernambuco*, which left for the Amazon on April 12, 1892. No trial was conducted. Brazil's guiding charter allowed any president to deport anyone to any point in the country while a state of siege was in effect. This, however, was simply a propriety that brought the law into alignment with standard practice. Ships referred to as "*presingangas*" had been used for just such removal purposes for years. The word was lifted from the English expression "press gang," and is indicative of not only the entire operation but of what transpired on vessels of this sort.

Floriano was not the first Brazilian ruler to utilize *presingangas* to rid himself

---

their interests behind the scenes, lobbying in their clubs, their yachts, their country houses. They shy clear of the risks and publicity of a political career, preferring to finance the ambitions of docile professionals, generally lawyers. Public office hinders rather than aids the maintenance or increase of their power. In the country's underdeveloped interior [,however,] the situation is reversed. A political career leads to wealth and provides one with the means to keep it. Scarcer opportunities tend to cluster in fewer hands. A seat in Congress or in a state assembly is an important asset that the local plutocracy cannot afford to vest in strangers. When a big landowner refrains from running for Congress it is not because he thinks, as does his urban counterpart, that checkbooks work better than speeches. He does so through fear that he, is a stammering redneck, hasn't the rhetoric to compete with well-educated professionals. Since the parliamentarian tool must not be wasted he tries to marry off a daughter or a beloved niece to someone able to represent him, and then goes about having the in-law elected. Only when this fails does he reach outside the family circle, the man chosen being normally a lawyer, doctor, or army officer. In the past he could also be a priest, but ecclesiastics are today deemed unreliable, some ordained members of the Catholic Church having lately acquired the scurvy habit of siding with the oppressed.

of his political enemies. At the conclusion of the successful movement for self rule it had also been used. As could be expected, not all of the country agreed to the separation from Portugal on September 7, 1822. In the Northeast, loyalists consequently freighted 271 pro-independence advocates back to Lisbon in the holds of a ship. About a third died on the way. The following year, the emperor sent a detachment of mercenaries under English Captain John Grenfell to Belém aboard the warship *Maranhão*. They were ordered to use force if necessary to win the allegiance of those still supporting the former mother country. Grenfell's presence gained many adherents for Rio de Janeiro; but it likewise ignited the passions of the lower classes, who began destroying loyalist property. By the time order was restored, the authorities had apprehended a minimum of 261 persons. Five were shot immediately. The remaining 256, with Grenfell's participation, were stuffed into the hold of the brig *Palhaço*. The vessel's name translates as "buffoon" or "clown" and must have prompted a number of sardonic comments once it was decided to use the craft as a suffocatingly small, floating prison.

Belém is one and a half degrees south of the Equator. It is one of the hottest and stickiest parts of Brazil. It did not matter that most of the captives were probably well acclimatized to these circumstances. Once they were loaded on board, all 256 fought and clamored their way over one another to get at the cracks of fresh air after the hatch cover had been banged shut. This same teeming effect occurred later when infrequent tins of dirty water were lowered to the swarming hands below decks. The liquid was naturally slopped all over the place. Such was likely the intent anyway, since the guards next poured sacks of lime down into the hold and then sealed off again. Days later when the lid was wrested open, there was but a solitary survivor.[22]

---

[22]*Cf.*: Bethell, Leslie, "The Independence of Brazil," *Brazil: Empire and Republic, 1822-1938*, Leslie Bethell (ed.), New York: Cambridge University Press, 1989, pp. 34-36; Neill Macaulay, *Dom Pedro: the Struggle for Liberty in Brazil and Portugal, 1798-1834*, Durham: Duke University Press, 1986, pp. 138-45; José Honório Rodrigues, *The Brazilians: Their Character and Aspirations*, Ralph Edward Dimmick (trans.), Austin: University of Texas Press, 1967, p. 72; and Julio José Chiavenato, *Cabanagem: o povo no poder*, São Paulo: Brasiliense, 1984, pp. 15-36. There are several estimates on the number of prisoners placed aboard the *Palhaço*. Macaulay (p. 145) as example states there were five executions, and that 253 captives were placed in the storage area of a makeshift prison ship. Nearly all, 249, died from suffocation. He does not mention the lime. The data in Chiavenato (*Cabanagem, loc. cit.*) is not based upon mere guess work, and is thus the source referred to here. An oil painting of this event, by the *Paraense* (someone from Pará) artist Maris Filho, can be seen in Figure 10. For another example

57

Following independence, the use of vessels for exile really came into its own with the *presingangas* of the Sabinada Revolt, which began in 1837. Floriano was merely improving on what had gone on before when he permitted large numbers of *indesejáveis*, or undesirables (i.e., blacks, racial hybrids, the poor, criminals, and the unemployed), to be included on the internal exile ships. Foreigners were subject to the same treatment until being deported back to their original country or last port of embarkation. In two years of Floriano's government, 1893 and 1894, a total of 76 foreigners were banned by presidential decree at the behest of the chief of police. Of these, 31 were expelled for theft (2 being women), 2 for pimping, 7 for counterfeiting (3 women), 16 for political crimes, and 20 for anarchism. There were a total of 17 deportees, 14 (82.4%) being Italians, Portuguese, or Spanish in 1893. The following year, 59 left the country, of which 30 (50.9%) were Italians, Portuguese, or Spanish.[23]

In 1893, Admiral Custódio de Mello resigned and declared himself in opposition to Floriano. A monarchist, the admiral lost no time in setting up an enclave favorable to deposed *Dom* Pedro II in Magé, at one end of Guanabara Bay. His forces held the area for four months before the army saved the day in a murdering and raping rampage. No less than 500 persons were executed during or

of this same use of lime against prisoners, eighty-eight years later, see *infra*, nn. 53-55.

[23]*Cf.*: Franco, *loc. cit.*; *Jornal do Brasil*, April 18, 1993, sec. Cidade, p. 21; Glauco Carneiro, *História das revoluções brasileiras*, Rio de Janeiro: Cruzeiro, 1965, vol. i, pp. 63-65; Paulo Sérgio Pinheiro, *Estratégias da ilusão: a revolução mundial e o Brasil, 1922-1935*, São Paulo: Companhia das Letras, 1991, pp. 88-89; Freyre, *Order and Progress*, pp. 9-10; Edgard Carone, *A República Velha: evolução política*, São Paulo: Difusão Européia do Livro, 1971, pp. 74-78; Souza, p. 109; Brazil, Senado Federal, *Constituições do Brasil de 1824, 1891, 1934, 1937, 1946 e 1967 e suas alterações*, Brasília: Subsecretaria de Edições Técnicas, 1986, vol. i, p. 102, title v, art. 80, sec. 2, no. 2; and United States, National Archives [hereafter USNA], letter, "Sackville to G-2," April 17, 1936, no. 1634, p. 2, MID 2657-K-70/34. The number of Brazilians and foreigners who were Shanghaied in this way to remote areas of Brazil, often to work under the lash as virtual slaves, can, of course, never totally be accounted for. Only a few cases will be touched upon in this text. For a new look at the *Sabinada*--a revolt in which 1,091 mostly non-whites were slaughtered, in three days of carnage once they surrendered to the government's forces--see the valuable work by Kraay (pp. 502, 520-21). The internal banishment feature of Brazilian law would reappear in all constitutions, with only slight wording changes, until the *Constitution of 1967. Cf.*: Brazil, Senado Federal, *Constituições do Brasil de 1824, 1891, 1934, 1937, 1946 e 1967*, p. 180, title viii, art. 175, sec. a; p. 221, art. 168, sec. a; and p. 296, art. 209, sec. 3. Arquivo Nacional [hereafter AN], document, Cx. 6C5/GIFI. In respect to the Italians, Portuguese and Spanish, note that these statistics are misleadingly reported in José Murilo de Carvalho (*Os bestializados: o Rio de Janeiro e a república que não foi*, São Paulo: Companhia das Letras, 1987, p. 24).

directly after the fighting.

Another grisly chapter while Floriano was president helped to solidify the position of this man called the "Iron Marshal." The Federalist Civil War (1893-1895) pitted republicans against yet another segment of those interested in a return of the Braganças.[24] Centered mainly in Rio Grande do Sul, it was a conflict with a shocking number of needless killings on both sides, many by beheading. Together with what had happened at Magé, both ordeals left the nation rife for some time with rumors and accusations concerning the monarchy and its reappearance.

Entering this nervous atmosphere, an aloof religious zealot, Antônio Vicente Mendes Maciel, or "Antônio Conselheiro" ("Antônio the Counselor"), founded an austere sect of folk Catholics in Canudos, Bahia. A curious sort of man, Conselheiro's grandfather had been lynched years before while in police custody. He himself had been battered about by the authorities no less than twice for crimes that were probably the figment of someone's imagination. At different times he had been a businessman, school teacher, salesman, and lawyer. It was while practicing law that he began to take the side of the oppressed. This metamorphosis resulted in a man noted for his special kindness to the victims of police and political wrongdoing. His benevolence involved no color lines and after arriving at Canudos in 1893, the composition of his community began to reflect this fact. Blacks, *mulatos*, *mamelucos*, many *caboclos*, and even whites, some of whom were well connected white women, were among the inhabitants.

Finally, and dangerously, there was a kind of confused yearning for the emperor. What this really was, however, was a nostalgia for the bygone days before the separation of Church and state that came with the republic. The new government had lost favor with Conselheiro after it passed a law in 1891 invalidating Church marriages. Overnight, legal matrimony became entirely a civil affair. It was perhaps an unwise decision on the part of legislators, since it untied the hands of most men, allowing those who chose to do so to abandon their freshly decreed illegitimate families.

---

[24]*Cf.*: *Jornal do Brasil*, April 18, 1993, sec. Cidade, p. 21; Franco, p. 423; Mocellin, pp. 159-63; José Maria Bello, *História da República, 1889-1954*, 4th ed., São Paulo: Nacional, 1959, pp. 133-42; and Samuel Bemis, *A Diplomatic History of the United States*, New York: Holt, 1936, pp. 758-59.

Antônio Conselheiro routinely dressed in a beltless, dirty-blue tunic and sandals. It was his standard garb long before Canudos. His lengthy hair and beard went unkempt on a gaunt frame. It was likely that he had body lice. Yet he was the most important type of rural layman, a counselor. He built churches, offered advice, and preached so well that his listeners were spellbound. He told them over and over again that whatever was not good was inherently evil, and that Free Masonry and Protestantism were the works of Satan. Conselheiro was careful not to encourage social revolution, promote miracles, or arrogate Catholic rituals. Nor did he offer healing to the drought-plagued *povos miseráveis*, or miserable masses.[25]

One need only look at the most terrible dry spell to understand what these people faced from climatic devastations. In the nearby province of Ceará, the drought of 1877-1879 brought a gush of peasants from the *caatinga*, or scrub-savanna rural areas of the region, to the provincial capital in Fortaleza. In 1877, the city's population was put at 40,000. Two years later the number of residents was estimated at 160,000. There were several thousand who died while on their way or after their arrival from the parched backlands. The rest were herded into large pens in the center of town. These enclosures would come to hold 7,000 or more people, and would be called "Concentration Camps" or "Corrals" by the locals. One grew to 1,640 sq. feet in size. The year 1878 was a calamity with as many as 56,791 people dying agonizing deaths. Starvation was not the main culprit. Most of these *retirantes*, or drought refugees, perished from the plague, cholera, beriberi, dropsy, dysentery, or smallpox. For the forty years between 1866 and 1905, Fortaleza's mortality statistics averaged just over 1,350 per year if

[25]*Cf.*: Levine, Robert, "Mud-Hut Jerusalem': Canudos Revisited," *HAHR*, vol. lxviii, no. 3, August 1988, pp. 526-27, 529-31, 534-36, 538, 545, 548, 562, 534n, 538n; ___, *Vale of Tears: Revisiting the Canudos Massacre in Northeastern Brazil, 1893-1897*, Berkeley: University of California Press, 1992, p. 140; Lori Madden, "Evolution in the Interpretations of the Canudos Movement: an Evaluation of the Social Sciences," *Luso-Brazilian Review* [hereafter *LBR*], vol. xxviii, no. 1, Summer 1991, p. 59; and João Batista Arruda Pontes, "Canudos: messianismo e conflito social," unpublished Master's thesis, Humanities Center, Universidade Federal da Paraíba, 1992, pp. 73-74. There have been numerous messianic/millenaristic movements in Brazil. For a discussion of some of the most important manifestations, *cf.*: Maria Isaura Pereira de Queiroz, *O messianismo: no Brasil e no mundo*, São Paulo: Dominus, 1965; and Levine, *Vale of Tears*. See also *infra*, n. 70 to the end of the chapter.

one subtracts 1878. If we also leave out the two years on each side of 1878, the average falls to 1,167 per year. Perhaps a more revealing way to visualize what took place is to note that the deaths for 1878 accounted for over half (51.9%) of all Fortaleza deaths during the entire forty-year span.[26]

Prisoners, particularly prisoners in the interior, also had a hard time. As they fled to the coast, many *retirantes* were arrested for committing some small crime in order to obtain food. At one lockup, in São Matheus, in 1878,

...the jail was a theater of the most absurd scenes. There were days in which the miserable inmates had nothing more to eat than four square inches of cow leather! Public charity could not provide more to ease their misfortune. Haggard men and women, like skeletons, laid on the floor because they had traded away their hammocks for a few handfuls of flour. Some cried, others swore hopelessly, and all were extremely unhappy. In the morning the guard opened the cell door and removed the cadavers of those who had starved to death. The following morning he did the same thing. On their knees, the prisoners begged him to go free. They at least wanted to die far away from the squalid jail, breathing fresh air again, not the putrid vapor of that dungeon! At this, the jailer shut the cell door, making an unbearable creaking sound, turned his back and walked away. He was accompanied by moans, expressions of grief, and curses.[27]

The underage were the ones who endured the most. If their parents died, they were left without anyone to help them. Many of the drought victims were consequently children. Of those that lived, the boys often became thieves and the girls prostitutes. With sickening infections and diseases, they wandered the streets looking for handouts. At each door, and from every person they staggered across, they would beg. Some did so out of necessity, others because of the bad company they had fallen in with. Their pleas were usually preceded with an appeal to one's religious nature that had been mumbled so many times they were memorized. One common version[28] went:

Eu peço por caridade,

[26]*Cf.*: Hall, Anthony, *Drought and Irrigation in North-East Brazil*, Cambridge: Cambridge University Press, 1978, Cambridge Latin American Studies xxix, p. 4; Rodolpho Theophilo, *Historia da secca do Ceará: 1877 a 1880*, Rio de Janeiro: Ingleza, 1922, p. 245; and ___, *A secca de 1915*, Fortaleza: Moderna-Carneiro, 1919, pp. 37, 142. These calculations assume that the later publication by Theophilo contains revised figures.
[27]*Ibid.*, pp. 358-59.
[28]*Cf.*: *ibid.*, pp. 245, 358, 387-91; and ___, *A secca de 1915*, p. 94.

> Pelos mysterios da cruz
> Meu irmão, me dê uma esmola
> Pelo sangue de Jesus
> . . . .
>
> I beg for charity,
> For the mysteries of the cross,
> My brother, give me something
> For the blood of Jesus

What Antônio Conselheiro offered those who came to him in droves was the promise of hard work and their redemption through the Christian creed. What he gave them was an alternative to starvation in an egalitarian community. It was an attractive offer covering a suggestive messianic core that went straight to the heart of rural Catholic beliefs.

Almost inherently, little of what Conselheiro was doing sat very well with the regional power-brokers. These men found it difficult to sit idly by and watch their extra laborers, their destitute customers, and their naïve parishioners run off to join up with a menacing religious extremist. There was perhaps one more reason for the exodus of these *fanáticos*, or usually poor rural people who blindly followed spiritual leaders. It was the fact that the 15,000 to 20,000 inhabitants of Canudos, by then Bahia's second biggest city, stopped paying any kind of taxes to the municipal, state, and federal authorities.[29] This provoked innumerable problems for Conselheiro, but it certainly did not hurt the feeling his people had for him. As an anonymous verse from Bahia would have it, the Canudos faithful came to view their leader as a religious shield who would act as their champion against exploitation and the constant fear of police repression:

> Antônio Conselheiro
> Por ser conselheirista
> Briga com o gôverno
> Não tem mêdo da poliça[30]

---

[29]*Cf.*: Levine, "Mud-Hut Jerusalem," pp. 525, 527, 535, 564; and "Canudos," TV Educativa, October 9, 1987.

[30]Silva, José Calasana Brandão da, *No tempo de Antônio Conselheiro: figuras e fatos da campanha de Canudos*, Salvador: Progresso, 1959, p. 62. By way of contrast, Levine observes ("Mud-Hut Jerusalem," pp. 528, 528n, 540) that despite near total illiteracy in rural areas, in the last years of the empire, Bahia expended much less on public education than it did on its police force.

62

. . . .

Antônio Conselheiro
Because he is a counselor
Fights with the government
And has no fear of the police

By 1894, complaints were being voiced by the Bahian establishment that the Counselor had gone mad, that he was a criminal preaching a rabid brand of royalism, and that his religious ceremonies included heretical religious practices. There were likewise slurs about the inferior flock the Conselheiro was gathering around himself at Canudos. The sources of power were then successful in blowing all this up into a threat to the young republic. Such a challenge could not be tolerated. In fact it was not even to be made by a horde of racially-mixed degenerates bent on bringing back the imperial family to rule the country.

Finally, in 1896, judge Arlindo Leoni impounded a shipment of wood bound for Canudos. The lumber was to be used on one of Conselheiro's pet projects: Canudos' new church. Joined by local *Coronel* João Evangelista Pereira e Mello, Leoni sent telegrams to the state governor pleading for protection, and for help in stemming the flow of peasant defectors to the Conselheiro's holy city.

It was not long before some one-hundred police soldiers were riding off to capture the self-styled religious adviser and put the fanatics in their place. Intercepted, the detachment was surprisingly defeated by the men and women making up the Counselor's rag-tag irregulars.[31] Then two federal armies were ceremoniously dispatched with the same objectives, and just as unceremoniously routed by the same partisans. If this were not enough, the commander of one of these government forces, national hero Moreira Cesar, was mistakenly shot and

---

[31]__, *Vale of Tears*, pp. 151-52. Chiavenato (*Cangaço*, p. 13), makes a key point about the kind of people fighting for Antônio Conselheiro.

Usually, the founders of Canudos are called *jagunços* [see *supra*, chap. i, nn. 1-2]: an error spread by Euclides da Cunha, in his bias vision of the followers of Conselheiro. A *jagunço* is a lawbreaker for rent. The *sertanejo* of Canudos was a peaceful farm worker, living in a religious community. The prejudice of Euclides da Cunha served to comprehensively associate with crime a people who only wanted to vindicate their use of the land.... There was nothing better to explain the blood bath that the army perpetrated at Canudos than to identify the leaseholder as the criminal.

Levine ("Mud-Hut Jerusalem," p. 528) adds that after the slaughter, the word "...*jagunço* took on a pejorative connotation, that of *cangaceiro* [see *infra*, chap. iii], or outlaw--one among many ways in which Canudos burrowed into the national psyche." See, for example, the mislabeling of survivors at Canudos in *infra*, 37n.

killed by one of his own soldiers.[32]

These events produced a corresponding panic down in Rio de Janeiro. The national administration became more and more desperate with each new disaster. Far removed from the parched backlands, the residents of the Brazilian capital were unaware that this enemy was conducting a quite cunning defense, one that would be called guerrilla warfare in the next century. In fact, had a refined gentleman on the streets of the old Federal District had such hit-and-run procedures explained to him, he probably would have thought they bordered on cowardice. There was no denying, on the other hand, their effectiveness. The hills, gullies, and other natural obstacles in and around the Canudos region were perfect for such tactics. The terrain was so fortified and familiar to the undermanned and under-equipped *sertanejos* that they could fight this way, and in so doing, stave off a limited invading force for some time.

Their historic struggle was doomed, however, despite more than one desertion to Conselheiro's side from the government's forces. It would fail because the War Ministry was sending larger numbers of men, and bigger guns, with each new assault. Whatever the price of victory, the ruling elite were prepared to pay it. In the end, the *sertanejos* were slowly made to retreat in the face of a massive army drawn from the capital and ten Brazilian states. As they thundered ever closer, the huge group of men and machines lobbed shell after artillery shell from the surrounding cliffs onto the earthen huts that were called Canudos. The final charge into the bombed-out cavity of a city, and the hand-to-hand savagery that followed, left most of the defenders dead.

Probably to the consternation of the government, Antônio Conselheiro had conveniently died some days before the decisive battle, most likely from dysentery. His corpse was dug up and decapitated anyway. The head was jammed onto a pike to the yelps and cheers of the victors. It was later shipped to Salvador and examined by forensic medicine specialist, Dr. Raimundo Nina Rodrigues. One of the few *mulatos* in Bahia who had succeeded against the odds and distinguished himself academically, Nina Rodrigues was a follower of Cesare Lombroso's evolutionary-throwback theories of criminology. Yet try as he might, no atavistic

---

[32]This information was provided by Manuel Ciriaco, one of the survivors of Canudos. *O Cruzeiro* (Rio de Janeiro), July 19, 1947, p. 60.

features were noted on Antônio Conselheiro's severed cranium by the good doctor or anyone else.[33]

Canudos was leveled, obliterated by a revenge-bent military. What male prisoners there were, were rapidly interrogated before being drawn and quartered, burned alive, or having their heads severed. Women, both young and old, were coerced into concubines, beaten, and raped. Others were turned into prostitutes, or compelled into slavery, which still existed in outlying areas. There was together with all this a forced march for part of the captives to a makeshift holding area. Anyone who could not keep up on this Brazilian "trail of tears" was a candidate for an immediate bullet. Even children were not spared. They either had their brains smashed into trees by soldiers or were taken to the coast and given to the families of the well-to-do.

A few of the lucky ones, those who escaped everything, slowly drifted back to Canudos. Survivor José Travessia stated that, "after the fighting I returned, but there wasn't anything left, only piles and piles of putrefying bodies without heads."[34] Manuel Ciriaco was another fortunate soul who managed to live. With the ground still smoldering, he re-entered the once flourishing community, noticing that "the decaying odor lingered for many miles. Vermin ran through the cadavers, and vultures made clouds in the skies. All of the bodies were abandoned; none were buried."[35] In the ensuing months, some of the other survivors made their way to Rio de Janeiro and began living on a hill just west of the downtown area. Their creation on Morro da Providência, a teeming legacy from Canudos, still exists. It became the first *favela*, or shantytown, in the national capital.[36]

---

[33]A picture of Antônio Conselheiro's corpse is presented here as Figure 19. Optato Gueiros (*Lampeão: memórias de um oficial ex-comandante deforças volantes*, 4th ed., Salvador: Progresso, 1956, pp. 220-21) claims that the head taken to the esteemed doctor was not that of Antônio Conselheiro. In his view, it belonged to the body of Manoel Quadrado. For other freshly removed skulls that were taken to the followers of Nina Rodrigues, see *infra*, chap. iii, nn. 94-95.

[34]*O Cruzeiro*, July 19, 1947, p. 36.

[35]*Ibid.*, p. 42.

[36]There are two versions concerning just who founded Morro da Providência. The first is that it was started by prostitutes who followed the troops. There were already a number of working-class individuals on the hill who had been forced out of the city center when Avenida Central was constructed (see *infra*, chap. iv). This theory would have to make room for some of the women from Canudos, forced into prostitution, who came back to Rio with the victorious soldiers. Once re-billeted, the troops could hardly take these females into the Quartel General, or headquarters of the Brazilian army, just below the slopes of Providência. Since some of the women were from the Morro da Favela in the interior of Bahia, they began using the word *Favella* when speaking

Dulling the sweetness of victory, the Brazilian army suffered a sharp drop in prestige at taking so many casualties in the Canudos affair. They not only lost men, they squandered too much equipment before casting tactics aside to overwhelm the uncouth *fanáticos*. This disagreeable chain of events was quickly blamed by them on what they claimed was an ineffectively run civilian government. Forgotten somewhere in all the accusations and explanations was the fact that thousands of lower-class Brazilians died in a war started by the all-powerful to save their profits, their careers, and their white republic.[37]

The spectacle in the Bahian badlands was not the only messianic movement requiring the attention of the elite's security apparatus during this period. Owing to the poverty of the agrarian population, tempered by provincial religious superstitions, a handful of rural personalities were propelled into the ranks of the influential. This was especially true, and sometimes especially quick, when these individuals were considered saint like. Ready for any kind of miracle that would deliver them, people in the interior were quite literally desperate to be saved from exploitation, privation, and all that went with it.[38]

---

of the encampment on Providência. The second position holds that it was the winning soldiers themselves who began Rio's first shantytown. According to this rendition, a number of veterans from the Canudos campaign went to the capital to ask for assistance from the government. In time the hovels they constructed on Providência came to be called Morro da Favella because the hills that surrounded Canudos were covered with a local plant that was known as *favela*. Note that it would be easiest to assume a degree of accuracy, depending on who told the story, in both accountings. *Cf.*: Anonymous-3, interviews, Rio de Janeiro, June 14, 1990; June 16, 1990; December 1, 1991; and *Jornal do Brasil*, November 29, 1992, sec. Cidade, p. 31. Statistics from the 1991 census list 394 *favelas* in the municipality of Rio de Janeiro. Brazil, Instituto Brasileiro de Geografia e Estatística, *IBGE revela: do total da população brasileira, 21% são indigentes (isto equivale à população Argentina)*, Rio de Janeiro: IBEG, 1994, informação para a imprensa, texto no. 73.

[37]*Cf.*: Levine, "Mud-Hut Jerusalem," pp. 528, 548, 550, 556-60, 568-70, 559n-560n; ___, *Vale of Tears*, pp. 183-192; *Isto É Senhor* (São Paulo), May 23, 1990, p. 42; "Canudos," TV Educativa (Rio de Janeiro), October 9, 1987; Henry Keith, "Soldiers as Saviors: the Brazilian Military Revolts of 1922 and 1924 in Historical Perspective," unpublished PhD thesis, Department of History, University of California, Berkeley, 1970, pp. 128-31; Pang, pp. 59-62; and Euclides da Cunha, *Os Sertões*, 22nd ed., São Paulo and Belo Horizonte: Francisco Alves, 1952, pp. 317-20, 325-26, 534, 542. Levine's "Mud-Hut Jerusalem" and *Vale of Tears* are excellent re-examinations of many of the events dealing with Canudos, including the cultural myopia of Euclides da Cunha. A photograph of some of the momentary survivors of Canudos, mistakenly claimed to be 400 *jagunços* and *jagunças* by the authorities, is presented here as Figure 22.

[38]Cava, Ralph della, *Miracle at Joaseiro*, New York: Columbia University Press, 1970, pp. 85-87. Although della Cava was concerned with *Padre Cícero* (see *supra*, 21n, *infra*, nn. 38-44, 63-70, and chap. iii), his remarks are equally applicable to Canudos.

Somewhat before Antônio Conselheiro gained national notoriety, there was *Padre* Cícero Romão Batista. Born in Ceará, in the Cariri Valley town of Crato, he eventually settled in the nearby hamlet of Juazeiro do Norte. *Padre* Cícero, or *"Padim* Ciço" in a rural Northeasterner's accent, become famous in 1889 when a communion wafer he was giving a black *beata,*[39] Maria de Araújo, turned to blood in her mouth. For some time thereafter, whenever *Padre* Cícero celebrated Eucharist with the woman, the same miracle occurred. Besides the blood, there were marks on her forehead where something, indicative of the scratches that could have been left by a crown of thorns, had irritated her skin. Her hands and feet showed the well known suggestions of crucifixion. A team of doctors was called in to examine Maria de Araújo but found nothing abnormal.[40] There was also a series of less absorbing mysteries attributed to Cícero over the coming years in an adjacent, outlying community

In Fortaleza, the Church hierarchy met much of this with skepticism because of jealousies harbored by the Bishop of Ceará, *Dom* Joaquim José Vieira. The bishop labeled the miracles as false irrespective of the evidence. He then had Cícero called to Rome to explain himself. And finally, Vieira made sure that Cícero was banned from the pulpit despite the favorable review he received from the Holy See. It has been suggested that the bishop of Ceará's real objection was based on the fact that he was first informed about the miracles through the press and not through the Church's chain of command. It did not help the situation either that Maria de Araújo was of African descent.

Vieira calculatingly empaneled a commission of trusted priests to evaluate the events at Juazeiro. He expected that they would prove him right. When the panel upheld the miracles, the bishop discarded their findings and set up a second commission. This new body, after one of its members received a sizable monetary inducement, voted the way the bishop wanted. Besides the opposition of *Dom*

[39]A religiously active lay person who has made vows of chastity, and who has no profession. *Beatos* or *beatas,* depending on their sex, lived off of charity. Xavier de Oliveira, *Beatos e cangaceiros,* Rio de Janeiro: Revista dos Tribunais, 1920, p. 39.
[40]Alencar, Generosa, interview, Juazeiro do Norte, May 11, 1993. An orphan, Generosa Alencar was partially raised by *Padre* Cícero. The priest's devotees referred to him as *meu padrinho* (my godfather, or my protector, or both). Candance Slater, "Messianism and the Padre Cicero Stories," *LBR,* vol. xxviii, no. 1, Summer 1991, pp. 120-21.

Joaquim José Vieira, the Cardinal down in Rio, *Dom* Joaquim Arcoverde de Albuquerque Cavalcanti never accepted the idea of the miracles. He consistently expressed his resistance, instructing Vieira to resolve the matter.[41] The provincial poor, however, never cared about these prelate maneuverings. They continued to venerate *Padre* Cícero. For them, he had been touched by the hand of the Almighty.[42]

Padre Cícero was to grow into the most influential (defrocked) priest of his time. Juazeiro itself mushroomed to some 15,000 inhabitants by 1909. There were even a number of sects within the city's boundaries or nearby. Cícero was not about to monopolize power as would Antônio Conselheiro. Administering to his congregation from his home, *Padim* Ciço saw after their religious needs, and those of his cherished Juazeiro.[43] He permitted his followers to work outside the city on neighboring *fazendas*. Cícero even placated the forceful through a strict policy of political neutrality until he found it beneficial to do otherwise. These were important concessions, helping him to pacify suspicious power barons, be they at home or all the way down in Rio.[44]

Other events were occupying the minds of the men in the Federal District. Another presidential election was shaping up. The contest was between the somewhat short, and very definitely gullible, Hermes Rodrigues da Fonseca, a marshal from the army, and Rui Barbosa, one of the few important political

---

[41]*Cf.*: Alencar, Generosa, interviews, Juazeiro do Norte, May 11, 1993; May 13, 1993; and Daniel Walker Almeida Marques, interview, Juazeiro do Norte, May 13, 1993.

[42]Lampião and his men (see *infra*, chap. iii) were among those who held this opinion of *Padre* Cícero. Billy Jaynes Chandler, *The Bandit King: Lampião of Brazil*, College Station: Texas A&M University Press, 1978, p. 207.

[43]*Padre* Cícero's political career is noted for the following chronology: **October 4, 1911:** nominated to the office of mayor of Juazeiro; **January 20, 1912:** elected the 3rd vice-governor of Ceará; **February 11, 1913:** dismissed from his post as mayor by *Coronel* Marcos Franco Rabelo (see *infra*, nn. 65-69), state governor; **July 22, 1913:** recognized as 1st vice-governor of Ceará; **1914:** reassumed the post of mayor after the military defeat of Rabelo and held the post until 1927; **April 16, 1925:** elected to fill the congressional seat of recently deceased Floro Bartolomeu but refused the position because he did not want to leave Juazeiro. *Cf.*: Daniel Walker Almeida Marques, interview, Juazeiro do Norte, May 13, 1993; and ___, *História do Padre Cícero em resumo: datas, fatos e fotos*, 2nd ed., Juazeiro do Norte: Mascote, 1989, pp. 16-17.

[44]*Cf.*: Slater, p. 118; Keith, "Soldiers as Saviors," p. 231; and Levine, "Mud-Hut Jerusalem," p. 564. Antônio Conselheiro, for example, ended up choosing the wrong patron for secular protection, state Conservative Party leader Luiz Vianna. *Ibid.*, pp. 537-40, 545-46. See also *infra*, nn. 63-65, 64n.

intellectuals of this or any period. Because Hermes was the official hand-picked candidate of the sitting president, and since the electors were made up solely of men of substance, the outcome was already decided. Recognizing this, Barbosa's campaign oratory was not encumbered by rhetoric designed to gain votes from all sides. He focused instead on a point that became the highlight of an otherwise boring contest. It was a risky theme too because Rui actually had the courage to say that politics was no place for the military.

This of course was the celebrated *Civilista* (i.e., "put a civilian in charge") election of 1909-1910. Rui captured the moral ear of the country; but was not thought to have much of a chance at the ballot box. His campaign speeches predictably proved unpopular in the barracks. In fact, they infuriated much of the army. Many idealistic members of this select group considered Hermes a honorable man; while viewing their own roles as "...the guardians of the republic they helped establish in 1889."[45]

Cadets taking the army's officer candidate course were coming more and more from middle-class backgrounds. Much of the time they spent in the classroom revolved around the memorization of courses that rested on nationalistic-positivistic foundations. This philosophical position was drilled into them by instructors following the lead of General Benjamin Constant Botelho de Magalhães. He in turn said he received his inspiration from the father of sociology, August Comte. It was an education that manufactured soldier-intellectuals who defined the best form of government--then and forever--as being a republican dictatorship, preferably with a strong, one-man rule. The single figurehead was naturally to come from the upper ranks of an unbiased, pristine, and well paid military.[46] It is clear that numerous men in uniform rejected as out-

[45]Hahner, June, *Civilian-Military Relations in Brazil, 1889-1898*, Columbia: University of South Carolina Press, 1969, p. 4. The quandary of Hermes was derided as a political cartoon in *O Gato*. It is recaptured here in Figure 15.

[46]*Ibid.*, p. 83. To be fair, and even if they felt that they could do no better, the military was not the only part of the Brazilian social fabric to be awed by positivism. It was an ideological approach, particularly the French version, which

...deeply infused the governments of this generation... [and] provided a rationale for neglecting the less fortunate. Society would progress, according to positivism, if led correctly by a scientific-minded and determined vanguard. The masses would be pulled along and up if society as a whole progressed. It was wrong to expend scarce resources on the poor, who did not know how to invest in progress. The stick (police repression) predominated over the carrot (better-living standards) for imposing social control.

of-hand any recommendations of the type made by Barbosa. The military would never leave politics. They believed that it was their duty to step in and save Brazil from itself.

The election was held, the votes were counted, and Hermes, as nearly everyone anticipated, was declared the victor. He assumed office but had barely settled into the presidential palace at Catete when everyone in the building, together with the 985,000 inhabitants of the Federal District, were blasted awake in the early morning hours of November 22, 1910. The capital had come under a full-blown naval bombardment.

It seems that the sailors aboard two brand new Brazilian battleships, the *Minas Gerais* and the *São Paulo*, were not as starry-eyed as some of their commanding officers. Joining the crews from these state-of-the-art warships, enlisted men on the aged dreadnought *Deodoro* and the cruiser *Bahia* had followed their brothers-in-arms by also seizing control of their vessels. It all took place after one of their numbers, Marcelino Rodrigues Menezes, was brutally flogged in front of the assembled ship's company on the deck of the *Minas Gerais*. The rebels were led by a tall charismatic seaman named João Cândido Felisberto. Of African heritage, he would one day be referred to in the Brazilian folklore as "The Black Admiral." On that Tuesday morning in 1910, the 2,379 mutineers under his command decided they'd had enough of the vicious system of discipline that remained a trademark of the fleet even though the days of legal bondage were supposedly long gone.

For decades, the lower ranks in the navy had been the last refuge of social misfits. Most were illiterate, many were described as being from undesirable races. Black and brown sailors were particularly numerous. So too were those who had been abducted into the navy from the Northeast. All were essentially treated as slaves while their superiors lived lives similar to former masters.

To the horror of the establishment and the new government, somehow these

---

Michael Conniff, *Urban Politics in Brazil: the Rise of Populism, 1925-1945*, Pittsburgh: University of Pittsburgh Press, 1981, p. 8.

For a manifestation of the racist side to positivism, see *supra*, nn. 28-37. There was finally the remunerative aspect, which is to say that since the time of the empire, the army usually began to seethe each time it felt that it was being underpaid. *Isto É*, November 4, 1987, p. 22.

ordinary seamen had commandeered their ships. They were rebelling for better rations, pay raises, and most importantly for an end to floggings with special whips studded with nails called *chibatas*. When these devices were put to use all hands were called to and obliged to watch. If the person being punished fainted it was not unusual for a physician to administer an injection to revive him so that the shredding bite of the *chibata* could be felt anew. In fact, there were only two types of penalties in the navy. For minor infractions, sailors were given bread, water and the brig for between three to six days. Major infringements meant a whipping with the *chibata*. The one saving grace was that no more than twenty-five lashes could be inflicted in a single twenty-four hour period.[47]

To keep the men pacified, some forms of gratification were offered, others were endured. Sailors had jobs, food, a roof over their heads, and free medical care, which was more than many of their countrymen could say. As men were isolated aboard their ships, sometimes for weeks or even months at sea, sexual relationships between older seamen and younger sailors were tolerated regardless of an avid *machismo* mentality among the general population. A few officers even went so far as to recognize the "marriages" of the men under them. Homosexual practices were evidently so common, in assorted forms, that it was said at the time that "...pederastism is the opium of the navy."[48]

It was a precarious way to run the fleet. By 1909, sailors were grumbling louder than ever on the *Benjamin Constant* as she circled the globe. One way those in the ship's ranks displayed these feelings was through a collective method of protest called "*promoção*," or "promotion," wherein they sabotaged their weapons. This caused no end of embarrassment for their immediate superiors. Intensifying the friction was another whipping and the subsequent events on the *Aquidaban* that same year. With nearly everyone standing at attention looking point blank at the flogging, a few sailors managed to sneak away and set fire to the craft's powder magazines. The *Aquidaban* exploded into flames and sank in ten

[47]*Cf.*: Carneiro, p. 166; and *Jornal do Brasil*, July 12, 1987, sec. 1, p. 14.
[48]*Cf.*: Arquivo do Departamento de Ordem Política e Social-Rio de Janeiro [hereafter ADOPS], document, "Palestra de um marinheiro na commemoração de *Revolta de João Candido*," [1936?], p. 1, comunismo/pasta 20; Brazil, *Anuário estatistico do Brasil, 1992*, Rio de Janeiro: IBGE, 1993, chap. 16, table 16.4; Carneiro, pp. 165-66, 169; Hahner, *Poverty and Politics*, p. 271; *Jornal do Brasil*, July 12, 1987, sec. 1, p. 14; and *João Cândido: O Almirante Negro*, directed by Emiliano Ribeiro, 1987.

minutes flat.

But it was the return of the crews aboard the *São Paulo* and *Minas Gerais* that really crystallized the aims of the mutineers. Cândido later stated that they were planning to rebel as soon as they left Europe with the new ships. While these vessels were being constructed in England, the crews witnessed the kind of duty seamen had in the British and French navies. This filled them with a desire for the same kind of treatment. They felt that changes had to be made and, since their lighter-skinned bosses were not about to make them, there was but one alternative.[49]

On the day of the revolt, the officer of the watch on the *Minas Gerais* discovered what was up. Without delay he communicated his finding to the ship's captain, Baptista das Neves, who inauspiciously happened to be inebriated on a visiting French craft in the harbor. Neves responded with exemplary logic, "Negroes don't revolt!..." When he sobered up and motored over to his ship in a launch, Captain Neves may still have been under this impression. Reaching the *Minas Gerais*, and learning from Cândido that black Brazilians did revolt, Neves pulled his sword and tried to attack a group of sailors standing nearby. Before he could realize his goal, however, he was hit in the head by one of them so crisply that he died almost instantly. Joviniano, the captain's aid, was also killed for trying to defend his commander. Later, a boat full of officers was sent out to the *Minas Gerais* to try to get the battleship to surrender. It returned to the docks without an agreement but with the officers' corpses. The rebels meant business.[50]

Holding Rio de Janeiro hostage this way produced the desired results. Within five days, Rui Barbosa presented a bill to the government that was voted on, passed, and signed into law. An amnesty was declared, and the antiquated methods of castigation terminated immediately. Yet there was an ominous side to the picture. Even though

> ...the mutineers only fired a few warning shots, this revolt deeply frightened the governing elite, as had slave revolts in the past. Fear of the lower classes, who now had guns and the capacity to use them, mingled with race prejudice. The revolt was not only a physical threat but also a

---

[49]*Cf. Progresso* (São Paulo), December 16, 1928, p. 1; and ADOPS, document, "Palestra de um marinheiro na commemoração de *Revolta de João Candido*," [1936?], *loc. cit.*, comunismo/pasta 20.

[50]*Cf.: ibid.*, pp. 1-2; and Raimundo Porfírio Costa, interview, Rio de Janeiro, June 9, 1993.

blow to elite pride. The rebellious sailors... [had held] for ransom the recently modernized capital of the nation, and... [used] as their weapon the newest European-built ships, which the elite... viewed as symbols of national strength.[51]

The storm burst just twelve days later. Another mutiny was provoked at the naval barracks on Ilha das Cobras and aboard the patrol ship *Rio Grande do Sul*. It was a move planned by the government to catch the defenders in a weakened position. The administration had used the intervening period to insure the loyalty of all the other warships in Guanabara Bay plus the city's shore batteries. With this guarantee of support, one could almost have predicted that Hermes and those who had his ear would have their revenge.

The *Rio Grande do Sul* was violently subdued and the navy's installations on Ilha das Cobras were nearly shot into oblivion. Out of approximately 600 revolting sailors, only seventy survived.[52] When the salvos stopped, and in defiance of the ban against the death penalty (outlawed in Brazil in 1890), Hermes personally ordered the execution by firing squad of one captive, and probably three others.

The authorities tried to discredit Cândido, claiming that he was behind the latest incident, that he committed breaches of naval discipline, and that his actions promoted disorder. The amnesty was suspended. This allowed the police to pick up the men off the *Rio Grande do Sul* and most of those from the first revolt. The majority were apprehended in the city, or as they left their ships, and deposited in the jails and prisons serving Rio de Janeiro. As this transpired, and before his own arrest, Cândido was offered sanctuary by one of the chief officers[53] to English

---

[51]Hahner, *Poverty and Politics*, p. 272. The father of Emiliano Ribeiro (*João Cândido: O Almirante Negro*) told him that *cariocas* evidently ran for their lives in desperation to leave the city. All of the northbound trains out of the capital, arriving in Petrópolis, were completely full. "Telecine Brasil," TV Educativa, February 18, 1989. For more on the "modernization" of the capital, see *infra*, chap. iv.

[52]*Cf.*: *O Cruzeiro*, June 27, 1964, pp. 112, 114; *Correio da Manhã* (Rio de Janeiro), November 23, 1910, p. 1; December 10, 1910, p. 1; and Raimundo Porfírio Costa, interview, Rio de Janeiro, June 9, 1993. The above issue of *O Cruzeiro* also presents a number of interesting photographs of the 1910 revolt. *Correio da Manhã* was usually in opposition to the government.

[53]Note that the *Progresso* (December 16, 1928, p. 1) interview (see *supra*, 49n) of Cândido took place eighteen years after the events of 1910. In the article, he states that he was offered asylum by "Admiral Sire Scotts." Either the short-lived black pride newspaper *Progresso* committed an error or João Cândido made one. Someone plainly garbled the title "Sir." Fortunately, *Jornal do Commercio* (December 9, 1910, p. 3) published a list of all the officers on the English warships

Admiral Arthur Farquhar. Farquhar had steamed north from Montevideo with four warships on the heels of the initial outbreak, entered Guanabara Bay, and begun a waiting game with Hermes. He said his mission was to protect British lives. There were still a few English technicians on board the *Minas Gerais*, not to mention the English community (i.e., entrepreneurs and their families) in Rio. Yet all this was another story because Cândido unwittingly refused the offer. He said that he believed in his president.

The British were the ones who started calling Cândido the Black Admiral. The Brazilians were the ones who tried to kill him. Along with seventeen of his fellow shipmates he was taken to the Ilha das Cobras' brig where every man was stripped and thrown nude into a single subterranean cell originally built to hold a solitary prisoner. Then, on orders that went at least as high as Marques Porto, the stockade's commander, a mixture of carbolic acid, water, and pure lime[54] was poured down on the caged rebels by the guards. As men screamed and their flesh burned, the door to their purgatory was slammed shut for six days. When it was pried opened again, at the insistence of physician Adão Pereira Nunes, only João Cândido and one other man were left alive. Some of those who died had drunk their own urine in a futile attempt to quench their thirst.

Dr. Nunes filled out papers attesting to the fact that Cândido had become mentally ill due to the treatment he received on Ilha das Cobras. He was not insane, but the trick worked. The Black Admiral was taken to a hospital where he stayed for a period before convalescing enough to be drummed out of the service. Up until the last years of his life he sold fish off of a box top at Praça Quinze (Plaza Fifteen) and always talked of returning to the sea. Whenever he tried to get a job that might allow him to do so, navy agents, who were always lurking in his shadows, stepped in to make sure he did not get hired.

Cândido began to look more and more disheveled although he was humble and never complained about his fate. Roberto Silveira, the governor of Rio de Janeiro (1959-1961), took pity on him and provided a modest house in Coelho da Rocha. When Leonel Brizola was governor of Rio Grande do Sul (1959-1963),

---

in Guanabara Bay, along with a number of the most prominent of His Majesty's subjects ashore. The only individual with the name close to "Scotts" was Albert C. Scott, one of the chief officers on Admiral Farquhar's flagship the HMS *Leviathan*.

[54]For a similar lime bath, this one in 1823, see *supra*, nn. 21-22, 22n.

João Cândido's home state, a pension was arranged. He never received anything from the federal government. In the navy, the mere mention of his name came to be prohibited. The officers' hatred of Cândido was so great that in the 1970s a *samba* composed to honor him was not released by the military-dictators' censors until the direct reference to João Cândido as "The Black Admiral" had been replaced with an imprecise "black sailor." It is said that at his funeral in 1968, any sailor who dared attend the service would have been arrested on the spot.[55]

As for the rest of the prisoners from the Naval Revolt of 1910, they remained locked up without benefit of a trial or legal council until Christmas Eve. Then, hidden by the mask of Yule Tide revelry elsewhere in the city, ninety-seven ex-seamen, together with a minimum of 292 *vagabundos* and petty criminals plus forty-four prostitutes from Rio's Casa de Detenção ("House of the Detained"), were all secretly put into the holds of the Lloyd Brasileiro steamer *Satélite*. This took place after the remaining leaders of the movement were stripped to their waists, strapped to the bulkheads at the prow of the freighter, and whipped. All had gone for naught. Following this example, and ritual, the *Satélite* sailed rapidly out of Guanabara Bay bound for the Amazon.[56] It was not to be a calm voyage.

In addition to fifty armed guards and the ship's crew, there were seven spies from the naval police mingling with the *Satélite's* prisoners below decks. Their job

[55]Cf.: Costa, Raimundo Porfírio, interview, Rio de Janeiro, June 9, 1993; Edmar Morél, *A Revolta da Chibata*, 1st ed., Rio de Janeiro:Pongetti, 1959, pp. 165-69; Victor Civita (ed.), *Nosso século, 1900-1910: A Era dos Bacharéis*, São Paulo: Abril Cultural, 1985, part ii, vol. ii, p. 65; Brazil, Ministério da Educação e Cultura, *Obras completas de Rui Barbosa: discursos parlamentares*, Rio de Janeiro: Fundação Casa Rui Barbosa, 1977, vol. xxxviii, 1911, book i, p. 66; ADOPS, document, "Palestra de um marinheiro na commemoração de *Revolta de João Candido*," [1936?], p. 2, comunismo/pasta 20; *Progresso*, December 16, 1928, p. 1; *Correio da Manhã*, November 24, 1910, 2nd ed., p. 9; November 28, 1910, p. 1; December 10, 1910, p. 1; December 10, 1910, 2nd ed., p. 1; December 11, 1910, p. 3; *Jornal do Brasil*, July 12, 1987, sec. 1, p. 14; and *João Cândido: O Almirante Negro*. One of the first published pictures of João Cândido leading the rebellion appeared in *Correio da Manhã*, November 27, 1910, p. 1 (here, Figure 17). Another photograph of the man in his eighty's can be seen in Morél (unnumbered plate between pp. 32 and 33). Note that this last depiction was not published in the subsequent editions of Morél's book.
[56]Cf.: Civita, *Nossa século, 1900-1910*, part ii, vol. ii, *loc. cit.*; and Brazil, Ministério da Educação e Cultura, *Obras completas de Rui Barbosa*, vol. xxxviii, 1911, book i, p. 11. Morél (*A Revolta da Chibata*, 1st ed., p. 151) states that all of the men taken from the Casa de Detenção were in fact thieves and murders, and that there were really 293 of them together with forty-five women. Hélio Leôncio Martins (*A Revolta dos Marinheiros, 1910*, São Paulo: Nacional, 1988, p. 193), agrees with the 293 figure.

was twofold. First, they were to report back to their supervisor, Francisco Mello, on all important gossip. If and when they got the chance, they were also to try to promote an insurrection so that as many of the deportees as possible could be dealt with quickly. Some rebels would not have to wait that long. They already had been secretly condemned to death before leaving Rio de Janeiro. An "X" was placed in the right-hand margin next to their names on the vessel's manifest. There appears to have been as many as twelve of these men. Out safely at sea, Mello ordered all of those so noted to be lined up and shot. Their remains were thrown overboard.[57]

When the *Satélite* reached the mouth of the famous river, she traveled upstream to Manaus, one of three stops on this journey, and dropped anchor. After the ship waited ten days in the tropical heat, the government telegraphed orders for the remainder of the voyage. The *Satélite* steamed back downstream until coming to the Madeira tributary. She then proceeded southwest down the Madeira for some distance before approaching her final destination on February 3, 1911. It was the tiny village of Santo Antônio do Madeira[58] in what is now the state of Rondônia.

Once the ship had come to a standstill, the more than 400 ragged prisoners-- they were fed only once a day during the entire voyage--were hoisted to shore in nets by the *Satélite's* cranes. Waiting on shore were several rubber *fazendeiros*. Always in need of more bodies for arduous work, they purchased half of the de-

---

[57]*Cf.*: ADOPS, document, "Palestra de um marinheiro na commemoração de *Revolta de João Candido*," [1936?], *loc. cit.*, comunismo/pasta 20; Pedro Calmon, *História do Brasil: século xx a República e o desenvolvimento*, Rio de Janeiro: José Olympio, 1959, vol. vi, p. 2124; and Morél, *A Revolta da Chibata*, 1st ed., pp. 154-58. A copy of the "X" list from one Rio jail is located in *ibid.*, p. 154. The number of executions is put at eight to ten by Rui Barbosa. Brazil, Ministério da Educação e Cultura, *Obras completas de Rui Barbosa*, vol. xxxviii, 1911, book i, p. 23. Barbosa made three speeches before the Senate denouncing what he called the "crime of the *Satélite* case." He was outraged at the summary execution of these prisoners; all without trial, without legal council, and without even so much as a priest to give them their last rights. During his oratory, he provoked the anger of his opponents through pointed and often times mocking questions, such as, "Where are we? In republican Brazilian or in Turkey of the sultans?" *Ibid.*, p. 25. For all three discourses, see *ibid.*, pp. 3-69, 71-134; and Brazil, Ministério da Educação e Cultura, *Obras completas de Rui Barbosa: discursos parlamentares*, Rio de Janeiro: Fundação Casa Rui Barbosa, 1981, vol. xlii, 1915, book ii, pp. 163-73. See also *infra*, nn. 57-63.

[58]Morél, *A Revolta da Chibata*, 1st ed., pp. 156-58. In the words of Rui Barbosa, persons who were shipped to this village were condemned to death. It was a place where "...you only die, you do not live, you are not born, you perish." Brazil, Ministério da Educação e Cultura, *Obras completas de Rui Barbosa*, vol. xxxviii, 1911, book i, *loc. cit.*

cimated cargo for their tracts of land where working conditions rivaled those from the days slavery. The rest, including the women, were bound over to the Rondon Commission to work at stringing up telegraph lines and at building the Madeira-Mamoré railroad.[59]

Under the terms of the Treaty of Petrópolis (1903) Brazil was ceded the area comprising Acre. Partially in return, she was to construct a 192.6 mile railway through dense jungle. The original concept was to link Santo Antônio do Madeira, Brazil with Villa Bella, Bolivia, at the junction of the Beni and Mamoré Rivers.[60] The Madeira has a series of impassable rapids between these two points. The plan was designed to provide an access for Bolivian rubber harvests via the railroad to the Amazon tributary system. The work went on for several years as Brazilian, British, and American crews vied with each other under the ultimate command of Brazilian army Lt. Colonel Candido Rondon.[61] The Americans were headed by Percival Farquhar,[62] a man whose great aim it was to control all the railroads in Latin America. To this end it did not hurt that Farquhar was a personal friend of *Coronel*-Senator José Gomes de Pinheiro Machado.

By the time the last spike was in place, the project had cost over 30,000 lives due to physical hardships, malaria, beri-beri, and sporadic Caripuna *índio* attacks. It is ironic that the line became useless almost as soon as it was completed owing to the collapse of the international rubber market. Of the captives off the *Satélite*, all the women died after returning to or being forced into prostitution to survive. Some of the male prisoners were butchered by their guards. None of the others were ever heard from again.[63]

---

[59]Morél, Edmar, *A Revolta da Chibata*, 2nd ed., rev., Guanabara: Letras e Artes, 1963, pp. 141-42.

[60]Brazil was also to pay Bolivia £2,000,000 within four years. Neville Craig, *Estrada de ferro Madeira-Mamoré: história trágica de uma expedição*, Moacir Vasconcelos (trad.), Rio de Janeiro: Nacional, 1947, pp. 436-37. The line was extended at both ends to connect Porto Velho with Guajará-Mirim, 227.2 miles away. Brazil, Conselho Nacional de Estatística, *Ferrovias do Brasil*, Rio de Janeiro: IBGE, 1956, p. 89. Numerous photographs depicting the history of the line, and what's left of it today, can be seen in the exceptional work by Christian Kaarsberg, *Djävulens järnväg: en resa i Amazonas historia*, Per Lennart Månsson (trans.), Nora: Nya Doxa, 1997.

[61]A picture of Rondon is displayed here as Figure 18.

[62]No known relation to Admiral Arthur Farquhar. See *supra*, nn. 53-54.

[63]*Cf.*: Civita, Victor (ed.), *Nosso século, 1910-1930: anos de crise e criação*, São Paulo: Abril Cultural, 1985, part i, vol. iii, p. 37; ___, *Nosso século, 1910-1930: anos de crise e criação*, São Paulo: Abril Cultural, 1985, part ii, vol. iv, pp. 46-49; Morél, *A Revolta da Chibata*, 2nd ed., pp.

Such was not the case for *Padre* Cícero. During these years, *Padim* Ciço had been busy with the growing number of his peasant faithful and with his beloved Juazeiro do Norte. He also had been keeping his political eyes and ears open. Cícero decided to end his long-noted neutrality by joining with fifteen *coronéis* plus one priest in the south of Ceará to support the state governor and *coronel*, Antônio Pinto Nogueira Aciolly.[64] Cícero was thus made a part of the elite of his part of the country. One cannot say that Antônio Conselheiro had such foresight.[65]

In spite of his troubles with the Church,[66] it would be fair to say that in essence time had been good to *Padre* Cícero. He had learned to cover himself. A good deal of this coverage was provided by the presence of the Bahian physician and *coronel*, Floro Bartolomeu da Costa. Bartolomeu was a strong personality. He was also part of a larger plan, one that wound its way back to Rio de Janeiro, to unseat the next governor of Ceará, *Coronel* Marcos Franco Rabelo. As protection implies obligation, Cícero too became involved with the conspiracy in Juazeiro when Bartolomeu returned to the city on November 22, 1913. Floro had been authorized to form an alternative state government in the community with himself as governor. Men-in-arms would be provided by the *coronéis* who signed the agreement backing Aciolly, and by the supporters of *Padim* Ciço.[67]

From the state capital, Rabelo attempted to check Bartolomeu. He also vowed to bring the head of *Padre* Cícero to Fortaleza skewered to the end of a pole.[68] Units of Rabelo's *Força Pública* (the *Polícia Militar* in some states) were soon dispatched to Juazeiro and the battle was underway. But unbeknown to

---

142-44; and *Enciclopédia Mirador Internacional*, São Paulo: Encyclopaedia Britannica do Brasil, 1975, p. 10065.

[64]*Cf.*: Menezes, Fátima and Generosa Alencar, *Homens e fatos na história do Juazeiro: estudo cronológico, 1827-1934*, Recife: Universitária UFPE, 1989, pp. 69-70; and Joaryvar Macedo, *Império do bacamarte: uma abordagem sobre o coronelismo no Cariri cearense*, 2nd ed., Fortaleza: Universidade Federal do Ceará, 1990, pp. 134-42. The agreement was of course the noted *pacto dos coronéis*, or "Pact of the Colonels." A penetrating analysis of its significance is presented in *ibid.*

[65]Keith, "Soldiers as Saviors," p. 232. See also, *supra*, 44n.

[66]See *supra*, nn. 38-42.

[67]*Cf.*: Menezes and Alencar, pp. 74-76; and Joaryvar Macedo, pp. 156-57.

[68]Memorial Padre Cícero [hereafter MPC], photograph, "*Coronel* Marcos Rabelo em 1914," exhibit 42. See the accompanying commentary to this picture.

Rabelo, the legal government in Ceará was to receive little support from the national capital. In Rio de Janeiro, the administration was still in the incapable hands of Hermes da Fonseca, who by this time was firmly in the back pocket of José Gomes de Pinheiro Machado. Machado liked to be called "The Chief." It was a nickname that suggested his real position in the government; a government that was out to destroy Rabelo.

The Chief deemed it best to use a stalling tactic to accomplish everything. It was all so easy. The administration, at the prodding of Machado, came up with one excuse after another for not sending men and material to Ceará. With this, Hermes let the rural fighters, including numerous backland bandits (usually called *cangacerios*) under Bartolomeu, batter the unaided *Força Pública* all the way back to the outskirts of Fortaleza. Ultimately a truce was arranged and elections were called in which Franco Rabelo lost.[69]

The point is that the army marshal and president, Hermes, under the sway of the *coronel*-senator, Pinheiro Machado, sided with extra-legal forces to depose a duly elected state governor. Several aspiring personalities in the army felt uncomfortable with this outcome. They thought it beneath the dignity of the president to let himself be compromised in such a way by a subordinate politician who was openly out to use the government and its institutions for his own purposes. In their opinion, Pinheiro Machado was attempting to realign the national *status quo* of already existing oligarchies into one more favorable to himself.

To this end the military had been trying to counter Machado for some time. Wherever the ambitious senator's influence in a given state was weak, the army tried to set up a "saved" state government. This took place over the entire span of Hermes' years in Catete. Whenever the president hesitated at cooperating, the soldiers simply rattled their sabers to get him to comply. "Salvations" (or

[69]*Cf.*: Freyre, *Order and Progress*, pp. 348-49; Keith, "Soldiers as Saviors," pp. 234-36; Cava, pp. 153-55, 287n; Generosa Alencar Papers [hereafter GAP], telegram, "General Pinheiro Machado to *Padre* Cícero Romão Batista," December 16, 1913; Irineu Pinheiro, *O Juazeiro do Padre Cícero e a Revolução de 1914*, Rio de Janeiro: Pongetti, 1938, pp. 168-69; and *Diário do Nordeste* (Fortaleza), June 29, 1993, sec. 3, p. 1. For the position held by *cangaceiros* in the scheme of things, see *infra*, chap. iii, nn. 3-6. Pinheiro Machado's photograph in 1911 is shown as Figure 16. Another snapshot, depicting Floro Bartolomeu and *Padim* Ciço together, is presented in Figure 30.

"*Salvações*" as the saved states were called), successfully came into being in Alagoas, Espírito Santo, Pará, Pernambuco, Rio de Janeiro, and Sergipe. They failed not only in Ceará, but in the more important states of São Paulo, Minas Gerais, and in Pinheiro's own backyard, Rio Grande do Sul. In each case, a military officer was placed in charge to become the new state governor. Sooner or later, however, the newcomer organized his own political machine, quite often more repressive than the one he replaced.

Together with a few elected officials, the army's protests at what was happening in Ceará greatly worried Hermes. It moved him to such an extent that he felt forced to rule under a state of siege in the Federal District, some surrounding cities, and up in Ceará until his term of office expired in November of 1914. Along the way there were numerous arrests, transfers within the armed forces, and a general air of dissatisfaction among the public and the military. These feelings were particularly strong among junior army officers. A large number of these men truly believed that their idealistic hopes and dreams for Brazil had been dashed by unworthy civilians and geriatric superiors.[70]

The political *Salvações* did not exhaust the areas of concern for Brazil's coming generation of young lions. There were actually several instances where questionable deeds were tolerated in the capital to soothe the nerves of the powerful in distant states. By far the most significant of these episodes, from the army's point of view, began in a disputed and largely unexplored region called the Contestado. Today this area mainly comprises the midwestern part of the state of Santa Catarina. It is a vast landscape, characterized by intermittent prairies, hills, and a lush vegetation rich in timber.

Sometime after 1870, an Italian mystic who went by the name of "*Monge* (Monk) João Maria de Agostini" wandered into Santa Catarina. He had been mocked by some and worshipped by others further to the north. As he continued on to the Contestado, Agostini went about his usual reclusive ways trying to cure the sick with homemade herbal remedies. *Monge* João Maria would accept no money for these services. During his travels he gave sermons and occasionally

---

[70]*Cf.*: *Diário do Nordeste*, June 29, 1993, sec. 3, p. 1. Keith, "Soldiers as Saviors," pp. 86, 198-200, 214-37; and Bello, *História da República*, p. 262.

erected large crosses in the fertile soil.

It was while on one of these journeys, in a gorge near the village of Catanduvas in Santa Catarina, that he predicted the future existence of a community named Santa Cruz (Saintly Cross) on the very ground from which he was speaking. A few years later, the town of Cruzeiro (or Large Cross) did come to life in the appointed area. Although the names were slightly different, the likeness was enough to convince a large part of the local population that Agostini was indeed a man close to God.[71]

Blessed or not, João Maria's behavior and accomplishments produced enemies. One report states that he was eventually arrested and imprisoned by the regional police. Some say he escaped. Others claim that he received a pardon and was released in Rio de Janeiro. Another story has it that he slowly moved on of his own accord, apparently without the help of the authorities. His adherents, however, found all of this speculation immaterial. They were certain that one day *Monge* João Maria would come back or somehow give them a sign that he was with them.[72]

It was not too long before they felt they were proven right. The only difference was that it was not Agostini who returned but a foreigner named Anastás Marcaf.[73] Due to several traits the two men had in common,[74] not the least of which were their fire and brimstone sermons, Marcaf was ultimately taken to be the reincarnation of Agostini. From then on he was known as "*Monge* João Maria de Jesus." Until he himself disappeared in 1908 or 1910,[75] the second João Maria

---

[71]*Cf.*: Cabral, Oswaldo, *História de Santa Catarina*, 2nd ed., Rio de Janeiro: Laudes, 1970, pp. 298-300; and Said Mohamad El-Khatib (ed.), *História de Santa Catarina*, Curitiba: Grafipar, 1970, vol. i, pp. 163-64.

[72]*Cf.*: El-Khatib, p. 164; and Cabral, p. 300.

[73]*Cf.*: *ibid.*; and Keith, "Soldiers as Saviors," p. 272. There are several spellings of this man's real name and no less than two countries from which he is suppose to have originated. Keith (*ibid.*) spells his name, Anastas Marcof, and claims that he came from France. Maurício Vinhas de Queiroz (*Messianismo e conflito social: a querra sertaneja do Contestado, 1912-1916*, Rio de Janeiro: Civilização Brasileira, 1966, p. 49), however, gives the spelling, Atanás Marcaf, and states that he was from Syria. The spelling in Cabral (*loc. cit.*) is the one used here.

[74]One dissimilarity between the two men that was overlooked was the fact that Agostini had three deformed fingers on his left hand. Marcaf's hands were normal. Cabral, pp. 299-300. A picture of the second João Maria is presented as Figure 20.

[75]*Cf.*: Cabral, p. 301; and Maurício Vinhas de Queiroz, pp. 49, 69. Both authors list different dates.

...was revered as a holy father figure through his miracles and good works, much as Antônio Conselheiro and Padre Cicero, healing the sick and the poor; in return, his followers lived by his strict codes of conduct, worshipping and obeying him in every particular. The faithful were spread throughout the Contestado region in several settlements; in each case, the settlements were closely organized, well-policed [by themselves], highly moral communities. Money transactions and commerce were forbidden, and a primitive kind of communism was practiced....[76]

The villages that João Maria de Jesus founded or revitalized in the Contestado began to grow noticeably in size after 1908. For it was in that year the scandal of "Telegram 9" took place. This was an affair in which Argentina accused Brazil, Chile, and the United States of plotting to make war against her. As hostilities seemed imminent, authorities in Rio de Janeiro decided that a rail link with Rio Grande do Sul on the Argentine border was imperative.[77] To put the plan into action the American owned, and Percival Farquhar[78] led, Brazil Railway Company was awarded a strip of land specifically for these purposes. The parcel was 18.6 miles in width by 285 miles in length, extending from the northern to the southern borders of Santa Catarina. It connected the *gaúcho* (something from the state of Rio Grande do Sul) rail system with those in the rest of the country.

The new American landlord wasted little time with the resident population, upwards of 150,000, who inhabited all this prime real estate. Everyone in sight was evicted. The company's intentions were to finish the line and sell the adjacent acreage to German, Polish, Russian, and Ukrainian immigrants. There was of course the long-range incentive of profits for many years to come, hauling the freight and produce of the new settlers to market. More persons were made homeless when a subsidiary of Brazil Railway, the Southern Brazil Lumber and Colonization Company, bought nearly 880 square miles of extra-investment property between 1909 and 1914. They then imported penniless workers from other states, and an even larger collection of Europeans, to function as debt peons. Local *grã-finos* (the upper classes) were allowed to recruit as well as directly

---

[76]Keith, "Soldiers as Saviors," *loc. cit.*

[77]*Cf.*: El-Khatib, *loc. cit.*; and E. Bradford Burns, "As relações internacionais do Brasil durante a Primeira República," *História geral da civilização brasileira: o Brasil republicano: sociedade e instituições, 1889-1930*, 2nd ed., Boris Fausto (dir.), Rio de Janeiro: Difel/Difusão, 1978, book iii, vol. ii, p. 393.

[78]See also *supra*, nn. 58-63.

control many of these laborers.

Each fresh male arrival was placed in a labor gang that either chopped down trees for lumber, worked in the newly assembled sawmill--which was the largest in Latin America--or helped in laying track. Guarded over by armed "assistants," when anyone broke the rules, they were placed in jails constructed along the right-of-way by the firm. Stiff penalties were rare, however, because these men had been brought in to work. When they committed an infraction, unless it was something serious, they were taken from their cells, whipped with the ubiquitous *chibata,* and put back on the job.

Once the line was constructed upwards of 8,000 workers were fired without any further ado, i.e., no passage was provided back to their home states or countries. At the same time there was some rather shady land speculation on the part of both Santa Catarina and nearby Paraná. In the real-estate boom propelled on by the selling of railroad property to immigrants, various tracts of land were sold in duplicate by both states to influential politicians and local strongmen. Whenever it went that far, these forceful individuals invariably won the legal and extra-legal battles with peasants to actually possess the acquired parcels. All of these things produced a flood disposed and the out-of-work on the roads and in the forests. Almost as if by gravity, no small number of them came to live in the religious communes of the missing João Maria de Jesus and his followers.[79]

In 1911 a part *índio,* former soldier, and deserter from the state of Paraná,[80]

---

[79]*Cf.*: Queiroz, Maurício Vinhas de, pp. 70, 75; Keith, "Soldiers as Saviors," p. 271; Civita, *Nosso século, 1910-1930,* part i, vol. iii, pp. 33-37; Levine, *Vale of Tears,* p. 223; Todd Diacon, *Millenarian Vision, Capitalist Reality: Brazil's Contestado Rebellion, 1912-1916,* Durham: Duke University Press, 1991, pp. 106-7; ___, "The Search for Meaning in an Historical Context: Popular Religion, Millenarianism, and the Contestado Rebellion," *LBR,* vol. xxviii, no. 1, Summer 1991, pp. 49-51; and Duglas Teixeira Monteiro, *Os errantes do novo século: um estudo sobre o surto milenarista do Contestado,* São Paulo: Duas Cidades, 1974, p. 31. The Brazil Railway Co., was originally incorporated in Portland, Maine. Maurício Vinhas de Queiroz, *loc. cit.*

[80]What exactly this man was running from is in disagreement. Gabral concludes (p. 298) that he had been in the military but fails to mention deserting. El-Khatib (p. 165) and Keith ("Soldiers as Saviors," p. 273) say that he was a former soldier and deserter from the *Força Pública* in Paraná. Writing in a military journal, infantry Major Luiz Antonio Rech does not mention a soldierly background but argues (p. 89) that he was a renegade from the Paraná police. Diacon (*Millenarian Vision,* p. 1) states that he forsook the security forces in Paraná, and later (pp. 115-18) that he deserted from the army. Lastly, there is Maurício Vinhas de Queiroz who, after some investigation into the matter, feels (p. 81) that he was in fact a soldier, and in

traveled south into the Contestado. He claimed that he was the brother of the missing João Maria de Jesus. Like both of his predecessors, this bearded and nearly toothless third version attempted to do something to help the sick. On one occasion, just a few months after reaching the region, it is said that he brought a small boy back to life. This helped to convince what disbelievers there were. Shortly thereafter the so-called "False Monk," Miguel Lucena da Boaventura, was accepted into the fold as a true apostle and transformed into "*Monge* José Maria de Santo Agostinho."[81]

The communities which José Maria inherited remained similar to those under the two João Marias. Religion was stressed. Communal praying was the day's big event. Property was largely held in common and commerce was prohibited, now under penalty of death. José Maria preached that a return to the monarchy was God's law. He put his military training to use by organizing the settlements for possible conflict with local luminaries. He also warned that the end was near, and that he himself would die in battle at the village of Irani. Meanwhile, scores of *cangaceiros* were easing away from their *patrões* to live in the religious sanctuaries. They were joined by a few army and police deserters plus a handful from the better-off classes.[82]

The same old story was unfolding all over again. The False Monk's activities began to try the patience of surrounding potentates. In fact it was probably one of these wealthy citizens, *Coronel* Francisco Ferreira de Albuquerque, the mayor of Curitibanos, who first called on the state government in 1912 to send a detachment of police to arrest José Maria and dissolve the redoubts.[83] José Maria had made several blunders. His final error was in traveling to Curitibanos for a religious holiday. Once there, his presence only served to incite the throng of needy persons recently dispossessed or fired by the American firms.

Realizing the inevitable, he did everything short of surrender to try to avoid violence. Together with forty or so men from his group, José Maria abruptly broke off the meeting and fled. The small party did not stop until it got to the

---

addition, that he joined an army road construction battalion from which he ultimately deserted.

[81]*Cf*.: Civita, *Nosso século, 1910-1930*, part i, vol. iii, p. 34; and Diacon, *Millenarian Vision, loc. cit.* A drawing of *Monge* José Maria taken from an old photograph is reprinted here as Figure 21.

[82]*Cf*.: Keith, "Soldiers as Saviors," pp. 272-73; and Diacon, *Millenarian Vision*, p. 116.

[83]*Cf*.: *ibid.*, pp. 128-29; El-Khatib, p. 166; and Monteiro, p. 271.

fateful town of Irani, one state away in Paraná. At first things went smoothly as José Maria attempted to reorganize his followers. He established Ministries of War, Agriculture, Finance, and the like. Titles of nobility, as well, were passed out to the *sertanejos* in a comic opera of elite society before the advent of the republic.

Monge Maria's congregation started to multiply again in Irani. But it was too late. One month after their arrival, the Paraná *Força Pública* caught up with José Maria and began shooting. The outcome, on October 22, 1912, was a bloody defeat of the state police. It also produced the deaths of the leaders on both sides: Colonel João Gualberto and *Monge* José Maria de Santo Agostinho. Gualberto's corpse was cut to shreds after the clash in accordance with rustic beliefs which held that such a disfigurement would keep a person's soul in limbo.[84]

As for José Maria, protagonists of his type die hard, especially since he predicted where he would die. It should have come as no surprise then when rumors began to creep through the Contestado the following year that he was still alive. The holy monk was reported to be in heaven telling his disciples that they should start construction of a celestial city at Taquaraçu[85] in the state of Rio Grande do Sul. Communication with him in paradise was mainly done through a fifteen year-old virgin, Maria Rosa.

Maria Rosa was the most influential of several young, untouched, female mediums who were said to possess the ability to speak with the departed leader. Her revelations were startling indeed. Not only did she say that José Maria would return, but that it would be in the year 1913 with the army of martyred Portuguese King Sebastião I.[86] The king had been killed fighting the Moors in 1578. His long prophesied reappearance was believed by some to be nothing short of the second coming of Christ. With the might of Sebastião's army and the power of his own followers, José Maria would be unstoppable. His forces would gain immortality,[87]

---

[84]*Cf.*: *ibid.*; Civita, *Nosso século, 1910-1930*, part i, vol. iii, pp. 38-42; and Marco Antônio da Silva Mello and Arno Vogel, "Monarquia contra República: a ideologia da terra e o paradigma do milênio na 'Guerra Santa' do Contestado," *Estudos Históricos*, vol. ii, no. 4, 1989, pp. 194, 198, 204-7.

[85]Spelled Taquaruçu in Civita (*Nosso século, 1910-1930*, part i, vol. iii, p. 41) and Beloch and Abreu (p. 683). The spelling here reflects current usage.

[86]Diacon (*Millenarian Vision*, p. 176n) points out that the legend of King Sebastião mixed freely in the Contestado with that of the Catholic Church's St. Sebastião. The latter was a Christian martyr in Rome who died about 288 AD.

[87]The religious rebels believed that if killed in battle they would be resurrected and return to

and drive out the infidels and all those supporting the evil republic. A peaceful millennium would then be ushered in throughout the land.

With Canudos still vividly in their minds, the professional politicians in the nation's capital had other plans for the new *fanáticos* gathering in the Contestado sanctuaries. The army was put on alert, perhaps in the hope that mere presence alone would bring about a rapid and total capitulation. It was wishful thinking just as it had been in the Northeast. Together with a few police units, the combined force eventually surrounded Taquaraçu and machine-gunned more than a hundred women, children, and old people. They then began a slow pursuit of the peasants from one section of the Contestado to another. Successes were few, and in the hunt the government's side suffered two humbling reversals. It was a shadowy, hopeless fight in over 15,000 square miles of land. As in other times and places, several area *coronéis* joined in the fray not just to do battle with the followers of José Maria, but also to take advantage of innocent homesteaders, to settle old feuds, and to get rid of the opposition.[88]

The Hermes administration finally came to the conclusion that a hero from the war with Antônio Conselheiro would be just the thing to bring about the desired results with the least possible cost. But General Carlos Frederico de Mesquita did no better than the officers sent into action before him. His failure was a product of two main factors. First, the provincials were exceptional fighters in the vastness of the well forested Contestado (whereas Canudos was but a single village surrounded by rows of fortifications). Second, in spite of the bombast in the halls of government, there was little material support from Rio de Janeiro. Mesquita ultimately came to the opinion he was in a no-win situation. He thereupon disbanded his troops and quit his command. His resignation speech reflected a growing anger on the part of the army at the government's intentions to use

> ...federal forces to chase bandits, like a *capitão do mato* during the time of slavery. It is the responsibility of the governments of Paraná and Santa Catarina, with their police forces, to exterminate outlaws as they appear; thus cleaning their zones of pernicious elements.[89]

resume the fight. *Ibid.*, p. 117.

[88] *Cf.*: *ibid.*, pp. 122-23; Mello and Vogel, p. 192; Civita, *Nosso século, 1910-1930*, part i, vol. iii, p. 42; and Cabral, p. 306.

[89] Soares, J.O. Pinto, *Guerra em Sertões brasileiros: do fanatismo á solução do secular litigio*

By the time Venceslau Brás Pereira Gomes took office as Brazil's next president in November of 1914, fainthearted views similar to Mesquita's were gaining a following in the army. Brás knew that he had to do something soon, and that he had to do it in a firm and decisive manner. Another grand legion was accordingly organized and ordered into the Contestado. This one was led by the army's champion of corruption, General Fernando Setembrino de Carvalho.[90] It had full complements of men, machines, and supplies. It even had two airplanes; the first time such craft were used by the Brazilian military in battle.

General Setembrino was newly returned from appeasing the forces of Floro Bartolomeu just outside Fortaleza. It had been a disagreeable assignment for a man of his rank. In the Contestado he wanted to show the mettle he was made of. On the other hand, he failed to realize that the operation would be far more difficult than anyone imagined. It required several bloody encounters and starvation tactics for Setembrino to gain the upper hand. Nearly 7,000 soldiers, or at that time about one half the Brazilian army, finished off the last sanctuary with a daily bombardment of Santa Maria. Following the shelling, the general's troops rushed in and put the torch to everything. Some 600 people died in the flames before they flickered out.[91] To reimpose order by the first part of 1916, the cost had been thirteen military campaigns and three years of ruthless fighting.

Was this what was required by the reputedly more modern and more professional army to subdue a few thousand hayseeds? Such was but one of the questions asked back at the seat of power with the conclusion of hostilities. True, the army had killed between 3,000 and 6,000 rebels, including all the *fanáticos'* spiritual leaders save one.[92] There was widespread agreement, nonetheless, that it had taken the ultimate providers of order too long to bring the *sertanejos* to their knees.

As a result of these military misadventures, which actually stretched back to the army's having a hand in the overthrow of *Dom* Pedro II in 1889, Brazil's armed

---

[90]*Cf.*: Keith, "Soldiers as Saviors," p. 275; and Nelson Werneck Sodré, *História militar do Brasil*, Rio de Janeiro: Civilização Brasileira, 1965, pp. 204-8.

[91]Diacon, *Millenarian Vision*, p. 4.

[92]*Ibid.*, p. 276. Another estimate (Monteiro, pp. 227, 277n) puts the number of dead as high as 8,000. Civita, (*Nosso século, 1910-1930*, part i, vol. iii, *loc. cit.*) states that when the fighting stopped in January 1916, the death toll had reached 20,000. A photograph of some of the survivors is offered here as Figure 23.

forces found themselves more and more in a position of ambiguity. They were undecided as to their ultimate role in defending the country and its current crop of statesmen. At least during the empire the military's duty was clear and firmly established. They were expected to defend their country and their sovereign. Statecraft was the historical right of the House of Brigança. Once the monarchy was gone, however, and because they effected its demise, many of the younger and the more romantic officers felt that their new posture called on them to interpret the form of this change. That the country had always been in the hands of the powerful was really only a secondary issue. The essential detail was that the true rulers of Brazil had been allowed to arrange things for generations in layers of ever increasing domination to suit their own regional, and when strength permitted, their own national interests.

Moreover, by the end of the nineteenth century, senior politicians had done nothing to stem the tide of foreign goods and services that were allowed in to cater to the appetites of the older order. With the start of World War I, many external markets dried up or were severely reduced. This in turn brought about an increased reliance on internal sources and the individuals who came to control them--the *nouveau riche* of a growing middle class. It would be from this group that men would arise who would alter the system but not the mentality of order.

These events, however, were still to come and the army was once again to play a part. It would be a role grounded on the tragic lessons of recent history. Their disparaging spirit would

...lay dormant during the term of President Venceslau, due to the diversion of World War I, but it would surface following the war with [a] strong conviction that Brazil must be 'saved' by young soldiers, untainted and unblemished by the corrupt politics of the past.[93]

---

[93]Keith, "Soldiers as Saviors," p. 276.

Chapter III

THE *CANGAÇO*: RURAL BANDITS?

Towards the end of the last century there was thus a growing number of freed blacks,[1] persons of mixed ancestry, and even poor whites, who could not, or who would not, eke out a life under the exploitative monopolies[2] that by then existed. To be sure, slaves had revolted or run away simply for want of liberty to *quilombos*. There were also other groups of the downtrodden, the vengeful (without the law behind them), and the rebellious for hire, who had terrorized Brazil in times past.[3] But largely by the 1870s, while many landowner *coronéis* were losing power due to fragmentation or to the increasing number of inter-elite disputes, the Northeast staggered through one drought after another.

Under such circumstances, it was almost predictable that banditry would become more and more of a problem. For some, there was no other way to survive. Others were maintained by large landowners attempting to continue their

---

[1]Aside from those who were deported back to Africa in the wake of the 1835 Bahian slave revolt (see *supra*, chap. i, nn. 65-68), those who worked in the navy, or those who were in the business of slaving itself, only a small proportion of freedmen, and a minuscule number of runaways, had returned to Africa by the year 1889. *Cf.*: Karasch, pp. 397-401; and Manuela Carneiro da Cunha, *Negros, estrangeiros: os escravos libertos e sua volta à África*, São Paulo: Brasiliense, 1985, p. 213.

[2]Facó, Rui, *Cangaceiros e fanáticos: gênese e lutas*, Rio de Janeiro: Civilização Brasileira, 1963, pp. 87-88.

[3]The *cabra, jagunço, capanga*, and *bundão* (singular of *bundões*) ruffians were not the only kinds of brawn put to use by people who could purchase intimidation (see *supra*, chap. i, nn. 1-2). By the last years of the nineteenth century Brazilians had also suffered under *marrões*, who were privately contracted bandits in Goiás and Bahia; *cacheados*, using hair-style as a notice of their role, they did the same thing in other parts of the Northeast; and the *vira-saias*. The *vira-saia* was a specialist in the assault of peasants and the raping of peasant women and their daughters. The latter often took place before pleading husbands and fathers. The *vira-saia*'s job was not necessarily to kill; but to humiliate the poor into submission. There were experts in murder too, like the *clavinoteiros*, who were never demonstrative about their exploits. They were hired singularly to eliminate someone as quietly as possible and then disappear. Others specializing in political murder were called *curimbabas* and *dungas*. Both had the fortune not to be punished because of the connections of their employers. There appears to have been an unwritten rule at work whenever a *curimbaba* or a *dunga* killed someone: "let them go about their business because an assassination here, an assassination there, stabilizes power in the interior." Chiavenato, *Cangaço*, pp. 11-13.

dominance of the *caatinga* and its peasant population. Additional desperados were merely the hired killers, the *capangas* of the *coronéis* whose star was on the decline or whose political party was out of favor. Consequently, in any one region *capangas* came to be called *cangaceiros independentes* ("independent bandits") if they went about their profession mostly on their own, such as when they were patronless by choice or when their sponsor was out of power. For those who used a protector, when he was back on top and they were safeguarded by, or even found themselves appointed to the first rung in his legal machinery, they were known as *cangaceiros mansos* ("house bandits").[4]

Being classified then as a "legal" outlaw or an "illegal" one depended in the first instance on if one had a *patrão*. Probably all sponsorless *independentes* were labeled illegal at one time or another. For those who had a protector, even if only in passing, legal or illegal status was related to the *patrão*'s power position at any given moment in the fluctuating backland social structure. If the benefactor was "in," the bandit would normally remain under his protection. If he was "out," the *cangaceiro* would ponder more earnestly the possibilities of exchanging the *patrão* for another. It was a procedure which trapped many a person into doing the *coronel*'s bidding. In fact, *mansos* were repeatedly

> ...transformed into his private army. In trade, they were given permission to operate in certain areas, attack specific peasants and take shelter in some *fazendas*. There, they received arms and ammunition, paid for by the booty of their raids. When necessary, they were recruited to eliminate the political enemies of their protectors or impose discipline among the hired help. Or, more common still, to expel families living on lands that the *coronel* wished to buy in a depreciated condition.[5]

Made up almost exclusively of persons from rural society's underside, the stated justifications for joining a group of provincial outlaws (the *cangaço*) were of course varied. Probably the most often cited motive was that an individual did so out of vengeance for unpunished crimes against him or his family. This explanation underscores the fact that the law in Brazil was largely enacted by the rich to protect the rich. In rural society, with sovereign power-brokers holding court over a vast range of territories and issues, an equitable application of the law

---

[4]Singelmann, pp. 62-63. Freyre (*The Masters and the Slaves*, p. 67n) points out that originally, *cangaço* signified the bundles of arms carried by law breakers in Brazil's Northeast.
[5]Chiavenato, *Cangaço*, p. 17.

in defense of the poor never existed.

There were naturally other factors that either singularly or together propelled peasants into this conditionally illicit venture. Hardships such as no land, loss of property, unemployment, no future, a weakened *patrão*, or no *patrão* where one was wanted, were all mentioned. All were important in their own secondary way. Some *cangaceiros* may have even mentioned that one or the other induced them into the *cangaço*. But it is shortsighted, on the other hand, to ignore or denude the lack of justice question since it was the larger foundation for nearly all of the other excuses.[6]

There is also the issue of the sources consulted, which adds a veneer of doubt to many of the published reports on individual *cangaceiros*. Especially questionable are the narratives on specific *independentes*. It has become almost foolhardy to accept these reports at face value, since they often contain reference material that was written or controlled by the enemies (i.e., some newspaper owners) of the *independentes* being investigated. Others, such as yellow journalists, can not be trusted because their work on *cangaceiros* comes from the realm of fabrication. Another group is apparently composed of those who have political or philosophical biases in looking at questions involving the rural poor. Finally, there are those who have never been closer to the Northeast than a trip through someone else's prose. When all of these creative forces are brought together, the results can be disastrous. False images abound about *cangaceiros*. And with each new generation of writers the whole process is retold, becoming more and more contaminated. Consider for example the cases of the last two major *independentes*. Both of these men have had a large share of less than factual accounts printed about them. What follows then will be an attempt to pay each a small but long overdue debt of fairness.

The first story begins in Paraíba with Antônio Silvino Aires Cavalcanti de Albuquerque.[7] He was known as "Silvino Torto," or "Deformed Silvino" because

---

[6]Mello, Frederico Pernambucano de, *Guerreiros do sol: o banditismo no Nordeste do Brasil*, Recife: Massangana (Fundação Joaquim Nabuco), 1985, pp. 47, 76, 97-98. Mello, as example, estimates that about 70% of the backland brigands joined the *cangaço* simply to survive, another 20% in order to hide-out, and only 10% for reasons of revenge.

[7]Oliveira, Aglae Lima de, *Lampião, cangaço e nordeste*, 2nd ed., Rio de Janeiro: O Cruzeiro, 1970, p. 328.

he only had one eye. Silvino Torto, together with the help of instrumental *coiteiros* (provincials, not always *coronéis*, who offered protection and assistance in return for favors[8]), eluded capture while terrorizing the backlands for a quarter of a century.[9]

His godson and relative,[10] who took over for him when he was taken prisoner in 1898,[11] was "Antônio Silvino." Of largely Dutch background, Manoel Batista de Moraes was born into more affluent than average family on May 5, 1875 in Serra de Colônia, Pernambuco. In homage to Silvino Aires, he took the first two names of his godfather as a *nom de guerre* the year this elder member of his family was arrested.[12] Manoel initially joined Torto's gang because he wanted to avenge the unpunished slaying of his father, Francisco Batista de Moraes.

Known by everyone as "Batistão" ("Big Batista"), Francisco Batista had been murdered on a Saturday afternoon in August of 1896. The scene was market day in Afogados da Ingazeira, Pernambuco, and the problem was a land dispute with José Cabaceira. Cabaceira coveted a section of property owned by Batistão. The case had gone all the way to court, with the decision going against Cabeceira. Not about to quit, Cabaceira took the matter to his cousin, José Ramos da Silva, a *macaco* (or monkey), as officers of the law were called in lively rural terminology. It was not long before policeman José Ramos, together with his two sons, Noé and Desidério, gunned down Batistão. The mayor of Ingazeira, L.A. Chaves, knew about the plan in advance but did not object. He even let his own brother, Grieco,

---

[8]A *coiteiro* could be anything from a local shop owner to an omnipotent *coronel*. All rural *coronéis*, without exception, were *coiteiros*. While some helped bandits out of fear, others obviously did so out of greed. The main kind of help provided was shelter and arms. *Cf.*: Chandler, pp. 86-90; and Chiavenato, *Cangaço*, pp. 44-45, 82, 120.

[9]*Jornal do Recife*, November 26, 1898, pp. 1-2.

[10]Silvino Torto was the maternal uncle or great-uncle of Antônio Silvino. This uncertainty is due to the fact that Silvino's parents were probably cousins. Lewin, p. 123.

[11]*Cf.*: Albuquerque, Ulysses Lins de, *Moxotó brabo*, Rio de Janeiro: Simões, 1960, pp. 93-95; Rodrigues de Carvalho, 2nd ed., p. 441; and *Jornal do Recife*, November 26, 1898, pp. 1-2.

[12]*Cf.*: Moraes, Severino Batista de, letter, [postmarked] July 5, 1993; ___, interview, João Pessoa, May 15, 1993; Linda Lewin, "Oral Traditions and Elite Myth: the Legend of Antônio Silvino in Brazilian Popular Culture," *Journal of Latin American Lore*, vol. v, no. 2, 1979, p. 161; Severino Rodrigues de Moura, *História de Frei Miguelinho: o bandoleiro, a fonte e o frade*, Recife: FIAM/Centro de Estudos de História Municipal, 1983, pp. 181-82; Mário Souto Maior, *Antônio Silvino: Capitão de Trabuco*, Rio de Janeiro: Arquimedes, 1971, pp. 13, 82; *Correio da Manhã*, November 2, 1938, p. 16; and Rodrigues de Carvalho, 2nd ed., p. 428. Many individuals changed their name when joining the *cangaço*. This was done for the protection it offered or to make themselves more colorful. *Ibid.*, p. 440.

act as a Judas to lure Batistão into relaxing his guard on his way out of town.[13]

Antônio Silvino only entered the *cangaço* because he was overwhelmed a by desire for vengeance. In the words of one of his sons, at first "he didn't have the sense to stop."[14] When he realized what he had done it was too late; the police were on his trail. For the next eighteen years, until his capture in 1914, Silvino would weigh his desire for justice against an avowal that he never wanted to be on the wrong side of the law. Silvino took no pleasure in being a *cangaceiro*. In the early days he was not even a good shot.[15] This changed out of necessity as the *macacos* would not leave him alone. His ability with a rifle became legendary. The incessant police pressure was likewise legendary, and more than once it prompted him to look for a permanent way out. Silvino was in Rio Grande do Norte four or five times with just such an end in mind. There and in other places he retreated to *fazendas* purchased for him in someone else's name. In spite of this, the subterfuge helped little. His every attempt to begin a new life only resulted in being recognized and turned into the police. One such episode took place in Ceará, near Crato in the Cariri Valley (This was the territory of *Padre Cícero*, although apparently the two men never met).[16]

It was not long before the rural elite were viewing Silvino as the most feared *independente* of his generation. During the apex of his years on the run he was often called "The Captain of the *Trabuco*," "The Lion of the North," "The Governor of the *sertão*," or "The Rifle of Gold."[17] He fancied "O Capitão" ("The Captain"), and routinely wore commandeered state police uniforms of different officer ranks. He and his companions used such attire to confuse adversaries and

---

[13]*Cf.*: Moraes, Severino Batista de, interview, João Pessoa, May 15, 1993; Manoel Batista de Moraes Filho, interview, Pirassununga, January 10, 1993; Rodrigues de Carvalho, 2nd ed., pp. 436-38; and Chiavenato, *Cangaço*, p. 115. Silvino was an amateur *repentista* (a *cordel* [see *infra*, nn. 25-26, 26n] orator who engages other *repentistas* in spontaneous duels of ability). Candace Slater (*Stories on a String: the Brazilian Literatura de Cordel*, Berkeley: University of California Press, 1989, p. 212) recounts that Silvino's initial encounter with one of those responsible for his father's death took place at a *cordel* recital. Silvino killed the individual.
[14]Moraes Filho, Manoel Batista de, interview, Pirassununga, January 10, 1993.
[15]*Ibid.*
[16]*Cf.*: Moraes, Severino Batista de, interview, João Pessoa, May 15, 1993; and ___, letter, [postmarked] July 5, 1993.
[17]*Cf.*: Lewin, "The Oligarchical Limitations of Social Banditry in Brazil," pp. 126-27; Francisco das Chagas Baptista, *História completa de Antonio Silvino: sua vida de crimes e seu julgamento*, Sebastião Nunes Batista (ed.), Rio de Janeiro: H. Antunes, 1960, p. 74; and Severino Barbosa, *Antônio Silvino: "O Rifle de Ouro,"* Recife: Editôra de Pernambuco, 1977, p. 15, *et passim*.

for the ease it afforded them in entering a community unrecognized.[18]

Silvino claimed that four *coronéis* had caused him, his family, and his friends no small amount of difficulty, even arresting seventy-two of the latter at a family funeral. Many years later, he would refer to these despots by giving each the first name of Brazil's then most notorious *independente*. Sarcastically, Silvino identified them as "Lampião" Gonçalves Ferreira, "Lampião" Segismundo Gonçalves, "Lampião" Herculano Bandeira, and "Lampião" Estácio Coimbra. Antônio Gonçalves Ferreira was a political big-wig in Pernambuco. He came to occupy the post of governor of the state from 1900 to 1904, and was a federal deputy and federal senator twice. Gonçalves Ferreira even became the national minister of the interior. Segismundo Gonçalves started out as a judge, then became chief of police in Pernambuco, senator, and finally, from 1904 to 1908, state governor. Antônio Herculano de Sousa Bandeira was the governor of both Paraíba (1885-1889) and Mato Grosso (1889). In 1895, Estácio de Albuquerque Coimbra began his career as a Pernambuco state assemblyman. Five years later, he became a federal congressman (1900-1912). He was out of politics in 1913 and 1914 due to revolutionary currents within Pernambuco. Coimbra later returned to elected office, eventually becoming state governor, and ultimately vice president of Brazil from 1922 to 1926.[19]

For Silvino, the real bandits were the crooked potentates and the ones chasing him. As for this last category, it was the police who, in his own words, were committing "the major part of the crimes that are being attributed to me...."[20] The men of law and order "...only want to stuff themselves with the money of the *sertão*."[21]

It was sad day indeed for his foes when he could stand it no more and turned the tables on such people. The experience of an affluent informer, Quinca

---

[18]Carvalho, Rodrigues de, 2nd ed., p. 438.

[19]*Cf.*: *Correio da Manhã*, November 2, 1938, p. 16; and Antônio Houaiss (ed.), *Grande enciclopédia Delta Larousse*, Rio de Janeiro: Delta, 1978, pp. 729, 1753, 2719, 3114-15. For more on Lampião, see *infra*, n. 44 to the end of the chapter.

[20]Albuquerque, Ulysses Lins de, *Um sertanejo e o sertão*, Rio de Janeiro: José Olympio, 1957, pp. 12-13. One should not forget that the police were as large or even larger than the army in some states. For more on this see *infra*, chap. v, nn. 11-13.

[21]Motta, Leonardo, *No tempo de Lampeão*, Rio de Janeiro: Officina Industrial Graphica, 1930, p. 10.

Napoleão, who brazenly passed a counterfeit bank note to the Captain, serves to underline how Silvino blended a renowned Robin Hood image with an ability to repay those who wronged him.

Quinca Napoleão and Antônio Silvino had never met. That did not keep Silvino from going to Pilar in Paraíba where Napoleão was the mayor. Once arriving and securing the town, he immediately freed the prisoners in the city jail and locked up their guards. Then, leaving his men to watch the streets, he went alone to the dry goods store over which Napoleão lived. Informed that Quinca was not at home (the doorman fainted on learning who doing the inquiring), Antônio entered anyway and began distributing all the food and clothing from the bottom floor business to the throng of people gathered outside. Upstairs, under the balcony, he discovered Quinca's strongbox. From it he took Napoleão's money and threw it to the crowd as well. For a couple of days thereafter, people wandered around the building scratching the sandy soil for anything left unclaimed. In the meantime, Silvino crossed the Paraíba River at the edge of the city and threw the keys to the jail into the gushing water. The Governor of the *sertão* topped off his visit by sending a telegram to the state governor which read,

> Senhor governador, Pilar [tem] governo novo. Antônio Silvino de Paz. Tudo que promete faz!
> . . . .

> Pilar [has a] new administration, Mr. Governor. The peaceful Antônio Silvino. Whatever he promises he does![22]

Silvino was perhaps most demanding of his men. He would accept no thieves into his group. Persons who were seeking justice were allowed in, but he insisted that they treat innocent provincials with respect. A good illustration of this occurred when he and his gang arrived at a small rural farm in need of something to eat. When the lady of the house asked who he was, Silvino gave his name, whereupon she began to tremble. Even though he tried to assure her that nothing would happen and that they were only hungry, she began to fix a meal with a great deal of nervousness.

---

[22]*Cf.*: Moraes, Severino Batista de, interview, João Pessoa, May 15, 1993; ___, letter, [postmarked] July 5, 1993; and Rodrigues de Carvalho, 2nd ed., p. 464. Note that Lewin ("Oral Tradition and Elite Myth," p. 166) has slightly distorted this quotation. Also observe that there are several versions to the story of what transpired at Pilar with Quinca Napoleão. The one used here was told by Antônio Silvino to his son, Severino Batista de Moraes.

And what a feast it was. She practically prepared everything she had, which was not much. In her haste and agitation, however, she forgot the salt. Sitting down to the meal, one of Silvino's men was about to bite into a piece of chicken when he noticed there was none of this basic seasoning. "What rubbish, there's no salt!"[23] he grumbled. Hearing this, and with the woman in tears, Silvino vehemently castigated the man in front of everyone for his bad manners.[24]

It is also said that he and his group abstained from customs like the "Rite of the First Night." Such was not the case for some *coronéis*. They customarily reserved this lopsided pleasure--sexual intercourse with the bride--for themselves following the weddings of peasants living within their spheres of influence. More than eschew such things, Silvino extended them, strictly enforcing a no-rape principle among his men with regard to rural women. Failure to follow this iron rule would bring the Captain's wrath down upon them. Those who went against the grain might be forced to marry the *sertaneja* they violated.

Silvino's protocols came to be well known. They generated the protection and hospitality of humble Northeasterners . These were people who could not be so sure that their loved ones would go untouched if they showed the same kindness to the police pursuing O Capitão.[25] One set of verse, from the mass-produced peasant literature called *cordel*, romanticizes him dangerously out of proportion. Yet the no molestation taboo is still easily apparent.

> Dizem que o Capitão
> Antônio Silvino era
> Um símbolo de malvadês
> Um coração de pantera
> Matava sem piedade
> Como se fôsse uma fera
>
> Outros dizem que êle tinha
> Um coração de bondade

---

[23]Moraes Filho, Manoel Batista de, interview, Pirassununga, January 10, 1993.

[24]Moraes, Severino Batista de, interview, João Pessoa, May 15, 1993. It is not true that Silvino asked her if she had any salt, and that on learning that she did forced the offending member of his gang to eat all of it. *Ibid.*

[25]*Cf.*: Chiavenato, *Cangaço*, p. 41; Severino Batista de Moraes, letter, [postmarked] July 5, 1993; Chandler, pp. 30-31; José Américo de Almeida, *A Parahyba e seus problemas*, Parahyba: Imprensa Official, 1923, p. 145; Lewin, "The Oligarchical Limitations of Social Banditry in Brazil," p. 129; and ___, "Oral Tradition and Elite Myth," pp. 167-68.

Que protegia a pobreza
E também a virgindade
De qualquer donzela que
Vivesse em honestidade[26]

. . . .

They say that Captain
Antônio Silvino was
A symbol of meanness
With the heart of a panther
Who killed without piety
As if he were a beast

Others say that he had
A heart of kindness
That protected the poor
And the virginity as well
Of any damsel who
Lived in purity

Silvino would enter a village demanding a tax, assessing a fine, or asking for donations for himself and his men. He never counted the money he received in front of the person giving it, and he may well have avoided asking for money if it was going to cause a hardship. Those who paid or contributed became his friends. Those who refused without good reason were on their way to making his list of enemies.[27]

Next he might cut the surrounding telegraph wires and, if the community had a link with the outside world by rail, steal whatever postal sacks he could gather. This included inter-company pouches of the English-owned Great Western Railway. The Great Western had tracks in Alagoas, Paraíba, Pernambuco, and Rio Grande do Norte. Silvino took a special delight in badgering this firm since he felt their rights-of-way trespassed on land he had inherited. Though in this harassment one should not discount the importance of the cut telegraph lines and snatched mail bags. Strategically effective, the interruption of communications in the

---

[26]Souto Maior, p. 45. The word *cordel* translates as twine or string. The name for this peasant literature thus comes from the fact that it is often sold hanging, one booklet after another, over some kind of string or line.

[27]*Cf.*: Moraes, Severino Batista de, interview, João Pessoa, May 15, 1993; Rodrigues de Carvalho, 2nd ed., pp. 445, 448-49; and Lewin, "The Oligarchical Limitations of Social Banditry in Brazil," pp. 130, 142n.

interior and the theft of postal sacks kept orders to the various police authorities and reports on his whereabouts from reaching their destinations.[28] In the ensuing confusion, Silvino virtually ran large areas of the *caatinga* in Ceará, Paraíba, Pernambuco, and Rio Grande do Norte. In so doing he intimidated jurors, magistrates, city, and state governments.[29] Moreover, while he occasionally campaigned for the election of some individuals, it was more common to find him rigging or attempting to insure the electoral defeat of others.[30]

His days as an outlaw came to a close as he waited for a meal to be brought to him by a farm boy on November 28, 1914. Resting in the shade of a tree with some companions, the group was jumped by a unit of the Pernambuco police commanded by 2nd Lieutenant Teofanes Ferraz Torres. Bullets started flying in all directions, and in the confusion Antônio was wounded in the back by one of his men. As the fighting raged, O Capitão's gang had to make a hasty retreat but were unable to take their leader with them. Left for dead, Silvino surrendered the following day when the police, learning that he wanted to give himself up, cautiously returned.[31] The bullet passed through his body at the fifth vertebrae. It was a wound that would leave him with a stiff back for the rest of his life.[32] Once

---

[28]*Cf.*: *ibid.*, p. 138; ___, *Politics and Parentela in Paraíba: a Case Study of Family-Based Oligarchy in Brazil*, Princeton: Princeton University Press, 1987, p. 291; and ADOPS, newspaper article, "*Juventude*," June 15, 1935, p. 1, comunismo/pasta 4B.

[29]Moraes, Severino Batista de, interview, Rio de Janeiro/Itabatinga, May 5, 1993. For an example that Silvino thought was humorous, the time he forced a community to repair and whitewash its own buildings, see *O Jornal* (Rio de Janeiro), December 8, 1968, sec. 2, p. 5. Shortly after its founding in 1919, *O Jornal* was acquired by Assis Chateaubriand and turned into his principle newspaper in Rio de Janeiro.

[30]*Cf.*: Daus, Ronald, *Der epische Zyklus der Cangaceiros in der Volkspoesie Nordostbrasiliens*, Berlin: Colloquium, 1969, pp. 38-39; Rodrigues de Carvalho, *Serrote prêto: Lampião e seus sequazes*, Rio de Janeiro: Sociedade Editôra e Gráfica, 1961, pp. 360-67; Maria Isaura Pereira de Queiroz, *Os cangaceiros: les bandits d'honneur brésiliens*, Paris: Julliard, 1968, pp. 63-67; and Severino Batista de Moraes, letter, [postmarked] July 5, 1993.

[31]*Cf.*: Severino Batista de Moraes, letter, [postmarked] July 5, 1993; ___, interview, João Pessoa, May 15, 1993; Manoel Batista de Moraes Filho, interview, Pirassununga, January 10, 1993; Lewin, "The Oligarchical Limitations of Social Banditry in Brazil," p. 126n; ___, "Oral Tradition and Elite Myth," pp. 161-62; and *O Jornal*, December 10, 1968, sec. 2, p. 7. Souto Maior (p. 72) incorrectly puts the date of Silvino's capture one day earlier. Lewin ("Oral Tradition and Elite Myth," p. 162, 162n) comments that by surrendering, he went against the image people had of him. The commonly held view was that he would kill himself before giving up. These attitudes, however, would serve to confirm the existence of spurious information at large about the man. The fact that he did try to take his own life later in jail is a not uncommon phenomenon by persons facing long prison terms.

[32]Moraes, Severino Batista de, interview, João Pessoa, May 15, 1993.

he regained his health enough to stand trial, he was hauled before the courts in Olinda. Six different judiciaries filed charges against him on twenty-six counts of murder. Found guilty of all charges, the sentence was the maximum under the law: thirty years consecutive confinement at the Casa de Detenção in Recife.[33]

Things might have concluded here but Antônio Silvino truly was a remarkable man. In prison he learned to read and was converted to Protestantism. Still charismatic and still called O Capitão, he became a mentor to many of the other men behind bars. This did not go unnoticed by the prison director who repeatedly sought his opinion on issues dealing with inmates. Due to being on the wrong side in the Revolution of 1930, Teofanes Torres was arrested and sent briefly to the Casa de Detenção. When the two met, Antônio Silvino told his captor, "No one will do any harm to you in here. You are my friend."[34]

A model prisoner, Silvino was admired and even allowed to make money from selling jewelry he made out of wood and painted horsehair. The adornments were mainly cufflinks, watchbands, bracelets, and necklaces. The cufflinks sold the best. His salesmen were his sons Manoel, Severino, and José Alves. On an alternating basis, each was allowed to live with their father at the Casa de Detenção for a number of years. They left the penitentiary on weekdays to go to school. After class they sold the trinkets to tourists and the sailors off foreign warships that occasionally called at Recife. Most of the profit was used to educate five of his eight children; but some of the money went towards helping out destitute prisoners.[35]

Meanwhile, his son José Alves joined the army in 1922. Promoted to sergeant, in 1930 he was commissioned a second lieutenant for capturing a city in the insurrection that swept Getúlio Vargas to power. He was later asked by General Newton Cavalcanti, head of the 4th Army stationed in Recife, to serve on

[33]*Cf.*: *ibid.*; Souto Maior, p. 133; *Correio da Manhã*, November 2, 1938, p. 16; *O Jornal*, December 10, 1968, sec. 2, p. 7; *Última Hora* (Rio de Janeiro), April 24, 1973, p. 5-polícia; and Cancelli, p. 2.

[34]*Cf.*: Moraes, Severino Batista de, interviews, João Pessoa, May 15, 1993; and Rio de Janeiro/Itabatinga, June 4, 1993.

[35]*Cf.*: Moraes Filho, Manoel Batista de, interview, Pirassununga, January 10, 1993; Severino Batista de Moraes, interview, Rio de Janeiro/Itabatinga, July 8, 1993; Lewin, "The Oligarchical Limitations of Social Banditry in Brazil," pp. 123, 127; ___, "Oral Tradition and Elite Myth," p. 162; Barbosa, p. 219; Souto Maior, pp. 79, 82; and *Correio da Manhã*, November 2, 1938, p. 16.

his general staff. Accepting, Silvino's son was shortly telling Cavalcanti about his father, and about how much he would like to see him freed. The general was soon convinced and sent a petition to that end to the new head of state.

So it was that in 1937, after serving twenty-three years, six months and five days of his sentence, Manoel Batista de Moraes was pardoned by the nation's leader for good behavior. Following his release, General Cavalcanti had a reception for him at the barracks. At one point in the festivities, some of the officers asked Silvino if he would give a display of his celebrated ability with firearms. Unwilling until the general added his urging, Silvino was given a rifle. His first target was a bottle set up at some distance away. He aimed carefully, fired, and blew it to bits. Next he had someone hold a burning cigarette. It was extinguished in like fashion. Both items were hit on the first shot after more than twenty-three years behind prison walls.[36]

At the age of sixty-five, the former *cangaceiro* stayed for a time in Recife. But Silvino became restless. In August of 1938, he decided to take a chance. He purchased a first-class ticket down to Rio de Janeiro on the Italian ship *Conta Grande*. He was not splurging with this more expensive passage. His extravagance was because he always had an aversion to dirt or anything unclean. It was the maiden voyage for Antônio on such a vessel. The journey was pleasant; the Atlantic was calm. He was treated as a celebrity by the other passengers.

After reaching the Federal District, he told waiting reporters that he wanted to meet the president. Somewhat embarrassed by all the dockside attention, Silvino mentioned with tongue in cheek that he did not want to be asked anything about his bandit days since he had never been a politician.[37] He also said that he was looking for a professional writer to help him do a book on the true story of his life.

Sometime later, José Lins do Rêgo and his publisher, José Olympio, contacted Silvino in Rio about writing just such a book. They offered the former *cangaceiro* ten *contos de réis* (written 10:000$000), or just over $500,[38] plus a

---

[36]*Cf.*: Moraes, Severino Batista de, interview, João Pessoa, May 15, 1993; and Manoel Batista de Moraes Filho, interview, Pirassununga, January 10, 1993.

[37]*Cf.*: *Correio da Manhã*, August 31, 1938, pp. 3, 12; and November 2, 1938, p. 16. A picture of Silvino following his arrival on the docks of Rio can be seen in Figure 24.

[38]*Correio da Manhã*, August 31, 1938, p. 14.

101

portion of the royalties. The project was ultimately scrapped, however, when it turned out that too many important people would be involved or slighted in some way. In the midst of the Vargas' dictatorship, Silvino's family was afraid that Getúlio might not like the manuscript and revoke their father's pardon.[39]

On the day before his sixty-seventh birthday, Antônio Silvino was interviewed again, this time in the Oswaldo Cruz suburb of the capital. Speaking with a journalist from *Correio da Manhã*, he said that since arriving in Rio he had sent two letters to Vargas asking for a monthly pension of one *conto de réis*. Confidentially, he added that he would be happy with 800$000. Silvino was always a man of action. Not long thereafter, he determined he could wait no longer. He and one of his sons, Manoel Batista de Moraes Filho, went to the mountains in Petrópolis where the president habitually spent the sweltering summer months. Following their arrival in the resort community, however, Silvino's boldness hurt his own case. He was ushered into Getúlio's presence. Vargas had just concluded a meeting with his ministers and the mayor of the Federal District, and he insured that everyone was standing as Antônio entered the room. Following the introductions, Vargas asked Silvino why he had ever entered the *cangaço* in the first place. O Capitão answered back, "Mr. President, it was because of the bandits who control government." Getúlio's only reaction was to smile one of his famous smiles and continue puffing on his ever present cigar.[40]

The two men then walked briefly outside the governmental compound. Following some probing about what Silvino was going to do next, Vargas offered to make him a doorman at the National Museum. But Silvino did not like the

---

[39]As an example, one of the implicated individuals was José Ermírio de Moraes, an out-of-wedlock son of Antônio Silvino. A *paulista*, when José Ermírio decided that he wanted to run for state senator, he did not try to get elected from the state of São Paulo. Instead, he traveled to Afogados da Ingazeira in Pernambuco (see *supra*, nn. 12-13), where he presented himself as a son of Antônio Silvino in need of the support of the local population. They gave it to him and he was elected a senator from their state. He then conveniently ignored the people from Pernambuco until the next election rolled around. They had not forgotten him though, and this time he was defeated. Later José Ermírio became the minister of agriculture in the national government of Janio Quadros. Later still, his son, José Ermírio de Moraes Filho, became the head of Votorantim, the largest industrial corporation in Brazil. *Cf.*: Severino Batista de Moraes, interview, João Pessoa, May 15, 1993; and Júlio Cesar Cruz de Oliveira, interview, João Pessoa, May 15, 1993.

[40]Moraes Filho, Manoel Batista de, interview, Pirassununga, January 10, 1993. See also *infra*, nn. 41-44.

thought of sitting down most of the time. He wanted to stay active. Getúlio then suggested a second position that was acceptable.[41]

Silvino went to work in Muriaé, Minas Gerais, on the highway that was being built from Rio to Salvador. Getúlio had sadistically arranged this second job to be one where Silvino broke stones with a sledge hammer; but when Antônio arrived the first day, he was transferred by a benevolent foreman to the post of timekeeper.[42] Some two months later, Antônio realized that despite his new job, he was not getting paid enough. At one point he confided that he would go along with reducing his still hoped-for pension to 20$000 a day, an amount equal to about ninety-six cents.[43] But Vargas put him off without ever answering his requests. Disappointed, the great Rifle of Gold finally quit the road gang and headed back to his beloved Northeast. He died there, impoverished, in the arms of his daughter Severina, on July 27, 1944.[44]

While he was in prison, Silvino use to say that "Lampião," or Virgulino Ferreira da Silva, was a prince with too many powerful people protecting him. He felt that Lampião would end up getting killed, but did not want to predict if it would be due to his temperament or because he knew too much. Antônio Silvino didn't like Lampião. The feeling was mutual.[45]

---

[41]Moraes Filho, Manoel Batista de, interview, Rio de Janeiro/Pirassununga, August 17, 1987. A snapshot of the remarkable meeting between these two men (here, Figure 25) was taken by an Agência Nacional photographer and sent to *Correio da Manhã* but never published. John W.F. Dulles located it in the newspaper's photo archives and included it as plate 33 in his landmark study, *Vargas of Brazil: a Political Biography*, Austin: University of Texas Press, 1967. The reference to Volta Sêca under Dulles' edition of the picture is incorrect. Volta Sêca was a different *cangaceiro*.

[42]Moraes, Severino Batista de, interview, João Pessoa, May 15, 1993.

[43]*Cf.*: *ibid.*; Arquivo José Americo, letter, "Manoel Batista de Moraes ['Antônio Silvino'] to José Americo de Almeida," April 26, 1939, CR p. 6, document 119; and *Correio da Manhã*, April 28, 1939, p. 12. The conversion was calculated at the black market rate.

[44]*Cf.*: Moraes Filho, Manoel Batista de, interview, Rio de Janeiro/Pirassununga, August 17, 1987; Souto Maior, pp. 80-83; Moura, p. 172; and *Manchete* (Rio de Janeiro), January 7, 1978, p. 107.

[45]*Cf.*: Moraes Filho, Manoel Batista de, interview, Pirassununga, January 10, 1993; and Chiavenato, *Cangaço*, p. 35. Lampião was always jealous of Silvino's fame. He also felt that his predecessor "...was a weakling" for surrendering. "A man who is macho," Lampião said, "doesn't give up. He dies fighting." *Ibid.* It is interesting to note, however, that the two men may have been related through Lampião's father and Antônio Silvino's mother. *Cf.*: Oliveira, p. 328; and Lewin, "The Oligarchical Limitations of Social Banditry in Brazil," p. 125n. Chandler (p. 22n), discounts this opinion, as does one of Antônio Silvino's sons. Manoel Batista de

Born in rural Pernambuco on July 7, 1897,[46] Virgulino's was a mix of Portuguese, African, and *índio*, with the Portuguese influence being the strongest. His alias, Lampião, or "Lantern," according to a glamorized view, came about because he could nearly turn night into day from the speed at which he could cock and fire a lever-action rifle.[47] Lampião was to go on to become Brazil's most notorious rural bandit; so much so that when today's Brazilians think about the *cangaço* they immediately envision this one man.

It all started over an accusation that he had trespassed on the property of a neighbor, José Saturnino. *Senhor* Saturnino was protected by two prestigious *coronéis* living in his area. There were several skirmishes. Finally, the Ferreira family began to move to avoid further trouble. This took place not once but three different times until they had traveled more than ninety miles from their original farm, and were trying to start over yet again in another state. The strain of the last relocation probably led to the early death of Lampião's mother.

Events, nonetheless, were to make such arduous and expensive changes of residence meaningless. Saturnino would not leave the Ferreiras alone. He continued to hound the family and eventually used his influence to have three of the Ferreira brothers branded as outlaws.[48] Shortly after Lampião's mother passed away, his father was slaughtered when police, friendly to Saturnino, arrived at the family's final homestead and shot up everything in sight--whether on two legs or four.

Eighteen year-old Virgulino and his brothers, Antônio and Livino, were away at the time of their father's murder. On returning home to discover the carnage, they did not bother with a formal complaint. The three young men knew that would lead nowhere. Instead, they opted for the one place where their kind of people could get revenge. The *cangaço* was the only choice.

First they sought out and found the group led by Antônio Maltides. Then

Moraes Filho, interview, Pirassununga, January 10, 1993.
[46]Oliveira, p. 20.
[47]Chandler, p. 33.
[48]*Cf.*: Gueiros, Optato, *Lampeão: memórias de um oficial ex-combatente de fôrças volantes*, 1st ed., Recife: Gráfica, 1953, p. 11; Oliveira, pp. 28-35; and Chandler, pp. 21, 25-32. There are several misinformed stories about how Lampião began his life of crime. Each has only added confusion to the man. For an example of one of these accountings--that it all began over the killing of a steer, a jail rescue of Lampião by his brothers, and the death of a policeman's daughter in the process--see, *Jornal do Brasil*, July 28, 1988, sec. 1, p. 9.

they drifted to the one headed by Antônio Porcino.[49] In both groups they learned valuable lessons; though they really came into their own as professional *cangaceiros* in 1920 when they joined the band of men headed by Sebastião Pereira. Known to everyone as "Sinhô"[50] Pereira, he was only a little over a year and a half older than Lampião. Famous for his bravery, and because he never robbed anyone, Sinhô had joined the *cangaço* seven years earlier to get even for the unresolved murder of his brother, Né Pereira. By the time Sinhô decided to quit rural banditry in February of 1922, because of acute rheumatism,[51] Lampião was ready to take charge.

Most people are convinced that Lampião did just that in the years that followed. Up until his own death in 1938--there is some evidence that Getúlio Vargas was ultimately responsible[52]--Lampião and his gang were reputed to have killed no less than 1,000 persons; although never anyone really important. It is said that they raped 200 or so women and some of these they branded. A few of their male victims were castrated. The group, which often numbered between forty and fifty men, set fire to some 500 structures, slaughtered over 5,000 head of cattle, stole innumerable amounts of money, and took part in more than 200 battles in six states. The sad truth, however (similar to the situation faced by Antônio Silvino), is that it was the police, supposedly in pursuit of Lampião, who were committing most of these offenses. Like many other *independentes*, in some places it was Lampião who provided the justice that police sub-elites refused to supply.[53]

---

[49]Chandler, p. 36.

[50]*Senhor* pronounced in antiquated Portuguese. Denise Sá, interview, Rio de Janeiro, June 1, 1993.

[51]*Cf.*: Oliveira, pp. 45-47; and Rodrigues de Carvalho, pp. 23-24, 30, 34, 41-42. See also *infra*, nn. 69-72.

[52]*Cf.*: Oliveira, pp. 46-49, 122; Chandler, p. 220; Frederico Pernambucano de Mello, pp. 197-200; *Fatos e Fotos* (Rio de Janeiro), December 8, 1962, pp. 43-44; and Antonio Amaury Corrêa de Araujo, *Assim morreu Lampião*, Rio de Janeiro: Brasília/Rio, 1976, pp. 59-60. See *infra*, nn. 80-82, for the Vargas connection. Note as well the suspicious events in *infra*, nn. 82-86.

[53]*Cf.*: Menezes, Fátima, interview, Juazeiro do Norte, May 11, 1993; Generosa Alencar, interviews, Juazeiro do Norte, May 11, 1993; May 13, 1993; João Oliveira, interview, Juazeiro do Norte, May 11, 1993; Aldenor Alencar Benevides, interview, Juazeiro do Norte, May 12, 1993; Lewin, *Politics and Parentela in Paraiba*, p. 343; Chiavenato, *Cangaço*, p. 96; Joaquim Góis, *Lampião: o último cangaceiro*, Aracaju: Regina, 1966, p. 146; Gueiros, 4th ed., Salvador: Progresso, 1956, p. 11; and Chandler, pp. 155-56, 188. Some of the disfigured persons appear in Oliveira (unnumbered plates between pp. 144-45).

This is not to say that Virgulino Ferreira da Silva was innocent. The exact ratio of crimes that he and his band did carry out versus those perpetrated by the police will always be disputed. Yet invariably, the blame for them was placed squarely on the shoulders of Lampião. This condemnation mushroomed to such a degree that he came to be vilified as "O Rei do Cangaço," or "The King of Banditry." While he may well have been the king of banditry in the minds of many people, Brazilian elites were not above contemplating the use of his abilities. For as improbable as it sounds, Lampião was offered the rank of captain in the government's forces (similar to his predecessor, he too was habitually called "O Capitão" after this). Although his commission was apparently not made in earnest--it may have been offered simply to get Lampião out of Juazeiro do Norte--there is the distinct possibility that he went along with the deception just to get arms from the government.[54] Lampião was, nevertheless, an obvious candidate when the men of law and order needed extra fighters, extra *cangaceiros mansos*, in their chase of someone more dangerous than Lampião himself.

A genuine captain, Luís Carlos Prestes, together with his men in arms, posed more of a threat to the government than did a group of lower-class *cangaceiros independentes* confined to remote areas in the Northeast. Prestes was a leader of one of two military uprisings in the 1920s, during the formation of the *tenentismo* movement,[55] which challenged the corrupt practices of the nation's *classe conservadora*. Ultimately, all of the ruling elite from the president down would view Prestes with apprehension if not outright fear.

Following a revolt in 1924, the then holder of Brazil's highest office, Artur da Silva Bernardes, unleashed loyal military units in an attempt to crush the insurrectionists once and for all. A series of battles took place on several fronts. The city of São Paulo was even occupied by the rebels. Owing to the superior number of government forces, the revolutionaries were soon forced to flee the city

[54]*Cf.*: Chandler, pp. 70-74: *Jornal do Brasil*, November 12, 1984, sec. B, p. 1; Fátima Menezes, letter, April 26, 1993; and ___, interview, Rio de Janeiro/Juazeiro do Norte, April 30, 1993. See also *infra*, nn. 66-78.

[55]Note that the aims and motivating philosophy of these mainly junior grade military officers in rebellion in 1922 and 1924, was not called *tenentismo* until after the victory of the Revolution of 1930. Jorge Amado, *A vida de Luís Carlos Prestes: O Cavaleiro da Esperança*, 4th ed., São Paulo: Martins, 1945, p. 93n. See *infra*, chap. v, especially nn. 18-19.

to the Southwest, where they formed the *Coluna* Prestes (or Prestes Column). From October 29, 1924 until February 3, 1927, the *Coluna* roamed more than 15,500 miles throughout the Brazilian interior, on the real "Long March,"[56] unsuccessfully attempting to arouse their destitute rural countrymen.

Included among his forces, President Bernardes gave the go-ahead to the formation of special unscrupulous[57]detachments, called *Batalhões Patrióticos* (Patriotic Battalions). A newspaper accounting from this period commented on the general duplicity of the *Batalhões* around the capital and in São Paulo in the following terms. One can imagine what these groups must have been like elsewhere.

> The *Batalhões Patrioticos* constituted another farcical aspect of the [Bernardes] state of siege. At the same time that Washington Luís was saying in São Paulo that they were organizing legionnaires, [prominent politician] Ataliba Leonel was stealing the funding. In Rio an energetic distribution of money created the most comic *Batalhões*. We had the Artur Bernardes [Battalion], the Francisco Sá [Battalion], the Legion Fontoura and others. They were given the satisfaction of proceeding to the post at Cruzeiro, only to desert *en masse*. Since the government possesses limitless credit, the *Batalhões* grew in size for some time. Out of them were born the famous *paulista* Legions that even today are being formed and incorporated into the police of São Paulo.[58]

As on other occasions, local members of the dominant class offered endless *independentes* promises of immediate amnesties if they would become members of Bernardes' *mansos*. The moral readjustment necessary in jumping from one side to

---

[56]*Cf.*: Amado, *A vida de Luis Carlos Prestes*, p. 98; Boris Fausto, *A Revolução de 1930, historiografia e história*, 9th ed., São Paulo: Brasiliense, 1983, p. 61; and Dênis de Moraes and Francisco Viana, *Prestes: lutas e autocríticas*, 2nd ed., Petrópolis: Vozes, 1982, p. 37. As there are several estimates of how far the *Coluna* actually traveled, it was decided to use the figures provided by Prestes (*ibid.*) himself, 25,000 kilometers. This converts to 15,534.3 miles, and should have earned the *Coluna* the name given to the feat begun in the next decade by Mao Tse-tung. That journey, by comparison, was a mere 6,000 miles in length. Edgar Snow, *Red Star over China*, London: Victor Gollancz, 1937, p. 189. See also *infra*, chap. v.

[57]*Cf.*: Pang, p. 159; and Neill Macaulay, *The Prestes Column: Revolution in Brazil*, New York: New Viewpoints, 1974, pp. 178-79.

[58]*O Globo*, November 15, 1926, p. 2. Ataliba Leonel was a federal deputy of the *Partido Republicano Paulista* (São Paulo Republican Party) during this period. Israel Beloch and Alzira Alves de Abreu (coords.), *Dicionário histórico-biográfico brasileiro, 1930-1983*, Rio de Janeiro: Forense-Universitária, 1984, p. 1803. For more on Bernardes, Washington Luís, and Fontoura, see *infra*, chap. v.

the other was the hardest part, since the police were universally more despised for their violence than the bandits themselves. This sub-elite aggression was a role requirement. *Mansos* who were not violent were of little use to their *patrão*.[59] In addition, there were always the perks. Everyone knew that the police were making a lot of money out of selling weapons to *cangaceiros*, so much money, in fact, that more than one police official was able to buy a *fazenda* in some distant state.[60] The thought of all this cash and land no doubt tempted many *independentes* to seriously consider becoming legal when and if the situation arose.

As the *Coluna* wound its way northward, *Padim* Ciço and his protector (by then a federal deputy) *Coronel* Floro Bartolomeu, deployed their men. Nearing Ceará in 1926, Cícero wrote a letter to Prestes calling on him and his companions in battle to surrender. In doing this, the former priest stated that his "...principal desire [was] to avoid moral ruin...."[61] Bartolomeu chose another course. Even before Cícero's dispatch, he had several stockades opened up to secure as much manpower as possible in the war against the rebels. He also had a budget to cover expenses of over $451,000.[62]

It should be added, however, that in his own war on local banditry, shortly before the appearance of the *Coluna*, Bartolomeu ordered the killing and subsequent decapitation in 1924 of a still-debated number of suspects being held in Juazeiro do Norte. Many of these victims were the *cangaceiros* used by Floro to defeat Franco Rabelo.[63] Shot on the road linking Juazeiro and her sister city,

---

[59]See *supra*, chap. ii, 4n. In the country as a whole, those involved in providing Bernardes' brand of law enforcement were noted for using "...methods which fifteen years later would make Heindrich Himmler the chief of the Gestapo." Edmar Morél, *Padre Cícero: O Santo do Juazeiro*, Rio de Janeiro: O Cruzeiro, 1946, p. 124. For more on these Nazi-like methods, see *infra*, chap. v.

[60]*Cf.*: Menezes, Fátima, interviews, Juazeiro do Norte, May 11, 1993; May 12, 1993; and Aldenor Alencar Benevides, interview, Juazeiro do Norte, May 12, 1993. See also *infra*, nn. 86-87.

[61]MPC, letter, "*Padre* Cícero Romão Batista to Captain Luís Carlos Prestes," n.m., n.d., 1926, exhibit 104.

[62]*Cf.*: Pang, pp. 158-60; Morél, *Padre Cícero*, pp. 124-28; and *O Globo*, November 16, 1926, p. 1. The exact amount was 3,000 *contos de réis*, or $451,127.81. Note that the figure in Menezes and Alencar (p. 136) of 3 *contos de réis* is a printing error. *Cf.*: Fátima Menezes, interview, Rio de Janeiro/Juazeiro do Norte, June 3, 1993; and *Jornal do Commercio*, January 1, 1926, p. 11.

[63]See *supra*, chap. ii, nn. 66-69. Following the victory over Rabelo, several of Floro's *cangaceiros* returned to the Cariri Valley to live and eventually harass local people by now and

Crato, the tortured bodies of these prisoners were taken to Crato and tossed on the sidewalk in front of the police station. The next victims were said to be the most dangerous prisoners from the Juazeiro jail. Just the heads[64] of these yet-to-be-tried individuals were left on the road to Crato as a warning to *cangaceiros* who were in the region. In the history of the Cariri Valley, these killings came to be called the *"mortes da rodagem,"* or "the murders on the road." They continued to occur at uneven intervals for several years.[65]

The writer Edmar Morél presented a limited retelling of these events in his 1946 book *Padre Cícero: O Santo do Juazeiro*. His description was taken from the anti-Floro newspaper *O Ideal* of August 15, 1925. In reality, the area was divided into two blocs that began forming in December of 1924 over the issue of whether the most common form of working-class gambling, *jogo do bicho*, or "The Game of the Animals, should or should not continue in Juazeiro. With this polarization process, the majority of the *rodagem* murders began taking place. Of the two factions, there were those in favor of Floro (pro-*bicho*) and those aligned with *Padre* Manoel Correia de Macêdo (anti-*bicho*). The Floro oriented group acknowledged that he was responsible for giving the order to kill a number of bandits. Those sympathizing with the priest, however, painted a much grimmer picture of Bartolomeu's activities, going so far as to say that he included town drunks, chicken thieves, and some children among those beheaded.[66]

---

again resorting to their former professions. *Cf.*: Daniel Walker Almeida Marques, interview, Juazeiro do Norte, May 13, 1993; and Generosa Alencar, interview, Juazeiro do Norte, May 13, 1993.

[64]This same kind of beheading scare tactic was copied at other times by out of power groups. See, for example, Euclides da Cunha's description of Antônio Conselheiro's *jagunços* in *Os sertões* (pp. 313-14).

[65]*Cf.*: Alencar, Generosa, interviews, Juazeiro do Norte, May 11, 1993; May 13, 1993; Fátima Menezes, interview, Juazeiro do Norte, May 11, 1993; Daniel Walker Almeida Marques, interview, Juazeiro do Norte, May 13, 1993; *Padre* Manuel Macedo, *Joazeiro em fóco*, Fortaleza: Autores Catholicos, 1925, pp. 43-50; Xavier de Oliveira, *O exercito e o sertão*, Rio de Janeiro: Coelho Branco, 1932, pp. 46-49; Joaryvar Macedo, pp. 210-15; Edmar Morél, *Padre Cicero*, pp. 103-4; and *O Ideal* (Juazeiro do Norte), November 4, 1924, p. 1; July 8, 1925, p. 1.

[66]*Cf.*: Menezes, Fátima, interview, Juazeiro do Norte, May 11, 1993; and Generosa Alencar, interview, Juazeiro do Norte, May 11, 1993. *Jogo do bicho* is a nation-wide, tacitly illegal numbers racket that uses both numbers and simple animal symbols. For more on *jogo do bicho*, see *infra*, chap. iv, nn. 27-28, 28n, and chap. v, nn. 47-48, 116-19. A January 5, 1928 photograph of five *cangaceiros* from the jail in Juazeiro about to be executed and left on the road to Crato is presented here as Figure 28. They were ex-members of Lampião's group. Menezes and Alencar, p. 151.

Even if the Patriotic Battalions were units that included a large number of *cangaceiros* in their ranks in the Northeast, the case of Lampião was clearly different. He was not asked to join until he let it be known that he could just as easily team up with the *Coluna* Prestes as fight it. At this, Floro asked João Ferreira, Lampião's non-*cangaceiro* brother, to deliver a letter to Virgulino inviting him to help the government. Later, in January of 1926, Floro had a change of mind and sent a telegram to his secretary and lawyer, José Ferreira de Menezes, who was in the *Patrióticos* staging area at Campo Sales, some seventy-five miles due west. The message read: "...communicate with our friend, Lampião, that we [don't] need him any longer because we've obtained [enough] people to pursue the rebels."[67] The following month, mortally sick, Floro left Juazeiro for treatment in Rio de Janeiro. He died there of heart problems on March 8th. Already on the 2nd, as a gesture of thanks, Bernardes conferred on him the rank of a honorary general in the Brazilian army.

Through his spies, Lampião was informed of Floro's new intentions. At this, the *cangaceiro* quickly gathered up his men, all forty-nine of them, and occupied Juazeiro on March 6, 1926. He stayed in the city for three days, residing at *Fazenda Nova*, owned by Floro Bartolomeu, and then at the home of João Mendes, a popular rural poet. Mendes' house was the town's only two-story dwelling; it offered a great vantage point to observe the coming and going of everyone. Some of the people Lampião met were important in the community. Others were members of the press. He even posed for photographs.[68]

While still at the *Fazenda Nova* he met with *Padre* Cícero. It was during this meeting, which journalist Benjamin Abraão,[69] the priest's secretary, attended, that Cícero offered to help Lampião start a new life in Goiás. Many *cangaceiros*, not just Antônio Silvino, attempted to return to a law-abiding existence. Some were

[67]GAP, telegram, "Floro [Bartolomeu da Costa] to José Ferreira [de Menezes]" January 23, 1926. A picture of a *Batalhão Patriótico* in Juazeiro in 1926 is reproduced here as Figure 29.

[68]*Cf.*: Menezes, Fátima, interview, Juazeiro do Norte, May 11, 1993; and Menezes and Alencar, pp. 140-42.

[69]Abraão had originally been contracted by *O Globo* to go to Juazeiro to cover the events in the city. MPC, photograph, "Padre Cícero e seu secretário Benjamin Abrahão em 1925," exhibit 75. The title of this photo translates as "*Padre* Cícero and his Secretary, Benjamin Abraão in 1925." It is depicted here as Figure 31.

too famous and were turned in by informers.[70] Others succeeded by themselves or with the help of intermediaries. One intercessor was *Padre* Cícero. He assisted several *cangaceiros* to change their names and move to Goiás, where he had good contacts. Perhaps the most famous case he sent there was that of Sinhô Pereira and his cousin Luíz Padre.[71] On the way to Goiás, however, the two men split up, each taking a few companions with them. The Sinhô group was discovered and attacked by a combined unit of *jagunços* and police in the state of Piauí. Fighting off this unusual alliance, Sinhô tried to go it alone, incognito, for a few days before he was recognized. He returned to the *cangaço*, only to abandon it for good in 1922. Eventually he found his way to Goiás, where he lived out the rest of his days.[72]

All Lampião had to do was to agree to leave the *cangaço*. But he refused, saying that he was responsible for the fifty or so people in his gang. If he accepted, what would happen to them? *Padim* Ciço next tried to convince Virgulino to leave the city. Lampião answered that to do so, he would have to have some kind of protection since the *macacos* were not far away. Cícero then departed to attend to other matters. Left alone with Lampião, Benjamin Abraão proposed a solution. *Padre* Cícero's secretary took it upon himself to offer Lampião a commission as a captain in the *Batalhões Patrióticos*.[73] As it was explained, Lampião and his group were to act as their own autonomous unit in the establishment's cause.

Lampião knew what awaited him should he refuse the offer. Semi-literate,[74] he may not have been able to read very well about events in the rest of Brazil. Much of his understanding of things was picked up through first-hand experiences. As his knowledge related to violence on the part of elites, he was obviously aware of the way the authorities treated innocent peasants. There is no doubt too that he had heard about the manner in which they took care of the provincials they called

---

[70]See *supra*, nn. 15-16 for Antônio Silvino. See also *infra*, 79n.

[71]See *supra*, nn. 49-51 for Sinhô Pereira.

[72]*Cf.*: Benevides, Alencar Aldenor, letter, May 14, 1993; and Rodrigues de Carvalho, 2nd ed., pp. 26-29, 41-42.

[73]*Cf.*: Menezes and Alencar, *loc. cit.*; Generosa Alencar, interview, Rio de Janeiro/Juazeiro do Norte, April 25, 1993; Fátima Menezes, interviews, Juazeiro do Norte, May 13, 1993; Rio de Janeiro/Juazeiro do Norte, April 26, 1993; April 30, 1993; Aldenor Alencar Benevides, interview, Juazeiro do Norte, May 12, 1993; Fátima Menezes, letter, April 26, 1993; Macaulay, *The Prestes Column*, pp. 189, 191; and Chiavenato, *Cangaço*, pp. 76-77.

[74]Carvalho, Rodrigues de, 2nd ed., p. 361.

fanáticos, once this group became bothersome.[75] And after several years in the *cangaço*, he knew from experience how the police dealt with the *independentes* they infrequently caught up with or who crossed their path.

In the last analysis, whatever desires he had to actually switch sides must have been met with displeasure at learning that his commission, so alluringly offered, was not being taken seriously. Of the approximately 2,000 *sertanejos* divided into eleven *Batalhões Patrióticos* in the Northeast, only one *Batalhão* commander, Lt. Francisco Chagas Azevedo, recognized Lampião's new rank.[76]

As if to show that he could cooperate, indeed, that he wanted to do so, Lampião and his followers left Juazeiro peacefully. The arms given them when they were superficially made *Patrióticos*, they sold to other *cangaceiros*.[77] They even refrained from all criminal activities for over a month. Only then, when they were repeatedly attacked by state forces, did Lampião give up his one attempt to switch sides. It is reported that when he traveled to Bahia in the period that followed, the killing of soldiers and the police, even ex-police, took on a new dimension and meaning for O Rei do Cangaço.[78] It was as it he and his bunch had finally said, "To hell with everything!"

For another twelve years, Lampião would continue his rampage. He did this in defiance of individuals from his own class, so that he might put fear into them to be sure of their help. A journalist who in his youth had interviewed Lampião recounts asking the famous *independente*,

> 'Captain, since you already have money and *fazendas*..., why do you insist on leading this dangerous life..., pursued by the police, being shot at here, shot at there?' Lampião answered, 'It is because, little *doutor*, I never shook the hand of a man at the side of the road that was not cold with fear.' He liked the feeling that men in front of him were filled with terror. His vocation was power, ...[and] domination, because of which he felt that everyone was inferior to him. If he was a *fazendeiro* he would disappear, dead by the age of forty, since he would have lost all of his

---

[75]It would be interesting to know which messianic/millenaristic movements, together with their all too often repression by the government, had come to Lampião's attention by the date of his commission. While he is certain to have known about Canudos (see *infra*, nn. 88-89), there had also been a profusion of such movements in the interior of Brazil before 1926.

[76]*Cf.*: Menezes, Fátima, letter, April 26, 1993; and *Jornal do Brasil*, December 27, 1992, sec. 1, p. 7.

[77]Menezes and Alencar, p. 143.

[78]Chandler, pp. 75-76.

hate, his advantage, his inclination to govern [and] to command.[79]

It all ended suddenly one morning in a ravine in usually safe Sergipe. He was shot down on July 28, 1938 in a *Polícia Militar* double-cross at a *fazenda* called Angicos.[80] Thanks to his connections in powerful places, Lampião had never been followed into or bothered in Sergipe. He was caught off guard at Angicos because he believed that one of his usual suppliers of arms, Lt. João Bezerra of the state police, was edging up to his encampment near a small ravine in order to sell him weapons.

That night, the *cachaça* delivered to Virgulino's encampment by a *coiteiro* was laced with some kind of sleeping potion. Lampião and his men, the women didn't drink the liquor, slept deeply. It proved to be their undoing, as Bezerra attacked at 4 A.M. The lieutenant was the kind of hypocrite that history would glorify. He had been a weapons supplier for years. He had also feigned hunting Lampião and then concocted excuse after excuse to tell his superiors. This time, however, Bezerra reluctantly carried out his assignment for fear of being fired. The state *interventor*, or governor, Eronildes de Carvalho, was a personal friend of Lampião but a personal appointee of Getúlio Vargas. Vargas forced Carvalho to order Bezerra to act. The *interventor* even went so far as to threaten the lieutenant with his suspicions that he was furnishing Lampião with guns.[81]

Why did the Vargas decide to push the button? It was most likely because in his view Lampião had insulted him. Getúlio felt offended by the film Benjamin Abraão made in 1936, depicting the bandit and his gang living the good life and dancing for the camera while theoretically on the run. In one scene, Lampião even made a group of defeated police troopers kiss his hand before killing them.[82]

Due to his earlier contacts with the *cangaceiro*,[83] Abraão had little trouble

[79]CPDOC, oral history, "Abelardo Jurema," 1977, p. 234. Lampião may well have changed his mind about leaving the *cangaço* some four months before his death. *Folha de São Paulo*, July 29, 1996, sec. A, p. 3.

[80]*Cf.*: Góis, p. 233; Fernando Portela and Cláudio Bojunga, *Lampião: o cangaceiro e o outro*. São Paulo: Traço, 1982, p. 73; Chiavenato, *Cangaço*, p. 43; and *O Globo*, February 24, 1985, p. 8.

[81]Chiavenato, *Cangaço*, pp. 46-49, 121-22. The information about the spiked *cachaça* was provided by Sila, one of the survivors of Angicos. Fátima Menezes, interview, Juazeiro do Norte, May 12, 1993. Note that Chiavenato (*Cangaço*, p. 122) spells this woman's name as "Cila." For more on *coiteiros*, see *supra*, nn. 7-8, 8n.

[82]Menezes, Fátima, interview, Juazeiro do Norte, May 11, 1993.

[83]See *supra*, nn. 68-74.

113

finding Lampião again. His initial plan was to live with Lampião's gang for a year while making his movie. But he couldn't stand the lifestyle and didn't last very long. Adhemar Albuquerque of Aba Film had contracted Abraão to shoot the picture. By the time Benjamin gave up, he had made a short work and snapped forty still photographs.[84] DIP (Departamento de Imprensa e Propaganda, or the Department of the Press and Propaganda), Vargas' *Estado Novo* censorship apparatus, obtained the out-takes and immediately locked them away. Aba Film, however, successfully hid the negatives.[85] The material that fell into DIP's hands was destroyed along with most of the rest of the DIP archives sometime before Vargas left office in 1945.

Abraão suffered a parallel fate. Following *Padre* Cicero's death on July 20, 1934, he began selling rifles and ammunition to the *cangaceiros*. By 1936, he had also amassed a large number of compromising letters and notes addressed to Lampião from several *coronéis* and members of various state police forces. Many of these communications dealt with trafficking in arms. Had they ever come to light, they certainly would have presented a different twist to the story of the Rei do Cangaço. While editing his film in 1937, Abraão was savagely hacked to death from behind in Aguas Belas, Pernambuco, after showing parts of his picture to outsiders and letting it be known that he had the Lampião letters. His body had thirty-eight stab wounds. The official story was that Benjamin's death was the product of a love triangle.[86]

Back in the gully at Angicos, the police sliced off the fingers and hands of the dead *cangaceiros* so that they could steal their rings as quickly as possible. Lt. Bezerra tried to stop this, making everyone turn in anything of value to him. It is said that he later bought three *fazendas* in Goiás with this booty.[87] The heads of Lampião and his common-law-wife, Maria Déa, together with those of nine members of his gang, were removed and lined up on the front steps of the nearest

[84]Figure 26, presented here, depicting Lampião and his gang in their prime, is one of these photographs.
[85]Arquivo Nirez in Fortaleza eventually obtained copies of Abraão's work. Miguel Ângelo de Azevedo, letter, October 27, 1992.
[86]*Cf.*: Menezes, Fátima, interviews, Juazeiro do Norte, May 11, 1993; May 12, 1992; and Aldenor Alencar Benevides, interview, Juazeiro do Norte, May 12, 1993.
[87]*Ibid.*

church for display.[88]

Maria Déa, known as "Maria Bonita" ("Maria Beautiful") by the *macacos*, was a descendant of one of the fighters who defended Antônio Conselheiro.[89] She was beheaded by the police after being captured and begging in vain to be spared.[90] Unaware that this was happening, Bezerra became so irritated when he found out that he yelled, "Who was the dog that killed this woman?"[91] *Cangaceiras* were renowned for their attractiveness, and Bezerra had plans to turn Maria Déa into one of his rapid sexual adventures or keep her permanently for himself. The *macacos'* treatment of captured women preceded them. Many apprehended females were appallingly tortured to death. So gruesome were the police in this one area that not even the dead escaped.

> One of the most awful cases was that of the *cangaceira* Nenê de Luís Pedro. She was killed in the early morning at a corral where *cangaceiros* had been drinking milk. The bandits fled, leaving her body. At daybreak, the *'macacos'* found Nenê's cadaver and gave it to the dogs. They then proceeded to excite and manipulate the canines in such a way that the dogs had 'sexual relations' with the deceased woman.[92]

In another instance, a policeman named Adbom, the individual who fired the first shot in the ambush of Lampião, stripped the clothes off of a freshly shot *cangaceira* with a knife, and then continued with

> ...deep incisions in the groin area, detaching the tissues, and cutting away 'the place where babies are made'.... He salted it, dried it, and cured the

---

[88]A photograph of this gory spectacle was taken and appeared first in *A Noite Illustrada* (Rio de Janeiro), August 9, 1938, pp. 24-25. It is reproduced here as Figure 27.

[89]*Cf.*: Oliveira, p. 257; and Fátima Menezes, letter, July 1, 1993. All too many authors refer to Maria by the nickname given her by the police. Lampião called her "Santinha" ("Little Saint") or simply by her given name. Other members of the group used the more respectful *Dona* Maria, or even "Maria de Lampião." *Ibid.* For the Antônio Conselheiro connection, see *supra*, 75n, and chap. ii.

[90]*Cf.*: Araujo, p. 53; and Fátima Menezes, interview, Juazeiro do Norte, May 12, 1993. That she was beheaded was later confirmed by the Nina Rodrigues Institute (see *infra*, nn. 94-95). *Ibid.* This view, nonetheless, is discounted by the policeman who claims to have shot her. Maria Christina Matta Machado, *As táticas de guerra dos cangaceiros*, 2nd ed., São Paulo: Brasiliense, 1978, p. 128.

[91]Sila (see *supra*, 81n) furnished this information too to Fátima Menezes. At Angicos the *cangaceira* escaped by running into the bush. While hiding she overheard Bezerra's outburst. Fátima Menezes, interview, Juazeiro do Norte, May 12, 1993.

[92]Chiavenato, *Cangaço*, p. 110.

115

leather. He carried the cured sexual organ with him as a talisman.[93]

Now already dead, Bezarra was not to have his diversion. Only the desecration remained. "The body of Maria was left in a grotesque position, its legs pulled apart and a large stick rammed up the vagina."[94] Lampião and Maria's craniums were ultimately sent to the Nina Rodrigues Institute in Salvador for classification. They remained on display there for nearly thirty years.[95]

Some of Lampião's gang were not present at the massacre. Principal among these were Christino Gomes da Silva and several people of his sub-group. Known as "Corisco," or lightning," he went on an immediate, revenge-bent killing spree but was severely crippled himself by police bullets. In 1940, semi-invalid and defenseless, *Coronel* José Rufino murdered Corisco with a machine gun barrage across the midsection.[96] Corisco's death effectively brought to an end the period in the Northeastern known as the *cangaço*.

Yet it was Virgulino Ferreira da Silva, one among many, who perhaps came closest to manifesting the desires of the displaced and the powerless from that era. These were and largely remain a people without any real monetary strength of their own. What would the hundreds of individuals from this strata hope to accomplish by joining up with Lampião in some fashion if not to show that despite their economic position, without justice they could be frightening?[97]

As has been suggested, it is important to remember that some aspects of what has become the legend of Lampião are completely distorted. True, he could be strategically daring and at times innovative. One of his most ingenious ideas, when he was in Bahia, was to divide up his group into units. Each had a nominal head, but all acted on his orders. This baffled the authorities into thinking that Lampião was in several places at once.[98] On the other hand, he was not, as is so often described, some kind of military genius or literally invincible adversary. These

---

[93]*Ibid.*, pp. 110, 123.
[94]Chandler, p. 226.
[95]*Cf.*: ibid., pp. 229-30; and *Grande enciclopédia Delta Larousse*, p. 3893. See also *supra*, chap. ii, nn. 32-33.
[96]Chiavenato, *Cangaço*, pp. 56-57, 125-26.
[97]*Cf.*: Chandler, p. 214; Lewin, "The Oligarchical Limitations of Social Banditry in Brazil," p. 116; and Eric Hobsbawn, *Bandits*, New York: Delacorte, 1969, pp. 50-53.
[98]Menezes, Fátima, interview, Juazeiro do Norte, May 13, 1993.

were myths put forward by police units bought off so as not to pursue him with very much enthusiasm. Those who continue to believe in this fantasy forget that Lampião was defeated at Mossoró when he tried his one and only raid in the state of Rio Grande do Norte.[99]

Before being arrested, Teofanes Torres[100] was in charge of the combined anti-*cangaceiro* police forces in Alagoas, Bahia, Paraíba, Pernambuco, and Sergipe. In this augmented role he also put in the appearance of chasing Lampião from time to time. His lack of eagerness arose in part from the fact that like Bezzara, he too was selling arms to Lampião.[101] Torres later stated that over 600 men affiliated with The King of Banditry during his long reign were either caught or killed. While there has been a discussion that this figure is way too high,[102] if we nevertheless accept Torres' statement, in light of his other frailties, then an interesting but suspect argument comes to light. For when one considers the number of additional personalities who escaped, and those who simply returned to more legal occupations along the way, the conceivable sum of people involved with Lampião might entice one to assume that they were witnessing some type of rural rebellion. But Lampião was no political radical, nor were a significant number of those from the world he represented. Rather, and in spite of the numbers, in turning to the *cangaço*, each opted for an individualized response that fragmented their power to provoke change.[103]

It was as if those persons who were behind the scenes pulling the strings of the regional police were primarily ignored or somehow excused from the vengeance of a repressed rural mass. As we have seen, it was the *coronéis*, political winds aside, who so predictably decided which persons were going to be *independentes* (the bandits) or *mansos* (the police).[104] That these two groups were

---

[99]Chiavenato, *Cangaço*, pp. 51-62. 115-16, 122.

[100]See also *supra*, nn. 30-34.

[101]Benevides, Aldenor Alencar, interview, Juazeiro do Norte, May 12, 1993.

[102]Both Chandler (pp. 107-8) and Gueiros (1st ed., pp. 31-32) feel that this figure of 600 may be inflated.

[103]*Cf.*: Blok, Anton, "The Peasant and the Brigand: Social Banditry Reconsidered," *Comparative Studies of Society and History*, vol. xiv, no. 4, September 1972, pp. 494-503; ___, *The Mafia of a Sicilian Village, 1860-1960: a Study of Violent Peasant Entrepreneurs*, Oxford: Blackwell, 1974, pp. 94-102; and Lewin, "The Oligarchical Limitations of Social Banditry in Brazil," p. 145.

[104]Joseph, Gilbert, "On the Trail of Latin American Bandits: a Re-examination of Peasant Resistance," *Latin American Research Review* [hereafter *LARR*], vol. xxv, no. 3, 1990, p. 10.

often interchangeable and drawn from the same class was a master stroke of the men of power. By turning one against the other, the dominant were able to rise above potential threats to their own positions. By keeping "outlaws" in the background as a possible substitute or reserve force and by giving an air of legality and respectability to the "police," justice could be sidestepped. In rural Brazil, the mighty were thus successful in playing the lower classes off against themselves.

See also *supra*, nn. 3-4.

Figure 1. Branding irons used on slaves before and/or after shipment from Africa. (Marfa Barbosa Vianna)

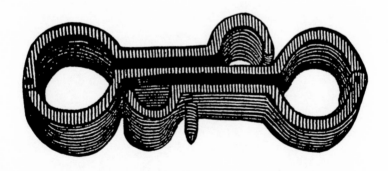

Figure 2. Shackles that bent slaves over, imprisoning the hands and feet, making sleep nearly impossible. (Thomas Ewbank)

Figure 3. Two of the metal masks used to keep slaves from drinking liquor or from committing suicide by eating dirt. (Thomas Ewbank, Luiz Edmundo)

Figure 4. A *feitor* in action. This technique of chastisement was the probable precursor to a contemporary torture called *pau de arara* or "Parrot's Perch." Note the whipping of another slave, tied to a tree, in the background. (Jean Debret)

Figure 5. A public thrashing. The slaves to the left are connected with a common rope tied around their necks. Today's police still use this effective method of prisoner constraint. (Jean Debret)

Figure 6. Galley or chain-gang prisoners, including one white inmate, bringing food to their fellow convicts. The original legend reads:
These Wretches have, in general, committed such atrocious crimes, that little commiseration is felt for their situation: the worst and most hardened are distinguished by Irons round the Leg, in addition to those on the Neck. (Henry Chamberlain)

Figure 7.
The log chained to one ankle, iron leg rings, and the *libambo*. (Jean Debret)

Figure 8.
Francisco
Alberto
Teixeira
de Aragão.
(Pacheco/Mello
Barreto Filho and
Hermeto Lima)

Figure 9. The Aljube.
(Mello Barreto Filho
and Hermeto Lima)

Figure 10. The hold of the brig *Palhaço* in 1823 as lime is poured down on prisoners already wet from scuffling for fetid water. (Maris Filho)

Figure 11.
A policeman in the 1840s.
(Pedro Ludwig and
Frederico Guilherme Briggs)

Figure 12.
A black *capitão do mato*
escorting his black victim.
(Maurice Rugendas)

Figure 13. A slave being
taken to the Casa de Correção
to be whipped for a "small sum."
(Pedro Ludwig and
Frederico Guilherme Briggs)

Figure 14. *Revista Illustrada*, February 18, 1886, pp. 4-5

(on the opposite page, translated from left to right)

Headline: "Scenes of slavery supported by the party of order under the glorious and wise reign of *Dom* Pedro II the great...."

Captions, **top row**:
1. "Slaves taken from prisons, tied, gagged, beaten, and placed into carriages for delivery to their owners."
2. "Some are transported in moving vans with their hands and feet bound all the while being subjected to ill-treatment by police spies."
3. "Others, like the slave Honorio, travel in this manner in wagons expressly rented by masters and the torturers of one Dr. Alfredo Ellis."
4. "Before arriving to face his owner, Honorio received his manumission documents. During his train ride of two days, without food and water, the Abolitionist Confederation telegraphed Dr. Antônio Bento, a distinguished humanitarian, to look after poor Honorio following his liberation--as he wasn't waiting on anything except death."

Captions, **middle row**:
1. "Another slave, who was being returned to his master, escaped from his guards and threw himself between the wheels of the train, where he was torn to bits."
2. "A different bondsman broke a wagon window with his head. Although it caused him excruciating pain, he then cut his neck with the broken glass."
3. "There are innumerable cases of slave suicide. Some hang themselves, others jump into the ocean or drown in rivers."
4. "Each of these forlorn people prefers the most appalling end over a slow, painful death from a *chicote*, dampened with vinegar and sand, which cuts the flesh to ribbons."

Captions, **bottom row**:
1. "They say horrible things about the atrocities of barbaric masters. [As example,] slaves have been shoved into flaming ovens."
2. "Others have been hurled into caldrons of boiling water on sugar mills."
3. "Still others, buried alive."
4. "Not long ago, the newspapers reported the horrible case of one *fazendeiro* who was furious at seeing a female slave who couldn't work because she was about to give birth. The man murdered her with kicks to her stomach."
5. "Despite all of these outrages, one can not find a single master confined to jail. But these lock ups are full of unfortunate slaves who had the courage to rise up against their tormentors. Holy Justice!"

Scenas da escravidão patrocinadas pelo partido da Ordem|sob o glorioso e sabio reinado do Senhor D. Pedro II o Grande...

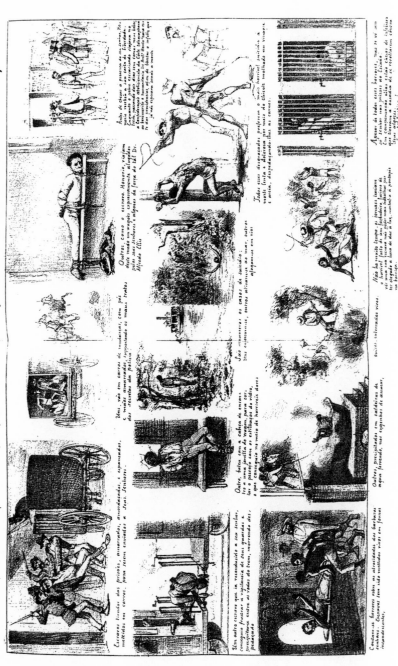

Figure 15.
Hermes da Fonseca
on Brazilian Republic Day.
"Viva the Republic or the Marshal?"
(Seth/*O Gato*)

Figure 16.
Coronel-Senator
Pinheiro Machado
in 1911.
(A Illustração Brazileira)

encar-
sceu
os dos
cou-
s.

:iaes
dos
l
1da-
os
1ssu-
os

O "Corre
nhã"
ante
vasos d
se
restitu
gov

E'cos e
form
sol
o movi
med

Figure 17.
"The Black Admiral" João Cândido (top),
and one of his fellow mutineers.
(Correio da Manhã)

Figure 18. Lt. Colonel Candido Rondon
in 1911 before going on to larger fame.
(Correio da Manhã/Arquivo Nacional)

Figure 19.
Antônio Conselheiro dead in
October of 1897. (Museu da República)

Figure 20.
The second João Maria,
Monge João Maria de Jesus.
(Claro Gustavo Jansson/
Dorothy Moretti collection)

Figure 21. José Maria, *Monge* José
Maria de Santo Agostinho. *(O Cruzeiro)*

Figure 22. Survivors of Canudos, erroneously said to be *"jagunços"* and *"jagunças"* as well as 400 in number. (Museu da República)

Figure 23. Survivors of the Contestado War (seated). To the left (standing, dressed in white) are four "virgins." (Claro Gustavo Jansson/Dorothy Moretti collection)

Figure 24. Antônio Silvino on August 30, 1938 after arriving in Rio de Janeiro aboard the Italian ship *Conta Grande*. He is flanked on his right by Hilda, a family friend. On his left in the naval uniform is Severino, one of his sons. *(Correio da Manhã/*Arquivo Nacional)

Figure 25. In Petropolis, Getulio Vargas offering to arrange a job for Antônio Silvino. *(Correio da Manhã/*John W.F. Dulles)

Figure 26. Lampião and a part of his gang in their prime in 1936. Lampião is in the front row, third from the left. Maria Déa is to his left. This photograph was among those taken by Benjamin Abraão which may have led to Lampião's extermination. (Benjamin Abraão/Arquivo Nirez)

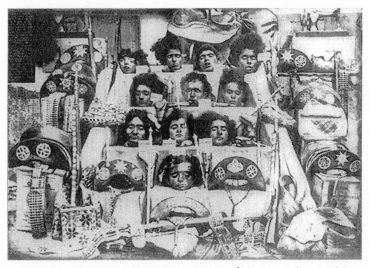

Figure 27. The heads of Lampião and some of his group after Angicos. Lampião's cranium is on the bottom row between the two hats. Maria Déa's head is directly behind Lampião's. (A Noite Illustrada)

Figure 28. A police execution squad in Juazeiro do Norte in early 1928. Commanded by Sergeant José Antonio (front row, left), all five of the *cangaceiros* to his left will have their bodies dumped on the road linking Juazeiro and Crato as a warning to other rural bandits. The victims were formerly members of one of Lampião's gangs. (Xavier de Oliveira)

Figure 29. A *Batalhão Patriótico* in Juazeiro do Norte in 1926.
(Fátima Menezes collection)

Figure 30.
Coronel-Dr. Floro
Bartolomeu and
Padre Cícero.
(Memorial *Padre* Cícero)

Figure 31. Benjamin Abraão and *Padre* Cícero. (Fátima Menezes collection)

"The Separation on the Island of the Snakes"

Figure 32.
Women: "Master, Doctor, Chief, for the love of God! Don't put our mens on the Acre boat! God bless you if yous grants us this favor."
Police Chief Cardoso de Castro: "It's all right. Be calm. I will choose very carefully. Only those who committed crimes will go.... Are your men innocent?"
Women: "They must be Master, Doctor. But if they makes noise again, by the light from heaven, we will put them fools in chains like dogs." *(O Malho)*

Figure 33.
"Big Daddy" (center, in top hat) inaugurating Avenida Central. *(O Malho)*

"Actualities"

Figure 34. "The police applying... the law." *(Gazeta de Noticias)*

"Police Inquiries"

Figure 35.
Deputy: "Please respond calmly. Was it or was it not my dear friend who stole the cheese?"
Man on ground: "No sir!"
Deputy: "One more stab buddy..." (K. Lixto/Correio da Manhã)

Figure 36.
An unsigned characterization of Artur Bernardes in December of 1928. *(Critica)*

Figure 37.
One-armed Tertuliano Potyguara
after being made a general.
(Centro de Documentação do Exército)

Figure 38. Chief of Police,
General Fontoura.
(Museu da Academia de Polícia)

Figure 39. A balding Carlos Reis,
partially hidden. (Arquivo Público Mineiro)

Figure 40. Waldemar Loureiro, Director of the Casa de Correção.
(Agência O Globo)

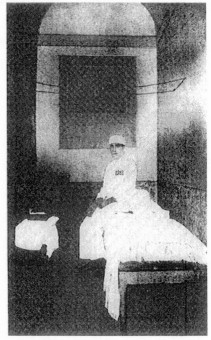

Figure 41. A staged photograph of "prisoner 2308" in his cell at the Casa de Correção in the mid-1920s.
(José Gabriel de Lemos Britto)

Figure 42. Meira Lima, Director of the Casa de Detenção.
*(Correio da Manhã/*Arquivo Nacional)

Figure 43. View of the galleries at the Casa de Detenção in the mid-1920s.
(José Gabriel de Lemos Britto)

Figure 44. "Mello das Creanças." (Agência O Globo)

Figure 45. General Santa Cruz alias "Scalped Coconut."
(Centro de Documentação do Exército)

Figure 46. The announcement of the "suicide" of José Nadyr Machado.
(Agência O Globo)

Figure 47. Attila Neves. *(Critica)*

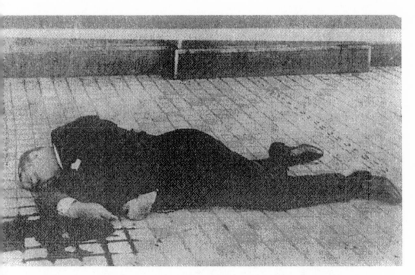

Figure 48. Conrado Niemeyer, dead on the Rua da Relação sidewalk. The numbers drawn on the tiles on each side of his body were to indicate the distance out from the side of the building that he had "jumped." (Agência O Globo)

Figure 49. A lad in knickers mopping up Niemeyer's blood. Conrado's corpse is to the left, covered with newspapers. (Agência O Globo)

Figure 50. The Polícia Central on the Rua da Relação. Niemeyer's body is covered with newspapers beneath the second-story window. (Agência O Globo)

Figure 51. From left to right, seated on the left side of the table: Chico Chagas, Moreira Machado, Pedro Mandovani, and "Twenty-Six," on the first day of their trial. (Correio da Manhã/Arquivo Nacional)

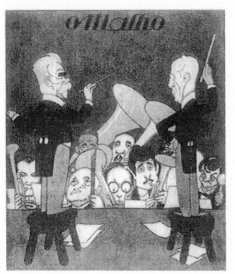

Figure 52.
Washington Luís and Artur Bernardes
"directing the band" on November 13,
1926 to the caption of "We're going to
hear a duet." The ensemble is made up
of some of the members of the incoming
government. *(O Malho)*

Figure 53. Coriolano de Góis.
*(Correio da Manhã/*Arquivo Nacional)

Figure 54. Luís Carlos Prestes during his *Coluna* days.
(Roberto/*Correio da Manhã*/Arquivo Nacional)

Chapter IV

CLEANING UP THE CAPITAL

In 1822, almost three months after the country proclaimed its independence, an acute fear of another slave revolt gripped Bahia. In Cachoeira, at one inlet of the Bahia de Todos os Santos across from Salvador, special orders were quickly passed for the entire province. The militia and police were put on alert and instructed to check local *quilombos* for runaways. They were likewise empowered to prevent slaves from carrying weapons (with a few specific exceptions) or from assembling in public, and were to detain every slave wandering about without a note from his master. In the cities, a curfew for bond servants began at 9 P.M. Violation of these ordinances brought from fifty to 200 lashes, depending on the rural or urban residence of the slave. Those in the more populated areas fared the worst.

The point to remember is that the arrest rates for black and brown males, enslaved or freed, may have remained high right through the period of difficulty in Bahia. If Cachoeira itself can be taken as example of the rest of the province, then the following graph (on page 120) would seem to demonstrate that the military, the militia, and the diverse policing agencies were indeed taking a hard look at every black and brown man all along. The type of justice that was accorded these two groups during this turbulent time served to indicate an important constant: the authorities' interpretation of the law in Bahia was probably a reflection of the biases and labor needs of the province's *classe conservadora*.

Similar patterns could be seen in other parts of Brazil. In Pernambuco, blacks were arrested a disproportionate number of times, more so than any other racial group, for disrupting public order. The most common charges were for breaking curfew, disorderly conduct, and running away.[1] Data from Rio de Janeiro indicate that from 1810 to 1821, 99.6% of all males arrested were either slaves or freedmen

---

[1]Huggins, pp. 87-89.

Male Arrests by Race as a Percent of All Arrests
Where Race Was Known in Cachoeira, Bahia from 1790 to 1833[2]

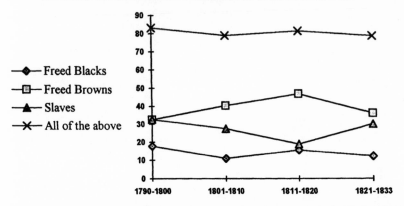

(99.7% from 1811 to 1820).[3] Following the major slave revolt in Bahia in 1835, the authorities in Rio prohibited more than three enslaved persons at one time from congregating in any type of shop, tavern or public house without permission from their masters. In addition, they were not to be encountered in the evenings or on the Sabbath without written authorization or they would be liable to suffer from twenty-five to fifty lashes. Both slaves and freedmen were likewise not to become peddlers. The bleak employment situation being what it was for emancipated males, this last proviso was probably intended at reducing the mobility and increasing the dependency of all ex-slaves.[4]

By the 1860s, as the number of imported slaves started to dwindle, and owing to the demands for even larger numbers of workers, the fate of the apprehended was decided rapidly. Once the formalities of being seized were over, many

---

[2]*Cf.*: Aufderheide, p. 375; and Conrad, *Children of God's Fire*, pp. 254-56. The actual percentages were as follows:

	1790-1800	1801-1810	1811-1820	1821-1833
Freed Blacks	17.8%	11.1	15.6	12.3
Freed Browns	32.7	40.4	46.9	36.3
Slaves	32.7	27.5	19.0	30.2
All of the above	83.2	79.0	81.5	78.8

[3]Algranti, Leila Mezan, "Slave Crimes: the Use of Police Power to Control the Slave Population of Rio de Janeiro," *LBR*, vol. xxv, no. 1, Summer 1988, pp. 40, 42.

[4]Conrad, *Children of God's Fire*, pp. 256-59. For the Bahia situation in 1835, see *supra*, chap. i, nn. 64-68, 40n. For the job market and freed males, see *supra*, chap. ii, nn. 8-9.

lawbreakers left legal confinement to try to find "honest employment" as dictated in their newly signed and issued *termos de bem viver*. All troublesome persons (*turbulentos*), refusing to accept jobs that were considered honest and useful, after being so advised by a *Juiz de Paz*, and who were without sufficient funds to prove that they weren't indigent, could be sentenced to between eight and twenty-four days confinement with labor. When there was no *Juiz* present, the remainder could be given between eight and thirty days with or without labor.[5]

In several areas of the country, what this honorable employment stipulation really indicated was a trip to the nearby plantations. Other prisoners, sometimes this included the underage, were simply taken to the *fazendas* of the rich, conscripted into the military, or put to work on different projects. In Rio, one of the most common penalties from 1816 to 1821 was to be placed on the road gang building a highway west to the suburb of Tijuca. Until their services were no longer needed, and even after their sentences had been completed, prisoners were kept on the construction crews and at other public works essentially as slaves. And not to be out done, one state away in São Paulo at the start of this century there were the hated agricultural centers and industrial workhouses that evidently were the favorites of future Brazilian president, Washington Luís.[6]

As for those who were actually sent on to prison, there are scant early figures at the national level. In one of the few available reports, from 1907, the ratio of black and brown men who were resident in Bahian penitentiaries at the end of the year was listed at an alarming 92.4%.[7] This was not some kind of isolated case

[5]Brazil, *Codigo criminal do Imperio do Brasil*, 3rd ed., Ouro Preto: Silva, 1831, pp. 212-13, arts. 295-96. See also *supra*, chap. i, nn. 81-84.

[6]*Cf.*: Hahner, pp. 49-50, 56; *Revista Illustrada*, November 30, 1885, pp. 4-5; Huggins, pp. 35, 68, 72-108; and Algranti, pp. 42-43. Heloísa de Faria Cruz, "Mercado e polícia - São Paulo, 1890-1915," *Revista Brasileira de História* [hereafter *RBH*], vol. vii, no. 14, March-August 1987, pp. 115-30. See also *infra*, 10n. For more on Washington Luís, see *infra*, chap. v, nn. 8-10.

[7]Brazil, Ministerio da Agricultura, Industria e Commercio, *Annuario estatistico do Brazil, 1908-1912*, Rio de Janeiro: Directoria Geral de Estatistica, 1916, vol. iii, p. 429. Since no racial statistics for the total population of Brazil were published between the 1890 and 1940 censuses, these two accountings will be used to define the parameters between which such figures most probably existed on a state by state basis. They are reproduced in Table 2 of the Appendix. Keep in mind that in both 1890 and 1940 there could have been differences in the way census takers recorded mulattos, who no doubt make up a majority of the "Brown" category used in all of the tables in the Appendix. Moreover, Brazilians are and have been known to classify many persons

limited to Bahia. It could just as easily be observed in the same data (see Appendix, Table 1) that in ten of nineteen states, the old Federal District, plus the country as a whole, white men were leaving prisons proportionately faster than they were entering them. Among blacks the situation was reversed with more men of African descent entering Brazilian penal institutions in 1907 than those who left. This took place in ten out of nineteen states, the former Federal District, and in the entire nation if added together. Brown males did slightly worse. They were imprisoned more often than they were released in the total figures for Brazil, in the former capital, and in twelve states. Finally, if one looks at the percentage of men still incarcerated at the end of 1907 in proportion to their actual occurrences in the state populations (see Appendix, Table 2), it is clear that whites were under-represented in the prison populations. This was true for all areas except Mato Grosso (which had only three inmates out of the country's total of 3,422). Black and brown males showed a distinctly opposite trend in this category, with distinctly higher numbers. It can be estimated that whereas white males were under-represented about 15% in the year-ending data for 1907, black and mixed-race men were over-represented 5% and 10% respectively. Had all things been equal, there would have been 1,432 whites in prison and not just 1,245; 635 blacks instead of 668; and 1,366 brown men in place of the higher figure of 1,518. There was one male of yellow heritage resident in a São Paulo prison on December 31, 1907.[8]

There are several intriguing interpretations of these countrywide figures. Each explanation lends partial support to the position that black and mixed-descent men continued to be treated unfairly as they became further entangled in the legal apparatus created and run by their former masters. One might assume, for example, that black and brown males were being given longer sentences and were confined more often than whites because they simply committed more serious crimes more frequently than whites. But, if true, one might qualify such a position

---

as *mulatos* or *pardos* (brown) that other societies would place in the "Black" category. Depending then on which definition one wishes to use, blacks could be under-represented in the Appendix, and in general throughout this work. See also *supra*, introduction, 2n, chap. i, 34n-35n.

[8] For a report on the situation in the city of São Paulo between 1880 and 1924, during which time 54.4% of all black and brown men and women (as opposed to 36.4% of all whites) were found guilty of those crimes for which they stood accused, see Boris Fausto, *Crime e cotidiano: a criminalidade em São Paulo, 1880-1924*, São Paulo: Brasiliense, 1984, pp. 235-36.

by asking what percentage of the non-whites perpetrated their offenses out of grinding economic desperation?

It may have been that non-whites were sentenced and whites were not, or maybe that the former were given longer terms for lesser or the same types of crimes than the latter? Also, whites could have been released sooner due to their race? Perhaps they got out quicker because of better connections (this would have included a knowledge of whom to bribe). It may be that their reduced time was due to larger incomes, and hence an ability to afford more capable legal counsel (this would have included an ability to bribe). There is some evidence to suggest, to the contrary, that while whites may well have been released earlier, just being white was *not* the most significant item in 1907. That is, if illiteracy plus menial labor can be taken to indicate poverty and low social class, then the majority of these convicts: white, black, and brown, were probably poor. This material (see Appendix, Table 3) was not made available by race in the government's accounting.

A more likely cause of the 1907 incarceration figures involved courts that continued to view all blacks and men of a combination of races with suspicion (nearly all were poor). These administrators of blind justice reacted differently, however, to the alleged crimes of whites (unless they were poor). Guarding the entrance to this legal mosaic stood the police sub-elites. What about those constables who were non-whites themselves? Unless these police wanted to be disciplined or even kicked off the force, they learned to carry out--indeed they learned to anticipate and believe in--their masters' choice[9] In so doing, the innocent and persons whose crimes would otherwise go unnoticed passed before the scrutinizing eyes of overly eager authorities. Down on the street this generally came to mean that despite the race of the policemen or the offender, there was a steady effort to get the black, the brown, and the impoverished white man who was not somehow protected.[10]

[9]These sub-elites were virtually urban *cangaceiros mansos* (see *supra*, chap. iii, especially nn. 3-4, 56-61, and n. 103 to the end of the chapter). Non-whites in such positions were not out of the ordinary. Brazilian elites historically used, and even specifically selected, trusted non-whites for a variety of roles as buffers to ameliorate the obtainment of goals. See, as example, the discussions of the *capataz* and the *captão de mato* (*supra*, chap. i, nn. 18-19, 52-53, 19n, 53n).

[10]Partial support for this position is given in Fausto for São Paulo (*loc. cit.*, Table 50), and in Huggins for Pernambuco (pp. 87-90, 124-27). In Rio, the majority of arrests in this period appear to have been for real or fictional public order violations. For male offenders the charges

As for women, the statistics on Brazilian female imprisonments for 1907 displayed something out of the ordinary only for non-white women in the old Federal District. Hence what took place in the capital during that era, an age inspired by its French counterpart and known as the *Belle Époque*, or Beautiful Epoch, deserves our attention.

The concern with things French had been evolving for nearly three-hundred years and as the nineteenth century drew to a close it really began to take hold. What it turned into, particularly in Rio, was the conspicuous consumption of European culture by the local *grã-fino*. This is not to say that all of Europe was favored equally. France and England, in that order, were the most popular. Whenever possible, the life-styles of the wealthy in these two nations were to be mimicked as a way of exhibiting social distance between persons of refinement and the scum down below. By the time Francisco de Paula Rodrigues Alves became president in 1902, the *Belle Époque*, complete with imitation European dandies and dilettante intellectuals, was in full swing. The new leader was a former monarchist and slaveocrat who fell asleep all too often during his abbreviated workday. Despite this small problem, sometime prior to 1903, "Big Daddy" (as he was occasionally called), decided on his main contribution to posterity. He would speed up the efforts to turn the capital into a Parisian-like showplace for indigenous and foreign elites.[11]

In the national changeover from a slave labor to a broader mercantile economy, Rio by the turn of the century had become the financial center for those

---

in this category of crimes included gambling, the use of arms, begging, drunkenness, vagrancy, disorderly behavior, and probably any other violation the apprehending policeman wanted to include. Sam Adamo, "The Broken Promise: Race, Health, and Justice in Rio de Janeiro, 1890-1940," unpublished PhD thesis, Department of History, University of New Mexico, 1983, pp. 242-47, 242n, 244n.

[11]*Cf.*: Lustosa, Isabel, *Histórias de presidentes: a república no Catete*, Petrópolis: Vozes, 1989, p. 39; Freyre, *Order and Progress*, pp. 56-57, 348; Jeffrey Needell, "Rio de Janeiro at the Turn of the Century: Modernization and the Parisian Ideal," *Journal of Interamerican Studies and World Affairs*, vol. xxv, no. 1, February 1983, pp. 83-103; Teresa Meade, "Civilizing Rio de Janeiro': the Public Health Campaign and the Riot of 1904," *Journal of Social History*, vol. xx, no. 2, Winter 1986, p. 307; and Bello, *A History of Modern Brazil*, pp. 173, 175-76. For what must be a small sample of the characterizations of Big Daddy's dozing problem, *cf.*: *O Malho* (Rio de Janeiro), October 22, 1904, p. 11; October 29, 1904, p. 28; November 5, 1904, p. 1; and November 26, 1904, p. 1. Founded in 1902, *O Malho* was one of the most important Brazilian magazines of criticism in the first decade of the twentieth century.

Brazilians, Europeans, and North Americans engaged in banking and the exchange of goods from abroad for Brazilian produce. To facilitate these interests, Rodrigues Alves felt that a new port close to the commercial area was called for and that the metropolitan region generally needed to be cleaned up. In everyday terms this meant that the city of Rio de Janeiro, long known overseas for its epidemics, vice, and rundown appearance, would be upgraded to meet plutocratic tastes. This was to take place regardless of the opinions and housing arrangements of those inhabitants who were not members of the international consortium of profit-makers.[12]

The undertaking was not to be an easy task but Big Daddy was determined to have his capital his way. As an opening step, a plan was put together that had a key byproduct (some might refer to it as an ingredient): the ejection of the unwanted classes from the city center. Somewhere it was decided that it would not be a bad thing to remove Rio's urban *povão* who crowded into eyesore tenements descriptively called *cortiços* or "bee-hives." A large number of downtown occupants lived in such dwellings on property that was potentially valuable.

The ingenious scheme revolved around a selective fight against disease. While residents in the old Federal District continuously suffered from tuberculosis and the ramifications of a bad water supply--when and where water was even available--it was smallpox and yellow fever that caused the most concern abroad. Interestingly enough then, yellow fever was the first malady chosen for executive action.[13] It can be granted that thousands of lower-class lives were eventually saved. Yet, as we will shortly see, this was not immediately a concern to those *cariocas* with the smallest piece of the turn-of-the-century economic pie.

---

[12]*Cf.*: Bello, *A History of Modern Brazil*, pp. 176-77, 179; Burns, pp. 226-28; Carlos Fico, "Movimentos de resistência na Primeira República: abastecimento e serviços na cidade do Rio de Janeiro," pre-publication manuscript, pp. 1-2; and Nicolau Sevcenko, *Literatura como missão: tensões sociais e criação cultural na Primeira República*, São Paulo: Brasiliense, 1983, pp. 27-28. The Rothchilds put up a loan for much of the port's construction. Hahner, p. 164.

[13]Aside from these two sicknesses, which were only dealt with by the government when there was a financial incentive to do so, a single example portrays the unhealthy conditions of life in Rio for the working classes by the start of the twentieth century. Since there was little indoor plumbing in their parts of the city, human excretion was carried to the windows and doors and, after the legally stipulated shouts of *Água vai! Água vai!* (Water coming! Water coming!), thrown into the street. *Cf.*: Bello, *A History of Modern Brazil*, p. 177; and Charles Dunlop, *Chronicas: fatos, gente e coisas da nossa história*, Rio de Janeiro: Americana, 1973, p. 40.

In 1903, mosquito inspectors and public health officials spearheaded the development plan. They swooped down on the shacks in the center of the capital occupied by the working poor. Ostensibly they were combating the now and again appearance of yellow fever. They sprayed here and they sprayed there, condemning just about everything in their path as unsanitary. A swank new boulevard ultimately to be renamed Avenida Rio Branco (after the Baron of Rio Branco[14]) was to be constructed right in the middle of this muddle. At first it was called Avenida Central (Central Avenue) and it was needed, so the explanations went, to facilitate work on the new port. No one would have guessed that it would be considered "the place" to be by the local aristocracy and assorted hangers-on after it was completed.[15] There was, following all this, a tune that began to be heard which went:

> A Avenida chic
> Eu sou a Central
> Da elegância o tic
> Dou à capital[16]
>
> . . . .
>
> The avenue of chic
> I am the Central
> Giving the spark of elegance
> To the capital

As for those forced to make way for progress, many of the urban poor were given forty-eight hours notice before eviction. The government then turned a virtual blind eye toward aiding these new homeless individuals. Since the city's urban renewal plans were no secret, there was more than one misgiving about the sanitation officials and all their health improvement endeavors.[17]

Tensions were heightened, as well, by positivist-minded men, particularly in the army, who feared some type of limit being placed on their autocratic powers. The defenders of Brazilian nationhood attempted to hide this fact behind the claim

---

[14]*Cf.*: Meade, pp. 302, 307-9; and ___, "Living Worse and Costing More': Resistance and Riot in Rio de Janeiro, 1890-1917," *JLAS*, vol. xxi, no. 2, May 1989, p. 246. For more on the *Barão* of Rio Branco, see *supra*, chap. ii, 12n.

[15]A photograph of Rodrigues Alves inaugurating the "Central" is presented here as Figure 33.

[16]Brasil, Geason, *História das ruas do Rio de Janeiro*, 4th ed., Rio de Janeiro: Brasiliana, 1965, p. 240.

[17]Hahner, p. 165.

that the real problem, and hence their real ire, was with the national administration's support of the "Politics of Governors." The latter was an agreement whereby the president was given a free rein in all economic decisions and foreign relations in return for largely overlooking what any governor did in his respective state.

By November 11, 1904, after most of the spraying had been done, obligatory vaccinations against yellow fever were to become law. At this juncture, fighting broke out in Rio de Janeiro by those opposed to the administration's designs for disease and downtown beautification. Foreign diplomats later wrote back to their governments that those who took to the streets were not what they would actually call citizens. Foreign diplomats labeled them "a mob," "dregs," "*foule*," "rabble," "social scum," and "a band of Negroes and *mestiços*."[18]

Four days later, the protesters were joined by a sizable group of revolting cadets from the Federal District's military academy, together with the facility's commanding officer, General Silvestre Travassos. These anti-government warriors wanted to bring down Rodrigues Alves and install a military dictatorship with Lt. Colonel (and Senator) Lauro Sodré as leader. It was not long, however, before loyal army and navy units arrived on the scene to smother the young cadets' side of the rebellion. The rescuers then merged with Rio's police to confront the civilians head on.

The ranks of the police had swollen in the years prior to the riot through the recruitment of unsavory characters. More than once, this "recruitment" was in fact very close to impressment. As a consequence, an ample number of new policemen came from criminal backgrounds. Others were former derelicts. Most had especially short fuses and all were more than willing to take a bribe.[19] In sum, the combined force resulted in a police-led rampage that was personally directed by the Bahian strongman, Minister of Justice and Internal Affairs José Joaquim Seabra. He in turn was aided by a particularly unethical chief of police, Antônio

---

[18]Carvalho, José Murilo de, p. 72. For more on positivism, see *supra*, chap. ii, nn. 45-46, 46n.

[19]*Cf.*: Nachman, Robert, "Positivism and Revolution in Brazil's First Republic: the 1904 Revolt," *The Americas*, vol. xxxiv, no. 1, July 1977, pp. 20-22, 30-31, 36-37; Brazil, Ministério da Educação e Saúde, *Obras completas de Rui Barbosa: discursos parlamentares*, Fernando Nery (ed.), Rio de Janeiro: n.p., 1952, vol. xxxi, 1904, book i, p. 353; Meade, "Civilizing Rio de Janeiro," pp. 308-14; and Adamo, pp. 188-89.

128

Augusto Cardoso de Castro.[20] Perhaps fearful of some kind of *coup*, or even of
an urban Canudos,[21] a state of siege was promptly put into effect. This mere
formality gave the government the legal pretext to deal with the disorder in a
heavy-handed way. What then followed in downtown Rio defies description. Uniformed men of justice were allowed to run amok, more than happy to "...settle
accounts and take revenge."[22] This excess, however, did know its place. The
treatment of military cadets and the officers leading them was milder than it was on
everyone else.[23]

> 'Without any right of defense, without any kind of inquiry, poorer
> citizens were gathered up in large police raids. No distinction was made
> as to sex or age. It was enough to look unemployed, tattered in ap-
> pearance or be unable to provide a place of fixed residence to be guilty.'[24]

Many of these "criminals" were taken straight away to police stations and
roughed up again. Then, by the hundreds, they were put into sealed cargo bins on
Lloyd Brasileiro steamships and summarily deported to the country's western-most
territory of Acre to work under the whip in the wild rubber tree groves. Others
were freighted off to the Amazon or unspecified states in the interior. São Paulo
too had a "tidying-up." There the occasion was used to expel the unsuitable to
Bauru, then a frontier district in the northwestern part of the state. Still more were
delivered to the Rio Branco tributary in Roraima or up the Xingu River in Pará.[25]

---

[20]*Cf.*: Bello, *A History of Modern Brazil*, pp. 182-83; and Hahner, pp. 258-59, 263-64. Hahner's remarks (*ibid.*) on Cardoso de Castro are most illuminating. See also *infra*, nn. 24-26, 26n. For another appalling installment of sub-elite violence during these years, this time involving several murders and beatings by the police in the state of Pará, see Benjamin Sodré (org.), *Lauro Sodré: vida, carater e sentimento a serviço de um povo*, Rio de Janeiro: Imprensa Oficial, 1956, pp. 19-20.

[21]Diacon, Todd, "Down and Out in Rio de Janeiro: Urban Poor and Elite Rule in the Old Republic," *LARR*, vol. xxv, no. 1, 1990, p. 247.

[22]*Correio da Manhã*, March 22, 1905, p. 1. For some of the two-fisted prerogatives at the government's disposal during a state of siege, see *supra*, chap. ii, nn. 21-23, 23n, and *infra*, chap. v, nn. 5-6. Additionally, a couple of illustrations of Rio's police dispensing justice, are presented here as Figures 34 and 35. Figure 34 (*Gazeta de Noticias* [Rio de Janeiro], February 7, 1904, p. 1) appeared some nine months before the riot. Figure 35 (*Correio da Manhã*, July 12, 1905, p. 1) was drawn nearly eight months to the day after the outbreak. Both figures are with the accompanying text in translation. That each rendition was front page material suggests that police violence was a common problem. *Gazeta de Noticias* was one of the principle newspapers of the Old Republic.

[23]Hahner, p. 183.

[24]Cited in Sevcenko, p. 66.

[25]Santos, José Maria, *A politica geral do Brasil*, São Paulo: J. Magalhães, 1930, pp. 414-15.

Back in Rio, Police Chief Castro had one of the main roles in deciding who would go and who would stay. Of 334 individuals deported to Acre on but a single freighter, the *Itaipava*, the young, the old, foreigners, and persons of various races were all heaped indiscriminately in the ship's hold, which when closed lacked a sufficient amount of air. When not guarded over by a diabolical black man, or members of the 12th Infantry Battalion, or when not being attacked by swarms of parasites, the semi-nude prisoners climbed over one another and their own blood, vomit, and feces to get at the little fresh air that was available. Almost all of these captives later became sick after breathing the noxious fumes in the bottom of the ship for a prolonged period.[26]

Naturally, there were lower-class residents of the Federal District who stayed indoors and out of the 1904 riot. Different plans, nonetheless, were underway to rid the city of this passive riff-raff. They were to be squeezed out into Rio's poorer suburbs.[27] Besides condemning their property, the out-migration goal was pursued through the aid of policies that supposedly banned *jogo do bicho*.[28]

---

[26]*Cf.*: Sevcenko, pp. 66-67; [Afonso Henriques de] Lima Barreto, *Diário íntimo: memórias*, São Paulo: Brasiliense, 1956, p. 49; Brazil, *Annaes da Camara dos Deputados*, Rio de Janeiro: Nacional, 1905, July 27, 1905, pp. 395-96; Afonso Arinos de Melo Franco, *Rodrigues Alves: apogeu e declínio do presidencialismo*, Rio de Janeiro: José Olympio, 1973, vol. i, p. 424; and *A Noticia* (Rio de Janeiro), December 27-28, 1904, p. 3. Founded in 1894 by Oliveria Rocha, *A Noticia* was one of Rio's most innovative and respected tabloids during the first part of the twentieth century. For a rendition of police Chief Cardoso de Castro in action, selecting those lawbreakers to be packed off to Acre or elsewhere, see *O Malho*, December 3, 1904, p. 24 (here, Figure 32). *O Malho* or the artist "A.A." inverted this drawing. In the background, Sugar Loaf is in reverse view. Keep in mind too that the text of lower-class ethnic Portuguese accompanying Figure 32 has been translated into lower-class ethnic English. Two photographs of this picking and choosing process can also be seen on p. 17 of the same issue of *O Malho*. Note that in one of these pictures (the other has too much contrast to tell), it appears that the majority of the victims are black.

[27]Meade ("Civilizing Rio de Janeiro," p. 304, *et passim*) provides a statistical breakdown of this movement between the renewal areas in the city center and the working-class areas of the North and West Zones. Her data covers the years 1872 to 1920 and shows that for the interval between 1890-1920 the following exodus from downtown districts took place: Candelária (-59%), Sacramento (-10), Santa Rita (-12), and São José (-25). Note, however, that this movement of people, and the influx of migrants from other parts of Brazil, did not noticeably alter the vast expanse of land even further to the northwest known collectively as the Baixada Fluminense. This area would remain under the control of a small number of *fazendeiros* with their vast orange groves until World War II. Only then would it begin to mushroom into today's satellite region of poor commuting workers. Victor Civita (ed.), *Nosso século, 1945-1960: A Era dos Partidos*, São Paulo: Abril Cultural, 1985, part ii, vol. viii, p. 32.

[28]This was simply political lip service. There was just too much money involved. Adamo (p.

Likewise tabooed was any manifestation of the religions that came to Brazil with the first African slaves. Even Carnival, which was still fundamentally a lower-class celebration, was to get a face-lift in the capital to make it more popular and palatable among the wealthier classes. Last, but by far from least, it was to be made a crime to be improperly dressed in the nation's *première* city.

Aimed at poorer males, it was proposed that in order to walk about in the downtown areas of Rio de Janeiro, everyone would have to wear proper shoes, a shirt, and no less than a sport-coat. Those who could not meet this standard would be subject to arrest, regardless of the heat, the humidity, or the circumstances. The proposed law, haughtily referred to as "The Sanitary Project Bill," can be translated as follows:

1907 - Project No. 82
PROHIBITION AGAINST PERSONS IN SHIRTS WITHOUT SPORT COATS
AND WITHOUT SHOES FROM USING THE STREETS AND PARKS IN
THE URBAN PART OF THE FEDERAL DISTRICT
The Municipal Council resolves:
Art. 1. No one will be allowed to pass through the streets
and parks of the urban part of the Federal District
in a shirt without a sport coat and shoes, and be
free from a fine of five *réis* for the first offense
or double thereafter.
Art. 2. All laws to the contrary are revoked.[29]

The proposal lasted through a first and second reading in the legislative chamber before being rejected.[30] The usually mundane *carioca* weekly *Fon-Fon,*

---

190) observes that official protection

...enabled gambling and prostitution to operate on a grand scale in Rio de Janeiro. Local newspapers and officials waged an unending campaign against gambling which was 'the worst of all habits,' responsible for the ruination of thousands of men and their families. Gambling houses operated throughout the city 'with the acquiescence of the police.' The illegal establishments paid officers a monthly fee so they could operate without interference. The profits and location of each business generally determined the amount of the payment made to local authorities.

For more on prostitution, see *infra*, n. 33 to the end of the chapter. For gambling, see *supra*, chap. iii, nn. 65-66, 66n, and *infra*, chap. v, nn. 47-48, 116-19.

[29]*Cf.*: Sevcenko, p. 33; and *Jornal do Commercio*, October 16, 1907, p. 4.

[30]*Cf.*: *Jornal do Commercio*, July 20, 1909, p. 6; and Nicolau Sevcenko, interview, Rio de Janeiro/São Paulo, February 28, 1985. While it was never approved, the moral tone of Project No. 82 was quite naturally a reflection of the rarefied opinions and tastes held by many persons, especially the upper classes, before, during, and after the *Belle Époque*. For a discussion of the antecedents leading up to this high-water mark of Brazilian dress snobbery, *cf.*: Hahner, p. 24;

in its issue following the bill's second deliberation, offered support for the measure. It likewise provided a glimpse of the era's cavalier desires to remove objectionable members of the working class, most of whom tended to have other than lighter shades of skin color, from public view.

In the Municipal Council the second reading of the Sanitary Project Bill has taken place. [This motion would] place limits on the unjustifiable and inadmissible disgrace of persons appearing in shirt-sleeves and without shoes in the streets of the city. The author of the project is the warm-hearted supervisor, *Senhor* Tertuliano Coelho, the current president of the council.

Fond of cleanliness and decency, and happily in near total agreement, the people of Rio anxiously await the end of the odor of armpits blocked only by simple tattered shirts imposed on them by this savage and vile habit. Repugnant with stink to the citizens next to them, coupled to the shame of a bunch of barefoot bumpkins, [such elements walk] through the most central and cleanest streets of the metropolis. They use the hypothetical pretext of poverty [for their actions, when everyone knows] a pair of pants costs five *réis* and there are work shoes at all prices.

These [sanitation] demands--it is well that one notes--were passed and respectfully observed, and even voluntarily adhered to according to modern customs, in all the honored cities of the old world and in almost all of the Americas.

In Europe, no one, absolutely no one, has the insolent shamelessness to walk through the streets of Paris, Berlin, Rome, or Lisbon, etc., shoeless and unashamedly in shirt sleeves.

Fon-Fon sends its best wishes to *Senhor* Tertuliano Coelho for the continued progress of his necessary proposal. And congratulations to the citizens of Rio for this additional improvement.[31]

The fine, or the price, of five *réis* was then equal to about forty hours labor for the typical worker. This meant of course that this new apparel could hardly have been within the budgets of those fortunate enough to be average employees. Few workers could buy such items when they did not even have the money to pay the higher rents that materialized as the capital was remodeled.[32] If what was

and Jeffrey Needell, *A Tropical Belle Epoque: Elite Culture and Society in Turn-of-the Century Rio de Janeiro*, Cambridge: Cambridge University Press, 1987, pp. 166-71.

[31] *Fon-Fon* (Rio de Janeiro), July 24, 1909, p. 7.

[32] Civita, Victor (ed.), *Nosso século, 1900-1910: A Era dos Bacharéis*, São Paulo: Abril Cultural, 1985, part i, vol. i, p. 41. Much of the early interest in the renovation proposals came from foreign transportation companies who stood to make enormous profits by transporting relocated residents from their new dwellings in the suburbs to work in the city center. Streetcars were thus

happening was still unclear, at about this point the press and the police started going after all kinds of "indigestible types" in the center of the city. This effort lasted throughout the *Belle Époque* and had as its apparent objective the removal of panhandlers, the underprivileged, lower-class inebriates, and trollops.[33]

The efforts on the part of Rodrigues Alves and succeeding administrations produced a metropolitan complex with its main sections more attuned to the wishes of the consorts of international wealth. At the same time, those persons jailed or in jail in 1907 in the simultaneous purge of the main urban areas formed a suggestive sundry of lower-class citizens. If one looks at both sexes in this group, and not just the male prisoners, particularly noticeable were black women accused of being unemployed, tramps, or prostitutes.

These females were lumped together and arrested on charges of *vadiagem* (vagrancy)[34] for failing to have a legal way of earning their living. One description points out that during the *Belle Époque*, suspect women came to be hounded arbitrarily, and at times even brutally, by the police and by all kinds of persons from sanctimonious society. Curiously, or perhaps by design, it was not uncommon for even guiltless women to be dragged in during this ruckus and charged with being prostitutes under the blanket *vadiagem* offense. This was especially the case after October of 1899 when the right to a courtroom appearance was taken away from those accused of *vadiagem*. From that point on, the police became the judge and the jury, and any woman out unescorted in the evenings became the victim. While this did not affect well-bred ladies, poorer women routinely walked about alone at night owing to their economic situations.[35]

a favorite target during the just ended riot. Foreign investors, often British, began to gobble up available real estate in the downtown area as the renewal got going. The ensuing speculation eased out small-time Brazilian entrepreneurs and former inhabitants. Meade, "Civilizing Rio de Janeiro," pp. 307, 313-14.

[33]Sevcenko, pp. 33-34.

[34]Those arrested were almost always charged with simple *vadiagem*. In a small number of cases, women were booked on *vadiagem e embriaguez* (vagrancy and drunkenness), *vadiagem e capoeiragem* (vagrancy and practicing *capoeira*), and *vadiagem reincidentes* (prior vagrancies). Women accused of one of these final transgressions, being sent on to serve prison sentences (see Appendix, Table 4), were clustered even further into *vadiagem e capoeiragem*. Since the Brazilian penal code had no statute specifically aimed at prostitution, seemingly in deference to more active double standards than those which exist today, hookers too were charged with *vadiagem*.

[35]*Cf.*: *Diario Illustrado* (Rio de Janeiro), October 19, 1910, p. 2 [*sic*, p. 7]; Rachel Soihet,

The Rio de Janeiro, D.F., police evidently began to ask selected individuals to move to other less distinguished byways beginning in 1896. They started making large scale arrests for *vadiagem* in 1903. If these last two reports are accurate, perhaps the reality of just which populations of women were being asked to move on and which were being apprehended can be deduced.[36]

"João do Rio" was a witness to much of this. Evidently writing about the year 1907, he reported that fifty-eight females had been removed from the capital's streets and taken to the Casa de Detenção. They were sequestered there in three rooms, one of which was the lockup's hospital. A notable shortage of space was evident, and lesbianism was prolific in the degrading cells that had been erected in each of the chambers. Most of the women were black or of mixed race from the needy classes. One of the urbane commentators of his day, João do Rio, was known for his vivid, if not racist, language. Some of these jailed females, he wrote,

> ...have the lively expressions of young *mulatas* with the libidinous eyes of monkeys. Others have deadened glances in puffy faces. Some possess the skeletal profiles of long-ago beautiful streetwalkers and smiles roughly slashed by razors on mouths without teeth. There are faces white with trembling lips. And in the middle of this characterization of abyss, the greasy heads of black women with flat noses and the filthy, matted

---

Condição feminina e formas de violência: mulheres pobres e ordem urbana: 1890-1920, Rio de Janeiro: Forense Universitária, 1989, pp. 201-16; Sidney Chalhoub, *et al.*, "Trabalho escravo e trabalho livre na cidade do Rio: vivência de libertos, 'galegos' e mulheres pobres," *RBH*, vol. lv, nos. 8-9, September 1984-April 1985, pp. 111-12; and Oscar de Macedo Soares, *Codigo penal da Republica dos Estados Unidos do Brasil: commentado e annotado segundo a legislação vigente até 1901*, Rio de Janeiro: Empreza Democratica, 1902, p. 233, law 628, art. 6. See also Marcos Luiz Bretas, "Policiar a cidade republicana," *OAB/RJ*, no. 22, July 1985, pp. 58-59; and ___, "A guerra das ruas: povo e polícia na cidade do Rio de Janeiro," unpublished Master's thesis, Departamento de Ciencias Politicas, Instituto Universitário de Pesquisas, 1988, pp. 80, 136-37.

[36]*Cf.*: Moraes [Filho], Evaristo de, *Ensaios de pathologia social: vagabundagem, alcoolismo, prostituição, lenocino*, Rio de Janeiro: Leite Ribeiro, 1921, p. 272; and Sidney Chalhoub, *Trabalho, lar e botequim: o cotidiano dos trabalhadores no Rio de Janeiro da Belle Époque*, São Paulo: Brasiliense, 1986, p. 240n. See also *infra*, 46n-47n. While another writer does not say if he is commenting about men or women or both, he nevertheless tells us that in respect to mistaken arrests

a visit to the Detenção [see *infra*, nn 36-37] and a rapid analysis of the cases of vagrancy convinces one of the worthlessness of the police in making judgements of any crime or infraction. We must stop the law of the *police being judge and jury*. It is time to limit the action of *police prosecutions*, which have become as inhuman as they are incompetent. *Correio da Manhã*, July 24, 1905, p. 4.

hair of alcoholics.[37]

It was an especially hard life for these women. João do Rio went on to report that they all had haggard-looking bodies and appearances older than their years. Many were tattooed, often excessively. Tattooing was a common practice among the working classes during this period. It was no surprise that those who catered to the lowest end of the social scale seem to have been tattooed in profusion on their arms, legs, hands, stomachs, shoulders and breasts. Some were even tattooed on their foreheads. The designs were crucifixes, fish, spades, the names of relatives, dead children, and lovers. One imprisoned *índio* named Carmelina was tattooed all over her body. She started with the name of her brother on the backside of her fingers and ended up with tattoos everywhere. Of particular note were her arms. They came to be dedicated to love. There she had a multitude of names, some on top of one another, some by initials only, and some in very large letters.

Older women who once offered passion for a price frequently removed all of their tattoos so that they could enter heaven with clean bodies. When spats developed between working prostitutes and their up-until-then steady paramours, not merely was the ex-client's name removed; it was removed from wherever it was and then reinscribed on the harlot's heels. The idea was that from that moment the out of favor name(s) would forever "...drag along in the dirt, flattened by the weight of the woman."[38]

Before being incarcerated, many females who actually walked the streets practiced their trade out of *zungas* (houses divided into small, cheaply rented rooms) or *casebres* (shacks). Such abodes were mainly located in the now beat-up district just west of the downtown area, near the navy arsenal, on the byways of Praça 15, and in the not too far away part of town known as Lapa. Men with a little more money to spend could satisfy their needs at any number of places on the most francofied street in the capital, the Rua do Ouvidor.

At the turn of the century, the Rua do Ouvidor had several risqué establishments. One of the more celebrated was the *Hôtel* Ravot where meals and lodging were supposedly available. Everybody knew, however, what really went

---

[37]Rio, João do [Paulo Barreto], *A alma encantadora das ruas*, Rio de Janeiro: Simões, 1952, p. 218.

[38]*Ibid.*, pp. 44-45, 47, 49, 220-21.

on there. It was a two-story building that "...occupied half a block, with the girls in wrappers seated in the windows or leaning on the sills beckoning the passers-by."[39] Not only in places like the Ravot, but in many other parts of the Brazilian capital, women for hire peered from their windows, bantered with their customers, and in the process, infuriated straight-laced citizens. Indeed, "one gets the impression that at the end of the nineteenth century there were more brothels than ordinary shops in Rio de Janeiro."[40]

Not far away from the *Hôtel* Ravot was a competitor, one that played havoc with the city's morals, the Alcazar. Named after its Parisian namesake, the Alcazar Lyrique Française in Rio was an at times anything-goes *théâtre* that offered the sexual charms of supposed French vamps to anyone who could pay the price. Although the wealthy frequented these enterprises, they usually traveled by coach (and more and more often by motorcar) to sumptuous bordellos cleverly called *pensions d'artistes*, or "artist's hotels." These luxurious cathouses were generally clustered in discrete sections of South Zone suburbs such as Catete, Botafogo, and Jardim Botânico.

Many of the women who attended to middle and upper-class sexual desires were referred to as *modistes* (saleswomen of refined garments), actresses or even *cocottes* ("Parisian" whores). While they may have been whiter skinned and foreign, these prostitutes were not always as French as they claimed to be. Some were from Eastern Europe, and more than one, French or otherwise, arrived in Brazil via white slavers. A fair number of this last group, and the accompanying pimps, appear to have been Jews.[41]

Of course, the total number of women arrested for vagrancy never reflected the actual occurrence of this type of crime. Furthermore, the number of females who actually wound up being sentenced to prison always constituted an even smaller figure. This is as true for many countries through time just as it was for

[39]Freyre, *Order and Progress*, p. 59.
[40]*Ibid.*, pp. 59-60.
[41]*Cf.*: Vainfas, Magali Engel, "Meretrizes e doutores: o saber médico e a prostituição na cidade do Rio de Janeiro, 1845 a 1890," unpublished Master's thesis, Instituto de Ciências Humanas e Filosofia, Universidade Federal Fluminense, 1985, p. 120; João do Rio, p. 219; Civita, *Nosso século, 1900-1910*, part i, vol. i, p. 44; Freyre, *Order and Progress*, pp. 57-61; Needell, *A Tropical Belle Epoque*, pp. 165-66, 171-74, 289n; and Mauricio Lamberg, *O Brasil*, Luiz de Castro (trans.), Rio de Janeiro: Lombaerts, 1896, p. 62.

Brazil in 1907.[42] Still, when examining the official published data for the country as a whole for 1907, and for Rio de Janeiro, D.F., through 1912 (see Appendix, Table 4), one is left to ponder the reasons behind a policy that arrested a disproportionate number of women who were non-white. Why was it that they were apprehended at all? Why were they picked up on real or mythical charges, sentenced to confinement more often, and kept there longer than white women indicted for the same crime during the same period? Nearly all the women involved in this procession in 1907, moreover, came from the very heart of the *carioca* capital.[43]

Unquestionably, Rio's black and brown women had a more difficult time finding legitimate employment than did their white sisters.[44] Those who were simple vagrants or simply unemployed had learned what to expect from the police for decades. With the start of the *Belle Époque*, however, selected prostitutes also came to feel this rancor much more frequently. Since only a small number of youthful and beautiful black women could get jobs in the better and safer *pensions d'artistes*, many black females who were in the trade were probably lower-class streetwalkers, part-timers, or even ex-prostitutes who were getting along in years.[45]

When those who had gone on to prison were finally released, their ordeals continued another way. Beginning in 1907, all first-time *vadiagem* offenders were given a *salvo conducto* (safe conduct voucher) upon being set free. This

---

[42]One stage back in these events, the race of those women in Rio de Janeiro D.F., who were simply arrested, in comparison to those entering prisons, as well as those leaving such institutions, on charges of *vadiagem* in 1907, can be examined in Table 4 of the Appendix.

[43]The female residents of Rio de Janeiro D.F., comprised 88.8% of those women entering prison, 84% of those leaving, and 96.5% of those still in prison at the end of 1907 on charges of *vadiagem*. See Appendix, Table 4. No racial breakdown was available.

[44]Fernandes, pp. 100-102. Writing basically about São Paulo, the situation presented by Fernandes is plausible to some degree in Rio de Janeiro, one state away.

[45]*Cf.*: Rio, João do, p. 175; *Jornal do Brasil*, June 15, 1994, sec. 1, p. 14; and June Hahner, "Women and Work in Brazil, 1850-1920: a Preliminary Investigation," *Essays Concerning the Socio-economic History of Brazil and Portuguese India*, Dauril Alden and Warren Dean (eds.), Gainesville: University Presses of Florida, 1977, p. 102. Freyre (*Order and Progress*, p. 59n) brings to our attention the following comments in a footnote drawn from Lamberg:

Speaking of the prostitution of mulattos in Rio de Janeiro, Lamberg observed that 'there are mulatto girls of eleven or twelve who already are mothers.' He noted, however, that these native prostitutes always 'preserved a certain decency--almost a certain dignity-- in their calling.' It was 'only in the large cities, under the bad example given by European courtesans, that these native customs are spoiled.'

document stipulated that former inmates were to find an approved vocation within a specified number of days. They could not be rearrested on a new charge of *vadiagem* during this period.[46] For those women who failed to secure suitable positions as the expiration date of their *salvo conductos* grew near, the incentive to leave town became an increasingly attractive option.

One could thus conclude that Rodrigues Alves, his successors and all their auxiliaries were rooting out unsuitable females from their remodeled city center to improve Rio's international reputation in the eyes of polite society. Part of this operation produced a period in which the nation's leaders went through the motions of chasing the world's oldest profession from the capital's streets. This was one of the convenient excuses used to try to remove non-white women from downtown areas. So efficient were the elites in this quest that they essentially ignored the rest of the country. So hypocritical were they in carrying out their task that they comfortably forgot about the brothels of the rich--brothels that they frequented.

In the cases of all of these usually poorer and often non-white *cariocas*, both male and female, there is a body of evidence that suggests a disturbing scenario. If only during the heyday of the *Belle Époque*, the unwanted were forced to get out of the central parts of the Federal District, or to be seen as little as possible, or to be prepared to suffer under the law.[47] By the time the new harbor and all the construction was finished, and this point had been made,

---

[46]Brazil, *Collecção das leis da Republica dos Estados Unidos do Brazil de 1907*, Rio de Janeiro: Nacional, 1908, vol. i, p. 574, decree 6440, chap. iii, art. 137, secs. 1-2. At the discretion of the police one alternative to a period of time behind bars for women accused of being prostitutes was for them, within eight days after being warned, to "...transfer their residences to other areas...." Aurelino Leal, *Policia e poder policia*, Rio de Janeiro: Nacional, 1918, p. 129. See also *supra*, 34n.

[47]While they were certainly there in supportive roles, behind the scenes, additional testimony for his point is suggested by the small number of blacks and obvious mixed-race *cariocas* in many of the photographs of the downtown area during this era. See as well the comments in Meade, Living Worse and Costing More," pp. 252, 255. Also suggestive is the fact that the vast majority of arrests for *vadiagem* (see Appendix, Table 4) took place in police districts in or near the main parts of the capital. *Cf.*: Brazil, Policia do Districto Federal, Gabinete de Identificação e de Estatistica, *Estatistica de 1909*, Rio de Janeiro: Nacional, 1910, pp. 284-89; ___, *Estatistica policial e criminal de 1910*, Rio de Janeiro: Nacional, 1915, p. 53; ___, *Estatistica policial e criminal de 1911*, Rio de Janeiro: Nacional, 1917, p. 53; and ___, *Estatistica policial e criminal de 1912*, Rio de Janeiro: Nacional, 1918, p. 53. See also *infra*, 48n.

ladies no longer felt ill at ease about walking on Rua do Ouvidor and other downtown streets, which were now cleared of prostitutes. Transatlantic steamers began to anchor at the modern harbor. A fondness for sports, especially water sports, and for open-air living was growing among the young [white] people. 'Rio is becoming civilized,' the papers said.[48]

---

[48]Bello, *A History of Modern Brazil*, p. 184. In respect to no less than water sports and Brazilians of African descent, until sometime beyond the 1930s, blacks did not fully use the public beaches in Rio de Janeiro. There was no formal prohibition, only the fear of causing a scandal and whatever else this might bring. CPDOC, oral history, "Nélson de Melo," 1978-1979, p. 33. Meade ("Civilizing Rio de Janeiro," p. 303) mentions that the use of the term "civilized," became a buzz word throughout the *Belle Époque* to identify with the excellence and hoped for transfer of European culture.

Chapter V

"O CRAVO VERMELHO"

A host of ignominious presidents took the reins of power for a time in Brazil, markedly more than the few that have been mentioned since the overthrow of the Braganças. During the Old Republic (1889-1930), these heads of state were chosen by a few rich men of European extraction--men not unlike the electors. The anointed candidates were voted on by a minuscule segment of the population made up of adult, literate, fair-skinned males in thoroughly corrupted elections. Women, enlisted men in the armed forces, persons with criminal records, those unable to speak Portuguese, and those incapable of reading and writing were all excluded from this democratic selection process.

To say that the number of legal electors was small is really to overstate the case. In 1894 when Prudente de Morais was elected president, just 2.2% of the population was allowed to vote. During the 1906 campaign of Afonso Pena, this figure was reduced to 1.4 per cent. A second go-round by Rodrigues Alves in 1918 witnessed a slight rise to 1.5%, which was the same number of persons who took part in the 1919 contest won by Epitácio Pessoa. As late as the last presidential election of the Old Republic, that which pitted Júlio Prestes de Albuquerque against Getúlio Vargas in 1930, the total electorate had risen to a grand total of 5.7% of the population.[1] The nominal winners, as one might have

---

[1]Women were prohibited from voting until 1933. But since Vargas was chief of the Provisional Government until 1937, and then dictator until 1945, their first opportunity to vote on a national scale for president was during the last month of 1945. In respect to military recruits, even today, all males reaching the age of eighteen are required to register with the military authorities. They are then expected to volunteer for the armed forces (getting a civilian job later on often depends on it). While there are exemptions granted, such as for students and the mentally incompetent, each "enlisted" man then serves from nine months to two years, depending on which branch of the service he chooses. During this period, he is not allowed to vote. As for non-whites and poor people, a literacy qualification was the most commonly used method to disenfranchise them for many years. In his maneuverings before the election of 1945, Vargas attempted to circumnavigate the literacy prerequisite in the cities for his own benefit. This eligibility requirement, however, remained a feature of the election law, and was only officially done away with on July 1, 1985. Cf.: Jordan Young, *The Brazilian Revolution of 1930 and the Aftermath*, New Brunswick: Rutgers University Press, 1967, p. 122n; *Encyclopédia Mirador International*,

predicted, were often disdainful of, dishonest to, and detached from the great bulk of their countrymen.

First there were the original military dictators, Manuel Deodoro da Fonseca and "Iron Marshal" Floriano Vieira Peixoto. Then there was the initial *paulista* to lead the nation in the name of king coffee, not to mention Canudos, Prudente José de Morais Barros. He in turn was followed by fellow *paulista* Manuel Ferraz de Campos Salles, a man perhaps best remembered for permitting the *coronéis* and unemployment to run wild. When Campos Salles left office he was so unpopular that the train carrying him back to São Paulo was stoned. The former president wisely went into hiding on a *fazenda*, only reappearing when public attention had shifted to the administration of his successor.[2]

That successor was the one and only builder of ports and thoroughfares, Rodrigues "Big Daddy" Alves. Next were the authoritarian regimes of Afonso Augusto Moreira Pena, who was from Minas Gerais, and the caretaker president, Nilo Procópio Peçanha. Following these two men there was "The Little Marshal," Hermes da Fonseca. Venceslau Brás, another *mineiro* (a man from Minas Gerais), then entered Catete not only to leave the tragedy of the Contestado but the ensuing and rather fitting observation:

...The people know the government through the chief of police, the authority that has the most contact with the masses, since he struggles against them the most, and who more than anyone else is a reflection of power and force.[3]

As we have seen, such displays of force by lawmen were nothing new or novel to the times of Venceslau Brás. The police had always acted on the whims of the *grã-fino* to keep the non-white subservient. More recently poor whites had been added. And by 1900, the guardians of law and order were beginning to keep their eyes peeled for suspicious looking foreign laborers and provocateurs. All of

pp. 3695-96; Brazil, *Coleção das leis de 1985: atos do poder legislativo e atos legislativos do poder executivo, leis de julho a setembro*, Brasília: Nacional, 1985, vol. v, p. 10, decree 7332, art. 18; ___, *Constituição [da] República Federativa do Brasil 1988*, Brasília: Centro Gráfico do Senado Federal, 1988, p. 18, art. 18, no. ii, c, par. 2; United States, Central Intelligence Agency, document, "Brazil," November 30, 1948, p. 7, SR-17; and John French, "Industrial Workers and the Birth of the Populist Republic in Brazil, 1945-1946," *LAP*, vol. xvi, no. 4, Fall 1989, p. 7.
[2]*Jornal do Brasil*, June 25, 1989, sec. 1, p. 12.
[3]Fontenelle, Oscar Penna, *Problemas policiaes*, Rio de Janeiro: Jornal do Commercio, 1927, p. 115.

this spawned a subtle expansion of former policies. It was also an aftermath of the unwillingness by mainly Italian, Portuguese, and Spanish immigrants to accept low pay, long hours, unsafe-working conditions, and savage treatment at the hands of employers.

Europeans were still being imported into Brazil in large numbers for two reasons: to bleach the country's gene pool, and to keep labor's competition for jobs at a fever pitch (thereby keeping the salaries paid out for them at a starvation level). In time, a fair number of these new workers refused to go along with the roles awaiting them. After living under autocratic dictates in their former countries, their new one failed to provide anything better for foreign wage-earners.

True, some arrived in the country with pre-established political agendas. More still became anarchists, conservative-laborites, or socialists especially in the largest urban areas. This radicalization process in turn was partly a reflection of the larger drama of worker unrest in Europe and North America. Both at home and abroad the results burst forth in a number of grueling walkouts all through these years. In the state of São Paulo, Brazil's blooming industrial giant, the number of strikes (displayed below by decades) soared with the turn of the century. This was especially evident for the period 1900 to 1919:

	1888-1899	1900-1909	1910-1919	1920-1929
City of São Paulo	12	61	54	41
State of São Paulo	23	90	96	37

Working conditions in São Paulo's manufacturing sphere, coupled with the physical violence used by owners to keep their employees obedient, were more akin to those found in a prison than to those of production. Nowhere was this more evident than in the textile field, which utilized large numbers of women and children. Textiles led all other professions in strikes by more than two to one in both the city and state of São Paulo during the above years. So terrible was the situation in this vocation that it not only touched off the massive general strike of 1917, but had any number of other manifestations. In one example, it was observed in 1919 that among the objectives of the striking employees at a single textile mill was the demand that overseers refrain from beating the children who also made up a part of the work force.[4]

---

[4]*Cf.*: Simão, Azis, *Sindicato e estado: suas relações na formação do proletariado de São Paulo,*

As for the rest of the country, the 1919 observations by Colonel R.H. Jordan, the American military attaché in Rio, are illustrative of what was already going on throughout this particular period of labor unrest:

Strikes in Pernambuco during the past month were accompanied by extreme violence, and on Sunday, September 7th, an outbreak occurred at Porto Alegre in Rio Grande do Sul in the extreme southern part of the Republic. During the past two days anarchistic demonstrations in Rio de Janeiro have assumed serious proportions. However, nothing has appeared to support the charge by 'A Tribuna'... that the Army and Navy are involved in the movement.

The happenings at Pernambuco were perhaps as much political as economic in their origin, a contested election being responsible for much of the disorder. It has been charged that the authorities to some extent ignored and even encouraged disorder to more easily sway the voting to suit the purposes of the Governor of Pernambuco and his circle of politicians in control. A general strike among laborers took place and some damage was done to the property of the Light and Power Company in Pernambuco. Reports from that district indicate that normal order was soon restored.

Sunday's outbreak at Porto Alegre was a strike among laborers. At the meetings held, the tone of the speeches became so frankly and openly anarchistic that the police interfered. The speakers assured the strikers that social justice is impossible so long as private property exists and that private property will exist so long as there is a State to protect it. Therefore the destruction of the State must be effected to secure the abolishment of private property. The police informed the leaders that such doctrines could not be permitted but the warning was ignored. Therefore the police started to disperse the meeting and the anarchists began firing. The police returned the fire and one man was killed and about thirty wounded. A large number of arrests were made, it developing, as had been expected, that the moving spirits are foreigners.

Following the seizure of the [newspapers] 'Spartacus' in Rio and the 'Plebe' in São Paulo, open meetings of protest were held by various labor organizations here in the capital. On Wednesday, September 10th, a parade was held which wound up at the headquarters of the "Union of Construction Labor" in Praça [da] Republica. Here speeches of a very inflammatory nature were delivered and the police interfered. They were met with a shower of bricks and stones and a few shots were fired. Thirty

São Paulo: Dominus, 1966, pp. 131, 133-34, 136-37, 139, 143, 145-46, 148-49, 151; Hall and Pinheiro, pp. 8, 11; ADOPS, newspaper article, "*Unidade Proletária*," December 1975, supplement, p. 2, comunismo/pasta 144; and *O Combate* (São Paulo), July 5, 1919, p. 1.

of the leaders of the mob were arrested, of whom only six were Brazilians, the others being Portuguese, Italians and Spaniards.[5]

As a countermeasure, in 1907 the nation's first political police were formed specifically to keep an eye on potential trouble by the working *pavão*. Blacklists had been kept up to this time by employers themselves. All job-seekers, in theory, had been checked against these rosters. But now, the *Corpo de Investigação e Segurança Pública* (or Public Investigation and Security Corps) were organized out of the *Polícia Civil* to take over that chore. Thus, commencing in 1907, the role of the police was formally expanded into the political process to harass workers, unionizers, strikers, and anyone who just happened to be standing around. Their regular preemptive dragnets paralleled similar efforts by other police units to now and again curb in the urban poor.

Likewise, the statutes governing deportation were successively changed beginning in 1907 to allow the authorities to expel foreign agitators. In practice this meant anyone even suspected of some infraction. Violations included such things as saying or writing something against the government, or its representatives, or becoming involved in the workers' movement in the slightest way. Keeping tabs on the foreign-born accordingly became one of the jobs of the political police. They were armed with laws that allowed all foreign mail (incoming and outgoing) to be opened and read by government agents. Police spies and informants at one's place of work, and in one's neighborhood, added the finishing touches. Not surprisingly, in the first year of the new ordinance the number of aliens who were shipped back to Europe jumped to 132.

The only foreigners left out of this enactment were those who had lived continuously in Brazil for two years, and 1) were married to a Brazilian, or 2) widowed and responsible for the care of a Brazilian child. In 1913, even these two exceptions were closed for several decades. The legal niceties of internal exile for native Brazilians, and deportation to other shores for aliens, were, of course, never followed to the letter of the law either before or after 1913.[6]

---

[5]USNA, letter, "Jordan to director of Military Intelligence," September 12, 1919, no. 265, pp. 1-3, MID 2052-84. See also *supra*, chap. ii, nn. 12-20, 12n-14n.

[6]*Cf.*: Arquivo Público do Estado do Rio de Janeiro, *Os arquivos das policias políticas: reflexos de nossa história contemporânea*, Rio de Janeiro: FAPERJ, 1994, p. 12; *A Revolução de 30*, directed by Silvio Beck, 1980; Pinheiro, *Estratégias da ilusão*, pp. 106, 114-15; John W.F.

Succeeding Brás, Epitácio da Silva Pessoa was selected president and varied only slightly from what had become *de rigueur*. There were actually but two noteworthy programs on his agenda. As a Northeasterner himself, he earmarked a considerable amount of funding to combat droughts in that part of the country. Money was also made available to provide the urban infrastructure for future elite suburbs (mainly Lagoa, Ipanema, and Leblon) in Rio's South Zone. The projects in the Northeast had to be canceled due to a slump in international coffee prices in the early 1920s. As for the not so noteworthy, Pessoa was a man whose racial beliefs were so strong that as president he would not let blacks or mixed-race Brazilians participate on the national soccer team. Following his three-year term, leftists claimed that he'd made the country a dungeon and common liberties a myth. It was their view that during his administration the nation's economic depression was remedied piecemeal through loans while bankrupt Brazilians were hidden under the spurious splendor of a needless World's Fair. There were those who protested. But they were silenced, whipped in jail, deported, or murdered.[7]

In respect to being exiled, the case of Everardo Dias is illustrative. Dias had arrived in Brazil with his parents at the age of two. As an adult, he was accused of having maligned the São Paulo state government. Dias was a political militant, and at one time editor of *O Livre Pensador* as well as chief proofreader for *O Estado de São Paulo*. He was arrested, stripped of his clothing in cold weather, starved, given twenty-five lashes with a *chibata*, and deported on the steamer *Benevente* to Spain. The only trouble was the Spanish wouldn't take him. A little over two months later, while still aboard the *Benevente* in the Spanish harbor of Vigo, he learned that São Paulo had reversed itself and he could come home. The fact that Dias was a prominent individual in *paulistano* society, and had influential friends,

Dulles, *Anarchists and Communists in Brazil, 1900-1935*, Austin: University of Texas Press, 1973, p. 22, 22n; and Brazil, *Collecção das leis da Republica dos Estados Unidos do Brazil de 1907*, vol. i, p. 527, decree 6440, art. 9, sec. 3, no. 9; p. 24, decree 1641, arts. 1, 3, secs. a-b; ___, *Collecção das leis da Republica dos Estados Unidos do Brazil de 1913*, Rio de Janeiro: Nacional, 1916, vol. i, p. 168, decree 2741. See also *supra*, chap. ii, nn. 21-23, 22n-23n, chap. iv, nn. 25-26, and *infra*, nn. 7-10, 84-88, 47n, 93n.
[7]*Cf.*: *Jornal do Brasil*, May 8, 1988, sec. B/especial, p. 8; Winston Fritsch, "Crise econômica," comments delivered to the seminar "Cenários de 1922," Fundação Getúlio Vargas/CPDOC, Rio de Janeiro, November 19, 1992; and ADOPS, newspaper article "*Juventude*," June 15, 1935, p. 1, comunismo/pasta 4B.

explains in part why the authorities changed their minds. He could count himself among the lucky.[8]

With the arrival of the *mineiro* Artur Bernardes, not only was Luís Carlos Prestes to become famous, but unrest would reach such a level that the new head of state was forced to rule under a state of siege. He would later say that as president of the Republic, he was only a leader of the police. Finally there was the last *paulista*: the authoritarian and pompous Washington Luís Pereira de Souza. Although he liked to be referred to as "The Builder of Roads," he was snickered at in the shadows as "Little Trepov." Washington Luís would face the collapse of a coffee-based economy, the world depression, and the cries for reform with a demeanor that was nevertheless reflective of a remark falsely attributed to him. It was said that during his administration labor questions would only be concerns for the special attention of the police.

The epithet Little Trepov was dreamed up by *A Voz do Trabalhador*, an anarchist-leaning newspaper in Rio de Janeiro. They tacked it on Washington Luís for being a cut-down version of Fyodor Fyodorovich Trepov, one of Tsarist Russia's most vicious St. Petersburg police chiefs. The Brazilian lower classes well-remembered that Washington Luís was the *paulista* secretary of justice and public security between 1906 and 1912. Thereby in charge of law enforcement, he was responsible for an intensive campaign of arrests against vagrants, hooligans, anarchists, laborers, and the unemployed. Many of these lawbreakers were sent to workhouses in the interior of the state. Others were forced to rebuild the São Paulo-Santos Road. A few years later when Little Trepov was the mayor of São Paulo, the city fathers decided to deal with striking laborers harshly.[9] The English consul-general in São Paulo, Arthur Abbott, subsequently observed in horror that protesters in Braz, then a working-class sector just east of the central area, "...were shot down by machine guns and rifle fire and given no quarter whatever.[10]

[8]Dias, Everardo, *Memorias de um exilado: episodios de uma deportação*, São Paulo: n.p., 1920, pp. 97-102.
[9]*Cf.*: ADOPS, newspaper article, *"Tribuna da Imprensa,"* May 25, 1971, p. 4, comunismo/pasta 103; Evaristo de Moraes Filho, *Temas atuais de trabalho e previdência*, São Paulo: LTr, 1976, pp. 102-13; *A Voz do Trabalhador* (Rio de Janeiro), June 8, 1915, p. 3; Beloch and Abreu, p. 1952, Pereira Reis Júnior, *Os presidentes do Brasil*, Rio de Janeiro: Divulbrás, 1975, p. 137; Cruz, pp. 117, 124-25, 130; and Civita, *Nosso século, 1910-1930*, part ii, vol. iv, p. 163. See also *supra*, chap. iv, nn. 5-6.
[10]United Kingdom, Public Records Office, letter, "[Arthur] Abbott to Seeds," February 4, 1935,

These issues, together with the special attention delegated toward their suppression, spilled over into many parts of Latin America as a result of a series of disruptive changes brought on by World War I. As has been commented, the European conflict provoked a short supply of overseas markets and credit used by South America's financier elites. In this void wealthier Brazilians were not long in attempting to create some semblance of the same opportunities at home. Urban labor paid the tab through wartime inflation and fueled the rise of the middle class which was able to reap some of the benefits. Along the way large numbers of foreigners and rural Brazilians were drawn into the cities to stoke the fires of industrialization. Looking at what happened another way, up until the end of the empire in 1889, there had been only 626 entrepreneurial establishments founded in Brazil. During the twenty-five year period from 1889 to 1914, there were 6,946 commercial ventures started. For just the five years of 1915 to 1919, 5,940 enterprises opened their doors for business.[11]

The election of Epitácio Pessoa as the nation's president in 1919 represented one of the final attempts by the older generation to maintain things as they were. Their goal was not merely to deter the political aspirations of the new bourgeoisie, but defuse the charges of that perpetual thorn-in-the-side, Rui Barbosa. This time Barbosa had the cheek to state in public what many understood to be taking place anyway: the governors of Minas Gerais and São Paulo had turned Brazil's most important job into a position to be rotated between themselves. In essence, these two state administrators were the most influential of the influential. Their states had become the most productive, the most wealthy, and hence the most powerful regions in the republic.

It was a republic whose main body of laws was contained in the *Constitution of 1891* that Barbosa himself had a large hand in writing. The finished document

no. 5, p. 3, FO 371/18655. As Abbott made this observation in 1935, some years after the fact, his listing of 1918 as the year of these shootings is probably incorrect. Nineteen seventeen or 1919 are more plausible. In this regard *cf.*: Beloch and Abreu, *loc. cit.*; and Hall and Pinheiro, pp. 11-12.
[11]*Cf.*: Lieuwen, Edwin, *Arms and Politics in Latin America*, New York: Frederick Praeger, 1960, pp. 44-45; and (Anonymous), "Evolução da conjuntura no Brasil de 1916 a 1929," *Conjuntura* Econômica, no. 11, November 1948, p. 25. See Hahner (*Poverty and Politics*, pp. 276-79), for a discussion of the poorer city dwellers' economic situation during the World War I era.

emulated much of the constitution of the United States. Not only did the country start calling itself "The United States of Brazil," but parts of Rui's new charter were lifted from its North American counterpart, almost word-for-word in some places. The drawbacks and omissions, however, were numerous, so much so that they permitted the policy of placating those few individuals at the top to continue. One of the main stumbling blocks was the ample autonomy given over to each state leader under the Politics of Governors. That these men exercised near unlimited prerogatives within their own orbits promoted a sizable obstacle to national unity. Most harmful of all was the fact that each states' massive police force was controlled by its respective governor. Moreover, in places like Rio Grande do Sul, São Paulo, and Minas Gerais, this alternative force was often better trained and better equipped than the army units stationed there. Whichever militarized police a state had, *Força Pública* or *Polícia Militar* (*Brigada Militar* in Rio Grande do Sul), it was a power to be reckoned with. This was one of the most potentially useful cards in the hands of the elites and the governors they elected. While complete data has yet to be published, official statistics on the total size of the army *vis-à-vis* the aggregate of military police in Brazil for 1917 through 1930 was as follows:[12]

Year	Army	(militarized police)
1917	37,228	28,744
1918	52,486	n.a.
1919	42,994	n.a.
1920	42,920-43,118	30,564
1921	41,121	n.a.
1922	59,066	n.a.
1923	47,455	n.a.
1924	44,086	35,263-35,342

[12]*Cf.*: Loewenstein, Karl, *Brazil under Vargas*, New York: Macmillan, 1944, pp. 11, 319: Brazil, Ministerio da Agricultura, Industria e Commercio, *Relatorio*, Rio de Janeiro: Directoria Geral de Estatistica, 1928, p. 98; ___, *Relatorios, 1928 e 1929*, Rio de Janeiro: Directoria Geral de Estatistica, 1930, pp. 198-99; ___, *Recenseamento do Brazil: população*, Rio de Janeiro: Directoria Geral de Estatistica, 1930, vol. iv, part 5, book i, pp. xii-xiii; and ___, Ministerio da Justiça e Negocios Interiores, *Relatorio*, Rio de Janeiro: Directoria de Estatistica Geral, 1936, p. 78. For years with two figures, the sources consulted give conflicting data. n.a. = Not available. See also *infra*, nn. 25-26, 26n. For more on the Politics of Governors, see *supra*, chap. iv, nn. 17-18.

1925	43,845	43,687-43,688
1926	40,815	41,924-41,959
1927	41,684	37,861-37,862
1928	46,877	37,767-37,777
1929	n.a.	38,025
1930	n.a.	37,688

With their loopholes of privilege sustained through this kind of strength, the king-makers probably felt secure enough to answer the accusations of Barbosa by choosing Pessoa. Epitácio was a man they expected they could manipulate because he came from the insignificant Northeastern state of Paraíba. It was a bad assumption since the new president, in the opinion of aspiring members of the armed forces, refused to bow down to the military. One did not have to go far to find the proof. Shortly after taking office, Pessoa vetoed legislation that would have increased military salaries--always a bad decision in the sweep of Brazilian history. To make matters worse, he then took the unheard-of step of naming civilians to the ministerial posts of the army and navy. This marked the first time that those formally outside of the military arts had had such positions in Brazil. It was only further proof to one faction of army officers, many of them in junior positions, that all was not right with the country's leaders.

During the term of Pessoa's predecessor, assorted concessions had been made to the army to improve professionalism in both equipment and training. The National Guard was reduced to a branch of the reserves. Civilian control over this once formidable body was removed from the portfolio of the minister of justice and internal affairs, and given to the war minister.[13] But after a short period the professionalism program had been allowed to lapse. Then, once Pessoa became president, he contracted with the French to upgrade Brazil's military forces in a highly unpopular move with Brazilian officers. It made them look incapable of the task themselves. Each of these endeavors only added fuel to the fires of military dissension lit years earlier.

Commencing before many of these men were even cadets, there were several smoldering affairs that had succeeded in warming things up indeed. The fiasco at Canudos, Rui Barbosa's *Civilista* campaign, the events leading to the military

---

[13]*Cf.*: Sodré, Nelson Werneck, pp. 198-201; and Keith, "Soldiers as Saviors," pp. 296-99.

Salvações, the Contestado, and World War I all contributed to a new militancy on the part of the youthful officers anxious for change. These men found it particularly frustrating to watch the government's return to a business-as-usual (i.e., boss-rule) routine following the War to End Wars.[14]

There was also the issue of the country's finances. Ever since taking office, President Pessoa had emphasized that the wartime prosperity of a boom economy would eventually cease once the countries of Europe and the rest of the world started to divert their production capabilities to peacetime, capitalistic consumption. While there certainly were other items that Brazil was trying to market abroad, coffee brought in seventy percent of the nation's income during the 1920s. Consequently, as the external price per bag started to drop,[15] coupled to a declining rate of exchange after the war, times began to get rough economically. Faced with this dilemma, the president opted to have the government itself buy up surplus coffee with a view to sell it later when prices at the world's trading centers were hoped to be more favorable.

As his term of office neared its conclusion, Epitácio topped everything off by rolling over for the political chieftains of Minas Gerais and São Paulo. Once again they were allowed to select an official candidate to become the country's next president.. Since it was Minas Gerais' turn, they soon settled on the *mineiro* governor, Artur Bernardes. In the ensuing ersatz election of 1921-1922, however, the forces opposing Bernardes used the opportunity to conduct a particularly effective mud-slinging operation. Portentously, these low blows finally drew the professional military lobby, the so-called Military Club, into the ruckus.

The biggest smudge was provided by the "Bernardes False Letters," in which the nominee was supposed to have insulted the dignity of the army and the Military Club's leader, the diminutive Hermes da Fonseca (among other things the communications had labeled Hermes an "overgrown sergeant"). Despite the fact that all the dispatches were proved to be forgeries some six months later, the intervening squabble was enough to turn an already irritable *cadre* of young officers completely against Bernardes. The letters raised such a stink before the final

---

[14]*Ibid.*, p. 295.

[15]*Cf.*: Young, p. 70; and Bello, *História da República*, p. 287. See also *infra*, n. 124, 124n.

verdict on their authenticity, that many civilians as well could not accept the decision much less forget the implications.[16]

While this was going on Bernardes' was naturally satirized on several levels. He was even mocked by a popular early *samba* in Rio during the 1922 Carnival. The hit "Ai seu mé," by Francisco José Freire Junior and "Caréca" Luís Nunes Sampaio, poked fun at Bernardes in his role as governor of Minas Gerais. Aside from the title, which can be translated as "It Hurts Mr. Baaa... (the sound of a sheep braying)," one line of verse said it all: "The cheese in Minas is rotten." Signing his work with the pseudonym "Scum of the Streets," Freire Junior was nonetheless found out and thrown in jail for his part in the composition.[17]

Mated to everything was the fact that when the election was finally held, it produced the closest returns of the entire republican period, with both camps naturally claiming victory. Then, as each side's validation committee toyed with the results, a gubernatorial election in Pernambuco became the usual fight between the state's two dominant *parentelas*. Involved with one faction were distant relatives of outgoing President Pessoa. As voting day approached, armed violence by both blocs and their *cangaceiros* occurred almost daily. To try to maintain order the president sent another relative, Jaime Pessoa da Silveira, to command the federal forces in the state. When the non-Pessoa candidate was declared the winner, Hermes da Fonseca, in the name of the Military Club, cabled Pessoa da Silveira to stay out of things and was thereafter soon arrested.[18]

The seizure of the ex-president and marshal was the final disgrace and produced an instantaneous call for action from the army. The plotters for change would come to be called *tenentes*, or lieutenants. Their immediate intentions were to promote synchronized rebellions at several military garrisons and thereby prevent Bernardes from taking office. In the process they felt they would redeem the army's tarnished honor. While honor is one thing; personal aspirations are quite another. These men were by no means idealists out to correct an authoritarian system. They merely wanted a louder voice within that system.[19] As such

---

[16]Keith, "Soldiers as Saviors," p. 318.

[17]*Cf.*: [Francisco José] Freire Junior and Caréca [Luís Nunes Sampaio], "Ai seu mé"; and *Enciclopédia da música brasileira: erudita, folclórica e popular*, São Paulo: Art, 1977, pp. 290-91.

[18]Keith, "Soldiers as Saviors," pp. 328-35.

[19]*Cf.*: *ibid.*, p. 336; and *A Revolução de 30*. See also *supra*, chap. iii, nn. 54-56, 55n, and *infra*,

things often go for conspirators, however, their plans became known. When the expected uprising broke out, the government was well-prepared and the rebellion was largely confined to the fort at the southern end of the beach in Rio's Copacabana suburb.

The insurgents in this reinforced structure began firing their main guns, two 7.5 inch cannons, across town at the War Ministry, shortly after 1 A.M. on July 5, 1922. The shells did some damage to the building and several additional targets, including the navy arsenal. Pessoa's countered by moving two battleships and a destroyer into position offshore. As these vessels came on line and opened fire, a seaplane flew over the fort and dropped its bombs. The rebels held out for awhile and even turned their twin guns on the presidential palace.[20] But the struggle was in vain as all the other planned insurrections had been or would be put down, and virtually no further help was forthcoming.

Finally, someone on the government's side cut off the fort's water and lights. Isolated, and with panic starting to spread, the garrison's leaders, Captain Euclydes Hermes da Fonseca, son of the imprisoned marshal, and Lieutenant Antônio de Siqueira Campos gave the men in their command two options. Either duck out of the stronghold after dark and escape into the city, or die a martyr's death by confronting the overwhelming number of government soldiers head on. Loyalist troops, made up *Policia Militar* units plus two companies from the 3rd Infantry Regiment, had already been dispatched to sections of Copacabana further to the northeast. Out of a complement of around three-hundred men in the fort, most of whom had already left, only twenty-three declined the chance to slither into the night. Five civilian employees joined the diehards, making a grand total of twenty-eight volunteers.

In the meantime Euclydes went alone to discuss a general surrender with the government. He was cold-shouldered by the president as long as his men back at the fort were armed. Epitácio's military aide went even further. He telephoned the fort and said that Captain Fonseca had been taken prisoner and would be executed if the twin artillery pieces were fired one more time. This was the deciding factor. In the morning the fortification's flag was hauled down and cut up. Each of the

nn. 26-27, 27n.
[20]Dulles, *Vargas of Brazil*, p. 22.

remaining rebels was given a piece. Some wrote patriotic expressions on their sections of the material,[21] and then those who could pinned the green, yellow, blue, and white swatches on their uniforms. Others put the bits of their national pride in a pocket or attached them in the best way possible. At the conclusion of this solemn ceremony in the early afternoon of July 6, 1922, with their rifles and pistols at the ready, the twenty-eight holdouts left the compound to meet eternity.

As soon as they marched onto Copacabana's beach front Avenida Atlântica two of their numbers deserted. A few of the people watching the little parade, now reduced to twenty-six dissenters, thought it comical. Others like the prostitutes at the *Mère Louise* brothel across the street offered water and tried to get the young men to go back or give themselves up. Three more soldiers and one of the civilians disappeared. A bystander, Otávio Corrêa, who knew some of the resisters, joined in. Soon, the two sides found each other and all hell broke loose after *tenente* Newton Prado cried out, "Friends! For life or for death!"[22] The rebels jumped down behind the sidewalk running parallel with the start of the beach a few feet below and opened fire. They had made it as far as Rua Barroso (now renamed Rua Siqueira Campos), about in the middle of Avenida Atlântica.

It must have seemed like hours but actually it was only minutes before the final shots echoed away over the sands. As the government's forces rushed to the sidewalk's edge, they had to protect the few *tenentes* crouching there still left alive. Infuriated *Policia Militar* soldiers under the command of army Lt. Colonel Tertuliano Potyguara wanted to strangle the rebels with their bare hands. If there had not been someone there to stop them, they would have murdered the shot-up survivors one at a time.[23]

The newspapers incorrectly stated that there were eighteen individuals fighting against the government on the sands of Copacabana because of a photo first published in *O Malho*. Eighteen rebels can be counted in the photograph. All twenty-three of those who actually took part in the battle have thus forever been referred to as "The Eighteen of the Fort." There was a cinematographer present

---

[21]Siqueira Campos wrote, "To my parents, my brothers, the memory of the twenty-eight companions, and to that which I cannot mention." Cristíana de Araujo Corrêa, interview, Rio de Janeiro, June 23, 1994.

[22]*Ibid.*

[23]*Cf.: ibid.*; June 17, 1994; and Keith, "Soldiers as Saviors," pp. 339-40. For more on Potyguara, see *infra,* nn. 31-32, 32n.

who filmed the march. His car was bombed and an assistant may have been killed. Nonetheless, the production got so far as to be given a name by director Salvador Aragão: *Ultimo encontro dos 18 heroícos revolucionários de Copacabana com as tropas legais*, or "The Last Encounter of the Eighteen Heroic Copacabana Revolutionaries with Loyalist Troops." The current whereabouts of Aragão's documentary, however, is unknown.[24]

In examining the administration's reactions to this first outburst by the *tenentes*, it has been stated that in comparison it would be

...interesting to speculate on the description in the historical perspective of Canudos, where anti-government *sertanêjos* were characterized as *malucos* (madmen); one does not have to stretch the parallel to realize any enemies of the Government would be [considered] deranged.... In a political and social system dominated by a small *élite*, fierce defensiveness could quickly turn into repressiveness when the dominant faction of that *élite* sensed itself threatened.[25]

After warnings that he would use the *mineiro Policia Militar* to support his taking office,[26] repression is just what the enemies of Artur Bernardes got when he moved into Catete in November of 1922. Under the state of siege he inherited from Pessoa, President Bernardes continued with the ongoing harassment. Among other things this meant the prosecution of those men in uniform thought to be associated with the July 5th revolt. Regardless of the fact that the new leader had implied there would be a general amnesty, *tenentes* opposing his government whose affiliations were uncovered found themselves facing their worst fears. These young officers,

...their military careers already brought to a sudden end in their youth, were now condemned to years of prison. Most of them remained at large, plotting new rebellions.... It would turn them into Brazil's most legendary figures, hardened by fighting, jailbreaks, and long forced marches.... Using fictitious names and posing as men engaged in a variety of trades, they were likely to travel constantly in their new work, visiting Army units and developing plans with [trusted] friends.[27]

[24]Corrêa, Cristíana de Araújo, interview, Rio de Janeiro, June 23, 1994.
[25]Keith, "Soldiers as Saviors," pp. 340-41.
[26]This point by José Murilo de Carvalho (*Jornal do Brasil*, December 6, 1992, sec. 1, p. 11) is often overlooked in the transition of Pessoa to Bernardes. See also *supra*, nn. 11-13.
[27]Dulles, *Vargas of Brazil*, p. 28. The conspiring by the *tenentes* did not die out with the demise of Artur Bernardes. They and their plotting continued to be major forces in Brazilian politics for

Since the new president also took steps to neutralize or rid himself of his political rivals from the election fight just concluded, it was soon evident that he was determined to modify that old refrain of power to the powerful. More than ever before, the chosen ones this time would be the faithful friends and adherents of the incoming president. Bernardes' total lack of compromise in this regard merely served to aggravate everything. One of the things it stimulated was a heightened number of revolutionary intrigues by members of the left-out elite, the military, and even a few ordinary civilians.[28] The conspirators were clearly out to "...rescue a Republic which had never existed, a 'Republic of their dreams....'"[29]

It was not long before one of these plots became a violent reality in the city of São Paulo, just two years to the day after the start of the incident in Copacabana. The new plan called for revolts at federal military bases in each of the states south of São Paulo.[30] But here too events went badly from the start, owing to stubbornness on the part of the rebel leadership, reducing the main area of combat to the *paulista* capital itself. Those in charge of the operation were determined that July 5, 1924 would be the date for the outbreak of renewed hostilities, regardless of the general unpreparedness of their men and material.

Of course, going into battle on this date was an important psychological gesture for both the conspirators and the nation. Being unyielding on their timetable, on the other hand, cost the rebels dearly. It resulted in a fight that was essentially limited to the state capital and to its nearby port city of Santos. Help from sympathetic detachments in other parts of the country arrived later, too little and too late, in uncoordinated batches. Help from any secrecy covering their plans failed them all together. The villain in this last regard was the commander of the army in São Paulo, General Abilio de Noronha. When he discovered what the insurgents were up to, he was able to put his own men and those of the state's *Força Pública* on alert. Noronha's decisiveness kept the revolutionaries from any

---

decades. In fact, one should remember that several of the *tenentes* of the 1920s, and the ones who took power in the *golpe* of 1964, were the same people. Aspásia Camargo, "Tenentismo," comments delivered before the seminar "Cenários de 1922," Fundação Getúlio Vargas/CPDOC, Rio de Janeiro, November 19, 1992.

[28]Fausto, *A Revolução de 1930*, p. 58.
[29]Keith, "Soldiers as Saviors," p. 404.
[30]*Ibid.*, p. 406.

155

chance at victory.[31]

The anti-Bernardes rebels were formally led this second time out by General Isidoro Dias Lopes. Actual power, however, was in the hands of junior officers such as Joaquim and Juarez Távora, Miguel Costa, and several others. With the fighters under them, they managed to take control of the metropolitan area of São Paulo for twenty-two days. Their stay might have been longer but Bernardes rushed in containing troops, took the upper hand, and compelled the rebels to give way in the face of superior firepower, hopeless odds, and their own desire to save the surrounding community from needless destruction.

It was a ghastly struggle. Prisoners falling into the hands of Colonel Tertuliano Potyguara (promoted because of his exploits in Copacabana) were sometimes taken to be mercenaries for the flimsiest of reasons. When this was the case, Potyguara invariably ordered the "foreign combatants" shot. Some insurrectionists, injured in combat, were taken from their hospital beds to be executed. As a way of thanking Potyguara, Bernardes made him a general--albeit eight days before he left office in November of 1926. In spite of this gesture, the revolutionary forces may well have had the last laugh on Tertuliano. Once São Paulo was subdued, Potyguara returned to Rio and to a posting at the city's Vila Militar. All went fine with his new assignment until the day he received a fancy package. Thinking it was another present, as he was known to be on the take, he opened it, provoking an explosion that ripped off one of his arms. But all of this was still to come. Back on the fields surrounding São Paulo, Colonel Potyguara urged a terrorist bombardment of the city. Bernardes liked the idea.[32] He liked it so much that he endeared himself to the *paulistanos* (persons from the *paulista* capital) by adamantly refusing to stop the artillery barrage on residential neighborhoods.

Naturalized French poet and writer Blaise Cendrars witnessed much of the devastation. A virtual guru to the Brazilian Modernist movement in the arts,

---

[31]*Ibid.*, p. 408.
[32]*Cf.*: Sodré, Nelson Werneck, pp. 204-8; *O Globo*, December 1, 1927, p. 1; December 3, 1927, p. 1; December 5, 1927, 2nd ed., p. 2; Arquivo Maurício de Lacerda [hereafter AML], telegram, "Tertuliano Potyguara to Arthur Bernardes," November 7, 1926; Arquivo Edgard Leuenroth [hereafter AEL] roll 16/2501; and *Correio da Manhã*, October 1, 1957, p. 2. Note that the newspapers reporting Potyguara's obituary consistently stated versions of the same wire service accounting of his career, including the erroneous description of his left arm being lost in the explosion. Actually it was his right arm that was damaged. A picture of Potyguara after he had made the rank of general is shown here as Figure 37. See also *supra*, nn. 22-23.

156

Cendrars began what would become a long relationship with Brazil in 1924. His association grew out of the esteem in which he was held by Brazilian literary figures, in particular those from São Paulo. As the fusillade began, he was near the downtown area and much of the mass destruction. With reminiscent nausea, Cendrars described what happened:

> After placing his artillery pieces in position on the hills dominating São Paulo, General [Eduardo] Sócrates, commander of the federal troops, unleashed on the... city--none of whose 800,000 [728,500] residents had been evacuated--a 'German' blitz. He knew how to take advantage of the lessons of the Great War in Europe. Not having a Reims Cathedral to demolish, Sócrates fired his cannons at a shining new hotel, then at a fine modern factory, and then at one of the new skyscrapers. The salvos fell and exploded in the center of the city, destroying a street car, blowing up a candy store, sneezing out a school, and blasted to bits a plaza or a bar. Airplanes directed the operation, dropping bombs that fell everywhere. Some detonated at random.
>
> This absurd barrage lasted for twenty-nine days and nights. One evening, the incendiaries launched by the big guns set off fires in the worker's suburbs of Luz and Moóca. This caused Shell's petroleum reservoirs and the coffee warehouses to explode. As the flames grew, they were accompanied by rifle and machine gun volleys. It all lasted until dawn. The intensity reminded me of the massive attacks at Verdun. But the anticipated charge against the capital never took place. During the day the artillery recommenced its pounding of the downtown area. It would seem that the 'legalist' officers did this with a light heart since their orders were unequivocal. 'Too bad for the city, it can be rebuilt. It was necessary to crush the sedition!'
>
> Bernardes, then president of the republic, was a man from one era with a mentality from another. He was a kind of Léon Bloy: strong and old fashioned; a convinced absolutist. ...They say he composed an opera while the guns... destroyed 11,000 houses.[33]

---

[33]*Cf.*: Cendrars, Blaise [Frédéric Sauser], *Etc..., etc... (um livro 100% brasileiro)*, Teresa Thiériot (trans. and ed.), São Paulo: Perspectiva, 1976, pp. 84, 88; and Brazil, *Anuário estatístico do Brasil, 1992, loc. cit.* Léon Bloy (1846-1917) was a writer from Cendrars' adopted country. He was noted for his belief that

> ...through pain and destitution man is redeemed by the Holy Spirit and is awakened to the hidden language of the universe. [As such, Bloy is revealed as]... a crusader of the absolute, launching onslaughts against lukewarm Christians. *Encyclopædia Britannica*, 15th ed., Chicago: Encyclopædia Britannica, 1994, Micropædia, vol. ii, p. 297.

As for Bernardes reasoning on why it all had to continue, the ignoble leader rephrased his orders another way:

> The material damages from a bombardment can be easily repaired... but the moral

Through his war minister, Bernardes emphasized that he would continue the shelling until the insurgents filed out of São Paulo. This was only a half truth. Once the rebels left, the bombing continued for another two days and nights before the government's forces entered what had been declared an open city. They paraded in to a specially composed victory march.[34]

Relinquishing control, General Isidoro's men moved by rail in a northwesterly direction out of São Paulo. As they did so, their leader issued a statement informing the nation that this was but one chapter in the struggle to free Brazil.[35] His forces were not leaving the city to surrender but to resume the fight elsewhere. Many of them would fulfill that promise. After several battles, in a failed attempt to establish an independent state, they finally joined up with the group headed by Luís Carlos Prestes near the Iguaçu Waterfalls in Paraná.

Prestes had led some 2,000 soldiers in Rio Grande do Sul against Bernardes not long after the breakout of hostilities in São Paulo. Even in the extreme south, however, the government had far too much strength. Gifted with abilities in both mathematics and military strategy, Prestes took one of the few options still open. He and his troops fought their way to the Iguaçu area and joined up with Isidoro. There, Prestes talked the rebel commanders into abandoning fixed-battle warfare. Instead they would fight a war of movement. Since he was in bad health, this meant that Isidoro could not keep up. The ailing general was thereupon talked into traveling with a small party to Argentina to try to start a new front in Rio Grande do Sul from across the border. Authority over the combined forces at Iguaçu was then given to Miguel Costa with Prestes shortly being made chief of staff. But it was Luís Carlos Prestes who proved to be the more capable leader and thus the entire group started using the name of their *de facto* commander, becoming the celebrated *Coluna* Prestes.[36]

They never lost a battle. Forever on the move, the *Coluna* played havoc with

damages [from the rebels], these are not susceptible to repair. José Carlos de Macedo Soares, *Justiça: a revolta militarem São Paulo*, Paris: Dupont, 1925, p. 71.

[34]Cendrars, p. 88.

[35]Keith, "Soldiers as Saviors," p. 418.

[36]*Cf.*: Amado, *A vida de Luis Carlos Prestes*, p. 111; Macaulay, *The Prestes Column*, pp. 60-61, 112-13; Luís Carlos Prestes, interview, Rio de Janeiro, August 13, 1987; and ADOPS, newspaper article, "*Imprensa Popular*," October 10, 1954, p. 4, comunismo/pasta 3. A rendition of Prestes during his *Coluna* days is presented here as Figure 54.

the government's legions. Prestes amazed his men with his energy. He could walk between thirty and forty miles a day, and he never seemed to get tired. He ate and slept little, and at all major encounters with the enemy he was in the front ranks leading his men onward.[37]

Years later, a politicized Prestes explained what the *Coluna* observed as it roamed all over the interior of Brazil with the government's forces usually in hot but feeble pursuit. As they moved from one region of the country to another, what impressed them the most was the widespread poverty, disease, and suffering that afflicted the *povão*. Wherever they could they accordingly destroyed municipal records and court documents favoring the rich over the poor. But it didn't help. The *fazendeiros* obtained the upper hand again as soon as the *Coluna* left. The landowners then convinced other rural laborers to travel to their holdings on the promise of a job, only to turn them into debt peons for the rest of their short lives. There was no such thing as a honest election. There was no freedom of the press. And there was especially no justice; except for the wealthy. Savage capitalism and its effects were everywhere.[38]

The *povo miserável* were afraid. They were afraid of what they didn't know and afraid of what their bosses would do to those who helped the rebels. In many places, the *Coluna* was thus met by provincial people thrown together into hastily organized *Batalhões Patrióticos*. One of the main goals of the *Coluna*, to turn the rural population against the national administration in Rio de Janeiro, consequently did not occur. Yet there were unexpected advances. Because the *Coluna* Prestes never suffered a defeat, it also came to be referred to as the *Coluna Invicta* or "Unbeaten Column." With each victory over the government's troops, or with each escape from their grasp, a mystique about Prestes began to take shape. He was eventually to become a living legend and compared to Napoleon, Caesar, and Alexander the Great. Numerous people, even those who knew nothing of his aims, called him "O Cavalheiro da Esperança" or "The Knight of Hope." Clearly, Bernardes had his hands full.[39]

---

[37]*Cf.*: ADOPS, newspaper article, "*Imprensa Popular*," October 10, 1954, p. 6, comunismo/pasta 3; and ___, October 19, 1954, n.p., comunismo/pasta 3. These observations of Prestes were made by Captain Italo Landucci, one of the members of the *Coluna*.

[38]Shoumatoff, Alex, *The World is Burning*, Boston: Little, Brown, 1990, pp. 38-39.

[39]*Cf.*: Alexander, Robert, "Brazilian *Tenentismo*," *A Century of Brazilian History Since 1865: Issues and Problems*, Richard Graham (ed.), New York: Alfred Knopf, 1969, p. 122; and *Jornal*

To those participants who were captured before the *Coluna* went into exile in Bolivia and Paraguay in 1927, to comrades in other branches of the military, or to persons on the home front who were sympathetic with the rebel's objectives, President Bernardes was unmerciful. This point was made early on in the uprising when the battleship *São Paulo* joined the opposition and steamed south to the waters off Rio Grande do Sul. Since the major battles were being fought inland, the warship sailed on to Montevideo and her crew turned her over to Uruguayan authorities. Some of the sailors then headed back to Brazil. Around a dozen or so were apprehended in Rio Grande do Sul only to have their throats cut.[40]

Bernardes let it be known that a reward would be given to anyone who executed any of the *Coluna*'s leaders.[41] This was but one of several areas in which he was willing to spend liberally to combat his enemies. By the end of 1926, he had used up the then extravagant sum of more than $100 million dollars trying to put down the rebellion. Needless to add, in the process the president surrounded himself with a wall of security. Catete was turned into a veritable fortress. The place was loaded with sentries, the so-called "Black Guards," who were nothing more than hired assassins. Bernardes even maintained a speedboat at the beach in nearby Flamengo just in case he had to make a fast get away. The public was kept away from the craft at all times by police who patrolled the adjoining streets.[42]

One of the president's main areas of suspicion was his junior army officers. There had been, for example, eighty arrests, primarily of young lieutenants, right after the start of hostilities. Amplifying this was the frightening wave of civilian arrests that never seemed to end. There were so many people being apprehended that as his term of office rolled on Bernardes came to be referred to by one caustic epithet after another. Among the most common were "Rolinha," (or "Little Dove," from a song that was then popular), and "O Réprobo" ("The Reprobate"). Almost as frequent were "O Calamitoso" ("The Calamity"), "O Cain da Familia Brasileira" ("The Cain of the Brazilian People"), "O Anti-Cristo" ("The Anti-Christ"), "O

---

do Brasil, March 8, 1990, sec. 1, p. 14. This *Jornal do Brasil* article points out that the *Coluna* likewise hoped to keep so many federal forces occupied in the country's interior, that it would weaken Bernardes' government and facilitate conspiratorial conditions in the capital.
[40]Macaulay, *The Prestes Column*, p. 57.
[41]*O Globo*, June 9, 1927, p. 1.
[42]*Ibid.*

Regabofe de Belo Horizonte" ("The Merrymaker from Belo Horizonte"), "Seu Mé" ("Mr. Baaa..."), and "O Cravo Vermelho," (or "The Red Carnation," from the flowers worn in their lapels by Bernardes' personal enforcers). There were likewise a host of prefixes in front of "...from Viçosa." Viçosa was Bernardes' hometown in Minas Gerais. Included in this list were such words as "Assassin," "Wretch," "Coward," "Reprobate," "Disastrous Politician," "Devil," "Renegade," and "Clown." Artur Bernardes was even called "Artur Lampião" by prominent opposition politician Maurício de Lacerda.[43]

If such titles were indicative of the regard in which he was held, Bernardes was certainly one of the most unpopular Brazilian presidents in the Old Republic. He was an obdurate man who had a hard time sitting down to negotiate issues when his mind was made up. His was the "government of legality,"[44] as he liked to call it. Because of this definition, Bernardes would accept nothing less than adherence to his every wish. To achieve the control he reasoned necessary, he extended the state of siege, and wound up using it in more and more parts of

---

[43]*Cf.*: Young, p. 27; Ilan Rachum, "From Young Rebels to Brokers of National Politics: the *tenentes* of Brazil, 1922-1967," *Boletin de Estudios Latinoamericanos y del Caribe*, no. 23, December 1977, p. 44; Hélio Silva, *1922 - Sangue na areia de Copacabana: o ciclo de Vargas, vol. i*, 2nd ed., Rio de Janeiro: Civilização Brasileira, 1971, caption to the unnumbered first figure between pp. 64-65; Maurício de Lacerda, *História de uma covardia*, Rio de Janeiro: Nova Fronteira, 1980, p. 184; Everardo Dias, *História das lutas sociais no Brasil*, 2nd ed, São Paulo: Alfa-Omega, 1977, p. 129; Tomé Cabral, *Novo dicionário de termos e expressões populares*, Fortaleza: Edições UFC, 1982, p. 665; Beloch and Abreu, pp. 368, 372; *A Rua* (Rio de Janeiro), October 29, 1921, p. 1; November 1, 1921, p. 1; November 28, 1921, p. 1; Arquivo Artur Bernardes [hereafter AAB], newspaper article, "*A Rua*," July 12, 1927. pp. 1, 6, AEL roll 2/107-8; *Correio da Manhã*, December 29, 1928, p. 1; December 30, 1928, p. 3; *Critica* (Rio de Janeiro), December 27, 1928, p. viii; December 28, 1928, pp. i, viii; December 29, 1928, pp. ii, v; December 30, 1928, p. i; January 2, 1929, p. i; "O governo mais infame que ainda viu o nosso paiz," [BN page fragment] n.p.; and "Continúam, no palacio sinistro da Rua da Relação, os mesmos processos dos tempos do 'Marechal Escuridão'!" [BN page fragment between December 30, 1928-January 3, 1929], p. ii(?). *Correio da Manhã*'s founder, Edmundo Bittencourt, and *Critica*'s director, Mario Rodrigues, were among those jailed by Bernardes' police. For the origin of the "Mr. Baaa..." nickname, see *supra*, nn. 16-17. I am grateful to Isabel Lustosa (Isabel Lustosa, interview, Rio de Janeiro, March 24, 1993) for clearing up the problem of translating "Seu Mé." Confirmation is provided in *A Rua*, December 15, 1921, p. 1. An unsigned characterization of Bernardes in December of 1928 is introduced here as Figure 36. Arrested and tortured, Maurício de Lacerda (*loc.cit.*) began calling Bernardes Artur Lampião for making the *cangaço* the law of the city as well as the law of the *sertão*.

[44]Observe also the comments of one of Bernardes' top policemen, Carlos da Silva Reis who later stated that he fought the enemies of Bernardes' administration in the "...holy cause of legality." AAB, letter, "Carlos da Silva Reis to Fontoura," April 1925, AEL roll 16/2234-35. For more on Carlos Reis, see *infra*, nn. 54-62, 95-96, 114-15.

Brazil, until it became a permanent nationwide feature of his four years in Catete. The army's allegiance was won by bribing various generals with funds purloined from the *Banco do Brasil* and the federal treasury. These bought-off officers came to be known as the "Generals with Clean Hands." It was stated that the money they received was to be used for expeditions against the enemy but the generals never had to account for any of it.[45]

In November of 1922, Bernardes placed the *Polícia Civil* in the Federal District under the command of one of the clean-handed generals, Manuel Lopes Carneiro da Fontoura. Fontoura was the head of the army in the state of Rio de Janeiro, and he too had nicknames preceding him that were routinely used by his adversaries. They knew him less than nobly as "General Ignorance," or "General Blackness," and even as "The Stupid Black." Because these titles cruelly played on his mixed-racial background, one can almost feel the public's scorn for this man who stepped outside the caste-based loyalties usually associated with persons of his heritage in Brazil. Fontoura, however, was only listening to his master's voice.[46]

Following military custom the general was formally addressed by the next higher rank, that of marshal, after he left the army to assume his new post. Once settling in, "Marshal" Fontoura turned out to be the anticipated yes-man to every presidential desire. It was a talent that enabled him to swiftly establish a program of repression in the nation's capital that meshed nicely with similar operations in other parts of the country.[47]

> Throughout his tenure as chief of the *Polícia Civil*, Mr. Fontoura produced officers of the law who took joy in their sadism. His policemen were other Fontouras. His closest advisors were dangerous mini-Fontouras. With the help of such people a literal commerce in prison sentences, along with the blackmail of big business, such as *jogo do bicho*, was put into operation. To be a cop, a servile member of

[45]*Cf.*: *Critica*, December 28, 1928, p. i; and *Correio da Manhã*, November 16, 1926, p. 1.
[46]*Cf.*: AAB, letter, "Manoel Lopes Carneiro da Fontoura to Arthur Bernardes," April 9, 1926, AEL roll 17/1127-28; Dulles, *Anarchists and Communists*, p. 242; and *Critica*, December 27, 1928, p. i. There are two meanings of "Escuridão," in "General Escuridão," no doubt amusing to Brazilians in the 1920s: "Ignorance" or "Blackness." For more on a master's wish *vis-à-vis* non-white policemen and police chiefs, see *supra*, chap. ii, nn. 5-6, and chap. iv, nn. 8-9, 9n. A photograph of Fontoura is presented here as Figure 38.
[47]Illustrating what took place elsewhere, there was reported to have been 10,000 arrests in São Paulo. Many of those prisoners were transported to Oyapock (see *infra*, nn. 83-94, 84n-89n, 92n-94n). Carone, p. 381.

Fontoura's inner circle, or merely someone trusted meant that as a pillar of law and order you would never have empty pockets.

Fontoura's police had one program: partake of what they falsely arrested, i.e. 'tidying up' the jails (making deals for captives' liberty or torturing those without funds). And, in special cases that interested Catete, murder. In the horrible darkness of the night, unnamable crimes took place, witnessed only by deaf dungeon walls. It was all carried out so well by Fontoura that the people didn't want retribution. They were afraid of their own shadows.[48]

As the noose tightened there seemed to be police undercover agents everywhere. Not merely rebellious soldiers but also those who sided with them, or those who questioned the president, or the economic order, were simply and efficiently taken into custody. Relatives of those known to have taken up arms against the government were brought in as hostage. No small number of persons-- on direct orders from Bernardes--may well have been whisked up and killed without any pretense of due process.[49] Others, including political idealists, various labor leaders, the unemployed, juveniles, numerous tramps, beggars,[50] petty hoodlums, unwanted foreigners, homosexuals, and "prostitutes" were all detained and held incommunicado in local jails. More than just a few were imprisoned because of tips provided by paid stool-pigeons whose names were naturally kept secret.[51] Others were taken in for the most trifling reasons.

One housewife who didn't like the two Corrêa do Lago boys denounced them over the telephone to the police for being in favor of the revolution. They were violently apprehended and spent weeks in the '*geladeira.*'[52]

There was likewise the case in which a launderer spent months in the Casa de

---

[48]*Correio da Manhã*, November 16, 1926, p. 1. For more on *jogo do bicho* and Fontoura, see *infra*, nn. 116-19.

[49]*O Globo*, June 9, 1927, p. 1.

[50]In respect to indigents, just by being in a 1926 report back to Washington DC, one might conclude that they were again becoming bothersome. The account stated that Rio de Janeiro had a fair number of "...whining beggars who drag themselves from door to door in the residential districts or crouch on the sidewalks in the business sections, exhibiting their sores...." USNA, letter, "Barclay to G-2," June 30, 1926, no. 589, p. 3, MID 2052-108/6.

[51]*Cf.*: Dulles, *Anarchists and Communists, loc. cit.*; Everardo Dias, *História das lutas sociais no Brasil*, p. 145; ___, *Bastilhas modernas, 1924-1926*, São Paulo: Obras Sociaes e Literarias, 1926, pp. 24, 121-28; [Carlos Saldanha da Gama] Chevalier, *Memórias de um revoltoso ou legalista?*, n.p.: n.p., n.y., p. 258; *O Globo*, November 15, 1926, pp. 2-3; and *Correio da Manhã*, January 8, 1927, pp. 1, 3.

[52]*O Globo*, November 15, 1926, p. 2. A description of the *geladeira* is given in *infra*, nn. 58-61.

Detenção for ruining a dress belonging to the wife of a policeman. In another instance, "...a man was thrown in jail because an [undercover] agent wanted his wife. As long as she refused, her husband was left to starve."[53] In a final example a young teacher, Souza Marques,

> ...was accused of having concocted a phrase, which he was going to use in a lecture, alluding to the events in São Paulo. As a result of this ridiculous accusation he had already languished forty days in prison. Half of that time was spent in solitary confinement. It appears that this poor youth is reliving the terrible adventures of those 'forgotten' in prisons during the regimes prior to the Marquis of Pombal in colonial Brazil.[54]

Those apprehended in Rio de Janeiro, in particular the political suspects, were routinely taken to the ornate Polícia Central (Central Police Station) and placed in the hands of torturers like Francisco Chagas, Alfredo Moreira do Carmo Machado (known more colloquially as "Moreira Machado"), Perminio Gonçalves, Inspector Barbosa, Colonel Tristão Araripe, Miguel Furtado de Mello (a.k.a. "Mello das Crianças"), Chief Fontoura's own son, João Lopes Carneiro da Fontoura (better known as "Bijuca"), José Nadyr Machado, Pedro Mandovani, Manoel da Costa Lima (alias "Twenty-Six"), and Carlos da Silva Reis. Twenty-Six, whose nickname came from his badge number,[55] was characterized as one of the Central's "...most grim brutes. Along with Mandovani, he was the policeman who had a predilection for 'surgery'...."[56]

Francisco Anselmo das Chagas, or "Chico" Chagas, had both medical and dental training. At the Central Police Station, one of his duties was not saving lives but ending them. Besides a profound knowledge of the human body's weak points, for use in information gathering sessions, Chagas had one other job. He

---

[53]*O Globo*, November 15, 1926, p. 2.
[54]*Ibid.*, p. 4. For more on the Marquis of Pombal, see *infra*, nn. 72-73.
[55]*Cf.*: AN, document, Cx. 1731/1927/Proc. 1992/27, p. 1788; ___, Estado-Maior do Exercito, *Almanak do ministerio da guerra, 1921*, Rio de Janeiro: Imprensa Militar, 1921, p. 22; Dias, *Bastilhas modernas*, pp. 34-47; *A Noite* (Rio de Janeiro), May 20, 1927, p. 3; May 25, 1927, p. 3; *Critica*, n.d., n.p. [page fragment, "O governo mais infame que ainda viu o nosso paiz," Biblioteca Nacional]; December 27, 1928, p. i; *O Globo*, November 15, 1926, p. 3; May 25, 1927, p. 3; May 30, 1927, 2nd ed., p. 1; October 19, 1927, p. 3; and *Correio da Manhã*, November 16, 1926, p. 2. Several photographs of these officers of the law are reproduced here in Figures 39, 44, 46 and 51. Moreira Machado's complete name is sometimes incorrectly listed as Alfredo Carmo do Moreira Machado.
[56]*Critica*, December 27, 1928, p. i.

was the jail's "suicide" specialist.[57] But everything was not a harmony of bone-crushing delight over at the Central. There were problems among the police themselves. For one thing, Carlos Reis and Chico Chagas did not always get along. Their differences probably triggered their mistreatment of the prisoners in a kind of morbid struggle to out do each other, and to impress Fontoura with their zeal. Chagas would use his abilities to torture then revive his victims, aiding the healing process with medicine. Reis ultimately won the little contest, however, and Chagas got transferred. His victory may well have been due to his positioning of bombs in different places in Rio. Attributing the devices to the revolutionaries, Reis and his men would then "discover" the explosives and bask in all the self-serving congratulations.[58]

It was thus a rogues' gallery that awaited anyone at the feared edifice on the Rua da Relação. Those who were not rich enough to have someone buy their way out by bribing Carlos Reis or Marshal Fontoura were often stuffed into the building's *geladeira*, or "ice box." This was a holding cell about twenty-six by thirty-three feet in size that at times held up to 190 prisoners. When crowded, it was not uncommon to have to sleep while standing up. More than one prisoner was beaten and robbed both by the jailers and other inmates. Reis is said to have stated "...whomever is sent to the *geladeira* is sent there to die...."[59] And as to the way these persons would be killed, he informed another inmate as follows: "Don't think that you are going to be shot. No...you are going to die very slowly, a little at a time...."[60] As for the beatings by other prisoners, the police had what must have been a very humorous system, to themselves, to promote this. They simply told individuals already being held in the *geladeira* that a new prisoner had money hidden on (in) his body that they could not find in the course of their interrogations.[61] When all else failed, special squads of men beat prisoners. This was largely abandoned later at the Polícia Central because the screams it produced kept Carlos Reis from having a good night's sleep, to say nothing of the neighbors. After that, prisoners were driven in handcuffs to the beaches of Leblon, mostly

[57]*Cf.: ibid.*; and *Correio da Manhã*, November 16, 1926, p. 1.
[58]*Cf.: O Globo*, November 15, 1926, pp. 3-4; and May 30, 1927, 2nd ed., p. 3.
[59]Dias, *Bastilhas modernas*, p. 30.
[60]*Ibid.*, p. 33.
[61]*A Plebe* (São Paulo), April 7, 1923, p. 4.

uninhabited in the 1920s, and whacked around until their tormenters became exhausted.[62]

Those who survived everything were sometimes transferred, or occasionally even delivered immediately after being apprehended, to either the Casa de Correção or the Casa de Detenção. At the first of these aging penal institutions they were mixed with common criminals on five floors containing 216 cells. None of these enclosures had a toilet or running water.[63] Besides the usual beatings, which were even carried out on minors,[64] the Correção had a special section for special treatment in the basement. Called the *novo raio*, or "New Horror," this inquisitional place was reserved for those who fell out of favor with the Correção's director, Waldemar Loureiro. One observer remarked that prisoners only left the New Horror

> ...to go to the infirmary, and from the infirmary to their coffins. The *novo raio* is a humid cement cubicle, without a bed or any kind of furniture. It's entirely empty. Prisoners [try to] escape the humidity by taking off their pants, tying them to the bars [like hammocks], and laying on them.
> Because of the revolt, a man who called himself engineer "X" and a well known *paulista* senator were in the *novo raio*. Weakened through various days of starvation, the engineer lost consciousness and ended up leaving the infirmary a paralytic. The senator wasn't fed for four days, [but somehow] obtained a strange kind of help--bits of bread and cigarette soup--to cheat his hunger.[65]

For those who were taken virtually next door to Rio's Casa de Detenção, the situation was not much better. They were thrown together into one of the dark and almost airless containers that ranged in sizes from 13'2" by 16'5" square.[66] *O Globo* presented a graphic narrative of two apparently innocent individuals who

[62]*Cf.*: Moraes [Filho], Evaristo de, *Minhas prisões e outros assumptos contemporaneos*, Rio de Janeiro: Edição do Autor, 1924, pp. 32-33, 56; and Dias, *Bastilhas modernas*, pp. 21, 24-28, 30-33, 35-36, 40-42.

[63]Britto, pp. 182, 199. Britto presents a number of orchestrated photographs dealing with prison conditions in his work. Two of these pictures, one with an all too neatly uniformed prisoner no. 2308 in his cell at the Casa de Correção and the other depicting the spic-and-span interior of Casa de Detenção, are reproduced here as Figures 41 and 43.

[64]*O Globo*, December 13, 1927, p. 3.

[65]*Cf.*: Chevalier, pp. 111, 129; and *O Globo*, November 15, 1926, p. 4. A picture of Waldemar Loureiro is displayed here as Figure 40.

[66]*Cf.*: Dias, *Bastilhas modernas*, pp. 67-68, 186; and [Heron] Herondino Pereira Pinto, *Nos subterraneos do Estado Novo*, Rio de Janeiro: Germinal, 1950, p. 25.

wound up at the Detenção:

> If after a chance meeting a couple of friends talked in a cafe or on the street about what was happening in São Paulo, an undercover agent might very well hear their conversation. Moments later they'd be taken to the famous '*geladeira*' at the Central Police Station. There, among vagabonds and criminals, they'd be subjected to starvation and cold until being taken to the Casa de Detenção. If they had friends who could arrange their release, it ended there. But if they were simple people, or poor workers, or unknown individuals, the brutality used against them took on a dark color.[67]

The uncultured director of the Detenção, Meira Lima, did his best to get prisoners to spy on one another. Known for his sadistic nature, he would call a captive into his office and try to browbeat him into betraying his fellow inmates. He would dangle an offer of freedom before the prisoner's eyes should he cooperate. But if he refused, Meira Lima frequently had the individual tossed into Cell 59. This infamous cubicle was one of the 13'2" square enclosures that served as home for ten to twelve of the most-hardened criminals, said to be from the lowest classes. Spiders, scorpions, and cockroaches were everywhere. Prisoners continuously stepped on these insects when moving about, since Cell 59 was so dark that one could barely make out the difference between night and day. There was no way to relieve oneself except in a greasy hole in one corner of the floor. The air was foul, especially at night, because of the plumbing. It was clammy. It was filthy. It was absolutely to be avoided in the minds of the political prisoners. This can be inferred from the fact that they always did more time in Cell 59 than anyone else.[68]

Similar to the New Horror at the nearby Correção, the Casa de Detenção was additionally said to have a heinous "Basement," "Tunnel," and a "Fort" where the stamina of selected prisoners was put to the test. The Basement consisted of a series of humid, dirty cells. Enough air trickled in under the doors to support four inmates, but the guards regularly filled each cell with up to twenty men. Sleeping was done on a straw mat if one was fortunate. If one was unfortunate, and the last to stake out a place to sleep, all that was left was the space on top of the latrine

[67]*O Globo*, November 15, 1926, p. 2.

[68]*Cf.*: *O Globo*, November 15, 1926, pp. 4-5; and Dias, *Bastilhas modernas*, pp. 67-68, 170, 186-87. A picture of Meira Lima is displayed here as Figure 42.

opening. The Tunnel and the Fort were small castigation cavities to one edge of the Basement. In reality they were little more than concrete coffins, measuring about 3'3" in width, by some 6'7" both length and height. Each was sweltering and pitch black. The lack of ventilation in both, together with the insects, drove weak men over the edge.[69]

It would truly be interesting to learn how many individuals died while incarcerated, or how many were helped to that end by the guards. The police all over Rio still used the ferule to slap hands, and they still used the *chibata* to apply corporal punishment. No favorites were played. The underage, adults, and the elderly were all slapped and whipped equally.[70] Most of the time, suspects lived long enough to be taken up to a government *fazenda* north of Guanabara Bay in Magé. This helped to ease the overcrowding, but the new prisoners kept coming. There were so many that some were locked up in diverse police facilities, military barracks, and even fire departments. Others were placed under guard on various ships. Among the vessels used were the *Alfenas, Campos, Benevente, Comandante Nascimento, Comandante Vasconcellos, Caxambu,* and the *Cayabá.*[71]

Most of the detainees were eventually freighted off to one of several prison islands. The jails, the ships, and the islands were all part of a Brazilian *gulag*, with prisoners being transferred from one to the other at the inclination of the authorities. Three of the first stops on this circuit were not even out of Guanabara Bay. They were the military stockades on Ilha das Flores and Ilha das Cobras, and the jail on Ilha do Bom Jesus.

"The Island of the Flowers," or Ilha das Flores, is located on the eastern side of the harbor just offshore from São Gonçalo. Persons who would never be tried

[69]*Cf.*: Dias, *Bastilhas modernas.*, pp. 63-65; and Leôncio Basbaum, *Uma vida em seis tempos: memórias*, São Paulo: Alfa-Omega, 1976, p. 130. A communist, Basbaum managed to make it through thirty-three days in one of these holes some years later. He stated that his confine was probably shorter by about eight inches.

[70]*Cf.*: *O Globo*, December 28, 1928, p. 1; and Dias, *Bastilhas modernas*, p. 40. For more on the *chibata*, see *supra*, chap. ii, nn. 46-47, 78-79 and *infra*, nn. 84-85. For the ferule (*palmatória*), see *supra*, chap. i, nn. 39-40 and *infra*, nn. 82-83, 97-98, 102-4.

[71]*Cf.*: Dias, *Bastilhas modernas*, pp. 49, 209; Pinheiro, *Estratégias da ilusão*, pp. 97, 100; *O Globo*, November 15, 1926, p. 4; and Chevalier, pp. 54, 92. Future military dictator Castelo Branco was among those army officers detained on the *Cuyabá*. *Ibid.*, pp. 88-89 [second to the last unnumbered plate].

or even charged made up the bulk of prisoners sent to this establishment. As one of the early batches of inmates arrived, they were met by some one-hundred soldiers armed with rifles. Escorted to the prison at a remote end of the island, they passed through two high fences topped with ten strands of barbed wire and came to a parade rest inside the front courtyard. Facing them were sentries every hundred feet, guarding a couple of shabby buildings. The two structures had been previously used to accommodate newly-arrived European immigrants. Those times, however, were long gone. Now the buildings were even further run down. Prisoners were kept in the most ragged of the two; the other was used to house the jail's officers and guards.

At sunset the new arrivals were ordered into the basement. The comfort of a cell, such as it was, would have to wait. Everyone was made to sleep in the cellar the first night. The following morning, the civilians were separated from those who had been in uniform. The latter were taken to the upper floors of the prisoners' building and placed two at a time into ample cells. Some of these confines had a view of the ocean. The civilians were left in the windowless basement. Cots were provided but it was crowded. The air was bad, hot, and humid.[72]

Ilha das Cobras was different. It had been a murky colonial lockup. In 1711, when the French under Duguay-Trouin invaded Rio, they occupied the island and began using its fortress as a prison. Since those times, many who opposed or resisted the government in power were incarcerated in the Ilha das Cobras stockade. From 1758 to 1777, during the dictatorship in Lisbon of the Marquis de Pombal, more than one political enemy of the Marquis arrived in chains to disappear forever into the subterranean holes on the Ilha.[73] Tiradentes and all the leaders of the *Inconfidência* (the Independence Movement of 1789) were held there. So too were João Cândido and the other members of the Naval Revolt of 1910. Most were never to walk out alive.

It was said that the brig on Ilha das Cobras had "...walls, galleys, tunnels, cells, bars [and] locks that [gave] it the aspect of having been made to imprison

---

[72]Dias, *Bastilhas modernas*, pp. 165-70, 185.
[73]*Cf.*: *Encyclopædia Britannica*, 15th ed., Chicago: Encyclopædia Britannica, 1994, Micropædia, vol. ix, p. 587; and Dias, *Bastilhas modernas*, p. 203.

wild animals, not human beings."[74] Used mainly for naval prisoners following the
1922 and 1924 revolts, most of its cubicles were below ground. Light and sufficient ventilation barely trickled in through cracks in the substantial gratings.
Prisoners were repeatedly packed up to four at a time into cells built to hold but a
single person. On another occasion, twenty prisoners were crammed into confines
designed for three.[75] Some of the newer cells were chopped out of the stone-hard
earth. They made up Ilha das Cobras' so-called "Third Prison," which contained
four divisions--two sections for solitary confinement and two for common criminals. All were dim and sticky. The enclosures for prisoners sent to solitary
confinement covered just over 3'3" by 6'7" of floor space. The usual sentence in
these reprimand vaults ranged from five days to one month.[76]

     The Ilha do Bom Jesus was situated not far from the Ilha das Cobras. On a
flat part of Bom Jesus the government constructed a pair of buildings next to the
docks. Similar to the organization of Ilha das Flores, the edifice to the left was
designated to hold political criminals, the one on the right the administration and
guards. The prison building had two large rooms or galleries for the inmates. This
living arrangement was done to save money. It certainly was not the plan to
promote conviviality as Ilha do Bom Jesus was known as another miserable institution. These negative feelings came about because of the total lack of hygiene, and
the main reasons for this lay just over a hundred yards away on the Ilha de Sapucaia.[77] Sapucaia was Rio's garbage dump. When the winds shifted, the odor from
the dump's rubbish pile was intolerable. So too were the accompanying parasites
and floating pieces of rotting debris.

     Captain Pedro Goytacazes was the man in charge on Bom Jesus. The captain
was not at all liked by the prisoners. It was said that he made life for his charges
"...an inferno capable of eclipsing Dante's,"[78] and there may well have been some
truth to these sentiments. Goytacazes seems to have be a master of deceit.
Among other things, he was extorting the supplier of food to the prison, a man
who just happened to be the father of one of the inmates. This may have resulted

---

[74]*Ibid.*, pp. 203-4. For what happened to João Cândido and some of the other rebels from 1910
on Ilha das Cobras, see *supra*, chap. ii, nn. 53-55.
[75]But see also *supra*, chap. ii, nn. 53-55.
[76]Dias, *Bastilhas modernas*, pp. 178, 202-7.
[77]Both the Ilha do Bom Jesus and the Ilha de Sapucaia are now part of the Ilha do Fundão.
[78]*O Globo*, November 15, 1926, p. 5.

in food being continuously in short supply on Bom Jesus. When one of the prisoners, Bruno Lobo, protested about the lack of things to eat, everyone's soup was mysteriously poisoned. There were sick men everywhere, and the medical attention they received was ineffective or slow in materializing. This prompted a vehement complaint to Goytacazes from Maurício de Lacerda, who was imprisoned on the island. Letters denouncing the situation were smuggled out to both the minister of justice and internal affairs, and the director of public health. The cries, however, brought no direct reply. The only fruit of their effort was when Bruno Lobo and Maurício de Lacerda were moved to other institutions.[79]

Just outside the entrance to Guanabara Bay stands the rock called Ilha Rasa. Ruled over by General Carlos Arlindo, chief of the *Polícia Militar*, the place was frequently unapproachable from the water due to the large waves that almost constantly buffeted the island. On those days when the weather was good, inmates could see the beaches of Leme, Copacabana and Leblon. Prisoners were housed in a one-story wooden outbuilding that was roughly 53' x 66' in size. It had a zinc roof that produced ovenlike temperatures most of the year. Since there was no electricity, light was provided at night by kerosene lanterns. Annoying mosquitoes and swarms of pesky flies were everywhere. Once in awhile medical supplies and other necessities had to be dropped by seaplane owing to the waves. Most drinking water also fell from the skies during storms. The joy of fresh water was offset by a leaky roof and the knowledge that the precious liquid was being gathered in the dirty lighthouse patio to be stored in a filthy canister. Bouts of diarrhea and even dysentery were the inevitable result.

The food on Ilha Rasa was said to be better than at the Detenção. This was usually true, at least for a few days anyway, after one of the ships from the mainland called and restocked the island's wares. The relative tranquillity of Ilha Rasa ended, however, following the escape of newspaperman José Eduardo de Macedo Soares. General Arlindo then began a strict eighteen-point military regime on the island. Prisoners dared not gripe too loudly about the new arrangement because from that point on, the forty-odd guards had permission to shoot anyone who was disrespectful or who refused to follow orders.[80]

---

[79]*Ibid.*

[80]*Cf.*: *ibid.*, pp. 4-6; Dulles, *Anarchists and Communists*, p. 256; and Dias, *Bastilhas modernas*, pp. 146-59, 168.

Even further out to sea, 800 miles off the coast of Espírito Santo, stands rugged Ilha Trindade. A Brazilian possession almost thirty miles in circumference, Trindade was only occupied as a result of the events of 1924. It was used at first for military prisoners believed to be planning still another uprising against Bernardes. The landfall had but three structures: a residence for the commander, Captain Melo Pena, a hut for the radio transmitter, and a barrack for the guards. Prisoners slept in tents or sometimes out in the open on the bare earth. Each day, the inmates were marched out and put to work. They also unloaded ships whenever one arrived offshore.

It is possible that Melo Pena was sent to Trindade because his superiors were suspicious of his political involvement with the rebels. Whatever his politics were, they did not keep him from having erected two kinds of castigation cells. The first were small, above-ground enclosures where prisoners were left for four or five days without food or water. The second type lacked roofs but they still did the job. Captives were tied into them in a laying position, and exposed to the intense rays of the sun for three days to a week at a time.

Eventually Melo Pena was replaced. Then, every three months, when a supply ship chugged on out to the island, a new administrator would take over. The vessels returned to the mainland with the old director, those few prisoners to be released, those to be transferred, and those who were seriously sick.[81]

Other ships hauled Bernardes' most worrisome political enemies to Ilha Grande. Located south along the coast, next to the state line with São Paulo, it was originally a leper colony, then a quarantine center for the passengers of infected ships. In 1908, during the term of President Afonso Pena, an old *fazenda* on the island was taken over by the government and used to create a "free colony of independent workers" (read: penal colony). Called "The Two Rivers Colony," it was a place where vagabonds, minors, gamblers and other small-time offenders

[81]*Cf.*: *ibid.*, pp. 209-16; *O Globo*, November 15, 1926, p. 6; USNA, document, "The Military Attache, Brazil, G-2 Report: 1170," February 11, 1925, no. 427, p. 2, MID 2052-105; AAB, photograph "Radio Station on Trindade," AEL roll 21/175-76; Arquivo Augusto do Amaral Peixoto, photograph, "Prisoners Waiting for Ships to Arrive," Fundação Getúlio Vargas/CPDOC, 004/4; and Arquivo Pedro Ernesto Batista, photograph, "Prison Complex on Trindade Island," Fundação Getúlio Vargas/CPDOC, 012/31. The Arquivo Pedro Ernesto contains the largest number of photographs of the prisoners and life on the island. Beriberi (caused by a bad diet and a lack of vitamin B_1) was one of the most common sickness on Trindade. *Critica*, December 28, 1928, p. viii.

were sent after leaving the larger lockups on land. This was done to keep these people, if they were destitute (no doubt most of them), off the streets following their release.

Men, women, and youngsters supposedly above the age of fourteen were all shipped to Two Rivers and placed under the constant stare of Commandant Horacio Malsonetti and his guards. In theory, these three groups were to be separated. In practice, it was another matter. Boys were sometimes promiscuously mixed in with adult males. Some of these adolescents were as young as eight. The actual place where the bulk of the minors were housed was described as "squalid, repellent, and infected."[82] As many as seventy-eight slept on the hard floor on occasional mats. Anyone who did not like these conditions, and anyone who squawked about anything, was likely to have a *palmatória* used against them. For prisoners who created more serious problems, there were three segregation boxes adjacent to the main house. Each was portrayed as horrible and muggy, without light or air. They were places where the lack of sanitation reached an unbearable limit. Compounding all of this on Ilha Grande, malaria took its toll on the prisoners. A lot of the detainees came down with the disease and little was done for them due to the lack of facilities and the lack of interest.[83]

As strange as it may seem, there was even a grimmer fate than confinement on Ilha Grande or any of the other islands. This nightmare began when a prisoner learned that he was being shipped to the federal concentration camp, euphemistically labeled the Clevelandia Agricultural Center, in the territory of Amapa.

Situated on one bank of the Oyapock (now spelled Oiapoque) River just adjacent to French Guiana, Clevelandia, like the Ilha do Bom Jesus, was depicted as a Dante's *Inferno*.[84] As of July 6, 1926, 419 deportees had already been transported nearly three thousand miles up the coast from Rio to Clevelandia in the holds of the ship *Campos*. Another 408 of the anti-Bernardes forces, who

---

[82]Britto, p. 207.

[83]*Cf.: ibid.*, pp. 202-8; and *O Globo*, November 15, 1926, p. 6.

[84]*Correio da Manhã*, January 8, 1927, p. 1. A characterization entitled "Oyapock! The symbol of bourgeois tyranny," was published in the São Paulo Anarchist newspaper *A Plebe* (February 12, 1927, p. 1). It is reprinted in Dulles' *Anarchists and Communists*, p. 261. Bernardes received a number of doctored photographs of Clevelandia showing the place as a well run camp with healthy-looking prisoners. Some of these snapshots are reprinted in Pinheiro, *Estratégia da ilusão*. They are all located in AAB, photographs, "Clevelandia in 1926," AEL roll 23/1033 106; and among the AAB collection at the Arquivo Pública Mineiro [hereafter APM].

survived the Battle of Catanduvas, came even further from Paranaguá, just outside Curitiba, aboard the *Cayabá*. A final 119 were shipped to Clevelandia from lockups in the Amazon River basin.

While en route, some of the politicals destined for Oiapoque were whipped with the pervasive *chibata* on orders from the government.[85] Around four hundred or so of these *desterros* (outcasts) were rebel soldiers, *Polícia Militar* dissidents, conspirators, or civilian sympathizers with the 1922 and 1924 revolts. The remainder were anarchists, associated political radicals, and the usual petty crooks, poor people, and vagrants.[86] There were more children and teenagers,[87] some of whom had fought against the government. Most of this underage group, however, were more than likely *abandonados* (abandoned children) who had become involved, often just to stay alive, with delinquent activities in the cities.

Using the figure of 946 prisoners at Oiapoque (from the shipments mentioned above), one report sent to Bernardes by the camp's superintendent, Gentil Norberto, stated that 404 had died of dysentery, tuberculosis, malaria, and assorted other sicknesses. Another eighty-seven were buried without a cause of death being recorded.[88] Although initially shocking, this mortality rate of 51.9 percent seems far too conservative when we reflect on the larger situation. There

---

[85]*Cf.*: APM, document, "Relatorio apresentado ao Snr. Ministro da Agricultura, Industria e Commercio pelo Director de Secção da Secretaria de Estado Oldemar Murtinho," July 6, 1926, dossiê Pr. AB/c. Clevelândia, p. 4; Dulles, *Anarchists and Communists*, pp. 260-62, 260n, 262n; and *O Globo*, January 28, 1928, 2nd ed., p. 1. The whippings reported here took place on December 14, 1924 aboard the *Campos* (see *supra*, nn. 70-71).

[86]*Cf.*: APM, document, "Relatorio apresentado ao Snr. Ministro da Agricultura, Industria e Commercio pelo Director de Secção da Secretaria de Estado Oldemar Murtinho," July 6, 1926, dossiê Pr. AB/c. Clevelândia, p. 22; Hall and Pinheiro, p. 15; Dulles, *Anarchists and Communists, loc. cit*; Dias, *História das lutas sociais no Brasil*, pp. 145-46; and *Correio da Manhã*, January 9, 1927, p. 3. Note that the number of soldiers and civilians actually shipped varies. The material presented by Hall and Pinheiro (*loc. cit.*) would appear to be the most accurate.

[87]*Cf.*: *Correio da Manhã*, January 8, 1927, pp. 1, 3; *O Jornal*, January 3, 1928, p. 6; and Pinheiro, *Estratégias da ilusão*, p. 95. *Correio da Manhã* (January 8, 1927, pp. 1, 3), whose owner Edmundo Bittencourt was once arrested for opposing Bernardes, mentions several youth who had been deported to the federal concentration camp at Clevelandia. The youngest age noted was fourteen. Another newspaper (*O Jornal*, January 3, 1928, p. 6) stated that forty-five "infants" were there in September of 1922.

[88]*Cf.*: Pinheiro, *Estratégias da ilusão*, pp. 103-4. The number of deaths are roughly confirmed in *A Rua*, February 21, 1927, p. 1. This same issue of *A Rua* laments the irony in the name of the man in charge at Clevelandia, Gentil Norberto. "Gentil" can be translated into English as "gentle," "genteel," and "well-bread," etc.

were additional persons who lost their lives trying to escape across the Oiapoque River into the jungles of French Guiana.[89] More were worked to death in the camp's forced labor regimens,[90] or suffered horrifying ends from barbarous acts[91] by the prison guards. For those taken sick, the hospital was a mere notch above the nonexistent. There was never enough bed space. To deal with

...the cases of malaria, bacterial dysentery, beri-beri, dropsy, and diarrhea --the fevers, vomitings, and convulsions[,] the standard cure was to provide quinine tablets, or quinine injections (which seemed to cause swellings). For injecting 120 persons daily, the hospital had only two syringes (and, more than once only one needle).[92]

No one wanted to become so incapacitated that they absolutely had to use this appalling excuse for a medical facility. The pointed comments to one new patient by the hospital's administrator summed up Bernardes' real purpose with his agricultural center.[93] "...You have come here to die. Resign yourselves to

[89]Dias, *Bastilhas modernas*, p. 243. A report in the Bernardes archives (AAB, document, "Relatorio apresentado ao Snr. Ministro da Agricultura, Industria e Commercio pelo Director de Secção da Secretaria de Estado Oldemar Murtinho," July 6, 1926, APM dossiê Pr. AB/c. Clevelândia, p. 45) states that 262 inmates managed to escape, many of them to San George in French Guiana. Observe as well the dispatch from Dionysio Bentes, the territory's administrator (AAB, letter, "Dionysio Bentes to Arthur Bernardes," July 15, 1925, AEL roll 14/8-9), in which he informs the president that many Oiapoque prisoners are escaping but that he can not send more men to guard duty there because he only has 600 individuals under arms in the entire region.
[90]*Correio da Manhã*, January 8, 1927, p. 1.
[91]*Ibid.*
[92]Dulles, *Anarchists and Communists*, p. 263. Dulles goes on to point out (p. 263n) that "...the official nurses (one the wife of the hospital administrator, the other the son of a Colônia official) were mere payroll names." Pictures of the structure, called the Hospital Simões Lopes, can be seen in AAB, photographs, "Clevelandia in 1926," AEL roll 23/1037-38.
[93]Bernardes claimed that the idea to use Clevelandia as a concentration camp was the inspiration of his minister of agriculture, Miguel Calmon. Calmon in turn gave the government's accounting of the matter to a special Senate tribunal at the end of December in 1927, once Bernardes' successor had been installed. Among other excuses offered, he apathetically declared that "...various persons of national notoriety..." had traditionally been banished ever since the times of Floriano Peixoto. The former minister of agriculture also emphasized that the camp was founded in 1920 during the term of Epitácio Pessoa. *O Jornal*, January 3, 1928, p. 6. Concerning the deportation of unwanted individuals to unknown fates in remote parts of the country, it was the view of one author that

the difference between Hermes da Fonseca and Arthur Bernardes was that the first handed hundreds of Brazilians over to the slavery practiced by inhuman rubber planters [see *supra*, chap. ii, nn. 55-63]. The second threw them to the beasts in a region isolated by malaria and other tropical diseases.... Morél, *A Revolt da Chibata*, 2nd ed., p. 144.

this[!]"[94]

Back in Rio, after O Cravo Vermelho left office, there was one case that boiled to the surface. It caught the public's attention even more than what unfolded offshore and up at Clevelandia. It all started when the transferred but not forgotten Chico Chagas learned about another revolutionary plot.[95] Oddly, his discovery took place at a time when Fontoura's influence with Bernardes was at a low ebb. The individual who had the president's ear was his military chief of staff, General Antenor de Santa Cruz Pereira de Abreu, also known behind his back as "Rapa Côco," or "Scalped Coconut." Since Fontoura protected Carlos Reis, Reis as well lost leverage and, for awhile, Francisco Chagas thought that he was running the police department. Chagas was just naïve enough not to understand that Bernardes was personally controlling things through Santa Cruz.[96] Unwittingly, Chico felt that his big chance had arrived.

It was not long before nineteen persons, including four army captains and four lieutenants, were arrested when a tip from a paid informant pointed them out as bomb-planting radicals. It was even said that their ultimate aim was to murder

---

[94]*Correio da Manhã*, January 8, 1927, p. 1. Photographs of the hospital's staff are located in AAB, photographs, "Clevelandia in 1926," AEL roll 23/1037-38.

[95]To be sure, there were plots throughout the Bernardes administration. In the tense atmosphere produced by the advent of the *Coluna* Prestes coupled to the government's suspicions that there were sympathizers everywhere, all kinds of reports dealing with sedition were sent to Catete from various points in the republic. For examples *cf.*: AAB, telegram, "Teffe to Felix Pacheco," December 5, 1924, AEL roll 17/2177; ___, telegram, "Felix Pacheco to Teffe," December 6, 1924, AEL roll 17/2178; ___, telegram, "Teffe to Felix Pacheco," December 8, 1924, AEL roll 17/2179; ___, telegram, "Agamenon [Magalhães] to Affonso Penna," February 1926, AEL roll 20/865-67; ___, telegram, "Borba to Minister of Justice and Internal Affairs," February 11, 1926, AEL roll 20/868-69; ___, telegram,"Sergio Loreto to Arthur Bernardes," February 10, 1926, AEL roll 20/877; ___, telegram, "Sergio Loreto to Arthur Bernardes," February 12, 1926, AEL roll 20/870; and ___, telegram, "[Pedro de] Toledo to Arthur Bernardes," April 22, 1925, AEL roll 16/1018.

[96]*Cf.*: USNA, letter, "Barclay to G-2," May 21, 1927, no. 732, p. 5, MID 2052-112; Brazil, *Ministerio da Guerra, 1921*, p. 150; *O Globo*, May 30, 1927, 2nd ed., p. 1; and June 9, 1927, p. 1. General Santa Cruz was scornfully called Rapa Côco in the parlance of Brazilian conscripts. The term was given him after he ordered all of his recruits to shave their heads. This was their penalty following a debate over who should be president while Bernardes was still a candidate. The actual inventor of this embarrassment to his commander was ultimately arrested and locked up for two years. The soldier nearly died of tuberculosis, yet the name Rapa Côco stuck. *Critica*, December 26, 1928, p. i. A photograph of General Santa Cruz is shown here as Figure 45.

the president. Among those picked up were Dr. Antonio Martins de Arajuo Silva, a physician, pharmacist and proprietor of the Elite Pharmacy in Catete; Accacio Rodrigues de Carvalho, a barber; Viriato da Cunha Bastos Schomaker, the landlord of the São Paulo Laundry; Narciso Ramalheda, the one-armed owner of a small fireworks factory; Rubens Bello, a worker at the factory; and the 16 year-old plant guard named Jorge.[97]

Turned over to Chagas and Moreira Machado at the Central Police Station, Dr. Martins was severely beaten with rubber hoses. Schomaker was maimed and abused for being the one who supposedly positioned bombs at various locations in the city. At one point he was made to sit in a chair that was said to be wired to produce shocks. Accacio was beaten nearly senseless, and Narciso Ramalheda had to sign papers saying that he had not been roughed up, which of course was exactly the opposite of what really had happened. With General Santa Cruz sometimes present, the police clobbered the hand on Ramalheda's remaining arm some forty-eight times with a *palmatória* until the nails were blue and oozing with blood.

The young man of sixteen received some of the special treatment that had been a part of the Central's reputation for years. He was hoisted upside down by his tied-together feet on a rope that had been thrown over a beam in one of the cells. Chagas and Machado kept Jorge in this position for hours, waiting for him to give them other names. But to their surprise and irritation, the youth stoically said nothing. He was only cut down when the guards saw blood and fluids coming out of his mouth, nose, and ears.[98]

As a result of a report by a disgruntled employee, Géo Vicente Parisi,[99] the police concluded that one of the heads of the conspiracy was Conrado Borlido

---

[97]*Cf.*: AN, document, Cx. 1907/1929/Proc. 199, p. 2122; *O Globo*, November 15, 1926, p. 3; and AAB, letter, "Carolina Bastos Schomaker to Arthur Bernardes," [December 1925], APM dossiê Pr. AB/polícia. In her touching letter to Bernardes, Carolina Schomaker reminded the president that Viriato had been in custody since July 24, 1925 (or at least 4½ months). Probably writing in December of the same year, she pleaded with the nation's leader to simply be allowed to see her husband on Christmas day. No answer to this request was found among the Bernardes papers.

[98]*Cf.*: *O Globo*, May 30, 1927, p. 3; *A Noite*, May 30, 1927, p. 3; June 20, 1927, p. 3; *Correio da Manhã*, November 16, 1926, p. 2; and May 31, 1927, p. 3.

[99]AN, document, Cx. 1907/1929/Proc. 199, p. 2108. Elsewhere (pp. 2113, 2117-18) in this trial docket (see *infra*, nn. 107-9), Parisi's last name is spelled: Paryse, Parize, or Parise.

Maia de Niemeyer.[100]   Niemeyer was a prominent *carioca* businessman and head of the Borlido Maia Company located on the Rua do Ouvidor.   His firm supplied the government with explosives.   Now, his bitter employee was saying that the businessman likewise provided the revolutionaries with volatile materials.

At first, Chico Chagas could not believe that a member of Rio's upper crust would commit such a crime.   But he quickly convinced himself that he had stumbled across the real thing after considering what an arrest and conviction would do for his career.   Rushing to Catete, he assured Bernardes and General Santa Cruz that he would get Niemeyer to confess "...or I won't be Chagas anymore."[101]

Niemeyer was called in for questioning.   Conrado went freely, assuring his wife that he'd be back shortly.   On reaching the Central, Chico Chagas confronted him with the charges.   He was told that the police had learned that he detested the president so much that he would not accept a 20$000 *réis* bank note because it had Bernardes' portrait on it.[102]   Chagas ranted on, claiming that due to his profound hatred of Brazil's elected leader Conrado had supplied the rebels with dynamite. Niemeyer unwaveringly denied everything.   When Chagas or Machado showered him with derogatory questions, he responded with a torrent of disavowing answers.

Around 7 P.M., Schomaker was dragged into Chagas' office.   Moreira Machado yanked him in by the hair after a beating he had just been given in the bathroom.   On seeing Schomaker's condition, Niemeyer protested the fact to Chagas.   This sent Chagas into a fury.   The acting chief of the *Polícia Civil* grabbed a *chicote* from Marshal Fontoura's son, who was watching, and went after the fifty-four year old Niemeyer.   Moreira Machado helped out by pinning back Conrado's arms.   A little later Rapa Côco visited the Polícia Central in order to witness Niemeyer's confession but went away disappointed.   All through the night he telephoned to find out what was happening.   Sadly, Chico Chagas had to tell his superior that Niemeyer had not caved in yet; but that he thought he would soon. The scene was growing ugly.   The authorities were running out of patience.

---

[100]This was Niemeyer's commonly used business name. His real name was Conrado Henrique de Niemeyer. AN, document, Cx. 1731/1927/Proc. 1992/27, p. 1742.

[101]*O Globo*, June 9, 1927, p. 1.

[102]AN, document, Cx. 1907/1929/Proc. 199, p. 2113.

In the morning, accompanied by Moreira Machado, Mandovani, and Twenty-Six carrying a *palmatória*, along with Bijuca and his whip, Chagas entered the cell where Niemeyer was being kept. Glaring at the businessman, Chico raised his voice, "You son-of-a-bitch! Are you or aren't you going to sign this confession?"[103] As they were standing there waiting for an answer, Niemeyer surprised everyone by attacking Chico Chagas, landing a powerful slap to his face. He then grabbed the policeman's neck with such force that Chagas' button collar popped loose. Momentarily stunned by what they had just seen, the other lawman quickly gathered their wits and pounced on Niemeyer. They began to beat and kick him. A rib and an arm were quickly broken. Then either Twenty-Six cracked Niemeyer's skull with the butt of his *palmatória*, or Moreira Machado did so with a blunt instrument. Niemeyer fell to the floor of his cell in a lump. He appeared to be dead. It was just before 9 A.M. on July 25, 1925.[104]

The problem was what to do with Niemeyer's body. If he had been poor[105] there would not have been cause for alarm, but Conrado Niemeyer was rich. When a wealthy member of the community was arrested, the authorities were instantaneous at providing excuses and lies about why the "citizen" had been picked up in the first place. Usually the *nata*, or upper-class individual, was already released and well on his way home. In keeping with this tradition, the police announced the day after he volunteered to come in for questioning that Niemeyer had broken free of his guards and committed suicide by jumping to his death from a second-story window at the Central Police Station.

Part of the story was true. The entrepreneur did fall from the second floor of the Central. There was a dull thud as his barely alive body smashed on to the Rua da Relação's waiting sidewalk. A bystander on the pavement came to Niemeyer's side in time to hear him gurgle what was probably the word "*miseraveis*," or "miserable ones."[106] As this was occurring, a policeman rushed forward with a

---

[103]*O Globo*, June 9, 1927, p. 1. The take-it-or-leave-it confession was dictated by Rapa Côco. *Ibid.*

[104]*Cf.*: AN, document, Cx. 1907/1929/Proc. 199, p. 2122; and *O Globo*, May 25, 1927, p. 3; May 30, 1927, p. 3; and June 9, 1927, p. 1.

[105]See *supra*, nn. 66-67.

[106]*Cf.*: *O Globo*, June 9, 1927, p. 1; *A Noite*, May 30, 1927, p. 3; and AN, document, Cx. 1731/1927/Proc. 1992/27, p. 1813. The defense (see *infra*, nn. 107-9) attacked this witness (pp. 1813-14) for the obvious ramifications that *miseraveis* brought to their clients. Under the pressure of cross examination, they got the individual to admit that he could have heard the word

handkerchief to wipe the blood from Niemeyer's mouth, almost as if he had been waiting to do so. Once order was restored and the gathering crowd moved back, a perfunctory examination was conducted. The position of the body was duly noted, its distance from the Central being carefully marked on the sidewalk tiles. Newspapers were placed over the still warm corpse and a lad in knickers began sweeping the accumulating blood into the gutter.

Niemeyer's lifeless form was eventually taken to the morgue to await the charade for his family. Suspecting foul play, they insisted on getting his body back. The authorities had other plans. The police refused to release the remains to a civilian undertaker or to the man's next of kin. They promptly buried Niemeyer and the evidence. His watch and the clothes he had on were kept by Chagas and his assistants. One was worth money, the others had too much soaked-in blood. The clothes the family did get back were completely different from the ones Niemeyer had on when asked to come downtown. His only real possessions ever returned were some innocent papers that had been in his pockets.[107]

At the end of the Bernardes presidency, Chico Chagas, Moreira Machado, Pedro Mandovani, and Twenty-Six were all charged with murdering Conrado Niemeyer. Their trial got underway on May 20, 1927. Coincidentally, the proceedings started on the very day that Bernardes returned to Rio de Janeiro to take up his seat in the Senate as an elected senator from Minas Gerais. After leaving office, he had returned to his home state and ran successfully for the legislature in February of 1927. Back in Rio, however, Bernardes found that he was detested to such a degree by the *cariocas* that he left for Europe within a week. That the former president could be called to account for what he knew about the Niemeyer affair was probably a major factor in his hasty departure for the continent. A witness to Bernardes' passing through the capital was the U.S. military attaché. In his down-played report (see the newspapers *Critica* and *O Globo* for more intense descriptions) to Washington DC, he commented that

yesterday ex-President Bernardes arrived from Minas by special train

---

in its singular form.

[107]*Cf.*: *Correio da Manhã*, May 28, 1927, p. 3; and *O Globo*, November 15, 1926, p. 3; June 9, 1927, p. 1. Three photographs of the dead Conrado Niemeyer, just outside the Central Police Station, are presented here as Figures 48-50. Note that the position of the body, parallel to the Central, lends support to the charge in *O Globo* (*ibid*) that he was thrown out the window by two or more persons who would have been lifting his body to get it over the concrete railing.

to assume his seat in the senate. His friends and supporters were within the station to give him a rousing welcome, and imposing body guard [*sic*] of police was on hand to protect him, and the populace awaited him outside the station.

Amid a chorus of hoots, jeers and insults an official automobile was forced through the crowd with the help of the police, and the new senator was transported to his brother's residence. When he had alighted, the vegetables [that had been thrown at his car] were removed from the vehicle. Moist towels were used for the eggs. A few arrests were made, but in general the affair passed off with little actual violence. The manifestation against the ex-President was led by the students who had declared it a holiday and who paraded the streets with banners bearing inscriptions far from flattering to the new arrival.[108]

The trial of the four defendants in the death of Conrado Niemeyer suffered from numerous problems, such as the "suicide" of one state's witness--political police Lieutenant José Nadyr Machado--and delays, like the 30-day wait so that a distraught Moreira Machado could regain his psychic composure. Moreira even had a chest x-ray entered into evidence as proof of his depressed mental condition. The four defendants, or "The Sinister Gang," as the press called them, were finally adjudged to be innocent. The victim's family appealed but the earlier verdict was upheld on June 2, 1931.[109]

Conrado Niemeyer's "suicide" was not the first staged by the police of Artur Bernardes,[110] nor the last once Washington Luís became president in 1926. The new head of state was an admirer of his predecessor. Already known as one who thought labor questions were questions for the police,[111] Washington Luís told a

[108]USNA, letter, "Barclay to G-2," May 21, 1927, no. 732, p. 2, MID 2052-112.

[109]*Cf.*: AN, document, Cx. 1731/1927/Proc. 1992/27, pp. 2171, 2187; ___, document, Cx. 1907/1929/Proc. 199, n.p., [page of original trial docket entitled: "N. 2115 Côrte de Appella-ção"]; ___, document, Cx. 1922/1927/Proc. 1992, pp. 1299-1305; Beloch and Abreu, p. 327; and *O Globo*, May 25, 1928, p. 1. José Nadyr Machado was an important witness against the defendants at their first trial. His mysterious death at an army barracks in Belém helped the defense. *Ibid.* Machado's front-page obituary picture is reprinted here as Figure 46.

[110]The first known case was that of Luís "Lulu" Barbosa. Lulu was a relative of former president Nilo Peçanha. He was accused of plotting to assassinate Bernardes at the behest of Peçanha, and was also thrown to his death from one of the windows at police headquarters. Lacerda, pp. 185-90.

[111]They apparently continued to be after Washington Luís took office. He had no less than one group of striking workers deported for wanting insignificant salary increases. *Cf.*: ADOPS, newspaper article, "*O Trabalhador Graphico*," February 7, 1928, p. 7, comunismo/pasta 4B; ___, May 4, 1929, p. 2, comunismo/pasta 4B; and ___, document, "O proletariado e o movimento

gathering in Belo Horizonte that "without Artur Bernardes, there wouldn't be a Brazil."[112] It is no wonder then that the new leader was not merely alluded to in whispers as Little Trepov. Some of his other titles were "Mr. Lulu," "Strong Arm," and "The *paulista* from Macaé."[113] This last designation came from the fact that Washington Luís was born in Macaé in the state of Rio de Janeiro. While he was still in his teens, the family moved to São Paulo. It is thus intriguing that following his inauguration he continued the secret policy of sending selected prisoners to *fazendas*, and to one in particular, near the city of Macaé, where they too "committed suicide."[114] It was an estate where inmates were essentially worked to death in the fields. With their last bits of strength, they were then forced to dig their own graves before being shot in the back of the head. There is speculation that Carlos Reis or some other Rio de Janeiro policeman owned this clandestine plantation.[115]

The new president continued to let the political police--by then known in the Federal District as the *4ª Delegacia Auxiliar*, or the police from the 4th Auxiliary Department--keep ordinary Brazilians and aliens under firm control. The *4ª Delegacia*, though, had an additional assignment over earlier versions of the political police. It spied on *all* threats to the sitting regime. In Rio de Janeiro, the division that dealt specifically with this last area was the *Seção de Ordem Política e Social*, or the Political and Social Order Section (SOPS). On December 30, 1924, in São Paulo, the entire umbrella of political police units began being called the *Delegacia de Ordem Política e Social* (or Delegation of Political and Social Order). By early 1928, leftists in Rio de Janeiro took this *paulistanos* cue. They replaced *Seção* with *Delegacia* in their own vernacular when referring to the political police. It didn't matter that SOPS was their real name in Rio. The *paulistano* version caught

---

[112]*Cf.*: *O Globo*, November 31, 1927, p. 1; and AML, newspaper article, "Washington-Bernardes: a fatalidade da politica professional," n.p., n.d., n.p., AEL roll 2/28a.

[113]Lustosa, p. 98. For Little Trepov, see *supra*, nn. 8-10. The connection, if at all, between "Mr. Lulu" and Luís "Lulu" Barbosa (see *supra*, 110n) remains to be proven.

[114]Many policies would continue with the new administration in addition to the manhandling of suspects. As if to illustrate this point, the front page of the magazine *O Malho* (November 13, 1926) (here, Figure 52) depicted both Washington Luís and Bernardes using "conductor's batons" to direct a band made up of some of the members of the incoming government. The caption to this drawing translates as "We're going to hear a duet." See also in this regard *infra*, nn. 122-23, 123n.

[115]*Cf.*: Beloch and Abreu, p. 1952; Mocellin, p. 214; *Critica*, December 29, 1928, p. v; *O Globo*, November 15, 1926, p. 3; and Lacerda, p. 191.

on elsewhere too and gave birth to the dreaded acronym, "DOPS." DOPS thus became the common expression for the "thought police" in practically all of Brazil, despite official designations, for most of the next sixty years.[116]

There was gossip all through his tenure as head of the *Policia Civil* that Fontoura was not serious about combating gambling.[117] One reason for his lack of ardor was the fact that he and his men were sharing in much of what they took in from bribes as well as from items confiscated in actual police raids. It appears that Mello das Creanças[118] was in charge of the division of the booty. Owing to these allegations, on April 9, 1926, Fontoura had some of his powers reduced. He followed up this affront by resigning.[119]

The fact that the chief left in disgrace meant nothing to Washington Luís. The man he chose as to replace Fontoura, Coriolano de Góis, was from the same mold.[120] Giving life to Góis's orders was a reconstituted gang of torturers down at the Central Police Station. With increased powers after mid-August 1928,[121] to

---

[116]*Cf.*: Pedeira, Waldecy Catharina Magalhães, interviews, Rio de Janeiro, June 30, 1994; October 18, 1994; Arquivo Público do Estado do Rio de Janeiro, *Os arquivos das policias politicas, loc. cit.*; AML, newspaper article, "*O Combate* [Rio de Janeiro]," February 2, 1928, n.p., AEL roll 2/79; and Brazil, São Paulo, lei no 2034 of December 30, 1924.

[117]There was a superficial attempt to do something about *jogos de azar*, or games of chance, of which *jogo do bicho* was certainly the most popular. For examples of Fontoura's police at work, *cf.*: AAB, letter, Fontoura to [Renato] Bittencourt," March 31, 1926, AEL roll 17/1105; ___, letter, "Renato Bittencourt to Chief of Police [Fontoura]," April 3, 1926, AEL roll 17/1104; ___, letter, "Renato Bittencourt to Chief of Police [Fontoura]," April 5, 1926, AEL roll 17/1095; ___, document, "Relação dos flagrantes de jogo, cavrados na 2ª Delegacia Auxiliar, 25 de março-3 de abril de 1926," AEL roll 17/1096-100; ___, document, "Relação dos flagrantes de jogo dos bichos, no periodo de 22 de junho de 1925, até a presente data, processados na Segunda Delegacia Auxiliar," AEL roll 17/1139-46; ___, document, "2ª Delegacia Auxiliar: serviço de repressão ao jogo desde 22 de julho de 1925," AEL roll 17/1136-38; ___, document, "Relação dos individuos recolhidos ao deposito de presos, Policia Central" [March 25-April 3, 1926], AEL roll 17/1101-3; and ___, miscellaneous documents, AEL roll 17/1105-9. For more on *jogo do bicho*, see *supra*, nn. 47-48, chap. iii, nn. 65-66, chap. iv, nn 27-28, 28n.

[118]See *supra*, nn. 54-55.

[119]*Cf.*: AAB, newspaper article, "*Gazeta de Noticias*," April 10, 1926, p. 1, AEL roll 17/1111; ___, document, "Caso das apprenhensões, 27 de maio de 1926," AEL roll 17/1110; and ___, anonymous letter, n.d., AEL roll 17/1147; ___, letter, "Manoel Lopes Carneiro da Fontoura to Arthur Bernardes," April 9, 1926, AEL roll 17/1127-28.

[120]A photograph of Coriolano de Góis is shown here as Figure 53.

[121]*Cf.*: *O Globo*, August 4, 1928, p. 1; August 7, 1928, p. 1; August 9, 1928, p. 1; August 10, 1928, p. 1; August 11, 1928, p. 1; August 14, 1928, p. 1; August 15, 1928, p. 1; and August 22, 1928, p. 2.

perform investigations free of judicial interference, the new men of pain were simply some of the old hands, plus several new faces. Chico Chagas was succeeded by Pedro de Oliveira Sobrinho. Assisting Oliveira Sobrinho were Renato Bittencourt, Mario Lucena, Raul Aguiar, Investigators Canuto and Orlantino, Martins Vidal, Octavio Peres, Alfredo Pinto Filho, and the two misogynists: Attila Neves and Jardemar San Pietro. Apparently, Attila and Jardemar actually enjoyed slapping women around. This included throwing them down flights of stairs while in police custody.[122] Little had changed. As one newspaper put it,

> ...Coriolano de Góis pursues the same debauched iniquity of the Stupid Black in the sinister building on Rua da Relação. For the former chief one can still find an excuse: the country was passing through abnormal times. It was in a state of siege. ...Now, however, no excuses are possible. ...Why then, re-institute only the practices of *fontourismo* among the capital's police? This is the question that the government can't answer. The facts are there, however, confirming that Fontoura's intellectual capacity is the dominate mentality at the Polícia Central. Substituting Chagas, Pedro de Oliveira Sobrinho presides calmly over the treachery and the beatings carried out by the *4ª Delegacia Auxiliar*. Under this demonic chief the "conductor's batons" [i.e., truncheons] of the *4ª* bust into homes in the dead of the night without the slightest respect for women, nor at least pity for children. ...With eyes fixed on the windows of the *4ª Auxiliar*, Coriolano waits for the "suicides." Inside at his post is Oliveira Sobrinho, and radiating from there the conductor's batons. What else is lacking?[123]

There was, however, a larger problem. Something smelled worse in Brazil than just the government's deficiencies in the field of justice for all. Rather precar-

[122]*Cf.: A Noite*, November 16, 1926, p. 2; *O Globo*, April 19, 1928, 2nd ed., p. 1; July 7, 1928, p. 3; September 22, 1928, p. 2; October 17, 1928, 2nd ed., p. 1; *Correio da Manhã*, November 16, 1926, p. 1; *Critica*, January 1, 1929, n.p.; January 3, 1929, p. i; "A inominavel violencia da policia na noite de São Sylvestre," [BN page fragment between December 30, 1928-January 3, 1929], p. ii(?); "Continúam, no palacio sinistro da Rua da Relação, os mesmos processos dos tempos do 'Marechal Escuridão'!" [BN page fragment between December 30, 1928-January 3, 1929], p. ii(?). A picture of Attila Neves is reproduced here as Figure 47. No know photograph of Jardemar San Pietro exists.

[123]*Critica*, January 3, 1929, p. i. Note also the implications of the conductor's batons in Figure 52. As concerns children being beaten by the Rio police during the administration of Washington Luís, see what may have been the tip of the iceberg in *O Globo*, November 14, 1927, p. 2; July 14, 1928, p. 3; and September 28, 1928, 2nd ed., p. 1. That this type of behavior was not confined to the capital can be seen in *O Globo*, December 2, 1927, 2nd ed., p. [2].

iously, the economy had been allowed to remain totally dependent on coffee sold abroad. As Washington Luís took control of the government, this policy continued. At the end of the decade, it would produce a sharp decline in wholesale Brazilian coffee prices in Europe and the United States. Beginning with 1925, the year before Washington Luís assumed power, and ending in November of the marketing year after he left office, the quotations in New York for the more sought-after variety of coffee (Santos Grade 4) averaged as follows:[124]

	1925	1926	1927	1928	1929	1930	1931
Cents per pound	24.5	22.3	18.7	23.2	22.1	13.0	8.4

For many generations, Brazil had been a country of one-product economies. Coffee came to be the major crop in 1853 when it finally overtook sugar to become the backbone of the nation's wealth.[125] Since the state of São Paulo produced the largest part of the Brazilian coffee crop, it was into *paulista* hands that the control of coffee was dumped by the federal government in 1925.[126] The move was in keeping with the laissez faire system of states' rights under the Old Republic. As a part of this general shift, the men of power in São Paulo also succeeded in another objective. They had long felt that only as a united group of coffee producers could they effectively deal with foreign bankers and buyers. To this end, after several failed attempts and other entities, the São Paulo State Coffee Institute came into being in 1926. It was an organization that grew to enjoy near dictatorial power over the sale of this Brazilian commodity. Single-mindedly, the São Paulo coffee barons began to speculate in futures while accumulating vast stockpiles of coffee. Slowly, the Institute came to reason that it was best to hoard their one product to drive prices up.[127]

The bubble began to burst of its own accord in May of 1929 when the price of coffee started to decline. This resulted from the prospect of one of the biggest Brazilian coffee harvests ever and the accompanying drop in the value of local

---

[124]Rowe, John W.F., "Studies in the Artificial Control of Raw Material Supplies: No. 3, Brazilian Coffee," *Royal Economic Society*, no. 34, February 1932, p. 86. The twelve monthly averages in cents per pound for 1930 were 14.7, 14.4, 14.2, 14.1, 13.8, 13.2, 13.1, 11.5, 12.1 at the end of September, 13.2 at the end of October, 11.6 and 10.5. *Ibid*.

[125]Taunay, Affonso de Escragnolle, *Historia do café no Brasil, no Brasil Imperial: 1822-1872.* Rio de Janeiro: Departamento Nacional do Café, 1939, book i, vol. iii, p. 307.

[126]Young, p. 71.

[127]*Cf.*: Bello, *A History of Modern Brazil*, p. 260; and Beloch and Abreu, pp. 1607-8.

currency. International lending centers in the Northern Hemisphere watched everything from the sidelines with nervous anticipation. Shortly, they began to put the brakes on Brazil's credit. In São Paulo, local banks were soon compelled to call in outstanding loans made to coffee growers.[128]

When the North American stock market crash occurred later in the year, the already sinking coffee prices took a headlong dive. At the end of September, the Brazilian government had a cash reserve of $151,265,600 in gold. By December of 1930, some fourteen months later, there would not be a single ounce of the metal left.[129] The aftermath of this chain reaction was economic disaster; especially since Washington Luís steadfastly refused to step in and do anything. In the eyes of the *paulista* elite, the attitude of the president turned him into a South American Herbert Hoover. The resulting lack of support for their adopted son, from people who counted, was to become a principal component in the success of the Revolution of 1930. But before this happened, hundreds of businesses folded and thousands of civil servants and others dependent on the government were fired.[130] Far beyond the business failures and government cutbacks,

> ...more than a million persons directly connected with the coffee industry in the states of São Paulo, Minas Gerais and Rio de Janeiro were affected by the adverse conditions. ...A feeling of unrest began to permeate the rural areas of the south.[131]

---

[128]Young, *loc. cit.*
[129]*Cf.: Isto É*, October 28, 1987, p. 74; and *Correio da Manhã*, October 1, 1929, p. 12.
[130]Young, pp. 73-75, 78-80.
[131]*Ibid.*, p. 77.

EPILOGUE

It was from the South that help finally came. *Gaúcho* Getúlio Vargas would replace Washington Luís. Vargas, however, would not replace the system of elite overreaction. Much less was he to ameliorate fear of contact with the police (the first line of sub-elite enforcement of that system) by the *povão*. In respect to the way violence was used to keep Getúlio in a position of command and privilege, the Revolution of 1930 only ushered in a change of jail keepers. Business continued as usual in remote areas. It also puttered along in the capital at the Central Police Station and at other lockups through out the city. Where once individuals like Manuel Fontoura used to play God with prisoners lives, little would be transformed with the demise of the Old Republic. Fontoura and his men had actually led the way in this century. They had tested the waters and found them safe. By 1933, the group of gangsters at the Central was led by another individual who was a personal appointee of the chief of the provisional government. Answerable only to Vargas, Filinto Müller's paramount responsibility was to maintain his superior in power at any cost.[1]

Only the faces at the top had changed. Long established policies of police interaction with the public remained unchanged, as did the newly redefined methods for dealing with unreliable members of the establishment. It was a continuous gloom out of which the reports of the burning, the ripping, and the tearing of human flesh began to circulate anew. In March of 1935 the commentary of one leading *carioca* newspaper, over what was becoming a reminiscent situation, went as follows:

> We are returning to what appears to be the days of Bernardes, when prisoners were thrown through the windows of the public building on the Rua da Relação, when the '*geladeiras*' functioned day and night, when Clevelandias existed, crowded with poor devils, and the 'bombs' prepared by the police themselves exploded all over the place to justify the most

---

[1]Beloch and Abreu, p. 2343.

incredible violence; crimes that were even more hideous.

Have we actually returned to practicing these same atrocities? Everything indicates that we have.[2]

---

[2]*Diario de Noticias* (Rio de Janeiro), March 3, 1935, p. 7. Founded by Orlando Dantas in July of 1930, *Diario de Noticias* was known as "The Newspaper of the Revolution." But it soon began to find fault with the Vargas' dictatorship.

APPENDIX

TABLE 1

MALES BY RACE (WHEN KNOWN) AND STATE, ENTERING AND LEAVING BRAZILIAN PRISONS DURING 1907 BY NUMBER AND PERCENT

	Black Males	Brown Males[a]	Black plus Brown[a] Males	White Males
Alagoas				
no. (% entering)	1(10.0%)	7(70.0)	8(80.0)	2(20.0)
no. [% leaving]	-	2[100.0]	2[100.0]	-
Amazonas	4(8.7)	34(73.9)	38(82.6)	8(17.4)
	-	2[66.7]	2[66.7]	1[33.3]
Bahia	17(21.5)	56(70.9)	73(92.4)	6(7.6)
	16[28.1]	33[57.9]	49[86.0]	8[14.0]
Ceará	2(12.5)	9(56.3)	11(68.8)	5(31.3)
	4[18.2]	10[45.5]	14[63.6]	8[36.4]
Espírito Santo	n.a.	n.a.	n.a.	n.a.
	n.a.	n.a.	n.a.	n.a.
Goiás	-	-	-	-
	-	-	-	-
Maranhão	-	3(66.7)	3(66.7)	1(33.3)
	1[25.0]	4[75.0]	5[100.0]	-
Mato Grosso	-	-	-	-
	-	-	-	-
Minas Gerais	60(24.5)	116(47.3)	176(76.8)	69(28.2)
	16[17.2]	50[53.8]	66[71.0]	27[29.0]
Pará	3(7.5)	27(67.5)	30(75.0)	10(25.0)
	4[8.7]	27[58.7]	31[67.4]	15[32.6]
Paraíba	-	7(58.3)	7(58.3)	5(41.7)
	1[4.8]	12[57.1]	13[61.9]	8[38.1]
Paraná	3(20.0)	2(13.3)	5(33.3)	10(66.7)
	1[7.1]	4[28.6]	5[35.7]	9[64.3]
Pernambuco	19(10.7)	90(50.8)	109(61.6)	68(38.4)
	6[10.3]	34[58.6]	40[69.0]	18[31.0]
Piauí	4(12.5)	22(68.8)	26(81.3)	6(18.8)
	1[16.7]	4[66.7]	5[83.3]	1[16.7]
Rio de Janeiro	27(32.1)	27(32.1)	54(64.3)	30(35.7)
	16[28.6]	21[37.5]	37[66.1]	19[33.9]
Rio de Janeiro DF	43(22.4)	74(38.5)	117(60.9)	75(39.1)
	20[16.4]	39[32.0]	83[48.4]	63[51.6]
R. Grande do Norte	-	1(33.3)	1(33.3)	2(66.7)
	-	-	-	1[100.0]
R. Grande do Sul	12(13.3)	36(40.0)	48(53.3)	42(46.7)
	9[10.6]	29[34.1]	38[44.7]	47[55.3]
Santa Catarina	3(23.1)	2(15.4)	5(38.5)	8(61.5)

TABLE 1 (continued)

	-	-	-	-
São Paulo	62(23.2)	58(21.7)	120(44.9)	147(55.1)
	29[14.1]	40[19.4]	69[33.5]	137[66.5]
Sergipe	-	5(83.3)	5(83.3)	1(16.7)
	2[10.0]	12[60.0]	14[70.0]	6[30.0]
BRAZIL	260(19.5)	576(43.3)	836(62.8)	495(37.2)
	126[15.4]	323[39.5]	449[55.0]	368[45.0]

Source:
Brazil, Ministerio da Agricultura, Industria e Commercio, *Annuario estatistico do Brazil, 1908-1912*, vol. iii, pp. 383, 407.
a = Includes *indios*.
n.a. = Not available by race.

TABLE 2

MALES BY RACE (WHEN KNOWN) AND STATE, RESIDENT ON DECEMBER 31, 1907 IN BRAZILIAN PRISONS AND THEIR OCCURRENCES IN THE 1890 AND 1940 CIVILIAN CENSUSES BY NUMBER AND PERCENT

	Black Males	Brown Males[a]	Black plus Brown[a] Males	White Males
Alagoas				
no. (% in prison)	1(8.3%)	9(75.0)	10(83.3)	2(16.7)
% 1890 census	10.0%	58.7	68.7	31.3
% 1940 census[b]	13.9%	29.3	43.2	56.7
Amazonas	4(9.3)	32(74.4)	36(83.7)	7(16.3)
	3.3	67.3	70.6	29.4
	7.6	61.0	68.6	30.9
Bahia	83(26.4)	207(65.9)	290(92.4)	24(7.6)
	20.0	54.0	74.1	26.0
	20.3	51.1	71.4	28.6
Ceará	10(8.6)	91(78.4)	101(87.1)	15(12.9)
	8.4	46.6	55.0	45.0
	23.4	23.9	47.3	52.5
Espírito Santo	n.a.	n.a	n.a.	n.a.
	16.4	40.8	57.2	42.8
	17.1	21.4	38.5	61.5
Goiás	19(63.3)	6(20.0)	25(83.3)	5(16.7)
	13.0	53.2	66.1	33.9
	17.0	10.7	27.8	72.1
Maranhão	5(16.1)	22(71.0)	27(87.1)	4(12.9)
	14.9	53.4	68.3	31.7
	27.9	25.5	53.4	46.5
Mato Grosso	-	1(33.3)	1(33.3)	2(66.7)
	14.4	55.8	70.1	29.9
	8.7	39.9	48.6	50.6
Minas Gerais	98(29.3)	158(47.3)	256(76.6)	78(23.4)
	18.4	40.6	59.0	41.0
	19.0	19.4	38.3	61.6
Pará	29(15.8)	110(59.8)	139(75.5)	45(24.5)
	6.5	53.8	60.3	39.7
	9.9	45.7	55.7	44.0
Paraíba	10(15.9)	42(66.7)	52(82.5)	11(17.5)
	6.8	45.7	52.5	47.5
	13.7	32.5	46.2	53.6
Paraná	6(9.2)	15(23.1)	21(32.3)	44(67.7)
	5.3	31.0	36.3	63.7
	4.9	7.5	12.4	86.4
Pernambuco	78(14.0)	303(54.5)	381(68.5)	175(31.5)
	11.1	47.0	58.1	41.9

TABLE 2 (continued)

	15.4	30.0	45.4	54.4
Piauí	16(14.4)	72(64.9)	88(79.3)	23(20.7)
	15.5	56.1	71.6	28.4
	32.1	22.5	54.6	45.2
Rio de Janeiro	29(37.7)	25(32.5)	54(70.1)	23(29.9)
	26.8	29.4	56.3	43.7
	21.3	18.4	39.7	60.0
Rio de Janeiro DF	80(38.6)	-	80(38.6)	127(61.4)
	10.1	21.8	31.9	68.1
	10.1	16.5	26.6	73.1
R. Grande do Norte	2(6.9)	21(72.4)	23(79.3)	6(20.7)
	8.8	46.4	55.1	44.9
	13.5	43.4	56.9	43.1
R. Grande do Sul	51(10.7)	196(41.0)	247(51.7)	231(48.3)
	8.7	20.7	29.4	70.6
	6.5	4.5	11.0	88.9
Santa Catarina	6(14.6)	10(24.4)	16(39.0)	25(61.0)
	4.6	10.4	15.0	85.0
	5.1	.3	5.4	94.6
São Paulo	124(20.1)	127(20.6)	251(40.6)	366(59.2)
	13.2	23.6	36.8	63.2
	7.3	4.7	12.0	84.8
Sergipe	17(14.2)	71(59.2)	88(73.3)	32(26.6)
	14.5	55.4	70.0	30.0
	18.9	34.7	53.5	46.2
BRAZIL	668(19.5)	1518(44.2)	2186(63.7)	1245(36.3)
	14.5	40.8	55.3	44.7
	14.5	21.0	35.5	63.8

Sources:

Cf.: Brazil, Ministerio da Agricultura, Industria e Commercio, *Annuario estatistico do Brazil, 1908-1912*, vol. iii, *loc. cit*.; ___, Ministerio da Industria, Viação e Obras publicas, *Sexo, raça e estado civil, nacionalidade, filiação, culto e analphabetismo da população recenseada em 31 de dezembro de 1890*, Rio de Janeiro: Directoria Geral de Estatistica, 1898, pp. 2-3; and ___, Instituto Brasileiro de Geografia e Estatística, *Censo demográfico: população e habitação [, 1940]*, Rio de Janeiro: IBGE, 1950, Série Nacional, vol. ii, p. 68.

a = Includes *índios*.

b = Includes persons not declaring race. Note: race was not enumerated in the censuses between 1890 and 1940.

n.a. = Not available by race.

TABLE 3

ILLITERATE PLUS MARGINALLY ILLITERATE MALES AND FEMALES, AND
ONLY THE PROFESSIONS OF DOMESTICS, INDUSTRIAL WORKERS,
AGRICULTURAL WORKERS AND THOSE PERSONS WITHOUT OCCUPATIONS,
AS A PROPORTION OF ALL PROFESSIONS (WHEN KNOWN) ENTERING,
LEAVING AND THOSE RESIDENT ON DECEMBER 31, 1907 IN BRAZILIAN
PRISONS BY STATE, NUMBER AND PERCENT

	Illiterate plus Marginally Illiterate		Domestics, Industrial Workers, Agricultural Workers, and those Without Professions	
	Females	Males	Females	Males
Alagoas				
no. (% entering)	-	10(100.0%)	-	10(100.0)
no. [% leaving]	-	2[100.0%]	-	2[100.0]
no. % remaining	-	12 **100.0%**	-	12 **100.0**
Amazonas	-	44(95.7)	-	34(73.9)
	-	3[100.0]	-	3[100.0]
	-	41 **95.3**	-	31 **72.1**
Bahia	-	73(92.4)	-	61(77.2)
	-	51[89.5]	-	57[100.0]
	-	291 **92.7**	-	265 **84.4**
Ceará	-	16(100.0)	-	12(75.0)
	-	22[100.0]	-	15[68.2]
	2 **100.0**	115 **99.1**	-	86 **74.1**
Espírito Santo	n.a.	n.a.	-	-
	n.a.	n.a.	-	-
	n.a.	n.a.	n.a.	n.a.
Goiás	-	-	-	-
	-	-	-	-
	-	30 **100.0**	-	1 **3.4**
Maranhão	-	4 (100.0)	-	2(50.0)
	-	5[100.0]	-	5[100.0]
	1 **100.0**	31 **100.0**	1 **100.0**	23 **74.2**
Mato Grosso	-	-	-	-
	-	-	-	-
	1 **100.0**	3 **100.0**	-	2 **66.7**
Minas Gerais	7(100.0)	236(96.3)	5(71.4)	154(62.9)
	3[100.0]	99[97.1]	3[100.0]	66[64.7]
	8 **100.0**	321 **96.1**	5 **62.5**	214 **64.1**
Pará	1(100.0)	34(85.0)	1(100.0)	27(67.5)
	2[100.0]	44[95.7]	2[100.0]	21[45.7]
	6 **100.0**	163 **88.6**	6 **100.0**	133 **72.3**
Paraíba	-	12(100.0)	-	11(91.7)
	-	21[100.0]	-	19[90.5]
	1 **100.0**	62 **98.4**	1 **100.0**	57 **90.5**

TABLE 3 (continued)

Paraná	1(100.0)	15(100.0)	1(100.0)	13(86.7)
	-	12[85.7]	-	8[57.1]
	4 100.0	63 96.9	-	51 78.5
Pernambuco	3(100.0)	173(97.7)	3(100.0)	166(93.8)
	-	55[94.8]	-	52[89.7]
	10 100.0	532 95.7	10 100.0	382 68.7
Piauí	2(100.0)	31(96.9)	1(50.0)	28(87.5)
		6[100.0]		6[100.0]
	7 100.0	109 98.2	5 71.4	98 88.3
Rio de Janeiro	-	84(100.0)	-	30(35.7)
	2[100.0]	56[100.0]	1[50.0]	17[30.4]
	-	77 100.0	-	29 37.7
Rio de Janeiro DF	73(100.0)	191(99.5)	34(46.6)	50(26.0)
	22[100.0]	121[99.2]	22[100.0]	43[35.2]
	111 100.0	308 99.0	23 20.7	95.30.5
R. Grande do Norte	-	3(100.0)	-	3(100.0)
	-	1[100.0]	-	1[100.0]
	-	29 100.0	-	13 44.8
R. Grande do Sul	-	90(100.0)	-	38(42.2)
	4[100.0]	85[100.0]	2[50.0]	34[40.0]
	12 100.0	331 69.2	1 16.7	198 41.4
Santa Catarina	-	13(100.0)	-	8(61.5)
	-	-	-	-
	2 100.0	41 100.0	-	27 65.9
São Paulo	14(100.0)	264(98.9)	13(92.9)	122(45.7)
	8[100.0]	194[94.2]	7[87.5]	89[43.2]
	14 100.0	597 96.6	7 50.0	333 53.9
Sergipe	-	6(100.0)	-	4(66.7)
	1[100.0]	20[100.0]	-	2[10.0]
	2 100.0	116 96.7	1 50.0	99 82.5
BRAZIL	101(100.0)	1299(97.6)	58(57.4)	774(57.4)
	42[100.0]	797[96.5]	37[88.1]	439[53.1]
	181 100.0	3272 92.5	61 33.7	2149 60.8

Sources:

Brazil, Ministerio da Agricultura, Industria e Commercio, *Annuario estatistico do Brazil 1908-1912*, vol. iii, pp. 391-393, 415-417, 437-439.

a = The category "Other Professions and Professions Ignored," in the source publication could not be included. Many of the above figures in respect to profession are therefore under-represented.

n.a. = Not available

TABLE 4

FEMALES BY RACE (WHEN KNOWN), ARRESTED, ENTERING, LEAVING AND STILL IN PRISON AT THE END OF 1907 BY NUMBER AND PERCENT, AND THOSE ARRESTED IN 1908 THROUGH 1912, FOR *VADIAGEM* IN RIO DE JANEIRO, D.F., BY THEIR ESTIMATED YEARLY OCCURRENCES IN THE POPULATION

	Black Females	Brown Females[a]	Black plus Brown[a] Females	White Females
Rio de Janeiro DF				
% of 1907 estimated population.[b]	14.3%	25.2	39.6	60.3
no. *% arrested*	373 *48.9%*	249 *32.6*	622 *81.5*	141 *18.5*
no. (% entering)[c]	50(68.5%)	18(24.7)	68(93.2)	5(6.8)
no. [% leaving][d]	11[50.0%]	7[31.8]	18[81.8]	4[18.2]
no. **% still in prison at end of 1907**	82 73.9%	20 18.0	102 91.9	9 8.1

Note: Data on the following years was published in complete form only in respect to the number of women arrested in Rio de Janeiro, D.F., for *vadiagem*.

% of 1908 est. pop.[b]	14.3	25.0	39.3	60.6
no. *% arrested*	297 *52.2*	166 *29.2*	463 *81.4*	106 *18.6*
% of 1909 est. pop.[b]	14.2	24.8	39.0	60.9
no. *% arrested*	242 *52.4*	156 *33.8*	398 *86.2*	64 *13.9*
% of 1910 est. pop.[b]	14.2	24.6	38.8	61.1
no. *% arrested*	195 *49.4*	150 *38.0*	345 *87.3*	50 *12.7*
% of 1911 est. pop.[b]	14.1	24.4	38.5	61.4
no. *% arrested*	164 *51.7*	90 *28.4*	254 *80.1*	63 *19.9*
% of 1912 est. pop.[b]	14.1	24.2	38.2	61.7
no. *% arrested*	200 *47.7*	157 *37.5*	357 *85.2*	62 *14.8*

Sources:

Cf.: Brazil, Ministerio da Agricultura, Industria e Commercio, *Annuario estatistico do Brazil, 1908-1912*, vol. iii, pp. 377, 383, 397-399, 402-403, 407, 421, 429; ___, Ministerio da Industria, Viação e Obras Publicas, *Sexo, raça e estado civil, nacionalidade, filiação, culto e analphabetismo da população recenseada em 31 de dezembro de 1890*, pp. 2-3; ___, Instituto Brasileiro de Geografia e Estatística, *Censo demográfico: população e habitação* [, *1940*], Série Nacional, vol. ii, *loc. cit.*; ___, Policia do Districto Federal, Gabinete de Identificação e de Estatistica, *Estatistica de 1909*, pp. 52-53; ___, *de 1911*, pp. 54-55; ___, *Estatistica policial e criminal de 1912*, pp. 54-55; ___, *Boletim policial*, Rio de Janeiro: Nacional, 1907, May 1907, p. 46; 1907, July 1907, Contravenções 2º trimestre de 1907 [no page]; 1907, October 1907, p. 36; 1908, January 1908, pp. 26-27; 1908, May 1908, p. 53; 1908, August 1908, p. 205; 1909, November 1908, p. 321; and 1909, February 1909, p. 412.

a = Includes *índios*.

b = There are no censuses between 1890 and 1940 listing individuals by race. This data includes persons from the 1940 enumeration who refused to declare race.

c = Includes two women, race unknown, imprisoned for begging or drunkenness.

d = Includes three women, race unknown: one died while imprisoned, a second was transferred to another institution, and the third had served out her sentence for theft.

SELECTED GLOSSARY

Africanos Livres - Africans slaves who landed in Brazil after the statute of 1831 declared them free. The law was ignored.

bacharel - A persons with a bachelor's degree.

barão - Baron.

Batalhões Patrioticos (singular *Batalhão Patriótico*) - "Patriotic Battalions" formed during the Bernandes administration to combat the *Coluna* Prestes.

Belle Époque - The "Beautiful Era."

caatinga - The scrub-savanna areas of the Northeast.

caboclo - A "civilized," pure-blooded Indian.

cabra - Usually a strong farm hand or other able-bodied worker who was pressed into service for his master as an assassin. The term is used interchangeably now days with *jagunço* and *capanga*.

cachaça - Sugar-cane bandy.

Calabouço - Jail.

cangaceiro - Normally a member of the rural poor who became an outlaw. Many of these persons did so for reasons of vengeance owing to the absence of justice for the lower classes.

cangaceiros independentes - "Independent bandits."

cangaceiros mansos - "House bandits." That is, outlaws employed by some powerful person or clique.

cangaço - The period of rural banditry that existed mainly in the Northeast until 1940.

capanga - "An armed bodyguard, privately hired. In addition to guarding bodies, he perform[ed] directly terroristic acts on behalf of the landlords when such acts [were] called for." Often used interchangeably with *cabra* and *jagunço*.

capitães do mato - Literally "forest captains," whose main job it was to capture and return runaway slaves and destroy their encampments.

capitão - Captain.

capitão do mato - (singular of *capitães do mato*).

carioca - A person from or something pertaining to the city of Rio de Janeiro.

capoeira - A dancing marshal art form of self-defense originally practiced by slaves.

Casa de Correção - House of Correction or prison.

Casa de Detenção - Literally "House of the Detained."

Catete - A small suburb in Rio de Janeiro where Catete Palace, one of the main presidential mansions, was located.

Central - The customary word used in referring to the Avenida Central (now Avenida Rio Branco) until sometime after 1910. In November of that year, with the completion of the Central Police Station, the term began to be applied to this police facility.

chibata - A special whip studded with nails.

chicote - A "...rawhide knout or whip."

Civilista **campaign** - The celebrated "Put a Civilian in Charge" election of 1909-1910.

classe conservadora - The upper classes.

coiteiro - A provincial individual, not always a *coronel*, who offered protection or assistance, or both, to *cangaceiros* in return for favors.

coluna - Column.

coronel (plural *coronéis*) - Literally "colonel," the word was applied liberally to string-pulling, rural potentates up to the 1930s, as a sign of respect. It does not necessarily imply that one served within the military.

coronelismo - The policies and system of control used by the *coronéis*.

dom - A honorific form of address, equivalent to "sir."

doutor - A term used when referring to a physician or anyone who has attended a university, despite the degree earned or lack of one.

duque - Duke.

escravo de ganho - A synonym for *prêto de ganho*.

fanáticos - A word usually given to destitute rural people who blindly followed a religious personality.

favela - Shantytown.

fazenda - A large, usually rural, estate.

fazendeiro - The landholder of a large estate.

feitor - Overseer.

figurão - A person of eminence.

Força Pública - The *Polícia Militar* in some states.

ferule - (see palmatória)

gaúcho - A man from or something pertaining to the state of Rio Grande do Sul.

geladeira - "The ice box" or large common cell in a police station. The one at the Central Police Station in Rio de Janeiro measured 26'3" x 32'10."

gente de cor - Literally "people of color."

grã-finos - The upper classes.

indígena (plural *indígenas)* - Adjectival of *índio.*

índio (plural *índios*) - A Native Brazilian (Indian).

intendente - A colonial police director whose job was modeled after the eighteenth-century French police system.

jagunço - An individual who did the killing for his bosses that was retained to supervise the slaves on large estates in times of peace. Often used interchangeably with *cabra* and *capanga.*

jogo do bicho - The "Game of the Animals" A tacitly illegal numbers racket that uses numbers and simple animal symbols. It is very popular among Brazil's working-class.

Juizes de Paz - Justices of the Peace.

macacos - "Monkeys" or policemen in Northeastern slang.

mameluco - A person whose parents were Indian and white (also called *mestiço).*

mendigo - Beggar.

mestiço - A person whose parents were Indian and white (also called *mameluco).*

mineiro - A man from or something pertaining to the state of Minas Gerais.

monge - Monk.

mulato - A person of European and African heritage.

O **Réprobo** - "The Reprobate" A nickname for Artur Bernardes.

O **Rolinha** - "The Little Dove" A nickname applied to Artur Bernardes.

Padre - "Father" (Priest).

Padim - *Padre* or "Father" (Priest) in a rural Northeasterner's accent.

palmatória - A holed, wooden paddle, or ferule, used to slap the palm of a hand.

parentela - A kinship network.

patrão (plural *patrões*) - A protector and benefactor.

paulista - A person from or something pertaining to the state of São Paulo.

paulistano - A person from or something pertaining to the city of São Paulo.

pensions d'artistes - Translated verbatim as "artist's hotels," but in fact, upper-class whorehouses.

Polícia Central - The Central Police Station in Rio de Janeiro.

Polícia Civil - "Civilian Police" The main function of this plain clothes police group was to carry out detective work. They were a separate entity from the *Polícia Militar*.

Polícia Militar - Literally "Military Police," these constables were not assigned to maintain order within the armed forces. Rather, they were supposed to provide the services of a regular, uniformed police force protecting the civilian population. They were a separate entity from the *Polícia Civil*, usually under the command of their respective state governors.

povo miserável (plural *povos miserávies*) - Literally "miserable people." A term usually employed by the upper classes to describe the destitute and out-of-work poor.

povão - The great mass of working-class Brazilians. Literally "the people," the word carries an aura of upper-class distaste when used by this latter segment of society.

presidente - Often the leader of something, from a president to state governor to even the head of a department at a university.

presigangas - A word lifted from "press gang" in English.

prêtos de ganho - Slaves who were put out on the streets to earn an income for their masters. Such people were also called *escravos de ganho*.

quilombo - Usually a small community of runaway slaves.

réis - Plural of *real* (royal): the Brazilian monetary unit until 1943. Note that in increments of one-thousand, a dollar sign was placed to the left of the third numeral, despite higher amounts. Ten-thousand *réis*, as an example, was accordingly written 10$000.

retirantes - Drought migrants in/from the Northeast.

Salvações - State governments that were "saved" (established) by the Army to counteract the influence of Pinheiro Machado.

salvo conducto - A "safe conduct" document.

senhor - Mister.

sertanejo - At first, this word referred to peasants from the Northeast. Later, the term was loosely applied to all peasants.

sertão - The arid region in the Northeast.

sub-elites - Situational and transitory muscle providers such as the police, guards, bodyguards, and all types of bullies in the employ of some higher authority.

tenentes - "Lieutenants" Often used in connection with *tenentismo*.

tenentismo - The movement of the "lieutenants" in the 1920s.

termos de bem viver - "Terms of Good Conduct" order.

vadiagem - Literally "vagrancy," but actually used as a catch-all offense for crimes not on the books. At one time, this included prostitution.

vagabundos - Vagabonds.

BIBLIOGRAPHY

For the sake of reference, the names of authors, titles of works, places of publication, and publishers appear exactly as they appeared at the time of publication on the entries listed below. Orthographic reforms between Portugal and Brazil may result in slightly different spellings in the text.

ARCHIVES

Arquivo Artur Bernardes, anonymous letter, n.d., AEL roll 17/1147.

____, document, "Caso das apprenhensões, 27 de maio de 1926," AEL roll 17/1110.

____, document, "Relação dos flagrantes de jogo, cavrados na 2ª Delegacia Auxiliar, 25 de março-3 de abril de 1926," AEL roll 17/1096-100.

____, document, "Relação dos flagrantes de jogo dos bichos, no periodo de 22 de junho de 1925, até a presente data, processados na Segunda Delegacia Auxiliar," AEL roll 17/1139-46.

____, document, "Relação dos individuos recolhidos ao deposito de presos, Policia Central," [March 25-April 3, 1926], AEL roll 17/1101-3.

____, document, "Relatorio apresentado ao Snr. Ministro da Agricultura, Industria e Commercio pelo Director de Secção da Secretaria de Estado Oldemar Murtinho," July 6, 1926, APM dossiê Pr. AB/c. Clevelândia.

____, document, "2ª Delegacia Auxiliar: serviço de repressão ao jogo desde 22 de julho de 1925," AEL roll 17/1136-38.

____, letter, "Carlos da Silva Reis to Fontoura," April 1925, AEL roll 16/2234-35.

____, letter, "Carolina Bastos Schomaker to Arthur Bernardes," [December 1925], APM dossiê Pr. AB/polícia.

____, letter, "Dionysio Bentes to Arthur Bernardes," July 15, 1925, AEL roll 14/8-9.

____, letter, "Fontoura to [Renato] Bittencourt," March 31, 1926, AEL roll 17/1105.

____, letter, "João Chaves to Pedro Goytacazes," May 11, 1926, AEL roll 17/1942.

____, letter, "Manoel Lopes Carneiro da Fontoura to Arthur Bernardes," April 9, 1926, AEL roll 17/1127-28.

____, letter, "Renato Bittencourt to Chief of Police [Fontoura]," April 3, 1926, AEL roll 17/1104.

____, letter, "Renato Bittencourt to Chief of Police [Fontoura]," April 5, 1926, AEL roll 17/1095.

____, miscellaneous document, AEL roll 17/1105.

____, miscellaneous document, AEL roll 17/1106.

____, miscellaneous document, AEL roll 17/1107.

_____, miscellaneous document, AEL roll 17/1108.

_____, miscellaneous document, AEL roll 17/1109.

_____, newspaper article, "*Gazeta de Noticias*," April 10, 1926, AEL roll 17/1111.

_____, photograph, "Clevelandia in 1926," AEL roll 23/1037.

_____, photograph, "Clevelandia in 1926," AEL roll 23/1038.

_____, photograph, "Radio Station on Trindade," AEL roll 21/175-76.

_____, photographs, "Clevelandia in 1926," AEL roll 23/1033-106.

_____, telegram, "Agamenon [Magalhães] to Affonso Penna," February 1926, AEL roll 20/865-67.

_____, telegram, "Borba to Minister of Justice and Internal Affairs," February 11, 1926, AEL roll 20/868-69.

_____, telegram, "Felix Pacheco to Teffe," December 6, 1924, AEL roll 17/2178.

_____, telegram, "[Pedro de] Toledo to Arthur Bernardes," April 22, 1925, AEL roll 16/1018.

_____, telegram, "Sergio Loreto to Arthur Bernardes," February 10, 1926, AEL roll 20/877.

_____, telegram, "Sergio Loreto to Arthur Bernardes," February 12, 1926, AEL roll 20/870.

_____, telegram, "Teffe to Felix Pacheco," December 5, 1924, AEL roll 17/ 2177.

_____, telegram, "Teffe to Felix Pacheco," December 8, 1924, AEL roll 17/ 2179.

_____, telegram, "Tertuliano Potyguara to Arthur Bernardes," November 7, 1926, AEL roll 16/2501.

Arquivo Augusto do Amaral Peixoto, photograph, "Prisoners Waiting for Ships to Arrive, Fundação Getúlio Vargas/CPDOC, 004/4.

Arquivo do Departamento de Ordem Política e Social-Rio de Janeiro, document, "O proletariado e o movimento nacional-libertador (feita por um 'leader syndical [']'), " [1936?], comunismo/pasta 20.

_____, document, "Palestra de um marinheiro na commemoração de *Revolta de João Candido*," [1936?], comunismo/pasta 20.

_____, newspaper article, "*Imprensa Popular*," October 10, 1954, comunismo/pasta 3.

_____, newspaper article, "*Imprensa Popular*," October 19, 1954, comunismo/pasta 3.

_____, newspaper article, "*Juventude*," June 15, 1935, comunismo/pasta 4B.

_____, newspaper article, "*O Trabalhador Graphico*," February 7, 1928, comunismo /pasta 4B.

_____, newspaper article, "*O Trabalhador Graphico*," May 4, 1929, comunismo/ pasta 4B.

_____, newspaper article, "*Tribuna da Imprensa*," May 25, 1971, comunismo/pasta 103.

_____, newspaper article, "*Unidade Proletária*," December 1975, supplement, comunismo/pasta 144.

Arquivo José Americo, letter, "Manoel Batista de Moraes ['Antonio Silvino'] to

José Americo de Almeida," April 26, 1939, CR, document 119.

Arquivo Maurício de Lacerda, newspaper article, "*A Rua*," July 12, 1927, AEL roll 2/107-108.

____, newspaper article, "*O Combate*," February 2, 1928, AEL roll 2/79.

____, newspaper article, "Washington-Bernardes: a fatalidade da politica professional," n.p., n.d., AEL roll 2/28a.

Arquivo Nacional, document, Cx. 6C5/GIFI.

____, document, Cx. 1731/1927/Proc. 1992/27.

____, document, Cx. 1907/1929/Proc. 199.

____, document, Cx. 1922/1927/Proc. 1992.

Arquivo Pedro Ernesto Batista, photograph, "Prison Complex on Trindade Island," Fundação Getúlio Vargas/CPDOC, 012/31.

Biblioteca Nacional, Rio de Janeiro, Manuscritos, document, C 453, 10 n. 1-2.

____, newspaper fragment, *Critica*, "A inominavel violencia da policia na noite de São Sylvestre."

____, newspaper fragment, *Critica*, "Continúam, no palacio sinistro da Rua da Relação, os mesmos processos dos tempos do 'Marechal Escuridão'!"

____, newspaper fragment, *Critica*, "O governo mais infame que ainda viu o nosso paiz ."

Centro de Pesquisa e Documentação de História Contemporânea do Brasil, oral history, "Abelardo Jurema," 1977.

____, oral history, "Nélson de Melo," 1978-1979.

____, oral history, "Osvaldo Trigueiro," 1977.

Generosa Alencar Papers, telegram, "Floro [Bartolomeu da Costa] to José Ferreira [de Menezes]" January 23, 1926.

____, telegram, "General Pinheiro Machado to *Padre* Cícero Romão Batista," December 16, 1913.

Memorial Padre Cícero, letter, "*Padre* Cícero Romão Batista to Captain Luís Carlos Prestes," n.m., 1926, exhibit 104.

____, photograph, "*Coronel* Marcos Rabelo em 1914," exhibit 42.

____, photograph, "Padre Cícero e seu secretário Benjamin Abrahão em 1925," exhibit 75.

United Kingdom, Public Records Office, letter, "[Arthur] Abbott to Seeds," February 4, 1935, no. 5, FO 371/18655.

United States, Central Intelligence Agency, document, "Brazil," November 30, 1948, SR-17.

____, National Archives, document, "The Military Attache, Brazil, G-2 Report: 1170," February 11, 1925, no. 427, MID 2052-105.

____, National Archives, letter, "Barclay to G-2," May 21, 1927, no. 732, MID 2052-112.

____, National Archives, letter, "Barclay to G-2," June 30, 1926, no. 589, MID 2052-108/6.

____, National Archives, letter, "Jordan to director of Military Intelligence," September 12, 1919, no. 265, MID 2052-84.

_____, National Archives, letter, "Sackville to G-2," April 17, 1936, no. 1634, MID 2657-K-70/34.

CONFERENCE PRESENTATIONS

Camargo, Aspásia, "Tenentismo," comments delivered before the seminar "Cenários de 1922," Fundação Getúlio Vargas/CPDOC, Rio de Janeiro, November 19, 1992.

Fritsch, Winston, "Crise econômica," comments delivered to the seminar "Cenários de 1922," Fundação Getúlio Vargas/CPDOC, Rio de Janeiro, November 19, 1992.

Hall, Michael and Paulo Sérgio Pinheiro, "The Control and Policing of the Working Class in Brazil," paper presented to the Conference on the History of Law, Labor and Crime, University of Warwick, September 15-18, 1983.

FILMS AND TELEVISION PROGRAMS

A Revolução de 30, directed by Silvio Beck, 1980.

"Canudos," TV Educativa, October 9, 1987.

"Fantástico," Rede Globo, February 21, 1988.

João Cândido: O Almirante Negro, directed by Emiliano Ribeiro, 1987.

"Telecine Brasil," TV Educativa, February 18, 1989.

GOVERNMENT AND OFFICIAL PUBLICATIONS

Brazil, *Annaes da Camara dos Deputados*, Rio de Janeiro: Nacional, 1905, July 27, 1905.

_____, *Anuário estatístico do Brasil, 1992*, Rio de Janeiro: IBGE, 1993.

_____, *Codigo criminal do Imperio do Brasil*, 3rd ed., Ouro Preto: Silva, 1831.

_____, *Coleção das leis de 1985: atos do poder legislativo e atos legislativos do poder executivo, leis de julho a setembro*, Brasília: Nacional, 1985, vol. v.

_____, *Collecção das leis da Republica dos Estados Unidos do Brazil de 1902*, Rio de Janeiro: Nacional, 1903, vol. i.

_____, *Collecção das leis da Republica dos Estados Unidos do Brazil de 1907*, Rio de Janeiro: Nacional, 1908, vol. i.

_____, *Collecção das leis da Republica dos Estados Unidos do Brazil de 1913*, Rio de Janeiro; Nacional, 1916, vol. i.

_____, *Collecção das leis do Brazil de 1808*, Rio de Janeiro: Nacional, 1891.

_____, *Collecção das leis do Imperio do Brasil, desde a independencia: 1832 e 1833*, Ouro Preto: Silva, 1833, vol. iv.

_____, *Collecção das leis e resoluções da assemblea legislativa da Bahia, sanccionadas e publicadas nos annos de 1835 a 1838*, Bahia: Antonio Olavo da

França Guerra, 1862, vol. i.

____, *Collecção de decretos, cartas imperiaes e alvarás do Imperio do Brazil de 1825*, Rio de Janeiro: Nacional, 1885.

____, Conselho Nacional de Estatística, *Anuário estatístico do Brasil, 1939-1940*, Rio de Janeiro: IBGE, 1941.

____, Conselho Nacional de Estatística, *Ferrovias do Brasil*, Rio de Janeiro: IBGE, 1956.

____, Conselho Nacional de Estatística, *O Brasil em números*, Rio de Janeiro: IBGE, 1966, vol. ii.

____, *Constituição [da] República Federativa do Brasil 1988*, Brasília: Centro Gráfico do Senado Federal, 1988.

____, Estado-Maior do Exercito, *Almanak do ministerio da guerra, 1921*, Rio de Janeiro: Imprensa Militar, 1921.

____, Instituto Brasileiro de Geografia e Estatística, *Censo demográfico: população e habitação* [, *1940*], Rio de Janeiro: IBGE, 1950, Série Nacional, vol. ii.

____, Instituto Brasileiro de Geografia e Estatística, *IBGE revela: do total da população brasileira, 21% são indigentes (isto equivale à população Argentina)*, Rio de Janeiro: IBEG, 1994, informação para a imprensa, texto no. 73.

____, Instituto Brasileiro de Geografia e Estatística, *Repertório estatístico do Brasil: quadros retrospectivos no. 1*, Rio de Janeiro: IBGE, 1941.

____, Ministerio da Agricultura, Industria e Commercio, *Annuario estatistico do Brazil, 1908-1912*, Rio de Janeiro: Directoria Geral de Estatistica, 1916, vols. i, iii.

____, Ministerio da Agricultura, Industria e Commercio, *Relatorio*, Rio de Janeiro: Directoria Geral de Estatistica, 1928.

____, Ministério da Educação e Cultura, *Obras completas de Rui Barbosa: discursos parlamentares*, Rio de Janeiro: Fundação Casa Rui Barbosa, 1977, vol. xxxviii, 1911, book i.

____, Ministério da Educação e Cultura, *Obras completas de Rui Barbosa: discursos parlamentares*, Rio de Janeiro: Fundação Casa Rui Barbosa, 1981, vol. xlii, 1915, book ii.

____, Ministério da Educação e Saúde, *Obras completas de Rui Barbosa: discursos parlamentares*, Fernando Nery (ed.), Rio de Janeiro: n.p, 1952, vol. xxxi, 1904, book i.

____, Ministerio da Industria, Viação e Obras Publicas, *Sexo, raça e estado civil, nacionalidade, filiação, culto e analphabetismo da população recenseada em 31 de dezembro de 1890*, Rio de Janeiro: Directoria Geral de Estatistica, 1898.

____, Ministerio da Justiça e Negocios Interiores, *Relatorio*, Rio de Janeiro: Directoria de Estatistica Geral, 1936.

____, Policia do Districto Federal, Gabinete de Identificação e de Estatistica, *Estatistica de 1909*, Rio de Janeiro: Nacional, 1910.

208

____, Policia do Districto Federal, Gabinete de Identificação e de Estatistica, *Estatistica policial e criminal de 1910*, Rio de Janeiro: Nacional, 1915.

____, Policia do Districto Federal, Gabinete de Identificação e de Estatistica, *Estatistica policial e criminal de 1911*, Rio de Janeiro: Nacional, 1917.

____, Policia do Districto Federal, Gabinete de Identificação e de Estatistica, *Estatistica policial e criminal de 1912*, Rio de Janeiro: Nacional, 1918.

____, *Recenseamento do Brazil: população*, Rio de Janeiro: Directoria Geral de Estatistica, 1930, vol. iv.

____, *Relatorios, 1928 e 1929*, Rio de Janeiro: Directoria Geral de Estatistica, 1930.

____, São Paulo, lei no. 2034 of December 30, 1924.

____, Senado Federal, *Constituições do Brasil de 1824, 1891, 1934, 1937, 1946 e 1967 e suas alterações*, Brasília: Subsecretaria de Edições Técnicas, 1986, vol. i.

INTERVIEWS

Alencar, Generosa, interviews, Juazeiro do Norte, May 11, 1993; May 13, 1993; and Rio de Janeiro/Juazeiro do Norte, April 25, 1993.

Anonymous-3, interviews, Rio de Janeiro, June 14, 1990; June 16, 1990; and December 1, 1991.

Benevides, Aldenor Alencar, interview, Juazeiro do Norte, May 12, 1993.

Corrêa, Cristiana de Araujo, interviews, Rio de Janeiro, June 17, 1994; and June 23, 1994.

Costa, Raimundo Porfirio, interview, Rio de Janeiro, June 9, 1993.

Lustosa, Isabel, interview, Rio de Janeiro, March 24, 1993.

Marques, Daniel Walker Almeida, interview, Juazeiro do Norte, May 13, 1993.

Menezes, Fátima, interviews, Juazeiro do Norte, May 11, 1993; May 12, 1993; May 13, 1993; Rio de Janeiro/Juazeiro do Norte, April 26, 1993; April 30, 1993; and June 3, 1993.

Moraes Filho, Manoel Batista de, interviews, Pirassununga, January 10, 1993; and Rio de Janeiro/Pirassununga, August 17, 1987.

Moraes, Severino Batista de, interviews, João Pessoa, May 15, 1993; Rio de Janeiro/Itabatinga, May 6, 1993; June 4, 1993; and July 8, 1993.

Oliveria, João, interview, Juazeiro do Norte, May 11, 1993.

Oliveria, Júlio Cesar Cruz de, interview, João Pessoa, May 15, 1993.

Pedeira, Waldecy Catharina Magalhães, interviews, Rio de Janeiro, June 30, 1994; and October 18, 1994.

Prestes, Luís Carlos, interview, Rio de Janeiro, August 13, 1987.

Prestes, Lygia, interview, Rio de Janeiro, August 6, 1994.

Sá, Denise, interview, Rio de Janeiro, June 1, 1993.

Sevcenko, Nicolau, interview, Rio de Janeiro/São Paulo, February 28, 1985.

Sveri, Knut, interview, Stockholm, April 10, 1985.

LETTERS

Azevedo, Miguel Ângelo de, letter, October 27, 1992.
Benevides, Aldenor Alencar, letter, May 14, 1993.
Menezes, Fátima, letters, April 26, 1993; and July 1, 1993.
Moraes, Severino Batista de, letter [postmarked] July 5, 1993.

NEWSPAPERS AND PERIODICALS

A Illustração Brazileira (Rio de Janeiro), 1911.
A Noite Illustrada (Rio de Janeiro), 1938.
A Noite (Rio de Janeiro), 1926-1927.
A Noticia (Rio de Janeiro), 1904.
A Plebe (São Paulo), 1923-1927.
A Rua (Rio de Janeiro), 1921-1927.
A Vida Fluminense (Rio de Janeiro), 1870.
A Voz do Trabalhador (Rio de Janeiro), 1915.
Correio da Manhã (Rio de Janeiro), 1905-1957.
Critica (Rio de Janeiro) 1928-1929.
Diario de Noticias (Rio de Janeiro), 1935.
Diário do Nordeste (Fortaleza), 1993.
Diario Illustrado (Rio de Janeiro), 1910.
Fatos e Fotos (Rio de Janeiro), 1962.
Folha de São Paulo, 1987-1996.
Fon-Fon (Rio de Janeiro), 1909.
Gazeta de Noticias (Rio de Janeiro), 1904-1926.
Imprensa Popular (Rio de Janeiro), 1954.
Isto É (São Paulo), 1987-1988.
Isto É Senhor (São Paulo), 1990.
Jornal do Brasil (Rio de Janeiro), 1973-1994.
Jornal do Commercio (Rio de Janeiro), 1830-1926.
Jornal do Recife, 1898.
Jornal O Povo (São Paulo), 1926.
Juventude (Rio de Janeiro), 1935.
Manchete (Rio de Janeiro), 1978.
New Orleans Price Current, and Commercial Intelligencer, 1835.
Newsweek (New York), 1997.
O Combate (Rio de Janeiro), 1928.
O Combate (São Paulo), 1919.
O Cruzeiro (Rio de Janeiro), 1947-1964.
O Dia (Rio de Janeiro), 1974.
O Gato (Rio de Janeiro), 1911.
O Globo (Rio de Janeiro), 1926-1997.

210

O Ideal (Juazeiro do Norte), 1924-1925.
O Jornal (Rio de Janeiro), 1928-1968.
O Malho (Rio de Janeiro), 1904-1926.
O Trabalhador Graphico (São Paulo), 1928-1929.
Progresso (São Paulo), 1928.
Revista da Semana (Rio de Janeiro), 1925.
Revista Illustrada (Rio de Janeiro), 1885-1886.
Tribuna da Imprensa (Rio de Janeiro), 1971.
Última Hora (Rio de Janeiro), 1973.
Unidade Proletária (Rio de Janeiro), 1975.

PUBLICATIONS, MANUSCRIPTS AND DISSERTATIONS

Adamo, Sam, "The Broken Promise: Race, Health, and Justice in Rio de Janeiro, 1890-1940," unpublished PhD thesis, Department of History, University of New Mexico, 1983.

Albuquerque, Ulysses Lins de, *Moxotó brabo*, Rio de Janeiro: Simões, 1960.

____, *Um sertanejo e o sertão*, Rio de Janeiro: José Olympio, 1957.

Alden, Dauril, *Royal Government in Colonial Brazil: with Special Reference to the Administration of the Marquis of Lavradio, 1769-1779*, Berkeley: University of California Press, 1968.

Alexander, Robert, "Brazilian *Tenentismo*," *A Century of Brazilian History Since 1865: Issues and Problems*, Richard Graham (ed.), New York: Alfred Knopf, 1969.

Algranti, Leila Mezan, "Slave Crimes: the Use of Police Power to Control the Slave Population of Rio de Janeiro," *Luso-Brazilian Review*, vol. xxv, no. 1, Summer 1988.

Almeida, Candido Mendes de (ed.), *Codigo philippino ou ordenações e leis do Reino de Portugal recopiladas por mandado d'El-Rey D. Philippe I*, 14th ed., Rio de Janeiro: Instituto Philomathico, 1870, book v.

Almeida, José Américo de, *A Parahyba e seus problemas*, Parahyba: Imprensa Official, 1923.

Almeida, Manuel Antônio de, *Memórias de um sargento de milícias*, São Paulo: Martins, 1941.

Alves, Marcio Moreira, *A Grain of Mustard Seed: the Awakening of the Brazilian Revolution*, Garden City, NY: Doubleday Anchor, 1973.

Amado, Jorge, *A vida de Luís Carlos Prestes: O Cavaleiro da Esperança*, 4th ed., São Paulo: Martins, 1945.

____, *Terras do sem fim*, 45th ed., Rio de Janeiro: Record, 1981.

____, *The Violent Land*, Samuel Putnam (trans.), 4th ed., New York: Avon, 1979.

(Anonymous), *Brazil: its History, People, Natural Productions, etc.*, London: Religious Tract Society, 1860.

(Anonymous), "Evolução da conjuntura no Brasil de 1916 a 1929," *Conjuntura*

211

Econômica, no. 11, November 1948.

Araujo, Antonio Amaury Corrêa de, *Assim morreu Lampião*, Rio de Janeiro: Brasília/Rio, 1976.

Arquivo Público do Estado do Rio de Janeiro, *Os arquivos das polícias políticas: reflexos de nossa história contemporânea*, Rio de Janeiro: FAPERJ, 1994.

Arraes, Miguel, *Brazil: the People and the Power*, Lancelot Sheppard (trans.), Middlesex: Penguin, 1972.

Arruda, Marcos, *et al.*, *The Multinational Corporations and Brazil: the Impact of Multinational Corporations in the Contemporary Brazilian Economy*, Toronto: Latin American Research Unit, 1975.

Asfora, Permínio, *Vento Nordeste*, Rio de Janeiro: José Olympio, 1957.

Aufderheide, Patricia, "Order and Violence: Social Deviance and Social Control in Brazil, 1780-1840," unpublished PhD thesis, Department of History, University of Minnesota, 1976.

Azevedo, Moreira de, *O Rio de Janeiro: sua história, monumentos, homens notáveis, usos e curiosidades*, 3rd ed., Rio de Janeiro: Brasiliana, 1969, vol. ii.

Baptista, Francisco das Chagas, *História completa de Antonio Silvino: sua vida de crimes e seu julgamento*, Sebastião Nunes Batista (ed.), Rio de Janeiro: H. Antunes, 1960.

Barbosa, Severino, *Antônio Silvino: "O Rifle de Ouro,"* Recife: Editôra de Pernambuco, 1977.

Barman, Roderick, "The Brazilian Peasantry Reexamined: the Implications of the Quebra-Quilo Revolt, 1874-1875," *Hispanic American Historical Review*, vol. lvii, no. 3, August 1977.

Barreto, [Afonso Henriques de] Lima, *Diário íntimo: memórias*, São Paulo: Brasiliense, 1956.

Barreto Filho, [João Paulo de] Mello and Hermeto Lima, *História da Polícia do Rio de Janeiro, aspectos da cidade e da vida carioca, 1565-1831*, Rio de Janeiro: S.A.A. Noite, 1939.

Basbaum, Leôncio, *Uma vida em seis tempos: memórias*, São Paulo: Alfa-Omega, 1976.

Beattie, Peter, "Exacting the Tribute of Blood: Army Impressment and the Troop Trade in Brazil, 1850-1916," pre-publication manuscript.

____, "National Identity and the Brazilian Folk: the *Sertanejo* in Taunay's *A retirada da Luguna*," *Review of Latin American Studies*, vol. iv, no. 1, 1991.

Bello, José Maria, *A History of Modern Brazil, 1889-1964*, Stanford: Stanford University Press, 1968.

____, *História da República, 1889-1954*, 4th ed., São Paulo: Nacional, 1959.

Beloch, Israel and Alzira Alves de Abreu (coords.), *Dicionário histórico-biográfico brasileiro, 1930-1983*, Rio de Janeiro: Forense-Universitária, 1984.

Bemis, Samuel, *A Diplomatic History of the United States*, New York: Holt, 1936.

Benci, Jorge, *Economia Cristã dos senhores no governo de escravos: livro bra-*

212

sileiro de 1700, 2nd ed., Serafim Leite (ed.), Porto: Apostolado, 1954.

Bethell, Leslie and José Murilo de Carvalho, "1822-1850," *Brazil: Empire and Republic, 1822-1930*, Leslie Bethell (ed.), New York: Cambridge University Press, 1989.

Bethell, Leslie, *The Abolition of the Brazilian Slave Trade: Britain, Brazil and the Slave Trade Question, 1807-1869*, Cambridge: Cambridge University Press, 1970.

____, "The Independence of Brazil," *Brazil: Empire and Republic, 1822-1930*, Leslie Bethell (ed.), New York: Cambridge University Press, 1989.

Blok, Anton, *The Mafia of a Sicilian Village, 1860-1960: a Study of Violent Peasant Entrepreneurs*, Oxford: Blackwell, 1974.

____, "The Peasant and the Brigand: Social Banditry Reconsidered," *Comparative Studies of Society and History*, vol. xiv, no. 4, September 1972.

Boxer, Charles, *Race Relations in the Portuguese Colonial Empire, 1415-1825*, Oxford: Clarendon, 1963.

____, *The Golden Age of Brazil, 1695-1750: Growing Pains of a Colonial Society*, Berkeley: University of California Press, 1962.

Brasil, Geason, *História das ruas do Rio de Janeiro*, 4th ed., Rio de Janeiro: Brasiliana, 1965.

Brasio, Antonio (ed.), *Monumenta missionaria africana: Africa Ocidental (1469-1599), suplemento ao século xv e xvi*, Lisbon: Agencia Geral de Ultramar, 1954, vol. iv.

____, *Monumenta missionaria africana*, 2nd ser., Lisbon: Agencia Geral de Ultramar, 1958-1964, vol. ii.

Bretas, Marcos Luiz, "A guerra das ruas: povo e polícia na cidade do Rio de Janeiro," unpublished Master's thesis, Departamento de Ciencias Politicas, Instituto Universitário de Pesquisas, 1988.

____, "Policiar a cidade republicana," *OAB/RJ*, no. 22, July 1985.

Britto, [José Gabriel de] Lemos, *Os systemas penitenciarios do Brasil*, Rio de Janeiro: Nacional, 1925, vol. ii.

Brockwell, Charles, *The Natural and Political History of Portugal: from...1090 Down to the Present Time...to Which is Added, the History of Brazil, and All Other Dominions Subject to the Crown of Portugal in Asia, Africa, and America*, London: T. Warner, 1726.

Burns, E. Bradford, *A History of Brazil*, New York: Columbia University Press, 1970.

____, "As relações internacionais do Brasil durante a Primeira República," *História geral da civilização brasileira: o Brasil republicano: sociedade e instituições, 1889-1930*, 2nd ed., Boris Fausto (dir.), Rio de Janeiro: Difel/ Difusão, 1978, book iii, vol. ii.

Cabral, Oswaldo, *História de Santa Catarina*, 2nd ed., Rio de Janeiro: Laudes, 1970.

Cabral, Tomé, *Novo dicionário de termos e expressões populares*, Fortaleza:

Edições UFC, 1982.

Callcott, Maria [Dundas] Graham, *Journal of a Voyage to Brazil and Residence There during Part of the Years 1821, 1822, 1823*, London: Longman *et al.*, 1824.

Calmon, Pedro, *História do Brasil: século xx a República e o desenvolvimento*, Rio de Janeiro: José Olympio, 1959, vol. vi.

Cancelli, Elizabeth, "O poder da polícia e o mundo da prisão na era Vargas (1930-1945)," pre-publication manuscript.

Carneiro, Glauco, *História das revoluções brasileiras*, Rio de Janeiro: Cruzeiro, 1965, vol. i.

Carneiro, Maria Luiza Tucci, *Preconceito racial: Portugal e Brasil-colônia*, 2nd ed., São Paulo: Brasiliense, 1988.

Carone, Edgard, *A República Velha: evolução política*, São Paulo: Difusão Européia do Livro, 1971, vol. ii.

Carvalho, José Murilo de, *Os bestializados: o Rio de Janeiro e a república que não foi*, São Paulo: Companhia das Letras, 1987.

Carvalho, Rodrigues de, *Serrote prêto: Lampião e seus sequazes*, Rio de Janeiro: Sociedade Editôra e Gráfica, 1961.

____, *Serrote prêto: Lampião e seus sequazes*, 2nd ed., Rio de Janeiro: Gráficos e Editores, 1974.

Cava, Ralph della, *Miracle at Joaseiro*, New York: Columbia University Press, 1970.

Cendrars, Blaise [Frédéric Sauser], *Etc..., etc... (um livro 100% brasileiro)*, Teresa Thiériot (trans. and ed.), São Paulo: Perspectiva, 1976.

Chalhoub, Sidney, *et al.*, "Trabalho escravo e trabalho livre na cidade do Rio: vivência de libertos, 'galegos' e mulheres pobres," *Revista Brasileira de História*, vol. lv, nos. 8-9, September 1984-April 1985.

Chalhoub, Sidney, *Trabalho, lar e botequim: o cotidiano dos trabalhadores no Rio de Janeiro da Belle Époque*, São Paulo: Brasiliense, 1986.

Chamberlain, Henry, *Views and Costumes of the City and Neighbourhood of Rio de Janeiro, Brazil: from Drawings Taken by Lieutenant Chamberlain, Royal Artillery, during the Years 1819 and 1820 with Descriptive Explanations*, London: Thomas McLean, 1822.

Chandler, Billy Jaynes, *The Bandit King: Lampião of Brazil*, College Station: Texas A&M University Press, 1978.

Chandler, Wayne, "The Moor: Light of Europe's Dark Age," *African Presence in Early Europe*, Ivan van Sertima (ed.), New Brunswick: Transaction, 1985.

Chevalier, Tenente [Carlos Saldanha da Gama], *Memórias de um revoltoso ou legalista?*, n.p.: n.p., n.y.

Chiavenato, Julio José, *Cabanagem: o povo no poder*, São Paulo: Brasiliense, 1984.

____, *Cangaço: a força do coronel*, São Paulo: Brasiliense, 1990.

Civita, Victor (ed.), *Nosso século, 1900-1910: A Era dos Bacharéis*, São Paulo:

214

Abril Cultural, 1985, part i, vol. i.

___, *Nosso século, 1900-1910: A Era dos Bacharéis*, São Paulo: Abril Cultural, 1985, part ii, vol. ii.

___, *Nosso século, 1910-1930: anos de crise e criação*, São Paulo: Abril Cultural, 1985, part i, vol. iii.

___, *Nosso século, 1910-1930: anos de crise e criação*, São Paulo: Abril Cultural, 1985, part ii, vol. iv.

___, *Nosso século, 1945-1960: A Era dos Partidos*, São Paulo: Abril Cultural, 1985, part ii, vol. viii.

Conniff, Michael, *Urban Politics in Brazil: the Rise of Populism, 1925-1945*, Pittsburgh: University of Pittsburgh Press, 1981.

Conrad, Robert, *Children of God's Fire: a Documentary History of Black Slavery in Brazil*, Princeton: Princeton University Press, 1983.

___, "Nineteenth-Century Brazilian Slavery," *Slavery and Race Relations in Latin America*, Robert Toplin (ed.), Westport, CT.: Greenwood, 1974.

___, *The Destruction of Brazilian Slavery, 1850-1888*, Berkley: University of California Press, 1972.

Corwin, Arthur, "Afro-Brazilians: Myths and Realities," *Slavery and Race Relationships in Latin America*, Robert Toplin (ed.), Westport, CT.: Greenwood, 1974.

Costa, Emilia Viotti da, "The Portuguese-African Slave Trade: a Lesson in Colonialism," *Latin American Perspectives*, vol. xii, no. 1, Issue 44, Winter 1985.

Coutinho, José Joaquim da Cunha de Azeredo, *Concordancia das leis de Portugal, e das bullas Pontificias, das quaes humas permittem a escravidão dos pretos d'Africa, e outras prohibem a escravidão dos indios do Brazil*, Lisbon: João Rodrigues Neves, 1808.

Craig, Neville, *Estrada de ferro Madeira-Mamoré: história trágica de uma expedição*, Moacir Vasconcelos (trad.), Rio de Janeiro: Nacional, 1947.

Cruz, Heloísa de Faria, "Mercado e polícia - São Paulo, 1890-1915," *Revista Brasileira de História*, vol. vii, no. 14, March-August 1987.

Cunha, Euclides da, *Os Sertões*, 22nd ed., São Paulo and Belo Horizonte: Francisco Alves, 1952.

Cunha, Manuela Carneiro da, *Negros, estrangeiros: os escravos libertos e sua volta à África*, São Paulo: Brasiliense, 1985.

Dallari, Dalmo de Abreu, "The *Força Pública* of São Paulo in State and National Politics," *Perspectives on Armed Politics in Brazil*, Henry Keith and Robert Hayes (eds.), Tempe: Arizona State University Press, 1976.

Darwin, Charles, *The Voyage of the Beagle*, New York: Collier, 1909.

Daus, Ronald, *Der epische Zyklus der Cangaceiros in der Volkspoesie Nordostbrasiliens*, Berlin: Colloquium, 1969.

Debret, Jean, *Voyage pittoresque et historique au Brésil*, Paris: Frères, 1835, vol. ii.

Denis, Pierre, *Le Brésil au xxᵉ siècle*, Paris: Armand Colin, 1909.

215

Diacon, Todd, "Down and Out in Rio de Janeiro: Urban Poor and Elite Rule in the Old Republic," *Latin American Research Review*, vol. xxv, no. 1, 1990.

_____, *Millenarian Vision, Capitalist Reality: Brazil's Contestado Rebellion, 1912-1916*, Durham: Duke University Press, 1991.

_____, "The Search for Meaning in an Histroical Context: Popular Religion, Millenarianism, and the Contestado Rebellion," *Luso-Brazilian Review*, vol. xxviii, no. 1, Summer 1991.

Dias, Everardo, *Bastilhas modernas, 1924-1926*, São Paulo: Obras Sociaes e Literarias, 1926.

_____, *História das lutas sociais no Brasil*, 2nd ed, São Paulo: Alfa-Omega, 1977.

_____, *Memorias de um exilado: episodios de uma deportação*, São Paulo: n.p., 1920

Dulles, John W.F., *Anarchists and Communists in Brazil, 1900-1935*, Austin: University of Texas Press, 1973.

_____, *Vargas of Brazil: a Political Biography*, Austin: University of Texas Press, 1967.

Dunlop, Charles, *Chronicas: fatos, gente e coisas da nossa história*, Rio de Janeiro: Americana, 1973.

Edmundo, Luiz, *O Rio de Janeiro no tempo dos vice-reis*, 4th ed., Rio de Janeiro: Conquista, 1956, vol. i.

El-Khatib, Said Mohamad (ed.), *História de Santa Catarina*, Curitiba: Grafipar, 1970, vol. i.

Enciclopédia Mirador Internacional, São Paulo: Encyclopaedia Britannica do Brasil, 1975.

Encyclopædia Britannica, 15th ed., Chicago: Encyclopædia Britannica, 1994, Micropædia, vols. ii, ix.

Ewbank, Thomas, *Life in Brazil: Or a Visit to the Land of the Cocoa and the Palm*, New York: Harper, 1856.

Facó, Rui, *Cangaceiros e fanáticos: gênese e lutas*, Rio de Janeiro: Civilização Brasileira, 1963.

Fausto, Boris, *A Revolução de 1930, historiografia e história*, 9th ed., São Paulo: Brasiliense, 1983.

_____, *Crime e cotidiano: a criminalidade em São Paulo, 1880-1924*, São Paulo: Brasiliense, 1984.

Fernandes, Florestan, *The Negro in Brazilian Society*, Phyllis Eveleth (ed.), Jacqueline Skiles, A. Brunel and Arthur Rothwell (trans.), New York: Columbia University Press, 1969.

Ferreira, Jose Carlos, "As insurreições dos africanos na Bahia," *Revista do Instituto Geográfico e Histórico da Bahia*, vol. x, no. 29, 1903.

Fico, Carlos, "Movimentos de resistência na Primeira Repúlica: abastecimento e serviços na cidade do Rio de Janeiro," pre-publication manuscript.

Flory, Thomas, "Judicial Politics in Nineteenth-Century Brazil," *Hispanic American Historical Review*, vol. lv, no. 4, November 1975.

Fontenelle, Oscar Penna, *Problemas policiaes*, Rio de Janeiro: Jornal do Commercio, 1927.

Franco, Afonso Arinos de Melo, *Rodrigues Alves: apogeu e declínio do presidencialismo*, Rio de Janeiro: José Olympio, 1973, vol. i.

Freire Junior, [Francisco José] and Caréca [Luís Nunes Sampaio], "Ai seu mé"; and *Enciclopédia da música brasileira: erudita, folclórica e popular*, São Paulo: Art, 1977.

French, John, "Industrial Workers and the Birth of the Populist Republic in Brazil, 1945-1946," *Latin American Perspectives*, vol. xvi, no. 4, Fall 1989.

Freyre, Gilberto, in Felix Cavalcanti de Albuquerque Mello, *Memorias de um Cavalcanti: trechos do livro de assentos de Felix Cavalcanti de Mello (1821/1901) escolhidos e annotados pelo seu bisneto Diogo de Mello Menezes*, São Paulo: Nacional, 1940.

Freyre, Gilberto, *O escravo nos anúncios de jornais brasileiros do século xix*, Recife: Universitária, 1963.

____, *Order and Progress: Brazil from Monarchy to Republic*, Rod Horton (ed. and trans.), New York: Alfred Knopf, 1970.

____, *The Mansions and the Shanties: the Making of Modern Brazil*, Harriet de Onis (ed. and trans.), New York: Alfred Knopf, 1963.

____, *The Masters and the Slaves: a Study in the Development of Brazilian Civilization*, Samuel Putnam (trans.), 2nd ed., New York: Alfred Knopf, 1966.

Gardner, George, *Travels in the Interior of Brazil: Principally through the Northern Provinces and the Gold and Diamond Districts, during the Years 1836-1841*, London: Reeve, 1846.

Góis, Joaquim, *Lampião: o último cangaceiro*, Aracaju: Regina, 1966.

Goulart, José Alípio, *Da palmatória ao patíbulo: castigos de escravos no Brasil*, Rio de Janeiro: Conquista, 1971.

Graham, Sandra Lauderdale, "The Vintem Riot and Political Culture: Rio de Janeiro, 1880," *Hispanic American Historical Review*, vol. lx, no. 3, August 1980.

Gueiros, Optato, *Lampeão: memórias de um oficial ex-combatente de fôrças volantes*, 1st ed., Recife: Gráfica, 1953.

____, *Lampeão: memórias de um oficial ex-comandante de forças volantes*, 4th ed., Salvador: Progresso, 1956.

Hahner, June, *Civilian-Military Relations in Brazil, 1889-1898*, Columbia: University of South Carolina Press, 1969.

____, *Poverty and Politics: the Urban Poor in Brazil, 1870-1920*, Albuquerque: University of New Mexico Press, 1986.

____, "Women and Work in Brazil, 1850-1920: a Preliminary Investigation," *Essays Concerning the Socioeconomic History of Brazil and Portuguese India*, Dauril Alden and Warren Dean (eds.), Gainesville: University Presses of Florida, 1977.

217

Hall, Anthony, *Drought and Irrigation in North-East Brazil*, Cambridge: Cambridge University Press, 1978, Cambridge Latin American Studies xxix.

Hall, Michael and Marco Aurélio Garcia, "Urban Labor," *Modern Brazil: Elites and Masses in Historical Perspective*, Michael Conniff and Frank McCann (eds.), Lincoln: University of Nebraska Press, 1989.

Hemming, John, *Red Gold: the Conquest of the Brazilian Indians*, Cambridge: Harvard University Press, 1978.

Henderson, James, *A History of Brazil*, London: Longman et al., 1821.

Henriques, Affonso, *Ascensão e queda de Getúlio Vargas: o maquiavélico*, Rio de Janeiro: Record, 1966, vol. i.

Hobsbawn, Eric, *Bandits*, New York: Delacorte, 1969.

Holloway, Thomas, "A Healthy Terror': Police Repression of *Capoeiras* in Nineteenth-Century Rio de Janeiro," *Hispanic American Historical Review*, vol. lxix, no. 4, November 1989.

____, *Policing Rio de Janeiro: Repression and Resistance in a 19th-Century City*, Stanford: Stanford University Press, 1993.

____, "The Brazilian 'Judicial Police' in Florianópolis, Santa Catarina, 1841-1871," *Journal of Social History*, vol. xx, no. 4, Summer 1987.

Houaiss, Antônio (ed.), *Grande enciclopédia Delta Larousse*, Rio de Janeiro: Delta, 1971.

____, *Grande enciclopédia Delta Larousse*, Rio de Janeiro: Delta, 1978.

Huggins, Martha Knisely, *From Slavery to Vagrancy in Brazil: Crime and Social Control in the Third World*, New Brunswick: Rutgers University Press, 1985.

Hutchinson, Harry, *Village and Plantation Life in Northeastern Brazil*, Seattle: University of Washington Press, 1957.

Joseph, Gilbert, "On the Trail of Latin American Bandits: a Reexamination of Peasant Resistance," *Latin American Research Review*, vol. xxv, no. 3, 1990.

Julião, Francisco, "The Practice and Preaching of Revolution," *Revolution in Brazil: Politics and Society in a Developing Nation*, Irving Horowitz (ed.), New York: E.P. Dutton, 1964.

Kaarsberg, Christian, *Djävulens järnväg: en resa i Amazonas historia*, Per Lennart Månsson (trans.), Nora: Nya Doxa, 1997.

Karasch, Mary, "Slave Life in Rio de Janeiro, 1808-1850," PhD thesis, Department of History, University of Wisconsin, 1972.

Keith, Henry, "Soldiers as Saviors: the Brazilian Military Revolts of 1922 and 1924 in Historical Perspective," unpublished PhD thesis, Department of History, University of California, Berkeley, 1970.

____, "The Nonviolent Tradition in Brazilian History: a Myth in Need of Explosion," *Conflict and Continuity in Brazilian Society*, Henry Keith and S.F. Edwards (eds.), Columbia: University of South Carolina Press, 1969.

Kent, R.K., "African Revolt in Bahia, 24-25 January 1835," *Journal of Social History*, vol. iii, no. 4, Summer 1970.

____, "Palmares: an African State in Brazil," *Journal of African History*, vol. vi, no. 2, 1965.

Kidder, Daniel and James Fletcher, *Brazil and the Brazilians: Portrayed in Historical and Descriptive Sketches*, Philadelphia: Childs and Peterson, 1857.

Kidder, Daniel, *Sketches of Residence and Travels in Brazil: Embracing Historical and Geographical Notices of the Empire and its Several Province*, Philadelphia: Sorin and Ball, London: Wiley and Putnam, 1845, vols. i-ii.

Kolabinska, Marie, *La circulation des élites en France*, Lausanne: F. Rouge, 1912.

Koster, Henry, *Travels in Brazil*, London: Longman *et al.*, 1816.

Kraay, Hendrik, "As Terrifying as Unexpected': the Bahian Sabinada, 1837-1838," *Hispanic American Historical Review*, vol. lxxii, no. 4, November 1992.

Lacerda, Maurício de, *História de uma covardia*, Rio de Janeiro: Nova Fronteira, 1980.

Lamberg, Mauricio, *O Brasil*, Luiz de Castro (trans.), Rio de Janeiro: Lombaerts, 1896.

Leal, Aurelino, *Policia e poder policia*, Rio de Janeiro: Nacional, 1918.

Leal, Victor Nunes, *Coronelismo, enxada e voto: o município e o regime representativo no Brasil*, 3rd ed., São Paulo: Alfa-Omega, 1976.

Leclerc, Max, *Cartas do Brasil*, Sérgio Milliet (trans. pref., & com.), São Paulo: Nacional, 1942.

Lesser, Jeff, "Are African-Americans African or American?: Brazilian Immigration Policy in the 1920s," *Review of Latin American Studies*, vol. iv, no. 1, 1991.

Levine, Robert, "Mud-Hut Jerusalem': Canudos Revisited," *Hispanic American Historical Review*, vol. lxviii, no. 3, August 1988.

____, *Pernambuco in the Brazilian Federation, 1889-1937*, Stanford: Stanford University Press, 1978.

____, *Vale of Tears: Revisiting the Canudos Massacre in Northeastern Brazil, 1893-1897*, Berkeley: University of California Press, 1992.

Lewin, Linda, "Oral Traditions and Elite Myth: the Legend of Antônio Silvino in Brazilian Popular Culture," *Journal of Latin American Lore*, vol. v, no. 2, 1979.

____, *Politics and Parentela in Paraíba: a Case Study of Family-Based Oligarchy in Brazil*, Princeton: Princeton University Press, 1987.

____, "The Oligarchical Limitations of Social Banditry in Brazil: the Case of the 'Good' Thief Antonio Silvino," *Past and Present*, no. 82, 1979.

Lieuwen, Edwin, *Arms and Politics in Latin America*, New York: Frederick Praeger, 1960.

Lobo, Antonio de Sousa Silva Costa, *Historia da sociedade em Portugal no seculo xv*, Lisbon: Nacional, 1903.

Loewenstein, Karl, *Brazil under Vargas*, New York: Macmillan, 1944.

Ludwig, Pedro and Frederico Guilherme Briggs, *The Brasilian Souvenir: a Selection of the Most Peculiar Costumes of the Brazils*, Rio de Janeiro: Ludwig and Briggs, 1846-1849.

Lustosa, Isabel, *Histórias de presidentes: a repúblic no Catete*, Petrópolis: Vozes, 1989.

Macaulay, Neill, *Dom Pedro: the Struggle for Liberty in Brazil and Portugal, 1798-1834*, Durham: Duke University Press, 1986.

____, *The Prestes Column: Revolution in Brazil*, New York: New Viewpoints, 1974.

Macedo, Joaryvar, *Império do bacamarte: uma abordagem sobre o coronelismo no Cariri cearense*, 2nd ed., Fortaleza: Universidade Federal do Ceará, 1990.

Macedo, *Padre Manuel, Joazeiro em fóco*, Fortaleza: Autores Catholicos, 1925.

Machado, Maria Christina Matta, *As táticas de guerra dos cangaceiros*, 2nd ed., São Paulo: Brasiliense, 1978.

Madden, Lori, "Evolution in the Interpretations of the Canudos Movement: an Evaluation of the Social Sciences," *Luso-Brazilian Review*, vol. xxviii, no. 1, Summer 1991.

Malheiro, Agostinho Perdigão, *A escravidão no Brasil*, Rio de Janeiro: Typographia Nacional, 1866, vol. i.

Marques, Daniel Walker Almeida, *História do Padre Cícero em resumo: datas, fatos e fotos*, 2nd ed., Juazeiro do Norte: Mascote, 1989.

Marques, João Martins da Silva, *Descobrimentos portugueses: documentos para a sua história publicados e prefaciados por João Martins da Silva Marques professor da faculdade de letras de Lisboa (1147-1460)*, Lisbon: Instituto para a Alta Cultura, 1944, vol. i.

Martins, Hélio Leôncio, *A Revolta dos Marinheiros, 1910*, São Paulo: Nacional, 1988.

Mattoso, Katia M. de Queirós, *To Be a Slave in Brazil, 1550-1888*, Arthur Goldhammer (trans.), New Brunswick: Rutgers University Press, 1986.

McCann, Frank and Michael Conniff, "Introduction," *Modern Brazil: Elites and Masses in Historical Perspective*, Michael Conniff and Frank McCann (eds.), Lincoln: University of Nebraska Press, 1989.

Meade, Teresa, "Civilizing Rio de Janeiro': the Public Health Campaign and the Riot of 1904," *Journal of Social History*, vol. xx, no. 2, Winter 1986.

____, "Living Worse and Costing More': Resistance and Riot in Rio de Janeiro, 1890-1917," *Journal of Latin American Studies*, vol. xxi, no. 2, May 1989.

Mello, Frederico Pernambucano de, *Guerreiros do sol: o banditismo no Nordeste do Brasil*, Recife: Massangana (Fundação Joaquim Nabuco), 1985.

Mello, Marco Antônio da Silva and Arno Vogel, "Monarquia contra República: a ideologia da terra e o paradigma do milênio na 'Guerra Santa' do Contestado," *Estudos Históricos*, vol. ii, no. 4, 1989.

Menezes, Fátima and Generosa Alencar, *Homens e fatos na história do Juazeiro: estudo cronológico, 1827-1934*, Recife: Universitária UFPE, 1989.

Mocellin, Renato, *A história crítica da nação brasileira*, 5th ed., São Paulo: Editora do Brasil, 1987.

Monteiro, Duglas Teixeira, *Os errantes do novo século: um estudo sobre o surto milenarista do Contestado*, São Paulo: Duas Cidades, 1974.

Moraes, Dênis de and Francisco Viana, *Prestes: lutas e autocríticas*, 2nd ed., Petrópolis: Vozes, 1982.

Moraes [Filho], Evaristo de, *Ensaios de pathologia social: vagabundagem, alcoolismo, prostituição, lenocino*, Rio de Janeiro: Leite Ribeiro, 1921.

_____, *Minhas prisões e outros assumptos contemporaneos*, Rio de Janeiro: Edição do Autor, 1924.

Moraes Filho, Evaristo de, *Temas atuais de trabalho e previdência*, São Paulo: LTr, 1976.

Morél, Edmar, *A Revolta da Chiabta*, 1st ed., Rio de Janeiro: Pongetti, 1959.

_____, *A Revolta da Chibata*, 2nd ed., rev., Guanabara: Letras e Artes, 1963.

_____, *Padre Cicero: O Santo do Juazeiro*, Rio de Janeiro: O Cruzeiro, 1946.

Morse, Richard, *Formação histórica de São Paulo: de comunidade à metrópole*, São Paulo: Difusão Européia do Livro, 1970.

Motta, Leonardo, *No tempo de Lampeão*, Rio de Janeiro: Officina Industrial Graphica, 1930.

Moura, Severino Rodrigues de, *História de Frei Miguelinho: o bandoleiro, a fonte e o frade*, Recife: FIAM/Centro de Estudos de História Municipal, 1983.

Nachman, Robert, "Positivism and Revolution in Brazil's First Republic: the 1904 Revolt," *The Americas*, vol. xxxiv, no. 1, July 1977.

Nascimento, Abdias do, *O quilombismo*, Petrópolis: Vozes, 1980.

Needell, Jeffrey, *A Tropical Belle Epoque: Elite Culture and Society in Turn-of-the Century Rio de Janeiro*, Cambridge: Cambridge University Press, 1987.

_____, "Rio de Janeiro at the Turn of the Century: Modernization and the Parisian Ideal," *Journal of Interamerican Studies and World Affairs*, vol. xxv, no. 1, February 1983.

Oliveira, Aglae Lima de, *Lampião, cangaço e nordeste*, 2nd ed., Rio de Janeiro: O Cruzeiro, 1970.

Oliveira, Xavier de, *Beatos e cangaceiros*, Rio de Janeiro: Revista dos Tribunais, 1920.

_____, *O exercito e o sertão*, Rio de Janeiro: Coelho Branco, 1932.

Page, Joseph, *The Revolution that Never Was*, New York: Grossman, 1972.

Pang, Eul-Soo, *Bahia in the First Brazilian Republic: Coronelismo and Oligarchies, 1889-1934*, Gainesville: University Presses of Florida, 1979.

Pareto, Vilfredo, *The Mind and Society*, A. Bongiorno and A. Livingston (trans.), A. Livingston (ed.), New York: Harcourt, Brace, 1935, vol. iii.

Pierson, Donald, *Negroes in Brazil: a Study of Race Contact at Bahia*, Carbondale: Southern Illinois University Press, 1967.

Pinheiro, Irineu, *O Juazeiro do Padre Cicero e a Revolução de 1914*, Rio de Janeiro: Pongetti, 1938.

Pinheiro, Paulo Sérgio, *Estratégias da ilusão: a revolução mundial e o Brasil*,

221

1922-1935, São Paulo: Companhia das Letras, 1991.

_____, "O proletariado industrial na Primeira República," *História geral da civilização brasileira: o Brasil republicano: sociedade e instituições, 1889-1930*, Boris Fausto (dir.), Rio de Janeiro: Difel, 1977, book iii, vol. ii.

Pinto, [Heron] Herondino Pereira, *Nos subterraneos do Estado Novo*, Rio de Janeiro: Germinal, 1950.

Pontes, João Batista Arruda, "Canudos: messianismo e conflito social," unpublished Master's thesis, Humanities Center, Universidade Federal da Paraíba, 1992.

Portela, Fernando and Cláudio Bojunga, *Lampião: o cangaceiro e o outro*, São Paulo: Traço, 1982.

Queiroz, Maria Isaura Pereira de, *O messianismo: no Brasil e no mundo*, São Paulo: Dominus, 1965.

_____, *Os cangaceiros: les bandits d'honneur brésiliens*, Paris: Julliard, 1968.

Queiroz, Maurício Vinhas de, *Messianismo e conflito social: a querra sertaneja do Contestado, 1912-1916*, Rio de Janeiro: Civilização Brasileira, 1966.

Querino, Manuel [Raymundo], *A raça africana e os seus costumes*, Rio de Janeiro: Progresso, 1955.

Rachum, Ilan, "From Young Rebels to Brokers of National Politics: the *tenentes* of Brazil, 1922-1967," *Boletin de Estudios Latinoamericanos y del Caribe*, no. 23, December 1977.

Rech, Luiz Antonio, "As guerrilhas no Brasil: considerações históricas - análise e conclusões," *A Defesa Nacional*, no. 639, September/October 1971.

Reis Júnior, Pereira, *Os presidentes do Brasil*, Rio de Janeiro: Divulbrás, 1975.

Rio, João do [Paulo Barreto], *A alma encantadora das ruas*, Rio de Janeiro: Simões, 1952.

Rodrigues, José Honório, *The Brazilians: Their Character and Aspirations*, Ralph Edward Dimmick (trans.), Austin: University of Texas Press, 1967.

Rose, R.S., "Slavery in Brazil: Does it Still Exist?" *Review of Latin American Studies*, vol. iv, no. 1, 1991.

Rowe, John W.F., "Studies in the Artificial Control of Raw Material Supplies: No. 3, Brazilian Coffee," *Royal Economic Society*, no. 34, February 1932.

Rugendas, Maurice, *Voyage pittoresque dans le Brésil*, Paris: Engelmann, 1835, parts ii, iv.

Russell-Wood, A.J.R., "Colonial Brazil," *Neither Slave nor Free: the Freedman of African Descent in the Slave Societies of the New World*, David Cohen and Jack Greene (eds.), Baltimore: Johns Hopkins University Press, 1972.

Santos, José Maria dos, *A politica geral do Brasil*, São Paulo: J. Magalhães, 1930.

Schlichthorst, Carl, *O Rio de Janeiro como é, 1824-1826: huma vez e nunca mais*, Rio de Janeiro: Getulio Costa, 1943.

Schwartz, Stuart, "The Manumission of Slaves in Colonial Brazil: Bahia, 1684-1745," *Hispanic American Historical Review*, vol. liv, no. 4, November 1974.

Schwarz, Lilla Moritz, *Retrato em branco e negro: jornais, escravos e cidadões*

222

em São Paulo no final do século xix, São Paulo: Compania das Letras, 1987.

Sevcenko, Nicolau, *Literatura como missão: tensões sociais e criação cultural na Primeira República*, São Paulo: Brasiliense, 1983.

Shoumatoff, Alex, *The World is Burning*, Boston: Little, Brown, 1990.

Silva, Hélio, *1922 - Sangue na areia de Copacabana: o ciclo de Vargas*, vol. i, 2nd ed., Rio de Janeiro: Civilização Brasileira, 1971.

Silva, José Calasana Brandão da, *No tempo de Antônio Conselheiro: figuras e fatos da campanha de Canudos*, Salvador: Progresso, 1959.

Simão, Azis, *Sindicato e estado: suas relações na formação do proletariado de São Paulo*, São Paulo: Dominus, 1966.

Singelmann, Peter, "Political Structure and Social Banditry in Northeastern Brazil," *Journal of Latin American Studies*, vol. vii, no. 1, May 1975.

Skidmore, Thomas, *Black into White: Race and Nationality in Brazilian Thought*, New York: Oxford University Press, 1974.

Slater, Candace, "Messianism and the Padre Cicero Stories," *Luso-Brazilian Review*, vol. xxviii, no. 1, Summer 1991.

____, *Stories on a String: the Brazilian Literatura de Cordel*, Berkeley: University of California Press, 1989.

Snow, Edgar, *Red Star over China*, London: Victor Gollancz, 1937.

Soares, J.O. Pinto, *Guerra em Sertões brasileiros: do fanatismo á solução do secular litigio entre o Paraná e Santa Catarina*, Rio de Janeiro: Papelaria Velho, 1931.

Soares, José Carlos de Macedo, *Justiça: a revolta militarem São Paulo*, Paris: Dupont, 1925.

Soares, Oscar de Macedo, *Codigo penal da Republica dos Estados Unidos do Brasil: commentado e annotado segundo a legislação vigente até 1901*, Rio de Janeiro: Empreza Democratica, 1902.

Sodré, Benjamin (org.), *Lauro Sodré: vida, carater e sentimento a serviço de um povo*, Rio de Janeiro: Imprensa Oficial, 1956.

Sodré, Nelson Werneck, *História militar do Brasil*, Rio de Janeiro: Civilização Brasileira, 1965.

Soihet, Rachel, *Condição feminina e formas de violência: mulheres pobres e ordem urbana: 1890-1920*, Rio de Janeiro: Forense Universitária, 1989.

Sousa, Antonio Caetano de, *Provas da historia genealogica da casa real portugueza, triadas dos inftrumentos dos archivos da Torre do Tombo, da serenijfima caja de Bragança, de diverfas cathedraes, mofteiros, e outros particulares defte reyno*, Lisbon: Sylviana, 1739, book i.

Souto Maior, Mário, *Antônio Silvino: Capitão de Trabuco*, Rio de Janeiro: Arquimedes, 1971.

Souza, Paulo Cesar, *A Sabinada: a revolta separatista da Bahia, 1837*, São Paulo: Brasiliense, 1987.

Taunay, Affonso de Escragnolle, *Historia do café no Brasil, no Brasil Imperial: 1822-1872*, Rio de Janeiro: Departamento Nacional do Café, 1939, book i, vol. iii.

Theophilo, Rodolpho, *A secca de 1915*, Fortaleza: Moderna-Carneiro, 1919.

____, *Historia da secca do Ceará: 1877 a 1880*, Rio de Janeiro: Ingleza, 1922.

Toplin, Robert (ed.), *Slavery and Race Relations in Latin America*, Westport, CT.: Greenwood, 1974.

____, *The Abolition of Slavery in Brazil*, New York: Atheneum, 1972.

Torres, Epitácio, *A polícia: uma perspectiva histórica*, Porto Alegre: Bels, 1977.

Tourinho, Eduardo, *Revelação do Rio de Janeiro*, Rio de Janeiro: Civilização Brasileira, 1964.

Vainfas, Magali Engel, "Meretrizes e doutores: o saber médico e a prostituição na cidade do Rio de Janeiro, 1845 a 1890," unpublished Master's thesis, Instituto de Ciências Humanas e Filosofia, Universidade Federal Fluminense, 1985.

Verger, Pierre, *Flux et reflux de la traite des nègres entre le golfe de Bénin et Bahia de todos os santos du dix-septième au dix-neuvième siècle*, Paris: Mouton, 1968.

Vianna, Marfa Barbosa, "O negro no Museu Histórico Nacional," *Anais do Museu Histórico Nacional*, vol. viii, 1947.

Vieira, Hermes and Oswaldo Silva, *História de Policia Civil do São Paulo*, São Paulo: Nacional, 1955.

Walsh, Robert, *Notices of Brazil in 1828 and 1829*, London: Westly and Davis, 1830, vols. i-ii.

Wied-Neuwied, Maximilian, *Reise nach Brasilien in den Jahren 1815 bis 1817*, Frankfurt: Brönner, 1820, vol. i.

Young, Jordan, *The Brazilian Revolution of 1930 and the Aftermath*, New Brunswick: Rutgers University Press, 1967.

INDEX

Numbers in boldface italics refer to the corresponding figures on the unnumbered pages between Chapters III and IV. Words in italics, from the Portuguese, are translated in the text at first use. A smaller number of Portuguese words, utilized repeatedly, are translated again in the Select Glossary.

Abbott, Arthur, 145, 145n. 10
Abraão, Benjamin, 109-10, 109n. 69, 112-13, *31*
and film on Lampião, 112-13, 113nn. 84-85
Batalhões Patrioticos, 110
death, 113
Getúlio Vargas and, 112-13
offers Lampião commission in
Padre Cícero and
See Cícero, *Padre*
Abreu, Antenor de Santa Cruz Pereira de,
See Santa Cruz
Aciolly, Antônio Pinto Nogueira, 77, 77n. 64
Africans
See race: blacks/Africans
Afro-Brazilian
See race: blacks/Africans
Agostini, João Maria de
See Maria, *Monge* João (1st)
Aguiar, Raul
See Polícia Central: agents/torturers at
Albuquerque, Antônio Silvino Aires Cavalcanti de
See cangaceiros: Silvino Torto
Albuquerque, Júlio Prestes de, 139
Aljube, the
See incarceration
Alves, Francisco de Paula Rodrigues
See Rodrigues Alves, Francisco de Paula
American cultural definitions, 1n
anarchists, 141-42, 145
Aragão, Francisco Alberto Teixeira
See police: *Polícia Militar*
Araripe, Tristão
See Polícia Central: agents/torturers at
Araújo, Maria de
See *Padre* Cícero
army, 17-18, 39n. 83, 86-87, 139, 139n. 1, and 1922 Rebellion, 151-52
Tertuliano Potyguara, 152

See also tenentes/tenentismo
and 1924 Rebellion, 154
Abilio de Noronha, 154-55
Antenor de Santa Cruz Pereira de Abreu, 175-77, 175n. 96, *45*
Bernardes suspicions against, 159, 175
bribes
"Generals with Clean Hands," 161
Manuel Lopes Carneiro da Fontoura
See police: *Polícia Civil*
Eduardo Sócrates, 156
Tertuliano Potyguara, 155, 155n. 32, *37*
See also Polícia Central: agents /torturers at; *tenentes/tenentismo*
and other men of power move to depose monarchy, 54-55
Antônio Conselheiro and, 62-65, 64nn. 33, 36, 65n. 37
Carlos Frederico de Mesquita, 85
Moreira Cesar, 62-63
See also Conselheiro, Antônio
blacks/Africans allowed to join, 45
deserters/dissenters from, 25, 82n. 80
idealism in, 68-69, 79, 85-87
impressment and, 38-39, 39n. 83, 121
in 1904 Rio de Janeiro Riots, 127, 129
Lauro Sodré
See Belle Époque: military action during 1904 Riot
Silvestre Travassos
See Belle Époque: military action during 1904 Riot
in Paraguayan War, 38-39
in Vintem Riot, 43
Luís Alves de Lima e Silva, 41
and dubious honor, 42
as Barão de Caxias, 41
as Duque de Caxias, 42
in Balaiada conflict, 41
in Battle of Porongos, 42

Monge José Maria and
  Carlos Frederico de Mesquita, 85-86
  Fernando Setembrino de Carvalho, 86
  João Gualberto, 84
  See also Maria, *Monge* José
Newton Cavalcanti, 99-100
positivism, 68-69, 68n. 46., 126
raping of peasant women by members of,
  89n. 3, 96
role conflict, 86-87
  See also tenentes/tenentismo
Rui Barbosa and, 68-69, 71, 75nn. 57-58
salaries and, 68, 68n. 46, 148
Salvações and, 78-79, 149
See also elites: sub-elites; incarceration;
  lower classes; police: *Polícia Civil:*
  Polícia Militar; slaves; violence
arrest
  See incarceration
Asians
  See race: Asians
Barão do Rio Branco [José Maria da Silva
  Paranhos], 51n. 12
Barbosa, Inspector
  See Polícia Central: agents/torturers at
Barbosa, Luís, 180n. 110
Barbosa, Rui, 55, 67-69, 71, 146
  and *Civilista* campaign, 68, 148
  and *Constitution of 1891,* 146-47
  and Naval Revolt of 1910, 71, 75nn. 57-
    58
  Satélite case, 75nn. 57-58
Barreto, Paulo
  See Rio, João do
Barros, Prudente José de Morais, 139-40
Bartolomeu, Floro [Floro Bartolomeu da
  Costa], 86, 107-9
  Lampião and, 109
  fights Franco Rabelo, 77-78, 107n. 63
  "mortes da rodagem," 108, **28**
  opens jails to fight *Coluna* Prestes, 107
  Padre Cícero and, 67n. 43, 77, 78n. 69,
    107, **30**
Batalhões Patrioticos
  See Abraão, Benjamin; Bernardes, Artur
    da Silva: 1924 Rebellion: repression
    and; *cangaceiros:* Lampião
Batista, Cícero Romão
  See Cícero, *Padre*
Battle of Catanduvas, 172-73
Belle Époque, 124-38, 197

military action during 1904 Riot, 126-27
  Lauro Sodré, 127
  Silvestre Travassos, 127
police action during 1904 Riot, 127-29,
  128nn. 20, 22, 129nn. 26, 28, 132n. 35
  Antônio Augusto Cardoso de Castro,
    127-29, 128n. 20, 129. 26
  José Joaquim Seabra, 127
Rio de Janeiro as financial center, 124-25,
Rio de Janeiro upgraded, 125, 127, 130,
  137-38
  by combating disease, 125-26, 125n. 13,
    127
  by removing urban poor, 125-38,
    129nn. 26-27, 132n. 35, 136nn. 42-
    44, 137nn. 46-47, 138n. 48
  creation of Avenida Central, 126
    ultimately renamed, 126
  The Sanitary Project Bill, 130
    Fon-Fon editorial, 130-31, 130n.
      30
  vadiagem (read: vagrancy and
    prostitution), 129n. 28, 132-38,
    132n. 34, 136nn. 42-45, 137nn.
    46-47, 195, 200
Bello, Rubens
  See Polícia Central: agents/torturers at:
    Francisco Chagas: deals with new
    revolutionary plot: suspects in
Bentes, Dionysio
  See incarceration: Oiapoque
Bernardes, Artur da Silva, 4-5, 105-6, 145,
  150, 154-57, 156n. 33, 171, 173, 173n. 87
  187
  election of 1921/22
    "Ai seu mé," 150
    "Bernardes False Letters," 149-50
    Military Club, 149-50
      Hermes da Fonseca, 149-50
  leaves country, 179
  leaves office, 175, 179
  Manuel Lopes Carneiro da Fontura
    See police: *Polícia Civil*
  1924 Rebellion
    "Black Guards," 159
    repression and, 155-63, 56n. 33, 160n.
      44, 161nn. 46-47, 175n. 95
    Batalhões Patrioticos, 106-7, 109, **29**
      cangaceiros in, 109
      composition of in Northeast, 111,
        158

corruption of, 106
Lampião asked to join, 109-11,
    111n. 75
Carolina Bastos Schomaker, 176n. 97
Conrado Niemeyer
    See Polícia Central: agents/torturers
    at: Francisco Chagas: deals with
    new revolutionary plot: suspects
    in
denies culpability for Oiapoque, 174n.
    93
probably orders killings, 162
rebel relatives taken as hostage, 162
sailors from the *São Paulo*, 159
Tertuliano Potyguara
    See army: and 1922 Rebellion: and
    1924 Rebellion
See also army; police: *Polícia Civil;*
    Polícia Central; Prestes, Luís Carlos;
    tenentes/tenentismo
other plots against, 154, 175-76, 175n. 95
threatens to use *Polícia Militar*, 153,
    153n. 26
vilification of, 159-60, 160n. 43, *36*
Bezerra, João
    See cangaceiros: Lampião
Big Daddy
    See Rodrigues Alves, Francisco de Paula
Bijuca
    See Polícia Central: agents/torturers at
Bittencourt, Edmundo, 173n. 87
Bittencourt, Renato
    See Polícia Central: agents/torturers at
blacks
    See race: blacks/Africans
Boaventura, Miguel Lucena da
    See Maria, *Monge* José
Bragança
    See House of Bragança
Brás, Venceslau [Venceslau Brás Pereira
    Gomes], 86, 140
    See also Contestado
Brizola, Leonel
    See Naval Revolt of 1910: João Cândido
brown
    See race: brown/*mulatos*
bundões
    See elites: sub-elites
cabra
    See elites: sub-elites
cachaça, 36, 112, 197

Calabouço
    See incarceration
Calmon, Miguel, 174n. 93
    See also incarceration: Oiapoque
Cândido, João
    See incarceration: Ilha das Cobras; Naval
    Revolt of 1910
cangaceiras, 114-15
Maria Déa, *26*
    aliases, 114, 114n. 89
    Antônio Conselheiro and, 114
    decapitated, 113-14, 114nn. 88, 90-
    91, *27*
    given name Maria Bonita by police,
    114n. 89
    mutilated, 115
    See also cangaceiros: Lampião
Nenê de Luís Pedro
    mutilated, 114
cangaceiros, 78, 78n. 69, 107, 107n. 63,
    109, 197
Antônio Maltides, 103
Antônio Porcino, 104
"Antônio Silvino" [Manoel Batista de
    Moraes], 92-102, 92nn. 10, 12, 93n. 13,
    95n. 22, 98n. 29, 100n. 37, 102nn.
    41, 45
    ability with a rifle, 93
    aliases, 93
    and biography of, 100-1, 101n. 39
    and Great Western Railway, 97-98
    and justice, 89-91
    and pension, 101-2
    and police, 92-4, 96, 98
        crimes vs., 92, 94
    and vengeance, 93, 93n. 13
    at Recife's Casa de Detenção, 99-100
    attempts suicide, 98n. 31
    attempts to leave *cangaço*, 93, 109
    demands made on his men, 95-96,
    96n. 24
    dies, 102
    employment after prison, 101-2, *25*
    four enemy *coronéis*, 94
    Francisco Batista de Moraes, 92-93
    Getúlio Vargas and, 101-2, 101n. 39,
    102n. 41, *25*
    in Rio de Janeiro, 100-2, 100n. 37,
    102n. 41, *24*
    Newton Cavalcanti and, 99-100
    on Lampião, 102, 102n. 45

Quinca Napoleão, 94-95, 95n. 22
released from prison, 100-1
Robin Hood image, 95
shot, 98
sons live with him in prison, 99
Teofanes Ferraz Torres and, 98-99
in *Batalhões Patrióticos*, 109
"Corisco" [Christino Gomes da Silva],
115
José Rufino, 115
"Lampião" [Virgulino Ferreira da Silva],
94, **26**
aliases, 105
ambush at Angicos
Benjamin Abraão's film, 112-13,
113nn. 84-85
decapitated, 113, **27**
Eronildes de Carvalho and, 112
Getúlio Vargas and, 112-13
João Bezerra and, 112-14
altered *cachaça*, 112
corruption, 112
plans for Maria Déa, 114
Maria Déa
See cangaceiras
and police
corruption, 104, 107, 113
crimes vs., 104-5
do not pursue with enthusiasm, 115-
16
kill family of, 103
mutilate bodies of and gang, 113
aptitude of, 110-11, 115
asked to join *Batalhões Patrioticos*,
109-11, 111n. 75, 197
endorsed by only one commander, 111
sells arms given him, 111
becomes more violent, 111-12
communications from Floro
Bartolomeu, 109
confusion on, 103n. 48, 105, 115-16
crimes, 104-5, 111
enters Juazeiro da Norte, 109
heads taken to Raimundo Nina
Rodrigues, 115
José Saturnino and, 103
kills police, 111-12
meets with Benjamin Abraão, 109-10
members, 115-16
on Antônio Silvino, 102, 102n. 45
on leaving the *cangaço*, 109-11, 112n. 79

origins, 103
Padre Cícero and, 67n. 42, 109-10
philosophy, 111-12
provides justice, 104
Teofanes Ferraz Torres does not pursue
with much enthusiasm, 116
police and *cangaceiras*, 114-15
police desecration of the dead, 114-15
"Silvino Torto" [Antônio Silvino Aires
Cavalcanti de Albuquerque], 91-92
"Sinhô" [Sebastião Pereira], 104
attempts to leave cangaço, 110
See also cangaço
cangaceiros independentes
See cangaço: and *coronéis*
cangaceiros mansos
See cangaço: and *coronéis*
cangaço, 4, 90n. 4, 197
and *coronéis*, 89-92, 92n. 8, 94, 96, 103,
107, 113, 116
cangaceiros independentes, 90-91, 93-
94, 104-7, 116-17
defined, 90, 197
kept as alternates, 116-17
treatment of if caught, 111
cangaceiros mansos, 90, 105-7, 150
defined, 90, 197
made police, 116-17, 123n. 9
not useful if not violent, 46n. 4, 116-
17
See also elites: sub-elites; police
coiteiros, 92, 92n. 8, 112, 197
composed of lower classes, 90
droughts, 89
end of, 115
problems in written accounts of, 91, 91n.
6, 103n. 48, 105, 115-16
reasons for joining, 90-91, 91n. 6
See also cangaceiros
Canudos
See Conselheiro, Antônio
Canuto, Investigator
See Polícia Central: agents/torturers at
capanga
See elites: sub-elites
capitão de mato/estrada/campo
See elites: sub-elites; slaves: escape
capoeira
See slaves: reactions by
Carvalho, Accacio Rodrigues de
See Polícia Central: agents/torturers at:

Francisco Chagas: deals with new revolutionary plot: suspects in Carvalho, Eronildes de
See cangaceiros: Lampião
Carvalho, Fernando Setembrino de
See army
Casa de Correção
See incarceration
Casa de Detenção
See incarceration
Castro, Antônio Augusto Cardoso de,
See Belle Époque: police action during; police: *Polícia Militar*
Catete, 69, 78, 135, 140, 153, 159, 161-62, 176-77, 175n. 95, 198
Catholic Church, 4
and Christianizing, 9, 11
and Contestado
See Contestado
and incarceration of clergy, 27
Antônio Conselheiro and, 58-59, 61-62, 62n. 31
clergy as relatives of slave owners, 14
enslavement processes
against *índios,* 9
Papal Bull of 1537, 9
Pope Paul III, 9
Pope Urban VIII, 9
against Moors, Muslims, and Africans
King Afonso V and request to, 11
Moors and, 10-11, 10n. 11
Muslims and, 10
Pope Calixtus III, 12
Pope Leo X, 12
Pope Nicholas V, 11
Pope Sixtus IV, 12
Romanus Pontifex, 11-12, 11n. 12
justified war, 12
refusal to become Christian, 11
early European grounds for, 10
failure to take an early stand against, 9, 9n. 7
profits as reason for, 9-13
See also slavery; slaves
following 1835 slave revolt, 33
Padre Cícero
See Cícero, *Padre*
Cavalcanti, *Dom* Joaquim Arcoverde de Albuquerque
See Cícero, *Padre:* and Church hierarchy

Cavalcanti, Newton
See army; *cangaceiros:* Antônio Silvino
Cendrars, Blaise, 155-56, 156n. 33
"Central" [Avenida Central], 126, 198
"Central" [Polícia Central]
See Polícia Central
Central Police Station
See Polícia Central
Cesar, Moreira
See army; Conselheiro, Antônio: Canudos: government's forces
Chagas, Francisco
See Polícia Central: agents/torturers at
chibata, 70, 82, 144, 167, 173, 198
chicote, 23, 23n. 43, 177, 198, **14**
Cícero, *Padre* [Cícero Romão Batista], 65n. 38, 66-67, 77, 77n. 68, 81, 107, 109-10, 109n. 69
and Church hierarchy, 66-6
Dom Joaquim Arcoverde de Albuquerque Cavalcanti, 67
Dom Joaquim José Vieira, 66-67
Benjamin Abraão and, 109-10, 109n. 69, 113, **31**
career, 67n. 43
defrocked, 66
different from Antônio Conselheiro, 67
Floro Bartolomeu da Costa and, 67n. 43, 77, 78n. 69, 107, **30**
in *pacto dos coronéis,* 77-79, 77n. 64
Maria de Araújo and, 66
meets/attempts to help Lampião, 109-10
See also cangaceiros: Lampião
Civilista campaign, 68, 148, 198
Clevelandia
See incarceration
coffee, 149, 183-185, 184n. 124
Coluna Prestes
See Prestes, Luís Carlos
Comte, August, 68
"Conselheiro, Antônio" [Antônio Vicente Mendes Maciel], 58-59, 61-66, 62n. 31, 81, 85, 108n. 64
and Catholic Church, 58-59, 61, 62n. 31
and monarchism, 58, 62
and taxes, 61
Canudos, 148
aftermath, **22**
bodies everywhere, 64
Brazilian "trail of tears," 64

first *favela* in Rio, 64, 64n. 36
defense, 63
  defenders equated with cowards/
    criminals/mentally deranged, 62n.
    31, 63, 65n. 37, 153
  Euclides da Cunha, 62n. 31, 65n. 37
  government's forces, 62-63
    Carlos Frederico de Mesquita, 85
    Moreira Cesar, 62-63
  various races at, 58
  chooses wrong protector, 67n. 44
  description of, 58-59
  dies, 63, 64n. 33, **19**
  head taken to Raimundo Nina
    Rodrigues, 63
conservative-laborites, 141
Constitution of 1891, 146-47
Contestado, 79-86, 80nn. 73-75, 82nn. 79-
  80, 83n. 81, 84nn. 85-87, 86n. 92, 149,
  23
  See also Maria, *Monge* João (1st); Maria,
    Monge João (2nd); Maria, *Monge* José
cordel, 97n. 26
coronéis [s. *coronel*], 17, 46n. 4, 76-78,
  83, 85, 89-90, 92, 92n. 8, 94, 96, 103,
  107, 116, 140, 198, **16, 30**
  and immigration, 51-52
  and relationship with state governors,
    45-47
  and relationship with the police, 46-47,
    113
  Antônio Conselheiro and, 62
  as *coiteiros*, 92, 92n. 8
    See also cangaço: coiteiros
  move to depose monarchy, 54-55
  other titles of higher rank, 17n. 29
  Padre Cícero and, 66-67, 67n. 43, 77-
    79, 77nn. 64, 68
  partido do coronel, 45
  types, 54n. 21
  See also army; *cangaço;* Catholic
    Church; elites; National Guards
coronelismo, 17-19, 17n. 29, 54n. 21, 198
Costa, Floro Bartolomeu da
  See Bartolomeu, Floro da
Costa Lima, Manoel da
  See Polícia Central: agents/torturers at
Costa, Miguel
  See tenentes/tenentismo: Rebellion of
    1924
Cunha, Euclides da

  See Conselheiro, Antônio: Canudos
"Curfew of Aragão," 37
Darwin, Charles, 25, 33-34
Déa, Maria
  See cangaceiras; cangaceiros: Lampião
Departamento de Imprensa e Propaganda
  (DIP), 113, 113n. 85
Dias, Everardo, 144-45
disenfranchisement
  enlisted men, 139, 139n. 1
  illiterates, 139
  non-Portuguese speakers, 139
  non-whites, 139, 139n. 1
  persons with criminal records, 139
  poor persons, 139, 139n. 1
  women, 139, 139n. 1
droughts 59-61, 60n. 26, 89
Duque de Caxias
  See army: Luís Alves de Lima e Silva
elites
  and abolition, 47-53, 50n. 7, 51n. 12,
    52nn. 13-14
  and achieved status, 1
    examples of , 1-2
  and ascribed status, 1
    examples of, 1
  and manumission, 34-35
  control of lower classes by
    See lower classes: controlled by elites
  fear of Luís Carlos Prestes, 105, 145, 158
  functional, 1
  move to depose monarchy, 54-55
  Padre Cícero and, 66-67, 67n. 43, 77-79,
    77nn. 64, 68, 78n. 69
  repression by, 2-4, 7, 153
  sexual oppression by, 19, 34
  social, definition of, 1
  sub-elites, 42, 89n. 3
    "Black Guards," 159
    bundões, 7, 89n. 3
    cabras, 7, 89n. 3, 197
    cacheados, 89n. 3
    cangaceiros mansos, 46n. 4, 90,
      105-7, 116-17, 123n. 9, 150
    capangas, 7, 51n. 12, 89n. 3, 90, 197
    capataz, 13, 13n. 19, 123n. 9
    capitão de mato/estrada/campo,
      26, 26n. 53, 85, 123n. 9, 197, **12**
      See also slaves: escape
    capoeira-adept bodyguards, 21
    clavinoteiros, 89n. 3

curimbabas, 89n. 3
definition of, 2-3, 8, 200
dungas, 89n. 3
feitors ("slave tamers"), 30, 30n. 63,
    198, *4*
jagunços, 7, 35, 62n. 31, 65n. 37, 89n.
    3, 108n. 64, 110, 199
marrões, 89n. 3
vira-saias, 89n. 3
See also army; *cangaceiros;* militia,
    colonial; National Guards; navy;
    police
united and disunited, 2, 82
Euro-Brazilian
See race: whites/Europeans
exiled
presingangas, 55-57
to locations outside Brazil, 56-57, 143,
to locations unspecified, 144, 180n. 111
to locations within Brazil, 57, 57n. 23,
    128, 143
Itaipava, 129, 129n. 26
Palhaço, 56
    lime bath on, 56, *10*
    See also Naval Revolt of 1910:
        João Cândido
Satélite, 74-76, 74n. 56, 75nn. 57-58
fanáticos, 61-62, 65, 85-86, 198
Farquhar, Arthur
See Naval Revolt of 1910
Farquhar, Percival, 76, 76n. 62, 81
favela, 198
    probable origin of term, 64, 64n. 36
fazenda, 7, 30n. 63, 51-52, 67, 90, 93, 107,
    109, 111-13, 121, 140, 167, 171, 181, 198
Federalist Civil War
    needless killings in, 58
feitors ("slave tamers")
See elites: sub-elites
Felisberto, João Cândido
See incarceration: Ilha das Cobras; Naval
    Revolt of 1910
ferule
See incarceration: *palmatória* used on
    prisoners; slaves: *palmatória* used on
Fonseca, Hermes Rodrigues da, 140
    and army, 79
    and Contestado, 79-85
    and Military Club, 149-50, 150
    and Naval Revolt of 1910, 69-76
    executions following, 72

repression following, 73-76, 74n. 56,
    75nn. 57-58, 174n. 93
and *Salvações*, 78-79
Civilista election of 1909-1910, 67-69
    derided, 68n. 45, *15*
Floro Bartolomeu and, 77
Franco Rabelo and, 77-78
Padre Cícero and, 77
Pinheiro Machado and, 78-79
Fonseca, Manuel Deodoro da, 55, 140
Fontoura, João Lopes Carneiro da
See Polícia Central: agents/torturers at
Fontoura, Manuel Lopes Carneiro da
See police: *Polícia Civil*
forced labor, 10
See also incarceration; slaves
gente de cor
See race: *gente de cor*
gente pequena, 19n. 33
Góis, Coriolano de
See Polícia Civil
Gomes, Venceslau Brás Pereira, 86-87, 140
See also Monge José Maria
Gonçalves, Perminio
See Polícia Central: agents/torturers at
governors, state
See state governors
Grenfell, John, 56
Himmler, Heindrich, 107n. 59
homosexuals
See incarceration
House of Bragança
    abdication of *Dom* Pedro I, 41, 45
    Antônio Conselheiro and, 58, 62
    deposed, 54-55, 139
    Dom João IV, 47
    Dom Pedro II, 43, 49, 57, 87
    Duque de Caxias and, 40-41
    move to Brazil, 16
    Princess Isabel, 49
    return to monarchy, 58, 62
    titles handed out by, 16-17
Ilha das Cobras
See incarceration
Ilha das Flores
See incarceration
Ilha do Bom Jesus
See incarceration
Ilha Grande
See incarceration
Ilha Rasa

See incarceration
Ilha Trindade
See incarceration
immigration
  as a way to whiten gene pool, 4, 51-52,
    51n. 12, 52nn. 13-14, 141
  for blacks/Africans after abolition, 49
  of Asians, 50
  of Europeans, 4, 14-15, 51-54, 51n. 12,
    52nn. 13-14
    ratios of Italians to native born
      Brazilians in São Paulo, 52n. 13
impressment, 38-39, 39n. 83, 69, 121, 127
incarceration, 38
  Aljube, the, 27-28, *9*
    deplorable conditions, 27
    Guiné, 27
      crowded conditions, 27-28
      deplorable conditions, 27-28
  and anarchists, 145, 173
  and blacks/Africans
    females, 124, 132-38, 132n. 34, 133n.
      36, 136nn. 42-43, 45, 137n. 46, 195
    males, 119-23, 120n. 2, 121n. 7, 122n.
      8, 123n. 10, 189-92
  and brown/*mulatos*
    females, 124, 132-38, 132n. 34, 133n.
      36, 136nn. 42-43, 45, 137n. 46, 195
    males, 119-23, 120n. 2, 121n. 7, 122n.
      8, 123n. 10, 129, 129n. 26, 189-92
  and conservative-laborites, 141
  and drought refuges, 60
  and foreigners, 53-54, 57, 57n. 23, 143-
    45, 162
  and gamblers, 171
  and homosexuals, 162
  and *indios*
    females, 124, 132-38, 132n. 34, 133n.
      36, 136nn. 42-43, 45, 137n. 46, 195
    males, 119-23, 120n. 2, 121n. 7, 122n.
      8, 123n. 10, 129, 129n. 26, 189-92
  and itinerants, 145, 162, 171, 173
  and minors, 38, 162, 165, 172-73, 173n.
    87
  and other small-time offenders, 171, 173
  and political idealists, 162, 173
  and poor people, 173
  and prostitutes, 74, 74n. 56, 132-38,
    132n. 34, 136nn. 42-43, 137n. 46, 162
    195
  and slaves, 22, 35n. 72, 119-21, 120n. 2,

    121n. 7, *14*
    following 1835 rebellion, 32-33
    made to whip other slaves, 29n. 60
  and socialists, 141
  and the Church, 27
  and the unemployed, 38, 57, 145
  and those in labor movement, 143-45,
    162, 180n. 111
  and whites/Europeans
    females, 124, 132-38, 132n. 34, 136nn.
      42-43, 137n. 46, 195
    males, 119-23, 120n. 2, 121n. 7, 122n.
      8, 123n. 10, 189-92
  by race in 1907, 121-24, 121n. 7, 122n. 8,
    123n. 10, 129, 129n. 26, 132-37, 132n.
    34, 136nn. 42-43, 137nn. 46-47, 189-
    92, 195
  Calabouço, 197
    as a place to take slaves to be tortured,
      28-29, 28n. 59
  Casa de Correção, 198
    as a place to take slaves to be tortured,
      29-30, 29nn. 60-61, 30n. 62
    fee involved, 29
    under Waldemar Loureiro, 165, *40*
      beatings, 165
      beatings of minors, 165
      description of conditions, 165, 165n.
        63, *41*
      novo raio (New Horror), 165, 199
  Casa de Detenção, 165, 198
    and prisoners for *Satélite*/Amazon exile,
      74-76, 74n. 56, 75nn. 57-58
    butchery by guards, 74-76
    description of female prisoners during
      Belle Époque, 133-34
    galleries in mid-1920s, *43*
    under Meira Lima, 162-63, 165-66, *42*
      Basement, 166
      Cell 59, 166
      description of conditions, 165-67,
        165n. 63, 167n. 69
      Fort, 166-67
      orchestrated photographs of, 165n. 63
      sadism by, 166
      Tunnel, 166-67
    chibata used on prisoners, 167, 173
    See also chibata
    during Bernardes' government at
      unspecified places, 163
    excess prisoners moved to

fire departments, 167
government *fazenda*, 167
police facilities, 167
ships, 167, 167n. 71
Ilha das Cobras, 27, 73, 167-69
  description of conditions, 168-69
  João Cândido, 168, 169n. 74
  Marques Porto, 73
  Marquis de Pombal, 168
  separation on, 129, 129n. 26, **32**
  Third Prison, 168
  Tiradentes, 168
  used mainly for naval prisoners
    following 1922/1924 Rebellions, 169
Ilha das Flores, 167-68
  description of conditions, 167-68
  military prisoners given best treatment,
    168
Ilha do Bom Jesus, 167, 169-70
  under Pedro Goytacazes, 169-70
  description of conditions, 169, 169n.
    77
  extortion and shortage of food, 169-70
  protests, 170
Ilha Grande [Two Rivers Colony], 171-72
  history, 171
  under Horacio Malsonetti, 171-72
  description of conditions, 171-72
  minors as young as eight, 172
  receives Bernardes' most worrisome
    political prisoners, 171
  receives prisoners government does
    not want released, 171-72
Ilha Rasa, 170
  under Carlos Arlindo, 170
  consequences of José Eduardo de
    Macedo Soares' escape, 170
  description of conditions, 170
  food better than Detenção, 170
Ilha Trindade, 171n. 81
  bad diet, 171n. 81
  description of conditions, 171, 171n. 81,
    174, 174nn. 92-93
  special castigation cells, 171
  under Melo Pena, 171
of drought refugees, 59-60
of lower classes, 22, 119-24, **14**
  in 1907, 121-24, 121n. 7, 122n. 8,
    123n. 10, 129, 129n. 26, 132-37, 132n.
    34, 136nn. 42-43, 137nn. 46-47, 189-95
  public order violations, 123n. 10, 132n.

34, 136n. 43, 137n. 46
Oiapoque [Clevelandia Agricultural
  Center], 172-175, 187
  Dionysio Bentes, 174n. 89
  under Gentil Norberto, 173, 173n. 88
    Bernardes sent doctored reports,
    172n. 84
  description of conditions, 172-74
    173nn. 86-88, 174n. 92
  escapes, 174, 174n. 89
  minors, 173, 173n. 87
  parliamentary inquiry, 174n. 93
  ships, 172-73, 173n. 85
  whippings on, 173, 173n. 85
palmatória used on prisoners, 167, 172,
  176, 178, 199
  See also slaves: *palmatória* used on
Santa Barbara Prison, 27
See also Polícia Central
Independence
  situation following, 56-57
Indians (Native Brazilians)
  See race: *indios*
Italian Parliament, 53-54
  See also immigration: of Europeans
itinerants
  exiled
    See exiled
  killed, 39, 39n. 84
  reports on, 162n. 50
  See also incarceration; lower classes
jagunço
  See elites: sub-elites
Jesus, *Monge* João Maria de
  See Maria, *Monge* João (2nd)
jogo do bicho, 108, 108n. 66, 129, 129n.
  28, 161-62, 182, 182n. 117, 199
  and resignation of Manuel Lopes
    Carneiro da Fontoura, 182
Jorge
  See Polícia Central: agents/torturers at:
    Francisco Chagas: deals with new
    revolutionary plot: suspects in
Juizes de Paz, 199
  and itinerants, 40, 40n. 90, 121
    bounties paid for apprehension, 40, 40n.
    90
  and justice, 39-40
  and slave/manumitted population, 39, 121
  concluded, 41
  following slave rebellion of 1835, 33

234

justice, 17n. 30, 128n. 22, 133n, 36
  and early Portuguese, 15
  and elites, 4-5, 8-9, 38, 175-80, 178n.
    106, 180nn. 109-10
  and itinerants, 40, 40n. 90, 121
    bounties paid for apprehension, 40, 40n.
      90
  and *Juizes de Paz*, 39-40
  and peasants, 80-86, 86n. 92, 89-91, 89n.
    3, 91n. 6, 93, 95-97, 103-4, 115-17
  and slave revolt of 1835, 31-33, 120
  and slaves, 20-24, 21n. 37, 28, 28nn. 58-
    59, 38n. 81, 119-24, *2, 4-7, 9, 12-14*
  legal limitations on masters, 28, 28n. 58
  See also lower classes: removal of
kinship
  See parentela,
Lacerda, Maurício de, 160n. 43, 170
Lampião
  See cangaceiros: Lampião
Lima e Silva, Luís Alves de
  See army
Lima, Meira
  See incarceration: Casa de Detenção
lime, used as torture 56, 73, *10*
Lobo, Bruno, 170
Lopes, Isidoro Dias
  See tenentes/tenentismo: Rebellion of
    1924
Loureiro, Waldemar
  See incarceration: Casa de Correção
lower classes, 3
  and Contestado, 80-86, 84nn. 86-87, 86n.
    92
  and droughts, 59-61, 60n. 26
  and Paraguayan War, 38-38
  and Vintem Riot, 43
  as *cangaceiros*, 90
  as cheap labor, 9, 50-54, 121
  as slave owners, 14
  controlled by elites, 2-4, 7-9, 8n. 4, 18,
    50-67, 57n. 23, 62n. 31, 69-76, 74n. 56,
    75nn. 57-58, 80-86, 86n. 92, 89-91, 94-
    95, 103, 115-17, 121, 125-38, 125n. 13,
    128nn. 20, 22, 129n. 26, 130n. 30,
    137nn. 46-47, 138n. 48, 139-41, 139n.
    1, 143-46, 158, *14*
  exiled
    See exiled
  fear, 158
  looked down upon during *Belle Époque,*

127-38, 130n. 30, 136n. 45, 137n. 47,
  138n. 48
massacre of, 41, 86, 86n. 92
murdered, 39, 39n. 84
removal of, 8-9, 39, 125-38, 129nn. 26-
  27, 130n. 30, 131n. 32, 132n. 34, 133n.
  36, 136nn. 42-44, 137nn. 46-47, 138n.
  48
termos de bem viver, 38-39, 121
See also elites: sub-elites; immigration;
  incarceration; itinerants; justice; police;
  Polícia Central; prisoners; *sertanejos;*
  slaves; violence; workers
Lucena, Mario
  See Polícia Central: agents/torturers at
Luís, Washington [Washington Luís Pereira
  de Souza], 121, 145,
  admiration for Artur Bernardes, 180-81,
    181n. 114, *52*
  and coffee/economic situation, 183-185,
    184n. 124
  and government "suicide" *fazendas*, 181
  and labor questions, 145, 180, 180n. 111
  and Revolution of 1930, 185, 187
  early career, 145
  vilification of, 145, 181, 181nn. 113-14,
    52
macacos
  See police
Macêdo, *Padre* Manoel Correia de, 108
Macedo Soares, José Eduardo de
  See incarceration: Ilha Rasa: under Carlos
    Arlindo
Machado, Alfredo Moreira do Carmo
  See Polícia Central: agents/torturers at
Machado, José Nadyr
  See Polícia Central: agents/torturers at
Machado, Moreira
  See Polícia Central: agents/torturers at
Maciel, Antônio Vicente Mendes
  See Conselheiro, Antônio
Madeira-Mamoré railroad, 76, 76n. 60
Magalhães, Benjamin Constant Botelho de,
  68
Magé, 57-58
maids, 50-51
Maltides, Antônio
  See cangaceiros
Mandovani, Pedro
  See Polícia Central: agents/torturers at
Marcaf, Anastás

See Maria, *Monge* João (2nd)
"Maria, *Monge* João" (1st) [João Maria de Agostini], 79-80, 80n. 74
"Maria, *Monge* João" (2nd) [Anastás Marcaf], 80-82, 80nn. 73-75, *20*
  and Southern Brazil Lumber Colonization Company, 81
  Brazil Railway Company, 81-82, 82n. 79
  Percival Farquhar and, 81
  treatment of laborers on, 81-82
  Telegram 9, 81
"Maria, *Monge* José" [Miguel Lucena da Boaventura], 83, *21*
  Carlos Frederico de Mesquita
    See army: *Monge* José Maria
  description of communities, 83
  deserter, 82n. 80
  Fernando Setembrino de Carvalho
    See army: *Monge* José Maria
  followers battle police/army, 84-86, 84n. 87, 86n. 92
    casualties, 85-86, 86n. 92
  Francisco Ferreira de Albuquerque and, 83
  João Gualberto
    See army: *Monge* José Maria
    killed, 84
  King Sebastião I, 84, 84n. 86
  Maria Rosa, 84
  St. Sebastião, 84n. 86
  survivors, *23*
  tries to avoid fight with elites, 83-84
  Venceslau Brás Pereira Gomes and, 86
masters
  slaves, 19n. 33, 31, 37
    children with, 19n. 33
    following 1835 rebellion, 32-33
    manumission of, 34-35
    most requests for arrest of made by, 29n. 60
    sexual oppression of, 19, 35
    treatment of, 3, 7-10, 13-14, 19, 22-40, 21n. 39, 22n. 40, 23n. 43, 24n. 48, 26n. 53, 27n. 54, 28nn. 58-59, 29n. 60, 30nn. 62-63, 35n. 72, 39n. 83, 40n. 90, *1-4*, *7*, *9*, *12-14*
Mello, Custódio de
  See navy
Mello das Creanças
  See Polícia Central: agents/torturers at

Mello, Miguel Furtado de
  See Polícia Central: agents/torturers at
Menezes, Marcelino Rodrigues
  See Naval Revolt of 1910
Mesquita, Carlos Frederico de
  See army; Conselheiro, Antônio: Canudos: government's forces; Maria, *Monge* José
messianic/millenaristic movements, 59n. 25 65, 79-86, 84n. 87, 110-11, 111n. 75
middle class, 43, 87, 146
Military Club, 149
militia, colonial
  description of in Bahia, 18n. 32
  overseen by minister of justice, 45
  power in hands of rural elites, 18, 18n. 32
  replaced, 45
  white leaders, 18, 18n. 32
minors, 64
  See also incarceration
mixed race
  See race: *brown/mulatos; caribocos; gente de cor; mamelucos; mestiços*
mocambos
  See slaves: reactions by
Moraes, Francisco Batista de
  See cangaceiros: Antônio Silvino
Moraes, Manoel Batista de
  See cangaceiros: Antônio Silvino
mulatos
  See race: brown/*mulatos*
Müller, Filinto, 187
  See also Getúlio Vargas
myth of Brazilian racial democracy, 13n. 18
Napoleão, Quinca
  See cangaceiros: Antônio Silvino
National Guards
  blacks/Africans not allowed to join, 45
  description of, 45n. 2
  difficult to join, 45
  officers come from elites, 45
  reduced to a branch of reserves, 148
Native Brazilians (Indians)
  See race: *indios*
Naval Revolt of 1910
  and English, 71-73, 72n. 53, 73n. 54
  Arthur Farquhar, 72-73, 72n. 53, 76n. 62
  Baptista das Neves
    See navy
  Candido Rondon Commission, 76
    Madeira-Mamoré railroad, 76, 76n. 60

butchery by guards, 76
Casa de Detenção prisoners, 74-76, 74n.
  56, 75nn. 57-58
Hermes Rodrigues da Fonseca,
  executions by following, 72
  repression by following, 73-76, 74n. 56,
    75nn. 57-58, 174n. 93
  See also Fonseca, Hermes Rodrigues da
João Cândido [João Cândido Felisberto],
  69-74, 72n. 53, 73n. 54, 74n. 55
  Adão Pereira Nunes, 73
  and English, 72-73, 72n. 53
  as "Black Admiral," 69, 73-74, **17**
  later years, 73-74
  Leonel Brizola, 73
  lime bath, 73, 73n. 54
    See also exiled: Palhaço
  1964 military dictators, 74
  Roberto Silveira, 73
  tortured, 72-74
  See also incarceration: Ilha das
    Cobras
Marcelino Rodrigues Menezes, 69
Marques Porto
  See incarceration: Ilha das Cobras
Rui Barbosa and, 71, 75nn. 57-58
Satélite, 74-76, 74n. 56, 75nn. 57-58
  executions on, 75, 75n. 57
  whippings on, 74
warships
  Aquidaban, 70-71
  Bahia, 69
  Benjamin Constant, 70
  Deodoro, 69
  Minas Gerais, 69, 71, 73
  Rio Grande do Sul, 72
  São Paulo, 69, 71
  whippings, 69-70, 74
navy,
  Baptista das Neves, 71
  Custódio de Mello, 57-58
  deserters/dissenters from, 25
  impressment, 69, 121
  in 1904 Rio de Janeiro Riots, 127
  punishments in, 70
  racial makeup of, 69
  See also Naval Revolt of 1910
Neves, Attila
  See Polícia Central: agents/torturers at:
Neves, Baptista das
  See navy

Niemeyer, Conrado
  See Polícia Central: agents/torturers at:
    Francisco Chagas: deals with new
    revolutionary plot: suspects in
1964 military dictators, 13n. 18, 74, 153n.
  27
  See also tenentes/tenentismo
non-whites
  See race: Asians; blacks/Africans; brown
    /mulatos; caboclos; caribocos; criou-
    los; gente de cor; índios; mamelucos;
    mestiços
Nunes, Adão Pereira
  See Naval Revolt of 1910
Oiapoque
  See incarceration
Old Republic
  ends, 185, 187
  exiled during
    See exiled
  veiled military rule, 55
Oliveira Sobrinho, Pedro de
  See Polícia Central: agents/torturers at:
Orlantino, Investigator
  See Polícia Central: agents/torturers at:
Palmares
  See slaves: reactions by
palmatória
  See incarceration: palmatória used on
    prisoners; slaves: palmatória used on
Paraguayan War, 38, 39n. 83, 45n. 1
Paranhos, José Maria da Silva [Barão do
  Rio Branco], 51n. 12, 126
parentela, 46, 150, 199
Parisi, Géo Vicente
  See Polícia Central: agents/torturers at:
    Francisco Chagas: deals with new
    revolutionary plot
Peçanha, Nilo Procópio, 140, 180n. 110
Pedro, Nenê de Luís
  See cangaceiras
Peixoto, Floriano Vieira, 57-58, 140
  and Federalist Civil War, 58
  marshal law, 55
  military autocrat, 55
  presingangas, 55-57, 200
Pena, Afonso Augusto Moreira, 140, 171
pensions d'artistes, 135-36, 200
Pereira, Sebastião
  See cangaceiros: Sinhô
Peres, Octavio

237

See Polícia Central: agents/torturers at:
Pessoa, Epitácio da Silva, 146
  administrative programs, 144
  and military chiefs, 148
  and military salaries, 148
  and military upgrade, 148
  and police repression, 144
  blamed for Oiapoque, 174n. 93
  coffee, 149
  economic depression, 144, 149
  liberties, 144
  1922 Rebellion, 151-53
  racial beliefs, 144
Pinheiro Machado, José Gomes de, 76, 78-79, 78n. 69, *16*
Pinto Filho, Alfredo
  See Polícia Central: agents/torturers at:
police, 35, 38-39, 38n. 81
  and criminal backgrounds of members, 127
  See also cangaço: coronéis: cangaceiros mansos; elites: sub-elites
  and desecration of the dead, 114-15
  and government, 140
  and non-whites, 35-38, 38n. 81, 39, 42, 42n. 93, 119-23, 120n. 2, 140
  and non-white women during *Belle Époque*, 132-37, 132n. 34, 136nn. 42-44, 137nn. 46-47, 193-95
  and poor whites, 43, 123, 123n. 10, 140
  Antônio Conselheiro and, 58, 61-62, 61n. 30
  as *macacos*, 92-93, 110, 114, 199
  Bragada Militar
    and size vs. army, 147-48
    See also elites: sub-elites; *Força Pública; Polícia Militar*
  corruption, 94, 94n. 20, 104, 107, 112-13
  despised for violence, 54, 106-7
  expenditures on vs. those for education, 61n. 30
  Força Pública, 147, 199
    and 1924 Rebellion, 154
    and size vs. army, 147-48
    deserters/dissenters from, 82n. 80
    used against *Monge* José Maria, 84
    used by Marcos Franco Rabelo, 77-78
    See also *Bragada Militar;* elites: sub-elites; *Polícia Militar*
  impressment, 127
  misfits in, 38n. 81

  mistaken arrests during *Belle Époque*, 133n. 36
  naval police, 74
  Polícia Civil, 41, 200
    Coriolano de Góis, 182, 182n. 120, *53*
      powers increased, 182
    created, 41
    Eusébio de Queiroz, 40, 40n. 90
      decides to clean Rio of itinerants, 40, 40n. 90
    Manuel Lopes Carneiro da Fontoura, 187, *38*
      and *jogo do bicho*, 161-62, 182
      and other corruption, 161-62
      "Marshal" Fontoura, 161
      relatives of 1924 rebels taken as hostage, 162
      resignation of, 182
      use of informants, 162
      vilification of, 161, 161n. 46
    See also Bernardes, Artur da Silva: 1924 Rebellion: repression and; elites: sub-elites; justice; Polícia Central: agents/torturers at: Francisco Chagas: deals with new revolutionary plot: suspects in
  Polícia Militar, 17, 17n. 30, 35-43, 42n. 93, 45, 200
    and 1922 Rebellion, 151-52
    and Paraguayan War, 45n. 1
    and size vs. army, 147-48
    Antônio Augusto Cardoso de Castro, See *Belle Époque:* police action during
    Carlos Arlindo
      See incarceration: Ilha Rasa
    created, 41
    deserters/dissenters from, 173
    earlier versions of, 17, 17n. 30, 35-39, 38n. 81, 41, 42n. 93
    Francisco Alberto Teixeira de Aragão, 37-38, *8*
      "Curfew of Aragão," 37
    João Bezerra
      See cangaceiros: Lampião
    Luís Alves de Lima e Silva
      See army
    Miguel Nunes Vidigal, 35-37
      "Shrimp Dinners," 36
      torturer/executioner, 36
    Teofanes Ferraz Torres

238

See cangaceiros: Antônio Silvino:
 Lampião
See also Bragada Militar; elites: sub-
 elites; *Força Pública*
political police
 and labor movement, 140-43
 *Corpo de Investigação e Segurança
  Pública,* 143
 Delegacia de Ordem Política e Social
  (DOPS), 181
 4ª Delegacia Auxiliar, 181, 183
 Seção de Ordem Política e Social
  (SOPS), 181
 raping of peasant women by, 89n. 3, 96
 repression by, 35-43, 38n. 81, 54, 46-47,
  53-54, 61, 107, 127-28, 128nn. 20, 22,
  132, 132n. 34, 137nn. 46-47, 140, 144-
  45, 153, 159-83, 161n. 47, 167n. 69,
  173nn. 85-87, 174n. 93, 176n. 97,
  179n. 107, 180nn. 110-11, 181n. 114,
  183n. 123, 187-88
 secret police, 43
 treatment of captured *cangaceiras,* 114
  -15, 114nn. 88, 90-91
 treatment of captured *cangaceiros
  independentes,* 111
 tropas de choque, 43
 unite with *jagunços,* 110
 whippings by, 144
 See also army; *cangaço: cangaceiros
  independentes: cangaceiros mansos;
  coronéis;* elites: sub-elites; incarceration; itinerants; justice; lower classes;
  Polícia Central; prisoners; race; slaves;
  violence; workers
Polícia Central, 163-65, 176, 200, *50*
 agents/torturers at
  Alfredo Pinto Filho, 183
  Attila Neves, 183, 183n. 122, *47*
  "Bijuca" [João Lopes Carneiro da
   Fontoura], 163, 177
  Carlos da Silva Reis, 160n. 44, 163-64,
   181, *39*
   contest with Francisco Chagas, 164
   out of favor, 175
   places bombs in Rio, 164, 187
  Francisco Chagas, 163, *51*
   contest with Carlos da Silva Reis, 164
   deals with new revolutionary plot,
    175-76, 175n. 95, 177-80
   Géo Vicente Parisi, 176

 suspects in
  Accacio Rodrigues de Carvalho,
   176
  Antonio Martins de Arajuo Silva,
   176
  Conrado Borlido Maia de
   Niemeyer [Conrado Henrique de
   Niemeyer], 5, 176-180, 177n.
   100, 179n. 107, 180n. 109,
   48-50
  Jorge (complete name unknown),
   176
  Narciso Ramalheda, 176
  Rubens Bello, 176
  Viriato da Cunha Bastos
   Schomaker, 176
 medical and dental training, 163
 suicide specialist, 164
Inspector Barbosa (complete name
 unknown), 163
Investigator Canuto (complete name
 unknown), 183
Investigator Orlantino (complete name
 unknown), 183
Jardemar San Pietro, 183, 183n. 122
José Nadyr Machado, 163
 "suicide" of, 180, 180n. 109, *46*
Mario Lucena, 183
Martins Vidal, 183
"Mello das Creanças" [Miguel Furtado
 de Mello], 163, *44*
"Moreira Machado" [Alfredo Moreira
 do Carmo Machado], 163, 163n. 55,
 176-77, 178-80, *51*
Octavio Peres, 183
Pedro de Oliveira Sobrinho, 183
Pedro Mandovani, 163, 178-80, *51*
Perminio Gonçalves, 163
Raul Aguiar, 183
Renato Bittencourt, 183
Tristão Araripe, 163
"Twenty-Six" [Manoel da Costa Lima],
 163, 178-80, *51*
beatings of minors at, 183, 183n. 123
See also Casa de Correção: under
 Waldemar Loureiro
geladeira at, 162, 162n. 52, 164, 166,
 187, 199
prisoners forced to bribe, 164
"suicide" at, 164, 178, 180, 180n. 110,
 187

See also Francisco Chagas
torture at, 163-65, 176-78, 187-88
trial of "The Sinister Gang," 179-80,
180n. 109
See also army; elites: sub-elites; incarceration; justice; lower classes; police;
prisoners; violence; workers
"Politics of Governors," 126-27, 146-47
Pombal, Marquis de
See incarceration: Ilha das Cobras
Porcino, Antônio
See cangaceiros
Porto, Marques
See incarceration: Ilha das Cobras
Portuguese, the
and carrying of weapons, 15-16
and excessive violence, 3-4, 8-9, 15-16
description of, 14-15
discrimination by, 14, 14n. 20
in slave trade, 10-14
tracts of land given to by king, 15
positivism, 68-69, 68n. 46, 126
Potyguara, Tertuliano
See army: and 1922 Rebellion: and 1924
Rebellion
povão, 2, 2n. 3, 43, 187, 200
povo miserável, 59, 158, 200
presingangas, 55-57, 200
Prestes, Luís Carlos, 105-7, 109, 145, *54*
Coluna Prestes, 109, 157
aims, 106-7, 158n. 39
and exile, 159
distance traveled, 106n. 56
observations, 158
description of, 157-58, 158n. 37.
glorification of, 158
prisoners
from Naval Revolt of 1910, etc., 73-76,
74n. 56, 75nn. 57-58
galley or chain gang, 22, *6*
itinerants, 39, 39n. 84
shoes, lack of, 25-26
slaves as, 22, *14*
vadiagem (read vagrants and prostitutes),
132-38, 132n. 34, 136nn. 42-43, 45,
137n. 46, 195
See also army; elites: sub-elites; incarceration; justice; lower classes; police;
Polícia Central; race; slaves; violence;
workers
prisons

See incarceration
prostitution
and children, 60, 136n. 45
and slaves, 21
during *Belle Époque*,
129n. 28, 132-38, 132n. 34, 136nn. 42-
43, 45, 137n. 46, 195
brothels, 134-35, 137
following Canudos, 64
from Casa de Detenção for Amazon exile,
74-76
incarceration for
See incarceration
See also justice; police; prisoners; race;
slaves; *vadiagem*
Queiroz, Eusébio de
See police: *Polícia Civil*
quilombos
See slaves: reactions by
Rabelo, Marcos Franco, 67n. 43, 77-78,
107, 107n. 63
See also Salvações
race
and classification systems, 1n. 2, 19,
19n. 33, 20nn. 34-35
Asians
immigration, 50
blacks/Africans, 3, 10n. 11, 19-20, 19n.
33, 20n. 35, 31-33, 47-50, 50n. 7
Africanos Livres, 48
after abolition, 49-55, 50n. 7, 53n. 16
and *cangaço*, 89
and disenfranchisement, 139, 139n. 1
and mark of Cain, 20
and Paraguayan War, 38-39, 39n. 83,
48
and police, 35, 37-39, 38n. 81
as a racial type used here, 1n. 2
as deserters/dissenters from military, 25
as "house servants," 50-51
as slaves
See slaves
as workers, 7-10, 14, 19, 19n. 33, 21-
29, 21n. 39, 23n. 43, 26n. 53, 27n.
54, 28n. 58, 29nn. 60-61, 30n. 62, 31-
35, 52-53, 53n. 16
at Canudos, 58
described, 20
exiled
See exiled
immigration after abolition, 49

in army, 39, 39n. 83, 45, 161, 161n. 46
incarceration of
  See incarceration
in colonial militias, 18n. 32
in navy, 69, 71
in police, 38n. 81, 45, 45n. 1, 123,
  123n. 9, 161-62, 161n. 46
killed defending House of Bragança, 55
looked down upon during Belle Époque,
  127-38, 130n. 30, 136n. 45, 138n. 48
Padre Cícero and, 66
returned to Africa, 89n. 1
slaughter of in Battle of Porongos, 42
too many, 21
See also Catholic Church
brasileiros, 19
brown/mulatos, 3, 19-20, 19n. 33, 20nn.
  34-35, 31-33, 47-50, 50n. 7
after abolition, 49-55, 50n. 7, 53n. 16
and cangaço, 89
and disenfranchisement, 139, 139n. 1
and Paraguayan War, 38-39, 39n. 83
and police, 35, 37-39
as a racial sub-type used here, 1n. 2
as "house servants," 50-51
as slaves
  See slaves
as workers, 7-10, 14, 19, 19n. 33, 21-
  29, 21n. 39, 23n. 43, 26n. 53, 27n.
  54, 28n. 58, 29nn. 60-61, 30n. 62, 31-
  35, 52-53, 53n. 16
at Canudos, 58
described, 20
exiled
  See exiled
in army, 39, 39n. 83, 45, 161, 161n. 46
incarceration of
  See incarceration
in colonial militias, 18n. 32
in navy, 69
in police, 38n. 81, 45, 45n. 1, 123,
  123n. 9, 161-62, 161n. 46
looked down upon during Belle Époque,
  127-38, 130n. 30, 136n. 45, 138n. 48
caboclos, 20, 20nn. 34-35, 197
at Canudos, 58
caribocos, 19, 20nn. 34-35
census accountings by, 50n. 7
crioulos, 19
filhos do reino, 19
gente de cor, 35, 38, 43, 199

See also race: blacks/Africans; brown/
  mulatos; caboclos; caribocos; crioulos; índios; mamelucos; mestiços
índios, 9, 20, 20nn. 34-35, 25, 50n. 7, 76,
  134
and mark of Cain, 20
as a racial type used here, 1n. 2
described, 20
incarceration of
  See incarceration
in colonial militias, 18
See also Catholic Church
mamelucos, 19, 199
at Canudos, 58
mestiços, 19
mixed race
  See race: brown/mulatos; caribocos;
    gente de cor; mamelucos; mestiços
mulatos
  See race: brown/mulatos
negros
  See race: blacks/Africans
non-whites
  See race: Asians; blacks/Africans;
    brown/mulatos; caboclos; caribocos;
    crioulos; gente de cor; índios;
    mamelucos; mestiços
termo de bem viver, 38-39, 121
whites/Europeans, 3, 10n. 11, 20, 20nn.
  34-35
after abolition, 49-51, 50n. 7, 51n. 12
and cangaço, 89
and Paraguayan War, 38
and police
as a racial type used here, 1n. 2
as slaves
  See slaves: white
at Canudos, 58
exiled
  See exiled
immigrants, 49-55, 51n. 12, 52nn. 13-
  14
incarceration of
  See incarceration
in colonial militias, 18, 18n. 32
lazy, 50-51
Ramalheda, Narciso
  See Polícia Central: agents/torturers at:
    Francisco Chagas: deals with new
    revolutionary plot: suspects in
Rebellion of 1922

See tenentes/tenentismo
Rebellion of 1924
See tenentes/tenentismo
Reis, Carlos da Silva,
  See Polícia Central: agents/torturers at
religion
  See Catholic Church; Contestado;
    messianic/millenaristic movements
retirantes, 59-60, 200
Revolution of 1930, 185, 187
"Rio, João do" [Paulo Barreto], 133-34
Rodrigues Alves, Francisco de Paula
  as "Big Daddy," 124, 139-40, *33*
  dozing off problem, 124
  main contribution to posterity, 124-25,
    132
Rodrigues, Raimundo Nina, 63, 114n. 90,
  115
Rondon, Candido, 76, *18*
Rondon Commission, 76
Rosa, Maria
  See Maria, *Monge* José
Rufino, José
  See cangaceiros: Corisco
rural banditry
  See cangaceiros; cangaço
Sabinada Revolt, 57, 57n. 23
Salles, Manuel Ferraz de Campos, 140
Salvações, 78-79, 149, 200
San Pietro, Jardemar
  See Polícia Central: agents/torturers at
Santa Barbara Prison
  See incarceration
Santa Cruz
  See army: Antenor de Santa Cruz Pereira
    de Abreu
Santo Agostinho, *Monge* José Maria de
  See Maria, *Monge* José
Saturnino, José
  See cangaceiros: Lampião
Schomaker, Carolina Bastos
  See Bernardes, Artur da Silva: 1924
    Rebellion: repression and
Schomaker, Viriato da Cunha Bastos
  See Polícia Central: agents/torturers at:
    Francisco Chagas: deals with new
    revolutionary plot: suspects in
Seabra, José Joaquim
  See Belle Époque: police action during
sertanejos, 111, 153, 200
  and Canudos, 59-65, 61n. 30, 62n. 31,

65nn. 37-38
  and Contestado, 80-86, 86n. 92
  massacre of, 41, 63-64
Silva, Antonio Martins de Arajuo
  See Polícia Central: agents/torturers at:
    Francisco Chagas: deals with new
    revolutionary plot: suspects in
Silva, Christino Gomes da Silva
  See cangaceiros: Corisco
Silva, Virgulino Ferreira da
  See cangaceiros: Lampião
Silveira, Jaime Pessoa da, 150
Silveira, Roberto
  See Naval Revolt of 1910: João Cândido
Silvino, Antônio
  See cangaceiros: Antônio Silvino
Silvino Torto
  See cangaceiros: Silvino Torto
Sinhô
  See cangaceiros: Sinhô
slavery, 3-4, 9-10
  abolition of, 23n. 43, 50n. 7
    Africanos Livres, 48, 197
    aftermath, 50-55, 50n. 7, 51n. 12, 52nn.
      13-14, 53n. 16, 54n. 20
    Brazilian statutes, 48-49
    delaying tactics, 47-49
    disgrace of, 53
    English stimulus to, 47-48
    treaties with/by foreign powers, 47-49
  and mining, 7, 13-14, 21n. 39
  and plantations, 7, 13-14, 21
  Brazil vs. United States, 3, 21, 21n. 39
  children, 19n. 33, 48
  debt peonage, 49
  enslavement processes against Moors,
    Muslims, *índios*, and Africans
    early European grounds for, 10
    See Catholic Church
  following Canudos, 64
  following Naval Revolt of 1910, 76-77
  profits as reason for, 9-13
  See also masters; slaves
slaves
  alcoholism of, 24
  and *Juizes de Paz*, 33, 39-41, 121
  and Paraguayan War, 38-39, 39n. 83, 48
  anti-congregating laws, 120
  assaults by, 21n. 39
  average hours of work by, 24
  average life spans of, 13

beating of, 23, *14*
boiled alive, *14*
branding of, 26, 27n. 54, *1*
buried alive, *14*
burning alive of, 24, 28, *14*
caning of, 38
    See also, 17n. 30
chicote use on, 23, 23n. 43, 198, *14*
curfew, 37, 119-20
dismemberment of, 22, 22n. 40, 26
drowning of, 28n. 58, *14*
escape, 25-26, 36, *14*
    capitão de mato/estrada/campo,
        26, 26n. 53, 85, 197, *12*
        See also elites: sub-elites
    jobs after, 25
    penalties if caught, 26, 29-30
    rewards for captors, 26, 40n. 90
execution of, 26, 32, 36
feitors ("slave tamers")
    See elites: sub-elites
gagging of, *14*
hanging, 22, 22n. 40, 24, *14*
incarceration of
    See incarceration
injure, 28n. 58
iron-leg rings, 29, *7*
libambo worn by, 29, *7*
logs chained to, 29, *7*
manumission of, 34-35, 39n. 83
marijuana use, 24
metal masks worn by, 24, 24n. 48, *3*
mortality and morbidity *en route* from
    Africa, 13
murder by, 22, 21n. 39, 22n. 40
murder of, 24, 28, 36, *14*
murder of due to pregnancy, 24, *14*
mutilation of, 26-27
palmatória used on, 22, 22n. 40, 199
    See also incarceration: *palmatória* used
        on prisoners
prostitution of, 21, 21n. 39
ratio vs. whites, 21
reactions by, 20-21, 31
    capoeira, 21, 21n. 37, 30, 37, 197
        See also elites: sub-elites
    quilombos/mocambos, 25-26, 29, 36,
        89, 119, 200
        Palmares, 25
    See also rebellions by
rebellions by, 3, 31-33, 31n. 65

1822 fear of, 119
1835 revolt, 31-33, 31n. 65
    possible English involvement, 31-32
    residence in Bahia following, 32-33
    See also Naval Revolt of 1910; reac-
        tions by
religious customs used against, 24
renting out of, 21n. 39
    escravos de ganho, prêtos de ganho,
        21n. 39, 198, 200
resold clandestinely, 26
returned to Africa, 89n. 1
shackles, 22-23, *2*
shoes, lack of, 25-26, 29n. 60, 42n. 93
starving of, *14*
stocks used on, 22, 22n. 40
stopped and searched, 37
suicide of, 24-25, *14*
    as a ratio of all suicides by race, 25
termo de bem viver, 38-39, 121
too few, 10, 13
too many, 3, 21, 49-50
torture of, 36
tying of, 23, 30nn. 62-63, *4, 14*
unnecessary noise by, 37
whipping of, 21, 21n. 37, 23n. 43, 24, 29-
    32, 29n. 60, 30nn. 62-63, 36, 49, 119-
    20, *4-5, 13-14*
whipping of females, 29n. 60, 39n. 83
whistling, 37
white/European, 22, *6*
    See also army; elites; elites: sub-elites;
        incarceration; justice; lower classes;
        police; prisoners; race; slavery; violence
"slave tamers"
    See elites: sub-elites: *feitors* ("slave
        tamers")
socialists, 141
Sodré, Lauro, 127
Souza, Washington Luís Pereira de
    See Luís, Washington
state governors, 62, 67n. 43, 77-79, 94-95,
    112, 127, 142, 146-47, 149-50
    and *Policia Militar*, 41n. 91
    partido do presidente, 46
    relationship with *coronéis*, 45-47
sub-elites
    See elites: sub-elites
sugar, 13, 21, 47, 184
Távora, Joaquim
    See tenentes/tenentismo: Rebellion of

1924
Távora, Juarez
See tenentes/tenentismo: Rebellion of
1924
tenentes/tenentismo, 4, 105, 105n. 55, 149-
53, 152n. 21, 153n. 27, 200
Rebellion of 1922
Copacabana Fort, 151-53
Epitácio Pessoa's reactions, 151
"18 of the Fort," 151-53, 152n. 21
documentary by Salvador Aragão,
153
Rebellion of 1924,
confined largely to São Paulo, 154
Isadoro Dias Lopes, 155, 157
Joaquim Távora, 155
Juarez Távora, 155
Luís Carlos Prestes
Coluna Prestes
See Prestes, Luís Carlos
Miguel Costa, 155, 157
São Paulo bombarded, 155-156, 156n.
33
unyielding on timetable for start, 154
See also army; 1964 military dictators
Torres, Teofanes Ferraz
See cangaceiros: Antônio Silvino:
Lampião
Travassos, Silvestre
See army
Twenty-Six
See Polícia Central: agents/torturers at:
unemployed, the
See workers
vadiagem (read: vagrancy and prostitution),
132-38, 132n. 34, 136nn. 42-43, 45,
137nn. 46-47, 195, 200
Vargas, Getúlio, 17, 99, 101-2, 104, 112-
13, 139, 139n. 1, 187, 188n. 2, **25**
Vidal, Martins
See Polícia Central: agents/torturers at:
Vidigal, Miguel Nunes
See police: *Polícia Militar*
Vieira, *Dom* Joaquim José
See Cícero, *Padre:* and Church hierarchy
Vintem Riot, 43
violence,
after independence, 56-57
after overthrow of monarchy, 55
and the police, 17-18, 17n. 30, 35-43,
38n. 81, 46, 46n. 4, 54, 58, 61, 85, 92,
103-5, 107, 110-11, 113-15, 127-28,
128nn. 20, 22, 133n. 36, 140-45, 145n.
10, 161-67, 176-83, 179n. 107, 180n.
110, 181n. 114, 183n. 123, 187-88
and the Portuguese, 8, 12-13, 15-16
antecedents of, 8
elites, directed towards lower classes as
social control, 2-4, 7-9, 8n. 4, 18, 50-
65, 52n. 13, 57n. 23, 62n. 31, 68n. 46,
69-76, 74n. 56, 75nn. 57-58, 82-87,
86n. 92, 89-93, 89n. 3, 96, 103-8, 107n.
59, 108nn. 64, 66, 110-17, 111n. 75,
119-124, 122n. 8, 123n. 10, 126-38,
128nn. 20, 22, 129n. 26, 130n. 30,
132n. 34, 133n. 36, 136nn. 42-44,
137nn. 46-47, 138n. 48, 140-45, 145n.
10, 155-56, 158-59, 161-83, 173-74,
173n. 88, 174n. 93, 179n. 107, 180n.
110, 181n. 114, 183n. 123, 187-88, *14*
inter-elite, 4-5, 8-9, 18, 56-57, 89, 150-
54, 153n. 27
lower classes, directed towards elites, 4,
8n. 4
sexual oppression, 19, 34
See also army; elites; elites: sub-elites;
incarceration; justice; lower classes;
police; Polícia Central; prisoners; race;
slaves
whites
See race: whites/Europeans
workers
and gambling (*jogo do bicho*), 108, 108n.
66, 129, 129n. 28, 161-62, 182, 182n.
117
and tattooing, 134
and working conditions, 7, 9-10, 13-14,
19n. 33, 21-22, 21n. 39, 24-27, 27n. 54,
32-33, 38, 47-53, 52n. 13, 57n. 23, 61,
62n. 31, 67, 75-76, 81-82, 102, 119-21,
124, 125n. 13, 128, 129n. 27, 130-31,
131n. 32, 141-43, 145, 145n. 10, 171-
74, 171n. 81, 172n. 84, 180-81, 180n.
111, 185
and World War I, 87, 146, 146n. 11
exiled
See exiled
expensive after abolition, 54
former slaves, 50-51
labor movement, 142
and arrests, 142-45, 180n. 111
and immigration, 49-52, 51n. 12, 52nn.

12-13, 141
children in work force, 141
murder of protesters, 145
police repression of, 140-45
    See exiled; political police
strikes, 141-43, 145
Washington Luís and, 145, 180, 180n.
    111
looked down on by elites, 53-54
poor, 50-53, 52nn. 13-14, 81-82, 89, 123,
    126, 193-94
and elections, 139, 139n. 1
removal of urban poor, 125-38, 129nn.
    26-27, 136nn. 42-43, 45, 137nn. 46-
    47, 143
unemployed, 38-39
    arrests of, 145
    exiled
        See exiled
    former slaves, 50-51
    impressment of, 38-39, 39n. 83, 69
    police repression of, 43
    sentencing of, 38-39
    termos de bem viver, 38-39, 121
    whipped, 82
See also elites; elites: sub-elites;
    incarceration; justice; lower classes;
    police; prisoners; race; slaves